ANCIENT INDIAN TRADITION & MYTHOLOGY

Translated by
A BOARD OF SCHOLARS

Edited by
DR. G.P. BHATT

VOLUME 62

ANCIENT INDIAN TRADITION AND MYTHOLOGY SERIES

[PURĀṆAS IN TRANSLATION]

Volumes Released

ŚIVA 1-4
LIṄGA 5-6
BHĀGAVATA 7-11
GARUḌA 12-14
NĀRADA 15-19
KŪRMA 20-21
BRAHMĀṆḌA 22-26
AGNI 27-30
VARĀHA 31-32
BRAHMA 33-36
VĀYU 37-38
PADMA 39-48
SKANDA, PARTS I-XX, 49-68
VĀMANA 72

Volumes Under Preparation

SKANDA, PARTS XXI-XXIV
BHAVIṢYA
BRAHMAVAIVARTA
DEVĪBHĀGAVATA
KĀLIKĀ
MĀRKAṆḌEYA
MATSYA
VIṢṆU
VIṢṆUDHARMOTTARA

THE SKANDA-PURĀṆA

Translated and Annotated by

DR. G.V. TAGARE

PART XIV

MOTILAL BANARSIDASS PUBLISHERS
PRIVATE LIMITED • DELHI

Reprint : Delhi, 2006
First Edition : Delhi, 1999

ISBN: 81-208-1698-6

MOTILAL BANARSIDASS
41 U.A. Bungalow Road, Jawahar Nagar, Delhi 110 007
8 Mahalaxmi Chamber, 22 Bhulabhai Desai Road, Mumbai 400 026
236, 9th Main III Block, Jayanagar, Bangalore 560 011
203 Royapettah High Road, Mylapore, Chennai 600 004
Sanas Plaza, 1302 Baji Rao Road, Pune 411 002
8 Camac Street, Kolkata 700 017
Ashok Rajpath, Patna 800 004
Chowk, Varanasi 221 001

UNESCO COLLECTION OF REPRESENTATIVE WORKS—Indian Series.
This book has been accepted in the Indian Translation Series of the UNESCO Collection of Representative Works, jointly sponsored by the United Nations Educational, Scientific and Cultural Organization (UNESCO) and the Government of India.

Printed in India
BY JAINENDRA PRAKASH JAIN AT SHRI JAINENDRA PRESS,
A-45 NARAINA, PHASE-I, NEW DELHI 110 028
AND PUBLISHED BY NARENDRA PRAKASH JAIN FOR
MOTILAL BANARSIDASS PUBLISHERS PRIVATE LIMITED,
BUNGALOW ROAD, DELHI 110 007

PUBLISHERS NOTE

The purest gems lie hidden in the bottom of the ocean or in the depth of rocks. One has to dive into the ocean or delve into the rocks to find them out. Similarly, truth lies concealed in the language which with the passage of time has become obsolete. Man has to learn that language before he discovers that truth.

But he has neither the means nor the leisure to embark on that course. We have, therefore, planned to help him acquire knowledge by an easier course. We have started the series of Ancient Indian Tradition and Mythology in English Translation. Our goal is to universalize knowledge through the most popular international medium of expression. The publication of the Purāṇas in English Translation is a step towards that goal.

Acknowledgements

It is our pleasant duty to put on record our sincere thanks to Dr. R.N. Dandekar and the UNESCO authorities for their kind encouragement and valuable help in the publication of the volumes in this series.

CONTENTS

ABBREVIATIONS

Common and self-evident abbreviations such as Ch (s)—Chapter(s), p—page, pp—pages, v—verse, vv—verses, Ftn—Footnote, Hist. Ind. Philo.—History of Indian Philosophy are not included in this list.

AGP	S.M. Ali's *The Geography of Purāṇas,* PPH, New Delhi, 1973
AIHT	*Ancient Indian Historical Tradition,* F.E. Pargiter, Motilal Banarsidass (MLBD), Delhi
AITM	*Ancient Indian Tradition and Mythology* Series, MLBD, Delhi
AP	*Agni Purāṇa,* Guru Mandal Edition (GM), Calcutta, 1957
AV	*Atharva Veda,* Svādhyāya Maṇḍal, Aundh
Bdp	*Brahmāṇḍa Purāṇa,* MLBD, Delhi, 1973
BG	*Bhagavadgītā*
BhP	*Bhāgavata Purāṇa,* Bhagavat Vidyapeeth, Ahmedabad
Br	*Brāhmaṇa* (preceded by name such as Śatapatha)
BsP	*Bhaviṣya Purāṇa,* Vishnu Shastri Bapat, Wai
BVP	*Brahma Vaivarta Purāṇa,* GM, 1955-57
CC	*Caturvarga Cintāmaṇi* by Hemādri
CVS	*Caraṇa Vyūha Sūtra* by Śaunaka, Com. by Mahīdāsa
DB	*Devī Bhāgavata,* GM, 1960-61
De or GDAMI	*The Geographical Dictionary of Ancient and Medieval India,* N.L. De/Dey, Oriental Reprint, Delhi, 1971
DhS	*Dharma Sūtra* (preceded by the author's name such as Gautama)
GP	*Garuḍa Purāṇa,* ed. R.S. Bhattacharya, Chowkhamba, Varanasi, 1964
GS	*Gṛhya Sūtra* (preceded by the name of the author such as Āpastamba)
HD	*History of Dharma Śāstra,* P.V. Kane, G.O.S.
JP	*Purāṇa* (Journal of the Kashiraj Trust), Varanasi
KA	*Kauṭilya Arthaśāstra*
KP	*Kūrma Purāṇa,* Veṅkaṭeśvara Press Edn., Bombay; also Kashiraj Trust Edn., Varanasi, 1971

LP	*Liṅga Purāṇa,* GM, 1960; also MLBD, Delhi, 1981
Manu	*Manusmṛti*
Mbh	*Mahābhārata,* Gītā Press, Gorakhpur, VS 2014
MkP	*Mārkaṇḍeya Purāṇa*
MN	*Mahābhārata Nāmānukramaṇī,* Gītā Press, Gorakhpur, VS 2016
MtP	*Matsya Purāṇa,* GM, 1954
MW	M. Monier-Williams' *Sanskrit-English Dictionary,* MLBD, Delhi, 1976
NP	*Nāradīya* or *Nārada Purāṇa,* Veṅkaṭeśvara Press, Bombay
PdP	*Padma Purāṇa,* GM, 1957-59
PE	*Purāṇic Encyclopaedia,* V. Mani, English Version, MLBD, Delhi, 1975
PR or PRHRC	*Puranic Records on Hindu Rites and Customs,* R.C. Hazra, Calcutta, 1948
ṚV	*Ṛg Veda,* Svādhyāya Maṇḍal, Aundh
Śat Br	*Śatapatha Brāhmaṇa*
SC or SMC	*Smṛti Candrikā* by Devanna Bhaṭṭa
Skp	*Skanda Purāṇa*
SP	*Śiva Purāṇa*
VāP	*Vāyu Purāṇa*
VR	*Vālmīki Rāmāyaṇa*
VdP	*Viṣṇudharmottara Purāṇa*
VmP	*Vāmana Purāṇa*
VP	*Viṣṇu Purāṇa*
VrP	*Varāha Purāṇa*

SKANDA PURĀṆA

BOOK V: ĀVANTYA-KHAṆḌA

SECTION III: REVĀ-KHAṆḌA

CHAPTER ONE

Purāṇa Texts Described

Obeisance to Śrī Gaṇeśa.
Oṁ obeisance to Śrī Puruṣottama.
Oṁ obeisance to Śrī Narmadā.
Oṁ obeisance to Hari, Hara and Hiraṇyagarbha.
Obeisance to Vyāsa, Vālmīki, Śuka and Parāśara.
Obeisance to Preceptors, Cows and Brāhmaṇas.

1. May the waters of Narmadā protect ye all—the waters which inebriate the swarms of bees with the fragrance of ichor washed off from the temples of elephants taking a dip in her, which are made tawny-coloured due to the saffron dissolved (and washed away) from the pairs of breasts of Siddha women while they take their holy bath in her, of which trees on either bank are strewn over with the flowers offered by sages every morning and evening, (the waters) the force of the waves of which is checked by alligators and trunks of elephants.

2. May Narmadā with sacred places on her both banks, who has washed off the masses of sins of all the worlds and is worthy of being venerated by Devas, sages and human beings, always dispel (our) sins.

3. Narmadā is possessed of meritorious waters. She has sanctified the entire earth. May she destroy all sins past, present or future, of the people taking birth on the earth.

4. Even ascetics desire her sandy banks. May Revā with Śiva as her deity, ever rendering service to multitudes of sages, be conducive to my welfare.

5. After bowing down to Nārāyaṇa and Nara, the most ex-

cellent one among men, to Goddess Sarasvatī and to Vyāsa one should recite *Jaya*[1].

6-16. In the meritorious place of Naimiṣa which was resorted to by many sages, Śaunaka who began a Satra (a sacrifice of long duration), asked Sūta in detail: "O Sūta, I believe that mastery of Dharma (holy rites and activities of piety) has been greatly esteemed always by you. As a disciple of Vyāsa, you alone are the propounder of the divine, nectarine stories of the Purāṇas. Hence, O Kavi (the seer of things beyond), I ask you something pertaining to piety and holy places. There are many holy spots and shrines. They have been heard by me too. The divine river pertaining to Brahmā (Sarasvatī), as well as the river pertaining to Viṣṇu (Gaṅgā) have been heard by me. The third excellent river (Narmadā) pertaining to Rudra has never been heard by me. O highly intelligent one, narrate unto me the details about that holy river having the Vedas as her sustaining basis—a river honoured and adored by the multitude of Devas and consecrated by (the presence of) excellent Tīrthas. What is that land which Revā has occupied? How has she originated from Śrī Rudra? Tell me all those Tīrthas which have resorted to Revā."

Sūta said:

O Kulapati (Head of the families) of sages, you have put a pertinent question as to the nature of Narmadā. She is wonderful, sacred, destructive of faults when described or listened to, O excellent one. The son of Satyavatī, who had a sense of fulfilment after analysing, redacting and compiling the Vedas, Upavedas, Vedāṅgas etc. is the expounder of the eighteen Purāṇas. After bowing down to him, I shall narrate the Purāṇas in due order. By giving discourse on them, there will be welcome increase in piety and longevity. The Śruti and Smṛti texts have been proclaimed as the eyes of Vipras (Brāhmaṇas). One bereft of one of these two is a one-eyed man and one bereft of both is loudly proclaimed as blind. The Śrutis, Smṛtis and

1. *JAYA*: This was the title of Mahābhārata. It was at first restricted to that epic but was adopted by the Purāṇas like *Vāyu* and *Brahmāṇḍa*. Finally *Kalpataru*, on the authority of *Bhaviṣya Purāṇa*, conceded it to Vālmīki *Rāmāyaṇa* (VR), 18 Mahāpurāṇas and *Manusmṛti*.

Purāṇas are the three eyes of learned men. He who sees through these three is considered as part and parcel of Maheśvara.[1]

17-28. The Vedic Vidyā (lore) of the Ātman was created by Īśvara himself. Then there is Śaunakīya lore (the Mantra lore such as Ṛgvidhāna, etc.). Then there is the Paurāṇikī lore in the form of Dharmaśāstra (treatises on ethics, piety and good conduct). These three lores are very important ones in taking definite decisions about all scriptural matters. This is the command of Brahmā that Purāṇa is (to be taken as) the fifth Veda. He who does not know the Purāṇa does not understand anything here, whether it is a holy rite or piety or an item of knowledge of any sort or anything else worthwhile. What is there that is not found in the Purāṇa?

The Vedas have been well-ensconced formerly in the Purāṇa. There is no doubt about it. The Veda is terribly worried about one with incomplete mastery of the Vedas apprehending, "He will distort me."

This is the conclusion arrived at earlier by Itihāsas and Purāṇas that the Purāṇa constitutes the soul of the Vedas; the well-known six Aṅgas (ancillary subjects) are the different limbs; what is found in the Vedas is seen in the Smṛtis and what is seen in both is narrated in the Purāṇas. Among all scriptural treatises it was the Purāṇa that was remembered at the outset by Brahmā. Thereafter the Vedas issued forth from his mouths. In this Kalpa and Manvantara there was only one Purāṇa, O sage. It was the means of acquiring the three aims of life. The meritorious text consisted of a hundred crores of verses. The Four-faced Lord remembered it and proclaimed it to the sages.

Thereafter the Purāṇa functioned as the source of all the scriptural treatises. As time passed on the sage noticed the inability of the people to comprehend the Purāṇa (due to their deficient intellect). The Lord assumes the form of Vyāsa during every Dvāpara Yuga always and abridges the Purāṇa to eight hundred thousand verses. This again is classified into

1. VV 16-28 describe the importance of Purāṇas. It is possible that originally there was one compendium called Purāṇa. Due to later accretions, the original Purāṇa was divided into many independent works, now known as eighteen Mahāpurāṇas. But the exorbitant claim that the original Pūrāṇa consisted of a hundred crore of verses and is retained in heaven is an exaggerated glorification of Purāṇas.

eighteen (separate Purāṇas) and put into currency in the world of mortals. Even to-day the Purāṇa extends to a hundred crore (verses) in Devaloka (world of immortals).

29-45a. Further, here it has been still abridged into four hundred thousand verses. These eighteen Purāṇas extant now are being enumerated here.[1] O excellent sage, listen; I shall mention them each by name.

The Purāṇa has five characteristic features, viz. creation, subsidiary creation, dynasties, Manvantaras and genealogical legends (of kings).

There in the collection, the first Purāṇa is Brāhma. There are ten thousand verses therein. It has a number of meritorious stories. Pādma Purāṇa is cited as consisting of fifty-five thousand verses. The third Purāṇa is Viṣṇu Purāṇa with twenty-three thousand verses. The fourth Purāṇa was originally proclaimed by Vāyu. It is remembered as Vāyavīya Purāṇa. Since devotion to Śiva has been propounded in it, the other name for it is Śaiva. O Śaunaka, there are twenty-four thousand verses in it. The fifth Purāṇa is cited as Bhaviṣya Purāṇa containing four Parvas (Books). There are fourteen thousand five hundred verses in it. The sixth Purāṇa contains nine thousand verses and it is glorified as Mārkaṇḍeya Purāṇa. Āgneya Purāṇa is the seventh one and it contains sixteen thousand verses. The eighth one is mentioned as Nāradīya Purāṇa. It consists of twenty-five thousand verses. The ninth one is Bhāgavata having two parts. The number of verses therein is eighteen thousand. The tenth Purāṇa, Brahma-vaivarta, has been mentioned as containing the same number of verses. Liṅga Purāṇa should be known as the eleventh Purāṇa. It has eleven thousand verses. O eminent sage, that Liṅga Purāṇa has two parts. They know that the twelfth Purāṇa is Vārāha Purāṇa with twenty-four thousand verses. O most excellent one among the illustrious ones, Skanda Purāṇa is divided into seven Khaṇḍas. It is observed that the number of verses in it is eighty-one thousand. Then the fourteenth Purāṇa is Vāmana by name. O Kulapati, ever since early days it is declared to consist of ten thousand verses. Kaurma

1. In this list of eighteen Purāṇas, Vāyu and Śaiva Purāṇa are regarded as one and the same, though actually they are separate (Tagare, *Intro. to Vāyu Purāṇa*, pp. XIX-XXV). *Matsya* (53.18-19), *Agni* (272. 4-5) regard *Vāyu* (and not *Śiva*) as a Mahāpurāṇa.

Purāṇa, the fifteenth Purāṇa, they say, has two parts. In Kali age, O Lord of Sāṅkhyas, it has seventeen thousand verses. Mātsya Purāṇa, the sixteenth one in the order, was narrated to Manu by the Fish (Lord in that incarnation). O most eloquent one, the verses number fourteen thousand. Gāruḍa Purāṇa is remembered as the seventeenth Purāṇa. It has nineteen thousand verses. The eighteenth Purāṇa is Brahmāṇḍa having two parts. The number of verses is twelve thousand eight hundred.

45b-53. Similarly there are Upapurāṇas which have been narrated by Vedhas (Brahmā).

The excellent Saura Upapurāṇa is a part of Brāhma Purāṇa. It has two versions. It is an easily accessible Upapurāṇa based on the meritorious story of Śiva. The first version is propounded by Sanatkumāra and the second one has been uttered by Sūrya. O great sage, it is well known by the name of Sanatkumāra. The second Upapurāṇa is Narasiṁha. It forms a part of Padma Purāṇa. Śaukeya (that of Śuka) is the third and is considered as a part of Viṣṇu Purāṇa. The fourth one is Bārhaspatya; it is always honoured as an ancillary to Vāyu Purāṇa. The fifth Upapurāṇa is Daurvāsasa. It is always ancillary to Bhāgavata. Nārada Upapurāṇa is mentioned by poets (learned men) as an ancillary to Bhaviṣya. (Then there are) Kāpila, Mānava and one narrated by Uśanas. Vāruṇa and the two Kālikā Upapurāṇas are ancillary to Brahmāṇḍa. Sāmba and Saura Upapurāṇas with the collection of all topics are Māheśvara (pertaining to Maheśvara—Śiva). Then there are Pārāśara, Bhāgavata and Kaurma the eighteenth. These eighteen Upapurāṇas have been enumerated by me in due order. He who listens to or recites this Purāṇasaṁhitā becomes sharer of infinite merit. On death he goes to the city of Brahmā.

CHAPTER TWO

The Greatness of Revā[1]

Sūta said:

1-8. Kṛṣṇa Dvaipāyana recounted the greatness of Narmadā. It was what you asked me and I shall fully narrate it to you. O excellent sage, with the exception of Lord Brahmā who is competent to recount the details of the holy spots on Narmadā? Formerly Janamejaya put this very question to a disciple of Dvaipāyana named Vaiśaṁpāyana. It has the meritorious reference to the Tīrthas on Revā. I shall mention it to you, O Śaunaka.

Formerly King Janamejaya, the son of Parīkṣita, was initiated in the holy rites concerning Yajña. All the articles for Havis (sacrificial offering) had been gathered together. The rites were going on. Eminent Brāhmaṇas were seated around and the sacrificial fire had been kindled with the holy offerings consigned to it. Everywhere pious discussions and discourses were being held. Day and night, O Kulapati, the words "Let it be given. Let it be consumed" were being uttered by the people, in the place of sacrifice. Those who were relaxed were indulging in different pastimes. Thus the Yajña was being performed in the chamber that was on a par with the heavenly assembly hall. Janamejaya then put this question to Vaiśaṁpāyana who was seated there:

Janamejaya said:

9-12. O Vaiśaṁpāyana, it is known to me that by the grace of Dvaipāyana, you have acquired knowledge. Hence, in the presence of the sages I am putting this question to you. Do tell me the events of the past regarding the holy pilgrimages of my forefathers. I have heard that they had experienced many kinds of painful calamities for a long time. After being defeated in the game of dice, the sons of Pṛthā, my grandfathers, began to wander all over the earth girt by the ocean, with a strong desire to visit holy spots. How did they fare in their wander-

1. This Purāṇa identifies Revā with Narmadā. But as De (p98) points out, some Purāṇas like BhP, Vāmana, treat Revā as an independent river.

ings, O Brāhmaṇa? By whom were they accompanied, O dear one, in their travels over many parts and regions of the earth? You have been considered by me as omniscient. Do tell me these details.

Vaiśampāyana said:

13-16. O Lord of the earth, O sinless one, after making obeisance to Lord Virūpākṣa (Śiva) and the great poet Vedavyāsa, I shall tell you what you have been asking.

The five Pāṇḍavas, your grandfathers, spent some time in the excellent Kāmyaka forest[1] along with Draupadī and Brāhmaṇas. In that forest where the chief person was Uddālaka, the highly intelligent Kaśyapa, Vibhāṇḍaka, the great sage, Guru, Pulastya, Lomaśa and others including their sons and grandsons lived. There they had their holy ablutions in all the Tīrthas, O eminent king. Then they went to the Vindhya mountain.

17-28. There they saw a holy hermitage surrounded by trees such as Campaka, Karṇikāra, Punnāga, Nāgakesara, Bakula, Kovidāra, Dāḍima, etc. It was rendered beautiful by Arjuna trees in full bloom, Bilvas, Pāṭalas, Ketakas, Kadambas, Āmras, Madhukas, Nimbas, Jambīras, Tindukas, Nālikeras (coconut trees), Kapitthas, Kharjūras and Panasas. It was crowded and overspread with various kinds of trees and creepers. It was spread over by various winding tendrils. The whole park was full of flowers and fruits. It was a big garden shining like Caitraratha forest. It was adorned with extensive ponds and tanks. It was embellished by clusters of lotuses. It was (as if) concealed by white, blue, yellow, whitish pink lilies, etc. It was scattered with Haṁsas (swans), Kāraṇḍava geese, Cakravākas (ruddy geese), etc. which enhanced its beauty. It was resorted to by many types of birds such as Āḍis, Kākas (a kind of raven), cranes, cuckoos, etc. It abounded in many types of beasts such as lions, tigers, boars, great elephants in their rut, huge-bodied buffaloes, deer, Citrakas, rabbits, Gaṇḍakas (rhinoceros), jackals, antelopes, bears (Bhallakas), bipeds as well as quadrupeds. It was resplendent and pleasing to the mind. There were many cuckoos too. Many kinds of birds such as Jīvañjīvaka flocks

1. One Kāmyaka Vana was on the banks of Sarasvatī while another was in the district of Mathurā (De 88).

adorned it. The place was free from miseries and grief. It was highly charming with smart and active animals. People were free from hunger and thirst and devoid of all ailments. The whole place attracted everyone. Here the deer used to suck at the udders of lioness with great affection. Cat and mouse licked each other with faces lifted up. The same was the case with lions and elephant cubs, serpents and peacocks. On seeing that beautiful forest the sons of Pāṇḍu entered it.

29-36. Dharmaputra saw there Sage Mārkaṇḍeya[1] who had the lustre like that of the midday Sun. He was attended upon by sages who were masters of the different scriptural texts. They belonged to noble families. They had the Sattva qualities and they strictly followed the conventions regarding cleanliness and good conduct. They performed Japa thrice everyday. They were endowed with great intelligence, patience and fortitude. They were particular in performing Japa three times a day. They were interested in regular performance of Homa with the chanting of the Mantras of Ṛk, Yajus and Sāma Vedas. Some of the attending sages were performing penances sitting in the midst of five fires. Some preferred to stay in secluded spots; some kept their arms raised up. Some remained without any support. Others kept on moving along with the movement of the Sun. Others took food in morning and evening. Still others took only one meal per day. Some took food once in twelve days. Some had food once a fortnight. Still others took food on every new-moon day. Some used to eat moss alone from ponds. Still others regularly took in only Piṇyāka (oil-cake). Some ate Palāśa leaves. A few had restricted regular food. Some took in only air or water. The sage was attended upon by eminent old sages of the types mentioned above. The glorious son of Dharma entered the hermitage and saw the quiescent, excellent sage, engaged in meditating on the greatest Being (Brahman). After circumambulating, he prostrated before him like a log of wood.

37-46. On seeing Dharmaputra fallen at his feet with devotion, the intelligent sage glanced at him for a long time and asked, "Who are you?"

---

1. Mārkaṇḍeya: A great sage who witnessed seven Kalpas. He was associated with Yudhiṣṭhira as a member of his Sabhā (Mbh, *Sabhā,* chs. 4-15) and in his exile in the forest (Mbh, *Vana,* chs. 186-232). He is the narrator of *Revā-Māhātmya.*

On hearing his words, a boy near him said, "Here is Dharmarāja who has come to meet you."

On hearing the words uttered by the boy, he respectfully said, "O dear one, O dear one, do come, do come." After moving a little from his seat, the sage lovingly sniffed at his head and made him seated. After he had been seated in the assembly, he honoured him duly by offering cereals grown in the forest, fruits, roots and juices of various kinds. All the Pāṇḍavas along with the Brāhmaṇas (accompanying them) were suitably honoured.

After resting for a short while, Yudhiṣṭhira, the son of Dharma, asked the excellent sage with curiosity: "Sir, it is known to me that you are the most long-lived one of all the people. O sinless one, narrate unto me the relevant events of all the seven Kalpas. Even when a Kalpa ends and when the mobile and immobile beings perish, you do not (perish), O eminent Brāhmaṇa. How is this? What is the reason therefor? O sage, there are many rivers including Gaṅgā. All of them flow into the seas. Among them which are those rivers that survive the Pralaya? What are those that become dissolved? Which of those rivers are always full of sacred waters? Which of them never get perished? O dear one, do tell me this with a delighted mind. I wish to hear it entirely along with the sages and kinsmen."

Śrī Mārkaṇḍeya said:

47-58. Very well, O highly intelligent Yudhiṣṭhira, O son of Dharma! I shall narrate duly what you have eagerly asked for, O sinless one. This is the ancient meritorious legend recounted by Rudra. It dispels all sins. Listen to the merit of one who listens devoutly to it. O king, there is no doubt about this that he will obtain that merit which is ordinarily obtained through a thousand Aśvamedhas and a hundred Vājapeyas. According to the statement of Rudra, a Brāhmana-slayer, a liquor-imbiber, a thief, a cow-slayer—all these men become freed from all sins.

These rivers are remembered (i.e. traditionally known) as those that dispel all sins: Gaṅgā, the most excellent one of all the rivers, Sarasvatī, Kāverī, Devikā, Sindhu, Sālakuṭī, Sarayū, Śatarudrā, Mahī, Carmilā, the meritorious Godāvarī, the river

Yamunā, Payoṣṇī, Śatadru and the splendid Dharmanadī. There are other rivers too.

O excellent king, I shall tell you the reason. The seas and all the rivers get destroyed in every Kalpa. But even when seven Kalpas passed away Narmadā has not perished. O great king, Narmadā is the only excellent river that stays for the longest time filled with water and eulogized by groups of sages, O blessed one. Gaṅgā and other rivers become destroyed at the end of every Kalpa. This divine river has been seen since long. This I shall explain to you, O sinless one. O great king, it is a miraculous river well-known in all the three worlds.

CHAPTER THREE

Mārkaṇḍeya Rescued in the Pralaya

Yudhiṣṭhira said:

1-11. O great sage, the terrible annihilation of seven Kalpas has been witnessed by you. There is no one else here, O holy Sir, who is so long-lived as you. Padmanābha (Viṣṇu with a lotus in the navel), the slayer of Asuras, who has a thousand feet[1], eyes and bellies has been seen by you when he was lying asleep in the vast expanse of water. When the mobile and immobile beings were being burnt, it was through the grace of that Lord that you were not destroyed. It was due to the boon granted by the Noble Soul. O sinless one, what were the miracles seen by you, as you were wandering about? O holy Sir, mention this. My curiosity is great. When the terrible end of the Yuga was imminent, when there was excessively terrible destruction, when all the worlds were formerly afflicted with drought extending to more than a hundred years, when the destruction of vegetation and medicinal herbs was awful, when there were neither the Devas nor the Dānavas, when everything was devoid of vigour, when there was no utterance of Vaṣaṭ, when everything was defiled much by Kali, when the rivers, lakes, ponds, puddles and parks became dried up, when,

1. An echo of Puruṣa-sūkta (RV X.90). Here Viṣṇu is identified with the Primeval Man.

O holy Sir, Maharloka merged into Janaloka, where were the noble-souled sages, the Brāhmaṇas, the Kṣatriyas, the Vaiśyas, etc. and the sages equipped with divine splendour? O great sage, when all beings are destroyed, which of the living beings remained stable (alive)? Did they disappear altogether? Do mention, O highly fortunate one, all these things severally. What are the elements? O eminent Brāhmaṇa, how can one attain Siddhi when the terribly hideous Kāla had caught hold of even Brahmā, Viṣṇu, Indra and Rudra?

On being enquired thus by Dharmarāja, the wise Sage Mārkaṇḍa surrounded by groups of sages, said thus:

Śrī Mārkaṇḍeya said:

12-22. O king, let all the sages along with you listen to the great Purāṇa narrated by Śaṁbhu to the Vāyudevatā[1]. This ancient work was heard by Skanda from Vāyu. Vasiṣṭha heard it from him and Parāśara from him. From him (Parāsara) it was heard by Jātūkarṇya and by the great sages from the latter. Thus it was traditionally narrated by hundreds of excellent Brāhmaṇas. The Saṁhitā consisting of a hundred thousand verses was narrated by Śaṁbhu indeed by thoroughly exploring earlier all the Śāstras and the deeper meaning of the Vedas in fact. Later it was classified into four, in accordance with the four Yugas, after due consideration by great sages, of the deficiency in the intellects of men. After propitiating Paśubhartṛ (i.e. Paśupati-Śiva), the great Lord, I heard this Purāṇa which I shall narrate entirely to you. On hearing this, O king, all the creatures are freed from all sins, mental and physical, accumulated in the course of seven births. With the favour of Viṣṇu Parameṣṭhin, the Lord of Devas, I have repeatedly witnessed the terrible destructions of seven Kalpas. When the whole universe was utterly burnt by the twelve Ādityas and everything was turned into a vast expanse of water, I had to swim through the ocean with the movement of my arms. Wandering (swimming) thus, I became utterly exhausted. Then, O king, I saw in the water the ancient Puruṣa, the Lord without beginning and

1. VV 12-14 give the Text-transmission of Revā Khaṇḍa through *Guru-paramparā* as follows: Śaṁbhu→Vāyu→Skanda→Vasiṣṭha→Parāśara→Jātūkarṇya→Vyāsa→ Sūta.

destruction, having lustre like that of the Sun. He had brightened the peak of the Lord of Mountains and all the ten quarters. A second person, Manu, was seen, accompanied by his sons and grandsons.

23-32. He too was drifting in the great deep sea enveloped in darkness. He was whirling round and round as though perched on the rim of a wheel, without resting even for a short while.

Swimming in the great sea with the movements of the arms, I became afraid and dispirited. Stationed there, I saw the great Fish in an inebriated state. O descendant of Bharata, he spoke to me on seeing me: "Do come; do come." He was Maheśvara in the form of a fish, the most important and the chief of all. Thereupon, O Lord of men, I hurriedly proceeded near the mouth of that Lord. I lost consciousness and became utterly exhausted and disgusted. Then I saw at the extremity (end) of the ocean, a meritorious river meandering as it wished[1]. She had many whirlpools and eddies. Waves were set in motion in the waters and she seemed to laugh boisterously by means of the foams. Fishes of diverse kinds swimming therein made the waters agitated. There was a young woman of comely appearance in the middle of the river. She was dark in complexion like the petals of a blue lotus. The current of the river was quite agitated with ripples. Her bodily limbs had the divine golden colour. She shone remarkably like molten gold. She had kept a big boat pressed on either side by the pair of her knees. Manu asked her: "O divinely excellent lady, who may you be? O celestial lady of great beauty, what may be the purpose for which you stand here? When both Suras and Asuras have perished, you are moving about in the ocean gracefully! The rivers, the oceans and the mountains have perished. O chaste lady, how is it that you alone among these many stay behind? I wish to hear the great reason therefor. O goddess, tell me without omitting anything."

The Abalā (the frail lady) said:

33-41. I am the sin-destroying meritorious river well known by the name Amṛtā. I have originated from the limbs of Īśvara.

1. Six Kalpas are described to affirm the imperishability of Revā. Sage Mārkaṇḍeya is a witness as he too was with her in those Pralayas.

Whence is fear if you resort to me? O Brāhmaṇa, I have brought this boat for your sake. Śaṅkara is stationed therein. Hence it will not get destroyed.

On hearing her words, my eyes became dilated with wonder. I got into the boat, O great king, along with Manu. With palms joined in veneration, I bowed down to the Lord, the all-pervading great Īśāna, the bestower of freedom from fear, and eulogized him:

"Obeisance to Lord Sadyojāta and Vāmadeva. Obeisance unto you in every birth. Obeisance to you who are attainable through devotion. Obeisance to Bhūḥ and Bhuvaḥ. Obeisance to the Lord senior to Rāma (Viṣṇu). Obeisance to you, O fair Lord Kāla; obeisance to one in the form of Kali. Obeisance to the incomprehensible one, the one of unmanifest form; to the great Lord and abode of brilliance. We do know the Lord of Lords, O Rudra. Obeisance, obeisance to you. Obeisance to the cause of the creation and annihilation of the universe. Obeisance."

Thus eulogized by me before the creation (of the world), the great Lord became pleased with me. Then he said: "O devotee of excellent holy rites, choose a boon."[1]

CHAPTER FOUR

Boons to Narmadā

Śrī Mārkaṇḍeya said:

1-6. Then I alighted from the sea (the boat) along with Manu and bowed to the pair of feet of Mahādeva saluted by all Devas. He was stationed on the peak of Trikūṭa[2] having the lustre of gold and comprising rocks of various colours. The Lord was seated on a great peak. He was accompanied by a crore of Rudras. The unborn, immutable Lord of the noble soul identical with all living beings was saluted by us both. O

1. This seems to be an abrupt end of the chapter.
2. A lofty mountain to the north of Panjab and south of Kashmir, the *Trikakud* of the Atharva Veda (De 106).

king worthy of esteem, O scion of the family of Kuru, I stayed in that terrible, vast expanse of water along with Rudra for a thousand Yugas.

Yudhiṣṭhira said:

O dear Sir, on hearing this a great deal of curiosity has been aroused in my mind. Hence even as I listen along with my kinsmen, please tell in detail who was that lady of eyes resembling lotus leaves? She was wandering like a Yogin in that vast ocean-like expanse of water enveloped by darkness. She introduced herself as the daughter of Rudra.

Śrī Mārkaṇḍeya said:

7-12. Formerly Manu was asked by me this same question. I shall recount the origin of that lady. The night of Brahmā Parameṣṭhin passed off and the bright day dawned. The creatures were being created. Then I bowed down my head to Manu, O Yudhiṣṭhira, and put to him this question: "Who is this lotus-eyed, dark-complexioned lady with a countenance resembling the Moon? She declares herself to have been born of Rudra and wanders in the vast expanse of waters. Is she Sāvitrī, the mother of the Vedas? Or is she Sarasvatī? Is she Mandākinī (Gaṅgā), the most excellent one of all the rivers? Is she Lakṣmī? Or is she Umā? She may be Kālarātri herself or she may be Prakṛti worthy of happiness. Do tell me this, O holy Sir. She is indeed Amṛtasaṁbhavā (origin of nectar, or originated from nectar). She wanders in the vast sea-like expanse of water of terrible appearance, where serpents and Rākṣasas have perished."

Manu said:

13-19. Listen, O dear one, I shall duly explain her origin, how this lady of excellent complexion originated from Rudra. Formerly Śiva Śaṅkara of quiescent body performed extensive penance along with Umā for the sake of the welfare of all the worlds. The Lord of self-control, the immanent soul of all living beings, climbed the Mountain Ṛkṣaśaila[1] and performed

1. *Ṛkṣa-śaila=Ṛkṣa-parvata*: The eastern part of the Vindhya range extending from the Bay of Bengal to the source of Narmadā and Śoṇa. (De 168-169)

a severe penance. He was invisible to all living beings. As that Lord was performing penance, perspiration issued forth from his body. The (drops of) sweat originating from Rudra flooded that mountain. The highly meritorious, excellent river was born of it. It was she of long eyes resembling the petals of a lotus, whom you saw in the sea-like expanse of water. Formerly in the first Kṛtayuga, she assumed the form of a woman and propitiated Rudra for ten thousand years.

Thereupon Śaṅkara, the great Lord, was pleased. Accompanied by Umā, he spoke to her: "O highly fortunate lady, speak out whatever there is in your mind."

The Sarit (*The River*) *said:*

20–33 By your grace, O Lord of Devas, let me be imperishable at the advent of Pralaya when all mobile and immobile beings are destroyed. When the rivers, oceans and mountains have perished, O Lord of Devas, let me be holy and imperishable, with your favour. Devout persons who have taken bath in me should be rid of all their sins, even if they have committed major and minor sins, O Śaṅkara. Jāhnavī destroys great sins in the northern region. I should become so in the southern region. Then only I shall be worshipped by gods. Just as the celestial river coming down from Svarga became well-known on the earth as Gaṅgā, O Lord of Devas, so let me be the Dakṣiṇagaṅgā (Southern Gaṅgā). A man who devoutly takes his holy bath in me, O Maheśvara, should acquire that merit which is usually obtained by taking holy bath in all the Tīrthas of the earth. O Lord, may the sin of Brāhmaṇa-slaughter and others like that which have remained accumulated be destroyed by taking the holy plunge for the period of a month. My desire is that, due to the holy dip in me, O Śaṅkara, one shall get all those benefits that accrue from the study of all the Vedas and performance of all the Yajñas. From my water, O Śaṅkara, let there be that benefit which usually arises from all sorts of Dānas and fasts and the holy plunge in all the Tīrthas. Those who adore Maheśvara on my banks should repair unto your Loka, O Śiva. Let this happen, O Lord, O Maheśāna; O Lord of the world, this alone is the boon. I desire that you do stay always on my banks along with Umā and other deities. Let every living being that dies in my waters go to Amarāvatī, whether they have done excellent Karmas or ignoble Karmas, whether they are mentally calm with full control over the sense-organs or not. O Lord of the chiefs of Devas, if you are pleased and if you consider it proper, let me be well-known in all the three worlds as the destroyer of great sins.

O excellent king, the Bull-vehicled Lord was requested for these and other divine boons by Narmadā. On being pleased he said:

Śrī Maheśa replied:

34-43a. O uncensured (i.e. praiseworthy) lady, O illustrious one, let what has been said (requested) by you, happen thus. O lotus-eyed one, excepting you, there is none else deserving the boon in all the worlds. O lady of excellent countenance, undoubtedly you have become one liberating devotees from all sins ever since the time you issued forth from my body. At the period when Kalpas come to a close, and specially at calamitous times, those men who reside resorting to your northern bank, and even insects, worms etc., trees, hedges, creepers etc. do attain excellent goal, O fair lady, after the fall of the bodies. Those Brāhmaṇas of great regard for piety and holy rites who resort to the southern bank and reside there till death, do go to the place of the Pitṛs. At your instance, as well as for some other reason, I shall always stay with Umā on your banks. O fair lady, O great lady, undoubtedly everything will happen thus. The deities will live on your northern bank along with Viṣṇu, Brahmā, Indra, Candra and Varuṇa and also Sādhyas, at my behest. Similarly, O celestial lady of great beauty, the others will stay on the southern bank along with me and the Pitṛs. This is your boon. Do go (hurry up), O blessed one; redeem men from sins. Do go there accompanied by the groups of sages, Siddhas, Suras and Asuras.

43b-54. After saying this, Lord Mahādeva, duly bowed down to by me and Manu, vanished along with Umā. Therefore this highly meritorious river is mentioned as the destroyer of great sins. This is the lady about whom you asked. Let there be no amazement on your part. This is (on a par with) Gaṅgā of great merit, well-known in all the three worlds. With her fifteen different branches it floods all the ten quarters. They are: Śoṇa, Mahānada, Narmadā, Surasā, Mandākinī, Daśārṇā, Citrakūṭā, Tamasā, Vidaśā, Karabhā, Yamunā, Citrotpalā, Vipāśā, Rañjanā and Vāluvāhinī. All these are born of the feet of Ṛkṣa mountain. All originated from Rudra. All are meritorious, auspicious and bestowers of welfare. They destroy all sins. She is eulogized by the masters of the Vedas, by these divine names as well as by the illustrious knowers of the Purāṇas, by Ājyapas and Somapas (varieties of Pitṛs). O excellent one among men, everything has been narrated. That which is conducive to good fortune and uttered by Manu is splendid. The origin of Amṛtā is incomparably sacred, since it is spoken by Rudra, O scion of the family of Bharata. Those men who glorify these fifteen names after getting up early in the morning, will attain the entire benefit of a holy plunge into the river. After casting off their human form, they will attain the highest place by riding an aerial chariot of solar lustre, reverberating with the sound of a hundred bells.

CHAPTER FIVE

Naming the River Narmadā

Yudhiṣṭhira said:

1-14. O excellent Brāhmaṇa, the entire story recounted is wonderful. The groups of sages along with me are extremely wonder-struck. It is very assuring that this divine, meritorious Narmadā, that has issued forth from the body of Rudra and hence has no human source of origin, causes the destruction of great sins. O sage of good holy rites, when seven Kalpas have come to a close (even as you have been a witness), this auspicious river along with you has not become dead. What else can be a more excellent merit? What are those Kalpas referred to, the seven ones, which come to an end, if this divine lady and you too, O great sage, have not become dead. When the whole universe had been converted into a vast expanse of waters without any trace of the flocks of birds, at the close of the Yuga, what was the form assumed by Mahādeva? How does he annihilate the universe? How does he remain in the great sea of waters? How does he create the universe? How does he sustain the subjects? What form does the divine river assume when everything has been converted into a single sea-like expanse of waters? Why is she called Narmadā? How is she remembered as Revā? Why this name Añjanā (or Rañjanā)? Why Surasā? Why was she called Kṛpā? Why the name Mandākinī? Why should she be (called) Śoṇa? Why (is she called) Trikūṭā? Why Vāluvāhinī? Crores and crores of Tīrthas have entered the great ocean. How many crores of these rivers serve Narmadā? How is she served by the sages with sacred threads and by the deities? O excellent sage, why is it heard that she is divided severally? Why is she called Vaiṣṇavī by those conversant with the Purāṇa? What are those Sthānas and Tīrthas where the excellent river has to be adored? Do mention the different Tīrthas separately where Hara is present. What is the size and magnitude of the divine river as created by Rudra? Of what nature are the Karmas (rites) mentioned by Rudra to you? O excellent Brāhmaṇa, how did this region become over-run by Mlecchas? O highly intelligent Mārkaṇḍeya, O holy Sir, narrate this unto me.

Śrī Mārkaṇḍeya said:

15-26. May all the sages, and you too, O Yudhiṣṭhira, listen to the Purāṇic legend regarding Narmadā as recounted by the Trident-bearing Lord. It was heard by me from the Vāyu Devatā and he had heard it from Maheśvara. Since human beings are incapable, the sages abridged it formerly. The first one is Māyūra.[1] O dear one, Kaurmya comes thereafter. Then Pura, Kauśika, Mātsya and Dvirada; Vārāha is what was seen by me. Vaiṣṇava is the eighth one. Then what was called Nyagrodha was evolved; then the excellent Ākāṁkṣā. Then Padma, Tāmasa, Saṁvarta, Udvarta and Mahāpralaya. These, the thinkers on the Vedas mentioned in regard to the Purāṇa.

These are the abridged versions condensed by those noble souls. They have been divided into four parts by Brahmā and others and the great sages. That I shall expatiate upon, O knower of the contents of Purāṇas. The highly terrible seven

1. These are later considered as names of Kalpas.

Kalpas during which this river did not die (had these characteristics): All mobile beings became enveloped in darkness without distinguishable characteristics and were not known clearly. The rays of the Moon and the Sun vanished. The living beings disappeared. At the extremity of the darkness, the Puruṣa, the preceptor of the universe, was known under his great name. The eternal one was both manifest and unmanifest. He moved about therein alone. Then the one consisting of Oṁkāra passed off and *Dvija* (the second-born from the original) created Gāyatrī. Then Īśāna, the Virāṭ (Cosmic) Puruṣa, sported about with her. From his own body he created the universe consisting of and named after the five elements. Sportingly he created the universe consisting of and named after the five elements. The being called Virāṭ sportingly created Hiraṇmaya (golden being) along with the *Bīja* (seed). That became the divine egg resembling the twelve Ādityas (Suns) (in brilliance).

27-37. Breaking it (the egg) the four-faced being, Pitāmaha, was born. He created thus the universe consisting of Devas, Asuras and human beings, animals, creatures and birds, the sweat-born, egg-born and the embryo-born ones. This egg is proclaimed as the first one in the Purāṇas.

O excellent king, Parameṣṭhin Rudra sported about with Umā in the vast expanse of sea-like water. A splendid girl was born out of the sweat of Umā due to her delight. When Śarva's chest pressed against the breasts of Umā, a great girl of lotus-like eyes issued forth from the sweat. This is the second birth, O Yudhiṣṭhira. That (lady, river) whirled around the worlds of Devas, Asuras and human beings. Unrivalled in beauty of form as she was, she maddened the three worlds. On seeing her, the leaders of Devas and Daityas were enchanted. They wondered: 'How is she to be obtained?' O scion of the family of Bharata, they searched for that girl here and there. She fascinated the entire universe through her seductive and graceful charms and coquettish manners. She moved about in her divine form like a lightning streak in the middle of clouds. The most excellent one among all maidens, she shone in her lustre. Then all the Suras, Daityas and Dānavas who were enamoured of that girl and overcome with Kāma (lust) requested Rudra for that girl to be given to them. Then Mahādeva said: "Of the two, Devas and Dānavas, he who will prove superior in strength and splendour will attain this girl, not otherwise, O excellent Suras."

38-44. Then all the Devas and Asuras approached the girl saying, "I shall seize her, I shall seize her." Even as all were watching her, the girl vanished. Then they saw her stationed a Yojana away. All of them then rushed to the place where she was seen. Then they saw her stationed three or four Yojanas away. Then the lady of elephantine gait vanished and stationed herself hundreds and thousands of Yojanas away. On account of her lightness she was seen hundred thousands of Yojanas away. They saw her sometimes ahead and sometimes behind in different directions and intermediate quarters. The beautiful lady appeared in one direction and many directions. Thus they were forced to wander about by her for a period of a thousand divine years. But that girl born of Mahādeva's limbs was not attained by them. Thereupon the Lord laughed boisterously along with Umā.

45-52. The Gaṇas joyously danced in accordance with the beating of the time. Suddenly the girl was seen very near Śaṅkara. On seeing her the wonder-struck Devas returned with faces turned away. Then the Pināka-bearing Lord himself gave her a name: "Since you humoured them by means of your pranks and gambols, O beautiful girl, you will become the excellent river *Narmadā* (*Narma*, humour+*dā*, giver)." The Lord resumed his form and joked. This river of cool water and auspicious features was called Narmadā by him. When the destruction of the seven Kalpas, as was said by Śaṁbhu before, took place, O great king, she did not die. She became well-known as Narmadā. Then he gave that well-behaved, splendid girl to the great Ocean. The Lord, the Lord of Devas, the Lord of all living beings and goblins gave her to the Ocean. Thereafter the divine river Narmadā laughing boisterously through the foams descended from the great mountain Ṛkṣa and entered the Ocean, the Lord of rivers. Thus she was born of Īśvara in the Brāhma Kalpa and was seen by me in Mātsya Kalpa. Listen as described by me.

CHAPTER SIX

Epithets[1] *of Narmadā Explained*

Mārkaṇḍeya said:

1-7. Again, O excellent king, when the end of the third Yuga approached, Lord Nīlalohita assumed the forms of the twelve Suns and burnt the entire ocean-girt earth along with the mountains and forests. Maheśvara then was in the form of Kāla, the destroyer. Thereafter he became an enormously big cloud and flooded the entire earth with water. His body assumed a dark physical form and the earth was marked with lightning and Moon as though hit with a weapon and flooded with water. The entire universe was turned into a vast expanse of water. By means of his Māyā, he withdrew the universe into himself and slept in the translucent water. In the ocean enveloped in darkness, when the element of Vāyu (Wind) assumed the activity of Maheśvara, I wandered about for a period of a thousand divine years. O great king, I meditated upon the Lord in the form of Oṁkāra, the Lord by whom everything was rendered impenetrable. I was meditating in the pure water when the mobile and immobile beings got merged in that terrible ocean. I suddenly espied a Mayūra (peacock) embellished with golden feathers with wonderful eyelike marks of various colours. The peacock was blue-throated and had excellent eyes.

1. The following are the epithets of Narmadā:
   - (i) *Trikūṭī*: The river descended from Mount Trikūṭa (vv 16-17).
   - (ii) *Mahatī*: (i) The river lifted up to Mount Ṛkṣa (vv 26-27): (ii) Of speedily flowing current (vv 30-31).
   - (iii) *Śoṇa*: That in which drops from Śiva's trident fell (v 28).
   - (iv) *Surasā*: A river of excellent *Rasa* or water (v 32).
   - (v) *Kṛpā*: A bestover of freedom from Saṁsāra (vv 32-34).
   - (vi) *Mandākinī*: A slow-flowing river (v 34).
   - (vii) *REVĀ*: Reverberating all the quarters with sound (*Rava*) while flowing (vv 37-38).
   - (viii) *Mahārṇavā*: Who broke away from the Ocean (v 39).
   - (ix) *Vipāpā* : Remover of sins (v 39).
   - (x) *Vipāśā* : Remover of the bond of Saṁsāra (v 40).
   - (xi) *Vimalā* : With clean, splendid waters (vv 41-42).
   - (xii) *Karabhā* : Of lustrous hands (waves) (vv 42-43).
   - (xiii) *Rañjanā* : Delighter of the world (vv 43-44).
   - (xiv) *Vāyu-vāhinī*: Carrier of every resident on her bank to heaven (v. 44).

8-20. Then the Mayūra (peacock) of great prowess moved about within the ocean-like expanse of water which it agitated much through its great shrill cry. The three-crowned peacock was Śiva, the protector of the three worlds. He agitated the waters in the form of a peacock. He saw the river of great flow of current, whirling within the great ocean. On seeing her whirling rapidly with waves after waves, Mahādeva in the form of Mayūra asked her: "Who are you, O splendid lady with a permanent physical form? In the course of the great annihilation you have not become destroyed, even when the multitudes of Devas and Asuras have perished in the great ocean-like expanse of rivers and lakes. Who are you, O lotus-eyed one, who continue to move about? How is it that you did not get destroyed?"

Narmadā said:

With your favour, O Lord of Devas, I have no death. Do create the universe once again, O Lord. The night has come to an end.

On being told thus, Mahādeva shook the cage-like plumage of feathers. Then from the middle of the cage, from the plumage issued forth all these: The great Daityas and Devas were born of his wings. The river Narmadā began to flow in between those two groups. Thereupon another great mountain was seen, O eminent scion of the family of Bharata. It had three huge peaks and it appeared like a horned bull. It was well-known by the name Trikūṭa. It was embellished with all jewels. The river descended from Trikūṭa and flooded the earth. Hence she became well known as *Trikūṭī*. She is the greatest saviour of the Pitṛs.

From the second peak Gaṅgā spread over the surface of the earth. The third peak split into seven pieces. They became the seven Kulaparvatas in Jaṁbūdvīpa.

All the things of the world were born, such as planets, constellations, moon, villages, rivers, four types of living beings, viz. the oviparous, the viviparous, the sweat-born and the germinating ones (i.e. trees and plants that pierce through the ground and grow). Thus the entire universe issued forth from the Mayūra formerly. Everything, O tiger among men, was born of Mahādeva.

21-27. Then the Lord of Devas separated the rivers and oceans and said to Narmadā: "You go to the southern quarter. Just as in the northern country Jāhnavī is the meritorious sacred river, destroyer of great sins, you shall be the splendid river in the South. Just as Gaṅgā originating from my head is highly meritorious, so also indeed better than Gaṅgā, you shall be meritorious undoubtedly. With a part of mine I shall be by your side. You shall be a panacea for those who are defiled by great sins."

On being told thus by the Lord, she became the Southern Gaṅgā and destroyer of great sins. She hurriedly went to the southern region of the country. With the blessings of the Moon-crested Lord, she went to the Ṛkṣa mountain whence she, being urged by Mahādeva, proceeded with the full complement of the currents of water. She was called *Mahatī* by Mahādeva, O Lord of the earth, because she was lifted up with great speed.

28-34. While the Lord was performing the penance, drops fell down from the tip of the trident. Hence she became known by the name *Śoṇa.*

Those rivers are seventeen in number. Of all the rivers, Narmadā is the most meritorious, since it had issued forth from the body of Rudra and also through the grant of the boon by the noble soul.

Due to the blessings of Śaṅkara, the divine river is the destroyer of great sins. She is called *Mahatī* also, because she was seen in the terrible, great ocean. Her limbs were prominent and she is huge in size. Hence also she is called *Mahatī.*

On being stirred and agitated by the elephants of the quarters comparable to clouds (in size), the waters became turbid, but she has excellent *Rasa* (water). Hence she is (called) *Surasā.*

Bestowing freedom from fear, she is sympathetic to all the worlds immersed in the ocean of worldly existence. Hence she is remembered as *Kṛpā.*

Formerly in the meritorious Kṛtayuga she was embellished with the divine Mandāra flowers strewn from the Kalpa trees. The river is full of Rohītaka fish. So she flows slowly. Hence she is remembered as *Mandākinī.*

35-45. She came to this world quickly piercing through the great ocean. She is worthy of being adored by Suras and Siddhas. Hence she is *Mahārṇavā.*

She has clusters of lilies of various colours. She is agitated by Ṛkṣas (bears) and Dvipas (elephants). She breaks through the large mountain and proceeds to the great ocean. With great *Rava* (sound) she makes all the quarters reverberate, flooding all places and shining everywhere. Hence she is remembered as *Revā.*

She makes those miserable (ones) on account of the sufferings of wives and children due to the curses, wherewith they are overwhelmed, free from sins. Hence she is remembered as *Vipāpā.*

She redeems and liberates from harassment due to bondage and the great misery caused by faeces, urine etc., as well as dust and mire and blood. Hence she is called *Vipāśā.*

She is the redeemer from the ocean of worldly existence. Narmadā has waters free from impurities. Her face is as splendid as the clear moon. In the great, awful envelopment of darkness, she is highly lustrous. For all these reasons, she is called *Vimalā* by learned men, O excellent king.

Her hands (waves) are as lustrous as the rays of the sun and moon. As she flows the whole universe rejoices. For all these reasons, she is called *Karabhā.*

Merely by her sight, she delights the worlds, O descendant of Bharata. The meaning of the root √*Rañj* is to delight, O excellent king. Hence she is called *Rañjanā.*

She takes even grass, creepers, hedges, creatures and birds to heaven (once they grow nearby). Hence she is called *Vāyuvāhinī.*

He who knows the (meaning of) names in this manner and particularly the way she flows, goes undoubtedly to Rudraloka after being liberated from sins.

CHAPTER SEVEN

The Advent of Kūrma Kalpa[1]

Śrī Mārkaṇḍeya said:

1-9. Again there was the advent of a vast expanse of ocean-like water with horrible features in which mobile and immobile beings perished. The whole world was submerged in water. Darkness enveloped everything and there was no light at all. Brahmā alone assumed the form of a *Khadyota* (Firefly, Glow-worm). For the period of a thousand divine years, he moved about in the great ocean enveloped in darkness. He then saw in the terrible expanse of ocean, the Lord asleep in the form of a tortoise. The excellent Lord, the incomprehensible, extended to a thousand Yojanas. He resembled the twelve Ādityas (Suns) in splendour. He had a thousand feet and eyes. On seeing him, Brahmā was surprised and roused him slowly by means of auspicious hymns taken from the Vedic and Vedāṅga texts: "O Vācaspati (Lord of Speech), do wake up. O Supreme Being, obeisance to you. O Parameśvara (Supreme Lord), the entire universe is stationed in your belly. Hence, O Mahāsattva (huge being of immense inner strength and good qualities), release what was withdrawn within by you. The night of Brahmā has passed off. The day has dawned. O Lord of all worlds, have a view, whereby the universe can take birth."

On hearing his words, Parameśvara (Great Lord) got up ejecting the three worlds that had been swallowed at the time of the close of the Kalpa. Devas, Dānavas, Gandharvas, Yakṣas, Uragas (Serpents) and Rākṣasas along with the Moon, the Sun and the planets, issued forth from his body.

10-20. After dividing the entire ocean-like expanse of water, Parameśvara espied the earth consisting of trees, medicinal herbs and puddles, extensively abounding in stones and flood of water and full of rivers and lakes. He saw Himavān the great mountain, Śveta the excellent mountain, the great mountain Śṛṅgavān as well as other Kulaparvatas. (He espied) the Dvīpas

1. This describes Narmadā in the form of a beautiful lady who survived Pralaya in Kūrma Kalpa.

such as Jambū Dvīpa, Kuśa, Krauñca, Gomeda, Śālmala, ending with Puṣkara and the seven great oceans, the great mountain Lokāloka— all these were stationed in front. That Maheśvara saw the entire universe consisting of the mobile and immobile beings with the fourfold Prakṛtis that had come out at the beginning of the Yuga. The Lord saw the earth with scattered pieces of rocks. The goddess (divine lady) was in the great ocean perched on the back of the tortoise. On the top of the shattered rocky hill where there was neither a river nor a lake, the waters of the ocean were moving in waves with agitated whirlpools and eddies. The medicinal herbs were shedding lustre on the surface of the earth where there were various rocks and stone slabs. The great Lord saw the river reverberated with warbling of birds and teeming with fish and tortoise. The divine river resembled an excellent cloud. She had divine charm and a number of incomparable eddies (stores of water).

The divine river Narmadā was in the form of a woman in the middle of the ocean and she had dark complexion like the colour of a cloud. The thighs, buttocks and the breasts were thick and huge. She had inimitable gorgeous garments and she was bedecked in ornaments. She had anklets and girdles of excellent chains. She was bedecked in necklaces and bracelets.

21-27. He saw Narmadā of unmanifest limbs and noble features. She was beautified by various ornaments of magical origin. The young woman had just risen above the water with half raised arms eulogizing the Lord of the chiefs of Devas. Her eyes were large like the petals of a lotus. On seeing that splendid lady, I was overwhelmed with surprise in the heart. I took my holy dip in her splendid water. I began to eulogize joyously by means of Mantras taken from the Vedic Scriptures. In front of her I saw the mobile and immobile beings created along with Devas, Asuras, Gandharvas, Pannagas and great Uragas. I saw that the highly esteemable lady did not undergo destruction before because she was born of the body of Mahādeva. With his favour she did not get dissolved. She was seen by me again and again. O excellent king, it has been recounted to you. Those excellent Brāhmaṇas who study this manifestation pertaining to Kūrma and the learned men who listen to it, are liberated from all sins.

CHAPTER EIGHT

The Advent of Baka Kalpa

Mārkaṇḍeya said:

1-10a. When the world was destroyed again and enveloped with water, I was caught in the middle of the great ocean and so I crossed the waters with my arms. When a hundred divine years elapsed, O excellent king, I was completely exhausted. I began to meditate on the Lord who could take me across the great ocean.

At that time, as I was meditating, I saw a great bird resembling a pearl necklace, Kunda flower, and the moon (in complexion). I saw a Baka (crane) white like cow's milk.

On seeing that crane, I was dismayed: 'Whence can there be the existence of a bird in this terrible, great ocean?' I thought. Untiringly I went on swimming (to it) and asked that crane: "O Lord endowed with divine Yogic soul! Assuming the form of a bird you seem as if to enchant me. Who may you be, wandering in this vast expanse of waters? Do narrate this to me completely. Whoever you are, I do obeisance to you."

He told me: "I am Mahādeva, Brahmā and Viṣṇu. O dear one, don't you understand that the entire universe has been annihilated (or taken within)? O great sage, I am the father and mother of the universe as well as of yours. Seeing everything submerged in the great ocean, I was moved with sympathy. Hence I have come here in the guise of a bird. Why are you getting agitated? Why do you wander like this in the great ocean? Quickly come within the fold of my wings, O Brāhmaṇa, so that you can rest."

10b-13. On being told thus by that Lord, O king, I ensconced myself within his wings and began wandering in the water. At the end of even a thousand Yugas I was not tired and I continued to be in the middle of the ocean. Then, O virtuous king, I suddenly heard in all the quarters an excellent, mysterious sound mixed with the sound of anklets. All of a sudden the entire mass of water in the ocean shrank in size. 'What could this be?' Thinking thus I looked in every direction.

14-22. Ten girls from all the quarters came to the ocean. They were clad in gorgeous garments and bedecked with anklets and other ornaments. One of them had the lustre resembling that of the moon. Another had the radiance of the sun. A certain girl had the lustre of a mass of collyrium. One of the maidens had the brilliance of a red lotus. They had different forms. All of them were gentle and they were bedecked in various ornaments. Those holy maidens worshipped the crane with Arghya, Pādya and garlands. The self-refulgent mountain entered that immutable, very terrible bird of mountain-like size. It became enlarged into thousands of Yojanas and hundreds of Yojanas. There was a distance of thirty thousand Yojanas from the terrestrial zone.

Then the earthly zone assumed a divine refulgence abounding in five kinds of gems. There was a divine flight of stairs of crystal rendered very charming with golden pillars. (The city built there) extended to a thousand Yojanas. Twice that was its length. It had a great many tanks and wells, palaces and towers. Kalpa trees abounded in the place. It was decorated with sixty flags.

In that beautiful, excellent city there was another beautiful city embellished with various kinds of gems. The altar was brilliant with flags and banners. The city was two hundred Yojanas in length and a hundred Yojanas in width.

23-31. There was a very splendid river in the middle of the city. It had meritorious waters and rocky banks studded with gems. It was a great river. On its bank I saw a great Liṅga too. It had the lustre of lightning and the Sun. All round, it was set with blue sapphires. In some places it resembled fire. In some other places it was smoke-coloured, yellow in some places, red in other places and white elsewhere. The Liṅga of diverse colours was very wonderful to behold. It was surrounded by Brahmā, Viṣṇu, Indra and Sādhyas. It was surrounded by Nandīśvara and other Gaṇādhyakṣas, Indra and Ādityas. I stared at that great Liṅga of Īśāna alone.

Thereafter I saw Devas and Dānavas with closed eyes lying asleep all round it. They were bedecked in divine jewels and ornaments.

Then after taking their holy bath in the waters of that river, those highly esteemed, excellent, ten young maidens duly offered Arghya, Pādya to the Liṅga along with that bird and worshipped them with divine flowers. Like lightning vanishing behind a cluster of clouds, all those ladies disappeared within that excellent city.

32-38. Neither the king of birds was there nor those women nor the Devas. The Liṅga alone which was being worshipped (by me?) remained there. I was surprised. On account of the grief, I was fainting as it were. I thought everything was an illusion created by Rudra. Then those girls emerged (from the water) brightening the entire universe with the divine garments and ornaments they were wearing, like lightning streaks brightening a cluster of clouds. After adoring the Liṅga with divine, golden lotuses those ladies of splendid countenances and excellent ornaments soon entered the water.

In the other excellent city I repeatedly saw a divine (immortal) girl adoring Maheśvara. Thereupon I asked that beautiful lotus-eyed girl: "Who may you be, O goddess staying in this city worshipping Śiva? Where have all those ladies gone? Where are those leaders of Gaṇas? I do obeisance to you, O illustrious Maheśvarī. O lady of holy rites! I wish to know this with your favour. Take pity on me, O great goddess! O sinless one, do tell me this."

The Strī (lady) replied:

39-48. O Brāhmaṇa, how is it that I have been forgotten by you? You had seen me in the previous Kalpa. Let there be no forgetfulness on your part. I am the same Kalpavāhinī well-known as Narmadā; I was born of Rudra's body. The girls seen by you adoring Maheśvara, the girls who have brought you along with the king of birds, O excellent sage, are the quarters. Mahāyogin Maheśvara has been brought here by these, Nandīśvara and others from Śivapura, O Brāhmaṇa. The same deity, Mahādeva, has established himself here in the form of a Liṅga. The preceptor of the Suras and Asuras is being worshipped by Brahmā, Viṣṇu and Indra. It is called Liṅga by the great sages conversant with the Purāṇas, because the entire universe consisting of mobile and immobile beings, becomes merged therein. Formerly, all the groups of Devas were taken together and dissolved by the Lord through Māyā. They are not seen now. On being created by the Self-born Lord, they will be seen again. I am engaged in adoring the Liṅga. My name is Narmadā. I have been the maid in attendance of Rudra for a period of a thousand Yugas.

O eminent Brāhmaṇa, you have become immortal with his favour. By worshipping Śiva, you have become a Siddha equipped with truth, straightforwardness and kindness.

After saying this the goddess vanished there itself.

49-55. The women, the Lord of Devas, Maheśvara in the form of a Baka—all vanished. On hearing her words I got down into the great river and took bath, with the recitation of Mantras duly worshipping the Liṅga. But when I rose up from the river I could not see the Liṅga or the river, O king. At that time itself all the worlds were born and also the earth with all forests. The same firmament became spangled with the stars, moon and sun. As before, what was rendered unseen was seen again. I mentally bowed down to the Lord and worshipped Maheśvara.

It was thus that in the previous Baka Kalpa, this immutable lady (Narmadā) was seen by me. Narmadā, the destroyer of the great sins of human beings, (was seen by me). Hence this esteemable (divine river) should always be resorted to by all Brāhmaṇas, Kṣatriyas, Śūdras, Vaiśyas and others of righteous nature if they wish to get piety increased. Those who devoutly take their bath in the waters of Narmadā even once and worship Maheśvara get all their sins dissolved undoubtedly.

CHAPTER NINE

The Origin of Narmadā

Śrī Mārkaṇḍeya said:

1-7. I shall recount to you another subsequent Yugānta (ending of a Yuga). Listen.

Formerly when the world consisting of the mobile and immobile beings was burnt by the Suns, when everywhere the rivers, lakes and oceans were completely dried up and destroyed, when the utterance of Vaṣaṭ became non-existent among men, when people began to transgress bounds of decorum, the entire sky was filled with clouds of various forms shining with rainbows and the world was filled with floods of water. Thereupon it formed a vast ocean-like water expanse. Lord Hara kept the entire universe within his belly and went to sleep.

Supporting his own Prakṛti that Lord of subjects, the Yogic soul, entered the ocean and lay down for a period of a thousand Yugas.

All the sages beginning with Bhṛgu and those beginning with Sanaka, all those who reside in Brahmaloka saw the Bull-emblemed Lord lying asleep along with his wife on a splendidly pure couch covered with many sheets.

8-18. That lady is omniformed. Maheśvara is also omniformed. I saw the immutable Lord who closely embraced her and lay asleep. At the foot of the Lord I saw that dark-complexioned girl characterised by lotuses, with well-shaped buttocks, massaging the feet of the Lord. That Śyāmā (Dark-complexioned one) was clad in pure, spotless garments. She had a python for the sacred thread. Her eyes resembled the petals of a lotus. She was bedecked in all sorts of ornaments. This knowledgeable Narmadā of excellent complexion serves and attends upon the sleeping Lord of the chiefs of Devas for the entire period of a thousand Yugas.

Brahmā, the great Lord too, eulogizes the immutable Śaṅkara along with his mental sons, Bhṛgu and others, by means of the four Vedas held by him, O king. With great devotion they eulogized Śaṁbhu free from ailments. With the Mantras originating from Īśvara, they continued the eulogy of the Lord of Devas there. All of a sudden, all those four Śrutis got submerged into the sea. With the Vedas got lost thus, the Lord (Brahmā) became enveloped with the darkness of ignorance. He approached Lord Īśāna who was asleep and began to wake him up. "O Hara, O tawny-eyed one, get up, O Mahādeva, O Maheśvara. All my Vedas have been taken away. Hence I am attempting to eulogize (you). The entire universe consisting of the mobile and immobile beings, whether divine or non-divine had been pervaded by the Vedas. It is due to them that I could remember the past and the present and performed the duty of creation. Without them I feel isolated. I am no better than a dumb, blind and senseless one, always. Without them there is no hope of any movement, vigour, strength or ardour. O

Lord of the chiefs of Devas, I cannot recollect anything without them.

19-28. It behoves you, O Lord of the chiefs of Devas, to give them (back) to me quickly. The entire universe consisting of the mobile and immobile beings is insentient, blind and deaf. O Lord of Suras, the fourteen worlds do not shine. Deprived of the Vedas, O Lord of Suras, I have become deficient in vigour and vitality. Hence I bow down (ardently). Whatever there is, whether mobile or immobile, is entirely born of the Vedas. O preceptor of the universe, the entire range of scriptural texts shines well only as long as the eternal treasure of the Vedas has not been removed. By keeping up and holding steadfast to the Vedas one can quell all sins as in the case of the darkness that is destroyed by the rising sun.

The eternal Brahman is the subtle mystery in the Vedas. O Lord, I used to know it as seated in the heart. It has gone now due to the roar of the Vedas. O Śaṅkara, I was reciting the Vedas before you to-day. All of a sudden, those Vedas have gone away. O Lord, I shall not be in a position to create the earth. All of them (the Vedas) have entered the ocean in front. They are being requested for by me. Let them stay in my memory. O Śarva, this daughter of wide eyes knows everything. O Bhava, no one else is like her. She has been in existence for a thousand Yugas. This illustrious sage Mārkaṇḍa is the most excellent one among intelligent ones. O Mahādeva, he attends upon you in every Kalpa. He performs excellent Vratas for the sake of the welfare of the three worlds."

29-39. On being told thus by Brahmā Parameṣṭhin, the Lord of Devas spoke to Narmadā, the most excellent one among rivers, in sweet and smooth words: "O blessed one, tell Brahmā what he is asking for? By whom have all the Vedas of Brahmā, the preceptor of the universe, been taken away?" On being told thus by Rudra, the fawn-eyed one said: "O Maheśvara, while you were asleep, Brahmā was reciting the Vedas. In this terrible expanse of water, two terrible Dānavas, Madhu and Kaiṭabha, spotted out a vulnerable point. These two Asuras were already born in the previous Kalpa. They could not be defeated by Suras. O Mahādeva, formerly it was you who had created them. Hence they were invincible to Suras and Asuras. They had all the glory and fortune. They became subtle like wind. They snatched off all the Vedas even as the Grandfather was reciting them. Thereafter they entered the great ocean."[1]

On hearing these words of Amṛtā that highly refulgent one remembered the Conch-discus-club-bearing Lord of Devas[2]. O great king, that excellent Sura, the Lord capable of bringing about the death of the Dānavas, the Lord adored by all the deities, came to the surface of the earth. The Lord then assumed the form of a fish and stirred up the ocean. There the Lord saw the Vedas kept in Pātāla. The Slayer of Madhu saw the two Daityas of great vigour and vitality. By means of his power he slew the two mighty-armed Daityas of great vigour and terrific strength. The Lord of the cosmos bedecked by the discus brought the Vedas kept hidden there in water and handed them to the Four-faced Lord.

40-50. Thereafter, having regained the Vedas Lord Pitāmaha became delighted. He again began the creation of the entire universe consisting of the mobile and immobile beings. The maid in attendance of Rudra, the meritorious divine river, the sanctifier of all living beings, diverted her water there.

Thereupon Devas and sages, with penance as their sole asset, began with highly delighted mind the worship of the Three-eyed Lord on her banks. The single form of Maheśa became for another reason triple and began to function in the forms of Brahmā, Viṣṇu and Īśvara.

Those who are deluded enough to emphasize absolute distinction among these are of sinful activities. How can they have piety and spiritual fulfilment?

In the same manner these three rivers born of Rudra are one and the same in the different forms of Gaṅgā, Revā and Sarasvatī. Gaṅgā is the form of Viṣṇu and is conducive to the destruction of all sins. Narmadā originating from the body of Rudra is also like that. The form of Brahmā, Sarasvatī, is well known in all the three worlds. The divine form of the goddess

1. The role of Narmadā as the reporter of Veda-snatchers, Madhu and Kaiṭabha, to Śiva who was lying asleep on the ocean of cosmic waters is meant for the glorification of Narmadā and Śiva. BhP, Mbh and other Purāṇas do not attribute this (Viṣṇu's) role to Śiva.
2. The credit of killing Madhu and Kaiṭabha and restoration of the Vedas is not denied to Viṣṇu. But it is said that he was commanded to do so by Śiva. This is a Śaivite twist to the episode.

can go wherever she desires. She stands for the richness (i.e. powers) of speech.

Narmadā is specially greatest and most auspicious form divinely bestowed with the power of going wherever she pleased. Everywhere she is adored by Suras. She is remembered as the subtlest of all subtle forms pervading all living beings. This is the immortal, everlasting, excellent flight of stairs leading to heaven (Svarga). She was created by Rudra as the redeemer of people from the ocean of worldly existence.

51-56. Those who drink the water of this river become liberated from the mass of great sins. They leave off the state of mundane existence that existed without beginning and attain the pure and permanent salvation.

As is Gaṅgā, so is Revā and Sarasvatī too is so. The merit acquired from holy bath, visiting and meditation is mentioned as equal. Due to the boon granted, the blessed one (Narmadā) is mentioned as superior by learned men. By the mercy (of the Lord) she does not get defunct. If she is approached (the devotee is liberated). Hence people are liberated from sins by due performance of holy ablution and other auspicious rites, if they bow down to the Three-eyed Lord on Narmadā, O excellent king. Since this great river has originated from the limbs of Umā and Rudra, she has become highly meritorious and she takes the devotees to Svarga.

He who listens to the activity of the divine river (after getting detached from the body of the excellent Īśāna) goes to Rudra, being sung about loudly by Gandharvas and Yakṣas.

CHAPTER TEN

The Benefits of Bath in Narmadā

Yudhiṣṭhira said:

1-12. O excellent Brāhmaṇa, in which Kalpa was this highly esteemable Narmadā divided by all the noble-souled sages endowed with the power of penance? Narrate this in detail, O most excellent one among eloquent persons.

What calamities have the people to face at the end of the

Kalpa? O Sir, describe the arrangement as existed in the last Kalpa? O sinless one, how was this in the earlier Kalpa that preceded it?

On being requested thus in the midst of the assembly, Mārkaṇḍa spoke these words:

Mārkaṇḍeya said:

I shall narrate (it). Let this be listened to by all. This story has been successively heard from the earlier days. This is the special story of the the great Kalpa beyond this one, when Kāla (Time, god of destruction) was terrible and hideous, causing the destruction of the worlds. Even in that highly terrible situation, this (river) did not die. Hence she was divided by the delighted (sages). Listen to that story. In the three days of Pitāmaha, when the Yuga was about to come to an end, the mental sons of Brahmā, excellent persons like Brahmā himself, viz. Sanaka and other noble souls, and those who were called Vaimānika Gaṇas (groups of people moving about in aerial chariots), the Guardians of the quarters, Yama, Indra, Varuṇa and others—all these remained awaiting Kāla (god of death). They were interested in the events of the world. Then, when the Kalpa came to a close, they had excellent knowledge that the life span of everyone comes to a close in accordance with the nature of the Yuga. They then left Bhūrloka (earth) and came to Bhuvaḥ world. Then they gradually (moved) to Svarloka, Mahaḥ, Jana and Tapas Lokas (regions). After all the other Lokas, they resorted to the excellent Satyaloka. For a period of a thousand Yugas, they remained in Satyaloka, accompanied by their sons and grandsons till the Cosmos was created again.

13-20a. Such of those sons of Brahmā as do not exist at the beginning of the Kalpa, leave off the three worlds and remain without any supporting base. The Brāhmaṇas who were with them and the ascetics as well, Yakṣas, Rākṣasas, Piśācas, the other Vaimānika Gaṇas, the highly esteemable sages, the different kinds of Varṇas —all these undergo suffering on the earth along with others dwelling on the surface.

A great drought extending to a hundred years happened to befall them. It was extremely terrible, bringing about the destruction of the worlds, causing trees and creepers also to perish.

It brought about a great agitation in all the three worlds and dried up the seven oceans. All the people were overpowered by hunger. They began to wander in all the ten quarters. In their miserable condition, they sustained themselves with fruits and roots and bulbous roots. The rivers, wells, oceans and sacred Tīrthas as well were resorted to. These too—all the oceans and rivers, got dried up. Thereat living beings of very poor intrinsic strength got perished at the outset, being deprived of a great quantity of water.

20b-27a. When the rivers and oceans got destroyed, sixty thousand sages living in Kurukṣetra, Vaikhānasa Brāhmaṇas, Dantolūkhalins (who just bit grains with their teeth making them their threshing and pounding rods), ascetics who lived in secret caves of Himācala —all these ascetics who were distressed due to hunger and thirst approached me. With palms joined together in veneration all said: "O great sage, we are in anguish. O Brāhmaṇa, the whole universe consisting of rivers, oceans and mountains has completely dried up. Where will we all go together until the times change? O eminent Brāhmaṇa, you are long-lived. You did not die even at the close of the Yuga. Everything of the past, future and present is retained in your heart (memory). Hence you know everything. O Brāhmaṇa of great holy rites, do tell us. How long will we have to spend, O highly esteemable sage of good Vratas? All the mobile and immobile beings are distressed on being assailed by drought. Save us from utter annihilation, O highly esteemable one."

27b-33a Thereupon, I mentally pondered and spoke thus urging those Brāhmaṇas: "All of you leave this Kurukṣetra along with your wives and sons. Leaving this northern quarter, let us go to the excellent southern region, abounding in towns, villages and milkmen's colonies, and beautified by cities and metropolitan areas. Let us go to the banks of Narmadā resorted to by many Siddhas. Let us see that highly meritorious (river) born of Rudra's limbs, conducive to the destruction of all sins, the highly esteemable one surrounded by Nyagrodha trees. Her waters have ripples and whirlpools; she abounds in frogs and fish. The chirping sound of different kinds of birds reverberates. Crores of sages resort to her. She is ardently attended upon by the devotees of Maheśvara, Sāṅkhyas and Siddhas. We are afraid of droughts but on both of her banks we shall build our hermitages without difficulty. We can successfully perform holy rites."

33b-36. On being told thus they came to the banks of Narmadā accompanied by their followers. They settled there without any fear from anywhere. They remembered the common difficulties at the beginning of a Kalpa. They came to the banks of Narmadā at the very beginning of Kali Yuga.

Then for a complete period of a hundred divine years they stayed on the banks of Revā. O king, I witnessed the miracle of the stay of the sages there for a period of thirty-six thousand human years.

37-52. When (the other parts of) the world were assailed by drought, when the mobile and immobile beings became dried up, when all the reckonings of the beginning of the Yuga had been changed, when there was loss of consciousness followed by a hue and cry, when the classification of the four Varṇas became extinct, when the order of *Balis* (oblations) and *Homas* became defunct, when the utterance of the phrases *Svāhā* and *Vaṣaṭ* ceased, when the purity of personal cleanliness and good conduct was no longer maintained, then this excellent river alone was resorted to by crores of sages. No other river was as beautiful as this in all the three worlds, O king. This region with the meritorious water shone like the city of Amarāvatī of Indra. The divine river Narmadā shone like Gaṅgā in Svarga.

The temples and shrines were splendid and the hermitages were well-planned. There were as many shrines adorning both the banks as there were trees and mountains up to the spot where she meets the ocean. When Agnihotras were performed, the sacrificial offerings and the smoke issuing forth gave the region around Narmadā the appearance of a night during rainy season.

Shining splendid with the adorations and consecrations in the many shrines, the area with many rivers blazed like the cities of Indra and of Bhāskara.

Some performed austerities in the midst of five fires. Some performed Agnihotras. Some of them were engaged in austere penance and they took in (inhaled) the columns of smoke. Some were engaged in Ātmayajña (meditation on the self). Others were engaged in devotional practices. Some followed the Vaiṣṇava tenets and others the Śaiva observances of vows.

In taking food also, they had varieties: Intake of food once in a day, once in two days, once in six days etc. Some practised Cāndrāyaṇa; some Kṛcchra and some Atikṛcchra. Thus they worshipped Lord Śaṅkara and Lord Keśava by means of these and similar kinds of austerities elaborately practised on the banks of Narmadā.

They worshipped the great Lord as a single entity or in different forms. In the extremely terrible Kali Yuga, they attained excellent Siddhi. Lord Īśa granted Siddhis to the different devotees in accordance with the nature of their devotion, extent of knowledge and the aspect of the deity adored with devotion. In accordance with the natural urge they attained Siddhi and got dissolved (in the deity?).

Those people who resort to different deities, wallow in the ocean of worldly existence. They are persons who leave the great tree of Īśāna and cling to the branches. They come back to the world and are born frequently. In the course of the four Yugas, they wander successively in various kinds of births as Devas, immobile beings etc.

53-61. Re-birth, off to Svarga and down to the terrible Raurava—that will be their lot. On the other hand, those who devoutly worship Bhava, Lord Īśāna, on the banks of Narmadā, are not born again. Some of those who had been adoring till their death had attained the greatest goal; some in twelve years; other ascetics in six years; some in three years; some in a single year. Some have become Siddhas in six months and others in three months. These sages had resorted to the Lord and Narmadā of great renown. After cutting off all the defects of the worldly existence, they have attained the eternal Brahman.

Thus in Kali Age, hundreds and thousands of sages have resorted to the banks of Narmadā and merged into Rudra. Those Brāhmaṇas who resort to the banks of Narmadā and put in effort to perform the Śaiva Vrata, devoutly take their holy bath thrice a day and adore the Lord, attain Śiva. Or those who constantly remember Nārāyaṇa along with meditations, adorations, Japas and Mahāvratas cross to the other shore of the ocean of worldly existence like royal swans with their white wings well-washed.

It is the truth. It is *the* truth. Again it is *the* truth. It is being proclaimed with raised hands. This has been excellently decided and concluded that Nārāyaṇa should be meditated upon always.

62-68. He who conquers his self, O king, resides for a month or a fortnight resorting to Revā and worships Hara, becomes a man of great esteem. He shall become identical with the Pinākа-bearing Lord of Devas.

Even worms, insects and ants that die in the waters of Narmadā, attain divine forms. They are born in noble families living for a hundred years engaged in pious rites.

Those trees whose roots have been eroded by the great waves and rapid currents and fall down in due course, get their sins destroyed through the waters of Narmadā. They shine refulgently and proceed to heaven.

Even senseless, deaf and mute ones having no vested interests and ardent desires or those who earnestly desire things, when they die on the banks of Revā, do go to heaven. Why should one doubt then about the Brāhmaṇas endowed with emotional fervour with Bhava as their object of worship?

The devotees who perform the worship of Śiva and direct their mental feelings towards Keśava and get their bodies purified by the waters of Revā, do attain, on being liberated from their bodies, that goal which those others who subject their limbs to desiccation through monthly fasts do not attain.

Those who resort to the banks of Narmadā and adore Śiva of immutable splendour or Nārāyaṇa with mental purity, do not taste the breast-milk of mothers again. There are other great sages who resort to the banks of Narmadā eulogized with hymns by Devas, and sustain themselves through grains of Nīvāra, Śyāmāka, Yava, Iṅguda etc.; they do not meet with death.

69-75. Those who approach the banks of the divine river and get themselves truly purified by the worship of the Lord thrice a day, do not lie down again within the belly of a young woman with faeces, urine, skin, bones and veins as their pillows. Of what avail to them are the many kinds of sacrifices and Dāna or the entire range of excellent Tīrthas resorted to by them? They resort to the northern or southern banks of Narmadā traversed previously by Rudra himself. Those men who do not resort to Revā who originated from Rudra's body and who functions like a flight of stairs unto heaven, have been cheated, are lame, sluggish and blind and are on a par with brutes.

The eminent Brāhmaṇas who never wish to see Kaliyuga again shall approach the banks of Narmadā, eschew association with all the others and worship Śarva. In spite of being overwhelmed by innumerable obstacles those who never leave the banks of Narmadā are worthy of being honoured: They should be venerated by all the people. They do what is beneficial to all the people.

Bhṛgu, Atri, Gārgeya, Vaśiṣṭha and Kaṅka along with hundreds of other persons have taken bath in the waters (of this river), have attained the greatest of Siddhis and have gone to the worlds of Maruts (Devas), not to others.

Those who are always pure in their inner thoughts and read this holy and highly meritorious narrative that yields wisdom, are really men of great esteem. They attain the greatest goal. Indeed the statement of Rudra himself is a valid testimony thereof.

CHAPTER ELEVEN

The Greatness of Narmadā

Yudhiṣṭhira said:

1-6. It is pleasantly wonderful that this river is very significant and highly meritorious as she has not been destroyed at the end of the Yuga. Hence she is the worthiest of being resorted to by leading sages eagerly interested in meditation, adoration and holy bath.

The sages earnest in pious rites attained salvation by resorting to that river. I understand from your statement that the rules and observances based on the Vedic passages and evolved by the sages, are conducive to the attainment of salvation. The different kinds of observances along with the adoration of the Lord of Devas, enable them to become liberated from the defects of Kali. They may be liberated in twelve, ten, eight, six, four or three years or even months. Undoubtedly one who adores Brahmā, the most excellent one of Suras, or Keśava, the preceptor of the universe, dispels all sins. Mention all these in detail, O sinless one. All the creatures are deeply immersed in the dense mire of worldly existence. How do they attain Svarga? This is my doubt. Do clarify it.

Śrī Mārkaṇḍeya said:

7-13. After a number of births human state is obtained. With great difficulty devotion to Śaṅkara is generated. This attainment is rendered possible through Tīrthas, Dānas, fasts, Yajñas, adorations of Devas and Brāhmaṇas and through great faith, O king. Hence faith has to be maintained by men fond of pious rites. Īśvara is also attainable by Śraddhā (faith). Hence faith is considered specially significant. Otherwise, if it is devoid of Śraddhā, everything is fruitless, O descendant of Bharata. Hence one should resort to devotion to Rudra Parameṣṭhin. Only the life of those is fruitful who have unswerving devotion. Bhakti (devotion) is of three kinds, namely Sāttvikī, Rājasī and Tāmasī and the benefit derived by all the people is also of three kinds. Men are reborn again and again as a result of their Karmas. After hundreds of births, wise worshippers of the deities obtain devotion to the three deities when sinful Karmas are destroyed.

14-19. Through (the kindness of) Īśāna, salvation is obtained thereafter without any doubt. Those excellent Brāhmaṇas who resort to the banks of Narmadā and follow the path of the Vedas, attain the greatest goal undoubtedly. Those excellent Brāhmaṇas who resort to the banks of Narmadā, who ardently follow the path prescribed in the three Vedas reach the highest goal. Those people who are of concentrated minds and who ardently worship the immutable Śiva attain spiritual progress quickly.

Embodied beings attain spiritual progress after lapse of a great deal of time in places other than the banks of Narmadā, but here the spiritual progress is attained quickly. Men conversant with Sāṅkhya (path of knowledge) attain Siddhi in six years. Vaiṣṇavas richly endowed with knowledge, also achieve progress before that. Like rivers joining the ocean, all those who know and practise Yoga become unified in the Māheśvara Yoga at the end of the Kalpa.

Of all the Yogas Māheśvara Yoga is the most excellent. Resorting to it, even those of sinful origins cease to have rebirths by adoring Śiva on the banks of the river.

This type of progress is very difficult to accomplish. It destroys all sins. By resorting to Revā all creatures are liberated quickly.

20. Even if they belong to sinful species, by worshipping Śiva on the banks of Narmadā they are not born again in (any of) the species.

21. This goal is difficult to attain. She destroys all sins. Beings get liberated from Saṁsāra after resorting to Revā.

22. Hence one should as a habit take the holy bath and smear oneself with holy ash. By approaching the banks of Narmadā, one shall quickly attain Siddhi.

23-32. A man who calmly and respectfully adores the Liṅga thrice a day, shall become freed from all ailments and attain the greatest goal.

Even if he be a sinner, he will attain Siddhi in six months. Those who have great purity of mind attain Siddhi in three months.

Just as snow touched by rays of the Sun breaks into fragments and vanishes from the top of a mountain, so also sin when touched by the splendid particles of holy ash gets destroyed.

Those Brāhmaṇas devoted to Rudra who are sprinkled with holy ash charged with the Mantra *Sadyojāta*[1] etc. shine like the Sun without impurities.

Just as serpents afraid of Garuḍa, perish, so also the sins when sprinkled with ash, perish.

Those who smear themselves with the holy ash sanctified by the waters of Narmadā, are immediately rid of masses of sins. There is no doubt about it.

Those who observe Pāśupata Vrata devoutly in the manner enjoined without eating Śūdra food attain the greatest goal.

Brāhmaṇa's food is (regarded as) Amṛta (Nectar); Kṣatriya's food is remembered as milk; Vaiśya's food is mere food, and Śūdra's food is proclaimed as blood.

Those excellent Brāhmaṇas who get nourished with Śūdra's food and juice and later die, become deprived of Tapas and knowledge and are born as crows and vultures.

1. The following are the sources of the Mantras:
   i) *agnimīḷe purohitam* (RV I. 1.1.)
   ii) *iṣetvo* (KS 3-6).
   iii) *agna āyāhi vītaye* (RV VI. 16.10).
   iv) *śanno devī abhīṣṭaye* (RV X.9.4).

Sinful action of men remains based on their food. If one takes anyone's food, he takes the latter's sin too.

33-40. Śaṅkara has declared that, more particularly so, in the case of those who are unsteady in the performance of austerities despite the fact that they have resorted to the holy rites of ascetics. Undoubtedly they go to Naraka.

Brāhmaṇas of this type, if they are well established in Pāsupatya Vrata, do undoubtedly burn the great mass of sins.

This has been urged by Śruti that those who associate with a cheat and are afflicted by avariciousness should not be talked to or associated with (accommodated in the party of the good).

People are ruined due to the faults committed by their parents; others are ruined as a result of their own actions; and still others are ruined due to vanity born of knowledge and egotism.

Those who have been excluded through the orders of the Smṛtis but still adhere to Śaṅkara's pious rite, undergo sufferings, but in due course they attain the greatest goal.

Fools, men who have no faith, those with increasing hypocrisy, wicked souls and those who glorify a bad doctrine do not attain Siddhi.

Those who adhere to Śāṅkara Vrata and are highly fortunate in practising the rites of Tīrtha, are born undoubtedly in base wombs, if they are avaricious.

Evil action is not quelled by Tīrthas and Dānas. But sins committed due to inadvertence or ignorance become dissolved.

41-50. After knowing this, all Brāhmaṇas should act in accordance with the injunctions (of religion). They must frequently recite in a low voice the great Brahman (the Vedic passages). He who recites the passages connected with Lord Virūpākṣa (Śiva) of the highest form and also the Rudra Mantras sees Īśāna directly within six months if he avoids undue attachment (to the world). He who has perfect self-control and recites the Saṁhitās ten times on the banks of Narmadā shall be liberated from all sins.

He who reads the Purāṇa Saṁhitā whether pertaining to Śiva or Viṣṇu, before a Śivaliṅga on the banks of Narmadā becomes identical with Śiva. Until the destruction of all living beings, he is honoured in Svargaloka.

This Nandigītā was formerly uttered by Nandin in order to dispel the sufferings of worldly existence.

He uttered this in a Śiva shrine in the assembly of celestial sages, Siddhas and Gandharvas. Listen to this splendid Nandigītā, O king, with full concentration of mind. It is meritorious. It gives heavenly pleasures and salvation. It destroys the fear of worldly existence.

"O people distressed at every step by worldly sufferings, if you wish to avoid the deep abyss of worldly existence, O people bound with different kinds of bonds of Karmas perpetrated by yourselves, listen for the sake of your own happiness to this beneficial thing recounted by me.

O Śakra, do not go along the crooked path. O Yama, do not torture me. O Pracetas (Varuṇa), subdue your own mind. O Vittapa (Kubera), eschew avariciousness.

If you are sick and disgusted with the tossings and upheavals of the waves of the ocean of worldly existence, distribute your entire wealth among the distressed and helpless people and also the people of distinguished characteristics.

51-60. The Pināka-wielding holy Lord protects the man who is disgusted with birth, is afraid of death and is overwhelmed by lust etc., but who does not slip from Yama (restraints), Niyama (observances) etc.

O Kīnāśa (god of death), do not be arrogant. If you inflict injury on a creature that has sought refuge in Śarva (Śiva), you will be laughed at. That alone will be your refuge.

What can cause fear unto men devoted to Śiva and Viṣṇu? The terrible Kāla is but a child. Who is Mṛtyu (god of death)? Who is base Yama? (They are negligible.)

Unto the creature distressed by the burden of mundane existence (but) habitually residing on the banks of Revā, Bharga and Bhagavān (Viṣṇu) are destroyers of the fear from worldly existence.

O pitiable fellow, if you wish for (spiritual) knowledge and salvation, resort to Śiva, meditate upon Śiva, eulogize Śiva, worship Śiva and bow down to Śiva. Recite the scriptural text of Pañcānana (Pāśupata Path); perform the Japa of the five-lettered Mantra (*namaḥ śivāya*). Meditate on the Tattvas consisting of five; worship the great Pañcānana (Śiva).

Of what account are those series of rites which have been differentiated due to diversity of nature, if the glorious Pañcānana, Śiva, is served exclusively?

Of what avail are the confident, maddening, trumpeting sounds of the elephant of worldly existence, if Lord Pañcānana (Śiva; a lion) is resorted to with the positive fragrance of faith and devotion? O foolish, deluded one, why do you grieve after seeing the futility of Karmas? Perform the Japa of Bhīma (the terrible one), the consort of Bhavānī, the destroyer of fear.

O deluded one, resort to Bharga, the Lord of Suras, the bestower of heavenly pleasures and salvation—Bharga who has his abode on the banks of Narmadā and who is the cause of the destruction of numerous miseries.

61-70. O deluded one, why do you go to distant quarters like a mad person (or) like one devoid of any feelings, after abandoning Revā worthy of being attended upon by even the celestial river, and where Lord Hara and Lord Hari are stationed on her banks?

Resort to the meritorious waters of Revā; worship the eternal Rudra; perform the Japa of the five-lettered Mantra (*namaḥ śivāya*) and go to the desired region.

Why torture your own body by pursuing innumerable means of Mokṣa? Resort to Revā. After attaining Śiva the greatest region is easily achievable."

What Nandin sang in the presence of Śiva in this manner after going to Kailāsa and meeting the Guardians of the Quarters, has been recounted to you now.

Mārkaṇḍeya said:

He who always protects pious rites and is devoted to the holy bath and Dāna after reaching the banks of Narmadā is rid of all sins.

One may recite all the Vedas for a hundred years disregarding the injunctions or perform the Japa of Mṛtyulāṅgala (Mṛtyuñjaya) Mantra, namely *tryambakam yajāmahe,* etc. (RV VII.59.12). This may equal the other or may be even superior to it in Guṇas (merits).

Just as a person who is not pure either in Bīja (semen i.e. Father) or in Yoni (mother) does not obtain (the benefit of) Rudra Mantra, so also Lāṅgala (Mṛtyuñjaya Mantra) does not stand by (save) the person bereft of life span.

A person of great self-control who performs the Japa of

Gāyatrī is superior in good qualities. Stationing himself on the banks of Narmadā, he who recites Mantras beginning with (1) *agnimīle,* (2) *iṣetvo,* (3) *agna āyāhi* and (4) *śanno devī,* is rid of sins.

One would perform Brahma Yajña. One who always performs, with concentration, the Japa of the Vedas along with the Aṅgas and Upāṅgas, does not obtain that benefit which a man of self-control obtains by the Japa of Gāyatrī.

71-80. A Brāhmaṇa equipped with the (knowledge of) Veda is rid of all sins by performing once the Japa of *Rudrādhyāya.* He goes to Viṣṇuloka.

By performing Japa of another Saṁsthāna, Sūkta or Āraṇyaka one is rid of all sins and goes to Viṣṇuloka.

Whatever Japa is performed and whatever Dāna is offered, if done so on the banks of Narmadā, shall become everlasting. Those who always resort to Narmadā with Vratas of this sort go to the Vaiṣṇava region or the immutable Śaiva region after death.

Some men go to Satyaloka and others go to Sūryaloka. There they remain surrounded by groups of heavenly damsels till all the living beings are annihilated. While this was the situation in this world, O great king, ten crores of sages, original inhabitants of Kurukṣetra, resorted to the banks of Narmadā along with me, O blessed one. They had their diet restricted to fruits and roots and they continued to adore Śiva.

The period of time extended to a hundred divine years which according to human reckoning comes to thirty-six thousand (years).

When the Sandhyā period elapsed, O excellent king, the remainder stood at a hundred years of human reckoning. Then there was a drought that destroyed all people, whereby everything met terrible destruction.

81-90. Due to the power of those sages who had mastered the Vedas and attained Siddhi earlier, Lord Indra, the slayer of Bala and Vṛtra, showered rain.

All round there was the downpour with profuse supply of water. As a result of the rain, their sustenance became possible.

A long period of time was spent by those desirous of great Siddhi (sustaining themselves) with Śyāmāka, Iṅguda, Bilva and other things growing on the banks of Narmadā.

Again when there was the advent of the closing period of

the Yuga and only a small part of Kali Yuga remained, all the mobile and immobile beings became entirely dried up.

The entire surface of the earth became denuded of trees, medicinal herbs and hedges, grasses and creepers too, as it was affected by drought.

Thereupon thousands of those sages became distressed due to hunger and thirst. As befitting the nature of the Yuga, O king, they became bereft of Sattva (intrinsic strength).

When the end of the Yuga was imminent, when people ceased to utter Svadhā and perform Homa, they were unable to decide: "What should be done? Where will we go? Who will be our refuge?"

I told them repeatedly: "Do not be afraid. Many such changes of times have been witnessed by me."

They were brought to the banks of Narmadā by me. "This divine (river) alone is our refuge when the close of the Yuga is imminent. O excellent Brāhmaṇas, we do not have any other refuge. This is the mother of all living beings, O excellent Brāhmaṇas.

91-96. It was by resorting to this great river that our grandfathers and great-grandfathers and other forefathers—all of them, went to heaven.

Seven of my earlier grandfathers beginning with Bhṛgu, Dhaumṛṇī, my wife, the highly virtuous lady of pure smiles, Manasvatī, my mother, Bhārgavas, Aṅgiras-s, Pulastya, Pulaha, Vasiṣṭha, Ātreya, Kāśyapa and other highly glorious ones practising vows and observances numbering hundreds of thousands attained Siddhi here.

Hence this highly esteemable river should never be abandoned. No other river is capable of giving the benefit of the three worlds.

The residents of the banks of Narmadā are rid immediately of many *Dvandvas* (mutually conflicting things) and also the great fear of hunger and thirst. Hence the excellent river should be resorted to with all endeavour by those who desire great welfare here in this world and hereafter."

CHAPTER TWELVE

Eulogy of Narmadā

Śrī Mārkaṇḍeya said:

1-6. On hearing this, O king, the sages became highly delighted. With palms joined together in veneration the Brāhmaṇas began to eulogize Narmadā.

"Obeisance to you, O divine river of meritorious waters. O alligator-gaited one, obeisance. Obeisance to thee, the redeemer from sins. Obeisance, O goddess of excellent countenance.

Obeisance to you, O splendid one, O reservoir of meritorious waters. O river of pure Sattva quality, served by Suras and Siddhas, obeisance to you, the excellent one originating from the limbs of Rudra.

Obeisance to you, O divine river, flowing towards the sea, O auspicious one, O bestower of boons. Obeisance to you, O bestower of the happiness of the two worlds (here and hereafter), O sinless one to whom many groups of living beings have resorted.

O excellent one among rivers, O remover of sins, O river of diverse varieties, your limbs have been resorted to by Gandharvas, Yakṣas and Uragas; O eternal one, you have mercy on groups of living beings; O bestower of salvation, O divine one, do what is beneficial to us.

O divine one served and attended upon by big multitudes of huge elephants, buffaloes and boars! You have great waves as garlands. O bestower of boons, O bestower of happiness, all of us bow down to you. Release us from the bondage of the (category) of Paśus.

7-15. Men wander through the various Narakas because they are fettered with many kinds of inauspicious sins. But their sufferings torment them only till they do not touch your waters emerging from the waves set in motion by violent gusts of winds. O lotus-faced one, you are the goal unto those who are tortured by the fear of many series of miseries, who are enveloped by many sins and overwhelmed by many Dvandvas (mutually opposing pairs e.g. pleasure—pain).

O divine river, there is no doubt about this that after attaining you all the rivers become sanctified and free from impurities. You grant freedom from fear to those who are distressed due to miseries. You have been honoured by many excellent and noble men.

The stones in you when touched by rays of the Moon and the Sun, shall grant the greatest region. On being flooded with your sacred waters, they attain great welfare and holiness. What wonder can there be here?

Men wander through hells, become distressed with miseries and their bodies become infested with sins only so long as they do not resort to your waves and ripples set in motion by great gusts of winds.

Mlecchas (barbarians), Pulindas (hunters) and Yātudhānas (demons) who drink your meritorious water, O divine river, become liberated from terrible fears, undoubtedly. What wonder is here!

All the lakes and rivers have become defunct in this terrible, defiled Kali Yuga; but, you, O divine river, shine with the full complement of water like Gaṅgā in heaven, the pathway of the constellations.

O excellent one, O giver of boons, we have waited so long. Now, with your favour, we shall go to Rudra. Do grant us your favour.

You are our goal like a mother or father who protects the sons; protect us till the end of the Yuga. With your excellent favour, we shall cross the adverse period when everything is overwhelmed by a severe drought."

16-18. The eminent Brāhmaṇas who read this eulogy and the quiescent men who listen to this attain Rudra by means of a vehicle drawn by a bull. They shall be adorned with divine garments too.

Those who read this prayer always after taking the holy bath in the waters of Narmadā, will ultimately be granted the purest goal by this excellent river.

A devotee shall get up in the morning everyday and recite this prayer. He may even recite it lying down on bed. He shall be liberated from sins and becomes purified in body. He attains the abode of Maheśvara.

CHAPTER THIRTEEN

The Story of Twentyone Kalpas[1]

Śrī Mārkaṇḍeya said:

1-8. On being eulogized thus by the leading sages, the divine, meritorious river thought thus: 'I shall grant excellent boon unto all.'

Thereafter, on coming to know that they were asleep during the night, the Divinity of sweet smiles appeared before every sage in dream.

When it was midnight, she arose from the midst of the water (in the guise of a woman) clad in clean garments and bedecked in divine garlands. She was a lady of excellent waist: She had an umbrella raised aloft. She was adorned in rubies. To each of them she severally said: "Do not be afraid. Do reside near me banishing the fear arising from hunger etc."

After saying thus to those great sages in the course of dream, the divine one entered her own waters and disappeared.

Later, in the morning, the sages joyously said to one another: "The Divinity was seen by me in such and such form in the course of a dream. She was excellent to look at. Freedom from fear has been granted to us (and its) fulfilment too ere long. Undoubtedly the vision of Narmadā is remarkable."

9-15 Another day, O king, they witnessed along with the members of their family in the vicinity of their own hermitages fishes of excellent form.

On seeing the fishes there, the great sages became struck with wonder. Without being excited they worshipped the deities with Havya and Kavya.

After obtaining shoals of fishes with the favour of the great goddess, they sustained themselves day by day along with their wives and sons.[2] Still there were further shoals of fishes, on seeing which they became struck with wonder.

There were the dead Pāṭhīna variety of fishes with well-

1. This chapter gives a list of twenty-one Kalpas (vv 42-45). Narmadā survived all these Kalpas but Mārkaṇḍeya lived for seven Kalpas from Māyūra to Vārāha (the present Kalpa).
2. The sages do not observe strict vegetarianism. Probably fish was a staple food of North Indian Brāhmaṇas then.

nourished limbs. O Yudhiṣṭhira, at every threshold of the hermitages of these ascetics, these fishes were seen dead.

Thereupon all the residents of the banks of Narmadā became well-nourished and delighted. All the sages eschewed every fear arising from hunger and thirst.

O leader of the descendants of Bharata, they stayed on performing penances and Japa. Resorting to the banks of Narmadā, they worshipped the Pitṛs and Devas.

16-23. With those excellent Brāhmaṇas performing Japa and penance for ever, the excellent river shone like the firmament with stars and planets.

Formerly Narmadā, the bestower of piety, was duly demarcated by numerous brilliant Brāhmaṇas who had mastered the Vedas. Narmadā, the bestower of welfare on men, was demarcated by ten crores of sages residing on the banks of Narmadā, the Divinity of well-defined limbs.

With resplendent sacred threads and rosary strings spread on both the banks, O descendant of Bharata, the highly meritorious Narmadā proceeding towards the ocean shone remarkably.

There were several shrines with splendid Liṅgas made of sand and clay, with which the excellent river shone like the night that shines by means of stars.

Propitiating the Suras and Pitṛs thus, all those sages resided on the banks of Narmadā till the ultimate annihilation of all living beings.

Thereafter, a little more than a hundred terrible years elapsed, O descendant of Bharata. Then at midnight, a girl with refulgence like that of a mass of lightning streaks rose up from the water. She had a python serving as the Yajñopavīta. She was gentle in appearance yet. In hand she grasped a trident. She spoke to them then:

24-31. "O ye groups of sages, do come. I am never born of a womb. Do merge unto me along with your sons and wives. Thereby you will achieve Siddhi. I shall grant you the several wishes each one has. I shall take you unto Viṣṇu, Brahmā, Īśāna or any other excellent Sura. Indeed I am the bestower of boons and am pleased. Be engrossed in Prāṇāyāma ('restraint of breath') and enter with concentration along with your sons and wives. Leave off your hermitages. You must not waste time. Pralaya is imminent. It is the annihilation of all living beings. The Kalpa conflagration is extremely terrible. I was the only one when there was the highly terrible destruction of people. All the remaining rivers and all the seas have become (dried up and) defunct. Due to the boon granted by Maheśa, I am not annihilated. Sthāṇu, the Lord, is immortal, the eternal Lord. What is it that he will not grant, O excellent Brāhmaṇas, if he is duly adored and prayed to?"

After saying this to the sages, Revā, that Divinity who had grasped a trident with her hand and who had the python serving as a sacred thread, entered the water.

32-39. On hearing her words their minds were overwhelmed with wonder. All of them venerated me and repeatedly craved for my pardon:

"While residing with your support we had uttered certain things which may kindly be forgiven."

All those highly fortunate ones abandoned their abodes along with their kinsmen and disciples. They recited the Japa of the sole imperishable Brahman (the single-syllabled OM) and meditated on Maheśvara in their hearts. They took their holy ablution in the waters sanctified through Mantras. After having successfully performed their holy Vratas, they entered the waters of Narmadā like winged mountains (entering the sea)[1]. With Kuśa grass in their hands and holding the sacred fires, they brightened all the quarters.

O great king, I alone remained there after their departure. I reached Amareśa and adored the river Narmadā. The seven Kalpas beginning with Māyūra were experienced by me, O king, O descendant of Bharata, due to the favour of Vedhas (god Brahmā). I spent all those years along with Revā.

But ever since my birth till to-day, I do not know (the nature of) her former existence. This Narmadā is the Śakti of Śaṅkara, the Kalā named Ilā of Śaṁbhu. She destroys all sins and redeems people from worldly existence.

40-47. O son of Pāṇḍu, in the fourteen earlier Kalpas, when I too was not born, this (divine river) was happily present. In those fourteen earlier Kalpas too Narmadā never ceased to exist. I shall recount them as that Divinity narrated to me.

---

1. It appears that Brāhmaṇas living on the banks were washed away in the flood of Narmadā.

The list of Kalpas:

Know that the first one is Kāpila; the second one is Prājāpatya. Thereafter the following: Brāhma, Saumya, Sāvitra, Bārhaspatya, Prabhāsaka, Māhendra, Agnikalpa, Jayanta, Māruta, Vaiṣṇava, Bahurūpa and Jyautiṣa is the fourteenth. These Kalpas which I enumerated are those in which Narmadā never ceased to be. The fifteenth Kalpa is Māyūra; the sixteenth is Kaurma. Then come the Kalpas: Baka, Mātsya, Pādma and Vaṭakālpa, O descendant of Bharata. The twenty-first current Kalpa is Vārāha. These seven Kalpas were lived through by me along with Revā.

Thus the twenty-one Kalpas lived through by Narmadā born of Śiva have been spoken by me in various ways.

O excellent king, they have been mentioned to you. What more shall I tell you?

CHAPTER FOURTEEN

Kālarātri Annihilates the Universe

Yudhiṣṭhira asked:

1-10. Then all those illustrious sages with austerities as their asset went to the highest world. What miracle did happen thereafter?

Śrī Mārkaṇḍeya replied:

After those residents of the banks of Narmadā had gone, there ensued the terrible annihilation causing the destruction of all living beings.

By means of Ṛk, Yajuḥ and Sāma passages, Brahmā and others eulogized Lord Śiva, the eternal great Lord seated on the peak of Kailāsa:

"O Lord, annihilate the universe along with Devas, Asuras and human beings. The end of a thousand Yugas has arrived. It is capable of destroying (them).

Adopting my form, all these visible worlds have been created by you. Assuming the form of Viṣṇu these have been sustained. The same form has become trichotomized as Brahmā,

Śiva and Viṣṇu for the purpose of creation, sustenance and annihilation, O great Lord."

On hearing these truthful words of Viṣṇu Parameṣṭhin, the great Lord Śiva pierced through the Cosmic Egg, greater than the greatest, beginning with Bhūrloka and ending with Brahmaloka. He was then accompanied by those two (Brahmā and Viṣṇu) and Umā and all his retinue. Lord Nīlalohita pierced through the seven worlds and entered the beginningless divine region of Śiva along with them.

There was no wind there; there was no firmament there; there was no fire; no surface of the ground where Śaṅkara, the Lord, was present along with Umā. There was no sun, no planets, neither constellations nor the quarters.

11-22. There were no Guardians of Quarters, O excellent king, nor even pleasure and pain. Wise men called it the region of Brahman; they call it the region of Śiva. Others call him Īśa and Kṣetrajña (the immanent soul). Sāṅkhyas praise him as the primordial liberation (Ādimokṣa).

Some call it the pre-eminent Brahman. Some call him Śarva, the age-old unborn Īśāna. Some call him single-formed; some, many-formed, the first and Avyaya (the immutable one). It is an entity having no colour, no name or lineage; the wise knowers call it the fourth state (*Turyaṁ Padam*)

It is of the nature of Vijñāna (perfect knowledge), the object of meditation. It is the subtlest one resting in Ātman, the most excellent Īśāna, the greatest one.

Then all those three came up to Lord Īśa and amalgamated themselves into one form. They alone in their separate forms protect the entire universe.

In the form of Rudra, the Lord causes the annihilation of all living beings; in the form of Viṣṇu he protects the worlds; he is the cause of creation in the form of Brahmā.

The great Lord becomes Kāla on being united with Prakṛti. The multiformed, esteemable Prakṛti abides at his side.

People conversant with it, who know the meanings of words, call it Prakṛti. It is Parameśvara who is the cause (of the distinction between) Prakṛti and Puruṣa.

From him issued forth the entire universe, the mobile and immobile beings. When the end of the Yuga arrives, it gets merged into him.

Everything marked by Bhaga and Liṅga is pervaded by Parameṣṭhin: Viṣṇu is in the form of Bhaga and Maheśvara is in the form of Liṅga.

Viṣṇu is remembered as Bhaga[1] because he shines (*Bhāti*) in all the worlds and is sung about (*Gīyate*) in the worlds. He has penetrated all the living beings in Bhūḥ and Bhuvar Loka.

He is said to be Viṣṇu because of *Viśana* (entrance). He is the great Lord identical with all the Devas. The appellation Bhaga is proclaimed due to *Bhāsana* (shining) and *Gamana* (moving about).

23-33. Learned men know it as Liṅga[2] because it is that in which everything in the world beginning with Brahmā and ending with a blade of grass gets merged and unified.

Thereupon Mahādeva said to the goddess who was standing nearby: "O splendid lady, do not delay. Annihilate the entire universe. Eschew this gentle form, resplendent like the white rays of the Moon. Assume a terrible form and annihilate the mobile and immobile beings.

O lotus-eyed goddess, be surrounded by the terrible and hideous groups of goblins and devour the entire world of living beings.

Thereafter I shall destroy the universe and make it flooded. After converting everything into a vast expanse of water I shall happily go to sleep along with you."

Śrī Devī said:

O highly brilliant Lord, I would rather not annihilate this universe. Having been its mother I would not devour it as it is motionless and extremely distressed. Due to the innate womanly nature, my heart melts with pity. O Lord of the universe, how can I burn down this universe? Hence, O Śaṅkara, you yourself do annihilate this universe.

On being spoken thus, Dhūrjaṭi Nīlalohita became angry. He rebuked the goddess Maheśvarī with a gruff, hissing *HUM* sound. With his eyes blazing with anger, he said thus: "*Oṁ hum*

---

1. A popular etymology of '*Bhaga*' and '*Viṣṇu*.'
2. A popular etymology of the word '*Liṅga*'. This is accepted in Vīraśaiva Texts.

phaṭ tvaṁ saḥ"[1] O descendant of Bharata, on being slighted with Huṁkāra, the wide-eyed goddess of plump thighs and hips became instantly hideous like Kālarātri (Nightmare). Producing hissing, gruff sounds of loud report, she made the ten quarters reverberate. Like a lightning streak of excessive hideousness, she increased in size.

34-46. She was too dazzling to be seen, like a lightning streak. She was swiftly moving as clusters of lightning streaks. She was excited and enraged like the flames (streaks) of lightning. Her eyes resembled the fiery lightning.

Her hairs were dishevelled and her eyes were wide; her neck and her belly were lean. She was clad in the hide of a tiger and a python served as the sacred thread. She was bedecked with scorpions and lizands blazing like the mass of flames. In height and magnitude she covered the three worlds. Her limbs shone and the black serpents served as earrings. She kept a stout stick of various colours raised aloft. She had covered herself with the hide of a tiger. Causing the destruction of the universe the highly terrible deity increased in size, licking the corners of the mouth. She hissed making the sound *Hum.* She opened her mouth wide making gruff sounds and causing excitement unto the entire universe. The goblins following her began to gambol and frisk. She took deep breaths exhibiting her anger. Laughing boisterously, she distorted the nostrils. Her eyes resembled a pit of fire. Making shrill sounds she burned the entire universe.

Being burnt thus, Suras fell on the earth. So also did Yakṣas, Gandharvas and Kinnaras along with the great serpents. The multitudes of Bhūtas crying *Hāhā* and *Hai-Hai* fell down. They tumbled down with loud lamentations and cries of distress. The entire universe with all the three worlds became filled with these howls and squeals. All the world became filled with these falling, flying and blazing beings. The entire earth was covered with the tumbling peaks of mountains making noise like *Caṭacaṭā* (crackling sound). In that violent festival, she heightened the delight of Rudra.

Injuring and torturing the living beings, munching and

1. These are the "Seeds" of Mantras (*Mantra-bījas*) of a destructive nature. Using these *Mantra-bījas*, Śaṅkara transformed the motherly Umā into a devouring ogress in order to destroy the universe.

crunching the immobile beings, she inhaled the odour arising from the various things that were consumed by the fire. She howled like a vixen.

In that violent destructive activity of annihilating the universe, Caṇḍī became all the more ferocious with the face rendered gory with streams of blood oozing out and the entire body smeared with blood gushing in currents.

47-57. Hundreds of the Brāhmaṇas, Kṣatriyas, Vaiśyas and others and the great sages beginning with Bhṛgu who had reached the Mahar Loka began to perish. Devas and Asuras became terrified. So also Yakṣas, Uragas and Rākṣasas. Some of them entered Pātāla and got them concealed in the caves and lakes.

That goddess pervaded all the quarters and stationed herself like death personified. She had been engaged by the Lord in that period of destruction of the Yuga.

Originally single, she transformed herself into nine and then into ten forms. Bursting into boisterous laughter she assumed sixty-four forms and then a hundred forms. Śivā, the goddess, became thousand-formed and then assumed millions and crores of bodies. Her forms were numerous, her sizes were diverse and she had innumerable weapons. Her movements were of various sorts. At the behest of Śiva the goddess assumed these forms, O king. The groups of the followers of Maheśvara wielded hideous weapons in the firmament in all the quarters checking and restraining the fleeing beings. Armed with tridents and Paṭṭiśas they wandered everywhere accompanying her.

Then some of the excessively fierce groups of Mātṛs in the company of Vināyakas rose up in size and started the act of annihilating the universe.

Thereupon her curved fang-like teeth resembling Kunda flowers and the moon lengthened into thousands, ten thousands and billions of Yojanas. The rows of fangs and the nails were sharp and rough. They ruthlessly scraped the sky and the quarters and overspread the earth consisting of the seven continents. The forests and the mountains were smashed to smithereens when struck with those fangs. The rocks and boulders crumbled into thousands of pieces.

58-66. Himavān, Hemakūṭa, Niṣadha, Gandhamādana, Mālyavān, Nīla, the great mountain Śveta, the centre of Meru,

Ilāpīṭha, all the seven continents and the oceans and also the mountain Lokāloka trembled and quivered, O excellent king. Great trees became shattered on being hit with the curved fangs resembling thunderbolt. Terrible evil portents overshadowed the quarters around along with the stars, planets and groups of beings moving about in aerial chariots. Surrounded by thousands of vixen and the great Mātṛgaṇas she wandered over the entire universe at the conclusion of the Yuga.

They were whirling, shouting and howling. Some were thrashing and some were blazing. All the ten quarters were pervaded by the Pramathas. The extensive range of mountains became shattered. The main entrance to the palatial buildings became broken. Hairs and dry bones lay scattered in confusing masses. The villages and cities stood razed to the ground by the conflagration. Ashes lay in heaps above them. All the three worlds consisting of the mobile and immobile beings were filled with the ashes of the funeral pyres. Laments and loud cries of *Hāhā* and *Ahāhā* spread everywhere. This universe lay helpless and bereft of refuge.

CHAPTER FIFTEEN

Turbulence of the Annihilation (Pralaya)

Śrī Mārkaṇḍeya said:

1-10a. Then Kālarātri of blazing (very bright) eyes, surrounded by thousands of terrible Mātṛs indulged in the destruction of the entire universe.

The fierce Mothers, the Śaktis identical with (or pertaining to) Brahmā, Viṣṇu and Śiva, the Śaktis of Vāyu, Indra, Anala (Fire), Kubera, Yama, Toyeśa (Varuṇa), Skanda, Kroḍa (i.e. Varāha) and Nṛsiṁha moved about striking terror.

In the course of that ultimate annihilation, the Mothers moved around armed with discuses, tridents, clubs, swords, thunderbolts, Śaktis, Ṛṣṭis, Paṭṭiśas, Khaṭvāṅgas and blazing torches urgently prompted by Umā—all of them overran all the ten quarters.

The entire range of the three worlds all over became completely burnt, when they heavily trod over with hissing sounds of *Huṁ* and resultant outbursts.

The entire earth all round became awful to look at, as skulls, variegated tresses of hairs etc., lay scattered all over along with hues and cries, laments and shouts of distress. The streets were split and cracked with the debris of the houses and ornamental gateways lying shattered.

The entire Jaṁbū Dvīpa that is said to have hundreds and thousands of sectors, lay demolished per force. People residing in Jaṁbū Dvīpa and (other) Dvīpas like Śāka, Kuśa, Krauñca, Gomeda, Śālmali and Puṣkara and those residing in mountains, were all seized by death and by goblins and groups of Mother-goddesses who were decked with the skulls of great Asuras. They were drunk with suet, marrow, blood and flesh. They were giving out terrific shouts. They were inebriated with smell of wine.

10b-13a. Mahāmāyā appeared surrounded with thousands of flames. Her earrings were dazzling like lightning. Her body became red with the blood gushing forth. She was very terrible (to look at). Fond of human flesh and suet, she was drinking blood there. With a skull in hand, the terrible (Mahāmāyā) was devouring Suras and Asuras. Dancing, boisterously laughing, shouting loudly, taking somersaults, she struck terror in the three worlds. Her laughter was like the peals of thunder.

13b-14. After having swallowed up the earth ending with seven seas, she came to the place where Lord Maheśvara lived on the bank of Narmadā, along with Mother-goddesses.

15. Laughing loudly, (the goddess) danced on the stout bodies of Amaras (immortal ones = Devas). The word '*Amaras*' means 'gods' and '*Kaṭa*' means 'a body'.[1]

16-17. O excellent king, as this mountain is scattered over (enveloped) with bodies, heaps of shattered bones and bodies dripping with suet, fat and blood, so it is called 'Amaraṅkaṭa' by the wise ones. It is greatly sanctifying and sacred all over the world as it is created by Śaṁbhu.

18-30. Śaṅkara is ever present there along with Umā. Hence I too stationed myself at the tip of its foot, with steady observances.

---

1. A popular etymology of mountain '*Amara-kaṇṭaka*', the source of Narmadā.

Humble with the fervour of obeisance I continued to eulogize Nīlalohita.

Along with Mṛtyu, the joyous Śaṅkara began to dance even as the Gaṇas and the groups of Mothers started beating the time.

The Gaṇas joyously danced in groups with flesh, fat and suet in their hands. They had Khaṭvāṅgas, firebrands, Paṭṭiśas and Parighas too. There were dwarfs, those with matted hairs, those with shaven heads and those with long neck, lips and hairs. Gaṇas with long penises, protruding bellies and arms loosely suspended were dancing and laughing. The faces of some were hideously distorted. The arms, mouths etc. were fiercely contorted and twisted.

When the transit of the (Yuga) period set in they made Amara as Kaṇṭaka (thorn). Among them, I saw the highly terrible Mṛtyu, the cause of fright for the entire universe.

I saw Mṛtyu dancing there. His hairs were tawny-coloured like a lightning streak. The goddess bedecked in clean garments was stationed near him. The earrings produced jingling sound near her cheeks. She had serpents serving the purpose of the sacred thread. She was adoring Maheśvara by means of diverse kinds of offerings.

There I saw Mother Narmadā revered and bowed to by the entire universe. There were waves and whirlpools therein. She resembled the ocean with excellent billows rising up. Invisible due to the great lake and the rivers falling therein, she had the visible form as well. O descendant of Bharata, she was being honoured by Suras, Siddhas and groups of sages.

In the middle I saw the terrible aspect of Narmadā called *Saptasaptaka.* She had great waves and foams. She flooded the entire universe. She was Mṛgakṛṣṇāṁbarā (clad in the skin of a black antelope). She was flowing in seven ways (currents) producing thunderous sound as of the rumbling sounds of smoking Aśani (thunderbolt).

Thus I saw the incomparable havoc of destruction, O excellent king. The rays of the sun and the moon disappeared from the world consisting of mobile and immobile beings.

31-36. There was a great evil portent. The stellar sphere had completely vanished. It caused everything to whirl continuously like *Alātacakra* (circular movement of a firebrand).

It was scattered over with millions of air-chariots of Kinnaras and great Uragas. There was a terrible, roaring wind which shook the mobile and immobile beings. It was the well-known Saṁvarta issuing from the mouth of Rudra. It dried up the seven oceans. May Hara protect you all day by day—Hara with dust particles smeared all over his body, with eyes and hairs tawny in colour, with his matted hairs tied up. He held a large resplendent trident and shouted loudly. He held the big brilliant Śūla (trident) and bow. There was a crown on his head. He had put on coat-of-mail. He had smeared all his body with the ashes of cremation ground. Garlands of skulls covered his neck. Great serpents were tied to the top of his head as though they were threads. *Goṇasas* (lizard-like serpents) entwined his limbs. There were the celestial river, the crescent moon, the poison and fire on the head. He was clad in the hide of elephant. He played on the Ḍamaru. The terrible Khaṭvāṅga and Pināka were held in the hands.

37-42. The divine being pervaded through the seven worlds. The great extending arms (serpents?) encircled all the limbs. His eye resembled the rising Sun with the centre like a tender sprout. It was pink in colour like the cloud at dusk, red lily, ruby, saffron and a streak of lightning. During the period of the conclusion of the Yuga, he played with heated Liṅga and blazing eye. Like Meru the Lord appeared as though he was discharging golden shafts. He walked there making the mountain shattered to pieces through the kicking with the tips of his feet. He was desirous of annihilating the entire heaven. He was laughing hideously. The sole Lord of the universe desirous of annihilating Svarga burst out his boisterous laughter, agitated and annihilated the entire heaven.

On seeing the excellent unborn Lord, the great Lord engaged in annihilating the universe, that Kālarātri accompanied by the Mothers and all the Gaṇas began to worship Śiva. Nandin and Bhṛṅgin and other Gaṇas bowed down to that Lord of all the living beings, the most excellent one in the universe, the cause of all, Hara the enemy of Smara. They bowed to him day and night.

CHAPTER SIXTEEN

Eulogy of Śiva by Brahmā

Śrī Mārkaṇḍeya said:

1-7. The Trident-bearing Lord was surrounded by the terrible groups of goblins along with the Mothers.

He continued his dance. Wearing two pieces of elephant hide he evinced his desire to annihilate the entire universe.

Śaṁbhu danced amidst the conflagration that consumed the three worlds. The entrails of all the leaders of Suras constituted his garland. Their fat, suet and blood smeared his limbs.

Accompanied by Kālarātri that noble-souled Lord annihilated the entire region of the three worlds at the proper time. Named Saṁvartaka and having the state of the fierce Sun, the noble-souled Śaṁbhu, the most excellent one in the universe, opened his mouth that resembled *Baḍavāmukha* (the entrance to the submarine fire) and laughed boisterously. It appeared like profuse outcome of sparks mixed with smoke or like the blow of a violent gust of wind wafting great firebrands and thunderbolts.

All the ten quarters were filled with that loud outburst of laughter arising from Hara. It had the forceful impact of a thousand thunderbolts. All the great oceans became agitated.

The loud sound reached the world of Brahmā. The entire Cosmic Egg shook and quaked violently. The sages became frightened and they worried wondering, 'What could this be?' All those frightened sages along with Suras and Asuras and the great Serpents bowed down to Brahmā, the Lord of the great chiefs:

8-11. "Who is this being that sports about stationed on the surface of the earth? His limbs are terrible and they blaze like the refulgence of a lightning streak. His body resembles the Kālānala fire and due to his boisterous laughter the whole universe is bewildered.

In a moment it has become utterly confused. Is it possible that he may wish to annihilate all the three worlds, along with you and all the seven oceans? Desirous of annihilating he proceeds towards Jana, Tapas and Satya worlds.

Who is this Lord? O incomprehensible being, recount all this. Never before has this difficult situation been faced. You do know the truth. You are considered by us as the greatest being."

On hearing their words, Brahmā consoled the groups of Suras and others and said:

Śrī Brahmā said:

12-15. He is Kāla (Death), the eternal Ātman desirous of annihilating the entire heaven and the whole universe. When the whole work is complete, he will be lying down. The Lord Īśāna will be lying down in the future *Parivatsaras* (years). It is not surprising.

This Lord himself is *Saṁvatsara, Parivatsara, Udvatsara* and *Vatsara* (different ways of reckoning years). Though seen, he is invisible. He is the one who illuminates everything. He is adored by means of Homa. He is gross. He is subtle. He is the ultimate atom.

There is nothing in this world here greater than this. He is the greatest and greater than the greatest. The Lord is proclaimed as Ātman. Of features similar to those Kāla will become pleased with me.

After saying this, the holy Lord, the chief of Suras, propitiated (Śiva) in the company of Sanatkumāra and others. He was of complete self-control.

Brahmā said:

16-20. Obeisance is done to Śarva of quiescent forms and features. Obeisance, obeisance to you in the form of Aghora. O Śarva, O immanent soul of all, obeisance, obeisance to you.

O Lord of goblins, obeisance to you, O great Ātman.

Obeisance, obeisance to you, O Svadhā and Vaṣaṭkāra, developed further into Oṁkāra and Huṁkāra. Obeisance to the Lord of the three Guṇas, to Maheśvara, identical with the Trayī (three Vedas), the immanent soul of the three Guṇas.

You are Śaṅkara. You alone are Maheśvara. You have penetrated into the foremost Pradhāna. You are Viṣṇu, Īśa and Prapitāmaha. You are the Fire-god with seven tongues of flames, with an infinite number of tongues of flames.

O Lord, you alone are the creator and the creation; you are the entity worthy of being known by the universe; you are the greatest support of the universe. The Brāhmaṇas who have mastered and understood the Vedas call you the most excellent and the greatest. You are greater than the greatest. They speak of you as subtler than the subtlest. The words along with the mind recede therefrom.

Śrī Mahādeva said:

21-24. I have been eulogized by you through diverse kinds of Mantras. O Lotus-born One, I shall increase the peace and calm in you. Look at me burning down this world, annihilating forcibly by means of many faces.

After saying thus and consoling Pitāmaha, the Lord of the universe vanished there itself along with the goddess.

By listening to this great and meritorious hymn, people attain the blissful goal. Even those who are infested by many sins proceed towards Rudra by means of aerial chariots free from impurities. They will never experience any fear—the excellent Brāhmaṇas who recite this, O dear one. There is no doubt about this that Śiva will be their saviour in the course of war, theft, fire, forest and ocean.

CHAPTER SEVENTEEN

Annihilation by Twelve Suns

Śrī Mārkaṇḍeya said:

1. On being eulogized thus by Brahmā and others and by the leading sages who had gone to the world of Brahmā, the Lord began the annihilation of the universe.

2. Brahmā saw the face of Mahādeva, the imperishable southern face (mouth) highly awful and hideous. Its great curved fangs produced loud reports while gnashing. The face resembled the abysmal depths of the nether worlds.

3-5. The eyes were tawny like fire and lightning streaks.

The face was frightening and causing the hairs to stand on end. The fangs and the tongues were huge. The neck was covered by great serpents, and the necklace was constituted of the great heads of the Asuras. It caused great Pralaya. It swallowed the Havis in the form of the waters and winds of the oceans. The face of Mahādeva resembled Baḍavāmukha (the open entrance to the submarine fire). He saw him licking up the entire world by the tip of the tongue.

6. It extended to thousands of Yojanas, nay hundreds of thousands of Yojanas. All the ten quarters appeared hideous with flesh, fat and suet abounding therein.

7. Hundreds and thousands of the curved fangs grew large. Pitāmaha saw Suras, Gandharvas, Asuras, Yakṣas, Uragas and Rākṣasas stuck up at the tips of the curved fangs.

8-9a. O great king, I too saw the universe caught as if in a machine within the structure of the curved fangs, with the necks shattered and thereafter it was found to enter his open mouth.

9b-10. Just as the rivers roaring due to the movement of different waves dashing against one another, with the confused mass of great foams, fall into the ocean and get merged therein, so also the extensive range of the entire universe having many living beings, impenetrable like a vast ocean, entered the blazing spacious mouth of Rudra. It was terrible with rumbling sounds as of clouds.

11. From his mouth a huge column of flames and hideous sparks issued forth, scattering smoke everywhere. They had different forms and they illuminated all the quarters with the brilliance of fire.

12. The face of Maheśvara of myriad miraculous forms with curved fangs and tremulous tongues seemed to be garlanded with thousands of solar flames. Though one and single he revealed himself in twelve ways.

13. Twelve Ādityas came out of the mouth of Rudra. Resorting to the southern quarter, they began scorching the earth.

14. All earthly creatures resting on the different trees and grass blades that had already been dried up earlier due to drought, became utterly confused over the entire range of the surface of the earth.

15. Being burnt suddenly by those Suns coming out of

Rudra, everything became enveloped in smoke. All the stars and planets got destroyed.

16. The entire terrestrial sphere became suddenly kindled and it blazed forth. All the mobile and immobile beings became enveloped in a garland of flames.

17. In all the seven continents and oceans, rivers and lakes the fire consumed the entire universe as though it were the sacred clarified butter being consigned to it in the course of a sacrificial rite.

18. The Ādityas born from Rudra, refulgent with extensive fiery brilliance and overwhelmed with great flames burnt the whole universe.

19. The rays of the Ādityas got mutually entangled. Thus the Lord burnt the three worlds consisting of mobile and immobile beings.

20. Maheśvara became the fire itself of the size of the seven continents and burnt completely the entire earth consisting of the seven continents and encircled by the seven oceans.

21. Then it burnt the earth with Sumeru and Mandara as its limit. Thereafter it pierced through the seven Pātālas and burnt Nāgaloka.

22. O Yudhiṣṭhira, the Agni continued to burn and blaze after completely burning down the seven Pātālas beneath the earth along with the stars.

23. When fanned with bellows a metal piece seems to blaze at night along with the burning charcoal. In the same manner everything in the universe blazed forth on being kindled by Saṁvartāgni.

24. Bereft of trees, grass-blades, springs, lakes, and rivers and with the clusters of the peaks of mountains scattered, the ground became comparable to the back of a tortoise.

25. After making the entire universe chaotically unsettled through the series of flames and sparks and merged in *Cit* (the conscious, sentient Being) Maheśvara, Rudra, remained in his own great form.

26. Accompanied by most of the Mātṛgaṇas, Yakṣas, Uragas and Rākṣasas, the goddess Harilocanā ('having green eyes', 'having leonine eyes') merged in Mahādeva.

27. Like the flame of fire that has become quiescent, the goddess attained the state of extinction. O sinless one, the

entire universe along with the three worlds became completely burnt down.

28. With the favour of Rudra, Narmadā not born of a womb, and I were excluded from this annihilation. Ten thousand Yugas were thus concluded by me as though subsisting in water (of Narmadā).

29-31. The Trident-bearing Lord was propitiated formerly by me. Hence I became immortal and free from old age. I had also recited the following scriptural passages: *Aghamarṣaṇa, Ghora Mantra, Vāmadeva Sūkta, Tryaṁbaka Sūkta, Ṛṣabha Sūkta, Trisuparṇa, Durgā Sūkta, Sāvitra Sūkta, Bṛhadāraṇyaka, Bṛhatsāman* and *Uttara Sāman*. So also, the great *Raudrī Gāyatrī, Śivopaniṣad, Pratiratha Sūkta* and *Mṛtyuñjaya Sūkta.*[1]

32. The earth extending to the rivers and oceans was reduced to ashes. But the highly esteemable Narmadā comparable to Amṛta, was excluded (spared).

33-34. The following are the Kulaparvatas: Mahendra, Malaya, Sahya, Hemakūṭa, Māḷyavān, Vindhya and Pāriyātra. These mountains were completely burnt down by the twelve Ādityas. (Due to heat) the rocks in them were severely shattered. They are seen reduced to ashes. But Narmadā did not perish then.

35-36. Himavān, Hemakūṭa, Niṣadha, Gandhamādana, the excellent mountain Mālyavān, Nīla, Śveta and Śṛṅgavān—these great mountains were resorted to by Devas and Gandharvas. All of them were completely burnt down by the Yugāntāgni (Fire at the end of the Yuga). The great rocks and boulders of all these were shattered.

37. Thus the utter annihilation of everything except that of the highly meritorious Narmadā was earlier seen by me at the close of the Yuga, O excellent king.

---

1. The author has confused Vedic Sūktas, individual Mantras and a Purāṇic compendium of seven chapters called "Śivopaniṣad."

CHAPTER EIGHTEEN

Glorification of Narmadā

Śrī Mārkaṇḍeya said:

1-7. When the world was completely burnt by the Suns originating from Īśvara, with the seven oceans rendered dry along with (the burning of) the seven continents, huge clouds issued forth from his mouth. When the world was dried up by the Suns and burnt down by Kālāgni, clouds issued forth from the mouth of Śaṅkara. Terrible clouds having features comparable to the weapon of Indra (i.e. Rainbow), urged by the most excellent Īśāna made the universe completely dark. Some of the clouds had the lustre of a blue lotus; somewhere they had the lustre of collyrium; some resembled cow's milk, Kunda flower and the moon; others resembled the eyelets on the feathers of a peacock; and some had the lustre of smokeless fire. Some clouds had the forms resembling great mountains; some could be compared to shoals of great fishes; some had excellent forms of huge elephants; and some clouds resembled great peaks. Some were similar in form to the moving waves and billows; some were akin to the domes in a big city; some resembled great towers and ornamental gateways; others appeared to be adorned at the extremities by comets, firebrands and thunderbolts characterized by lightning streaks. A Gaṇa of Rudra named Saṁvartaka got his limbs concealed. The Lord showered limitlessly and made the universe one vast expanse of water.

Utterly terrified and flooded with the currents of the waters of Gaṅgā, I dared not look at Īśāna increasing in size along with the great clouds and having limbs covered with Indra's thunderbolt.

8-13. Devouring the burning universe all round repeatedly, the elephants (clouds resembling them) covered the ground completely. They filled the universe (with waters). and vanished all of them.

The seven great oceans, the lakes, the continents, all the rivers, Bhūḥ and Bhuvaḥ were filled with waves and waves of waters. Everything became a vast expanse of waters.

In the entire range of mobile and immobile beings, devoid

of fire, the Moon and the Sun, in the darkness caused by the disappearance of the stars, when all the winds subsided into a calm atmosphere, nothing was visible.

O king, then, in that vast expanse of water I eulogized him (the Lord) with the purity of mind retained. Thereafter, I thought thus: 'In whom shall I seek a quiescent refuge?'

I then remembered the Lord within my heart. Remaining within the water, I thought of the Lord as worthy of seeking refuge in. I bowed down to him, sought refuge in him and then I meditated upon him. After meditation, I forded the watery expanse, with his favour, never losing sense and fortitude. O son of a great man, due to the favour of the goddess, fatigue and anguish disappeared from me.

CHAPTER NINETEEN

Vārāhakalpa

Śrī Mārkeṇḍeya said:

1-7. I was about to die in that vast ocean-like expanse of water and was distressed. Muttering to myself and sighing, O excellent king, I swam across the water with my arms.

Stationed in the middle of the sea-like expanse, when everything was quiet and motionless, I heard an inimitable "*Ambho*" sound (the sound of a cow) causing reverberation in all the ten quarters. Despondent as I was, I saw a cow standing before me. She resembled a swan, a Kunda flower and the moon, white in colour like a pearl necklace and cow's milk. Her body was bedecked with many gems of diverse colours. The horns were bedecked in gold. Her boofs were covered with coral. She was fascinating with the tail lifted up and shining like a banner. With her snout stooping down she was making bellowing sound. She was crossing the ocean with her hoofs. She was encircled by golden strings of small tinkling bells and pearls. By the movements of her legs (when she waded through) in the water of the vast ocean-like expanse a mass of foams formed around her and she appeared to dance. She shouted loudly as she stirred up the ocean sending up columns of waters. O fortunate one, in smooth and majestic voice she said to me:

8-14 "O dear child, do not be afraid. O dear one, you have no death. With the favour of Mahādeva, neither you nor I have to face death. Support yourself holding on to my tail. I shall take you across this ocean. I shall save you, O Brāhmaṇa, from this fearful situation as long as the universe is flooded. In order to ward off hunger and quench thirst, suck at my udders. Be satisfied by drinking the divine milk with Amṛta as its basis."

On hearing her words, I joyously sucked at her udders. No sooner had the udders been sucked than hunger and thirst vanished. I had a divine strength and vitality capable of swimming across the sea. Then I spoke to her: "Who are you wandering here in this vast ocean-like expanse? Tell me the truth. There is a great curiosity in me. You alone are my refuge even as I wander here and there lashed about and on the point of death as it were. It was due to the residue of my good fortune, O Divinity of holy rites."

The cow said:

15-32. Have I been forgotten by you? I am Maheśvarī (Great Goddess) of diverse forms. I am Narmadā, the bestower of piety on men, the bestower of heavenly pleasures, happiness and strength. On seeing you distressed Rudra has despatched me saying: "O noble lady, redeem that Brāhmaṇa. Let him not lose his life in the water." At the instance of the Lord, I have come near you in the form of a cow. I hurried lest Śaṁbhu should be one of false speech.

On being told thus by her, I came to know that her tail was splendid and indestructible and comparable to Indrāyudha (Vajra). I held on to it with my arms. Resorting to the banner-like tail, I crossed the ocean. She told me that the deity therein was Lord Mahādeva. Thereafter, for a period of a thousand Yugas, I wandered about along with her in that darkened atmosphere encircled all round by the waters of the great ocean.

I continued wandering, holding on to the tip of the tail of the cow. There was no movement of wind. There was no light. There was darkness. It was free from ailments.

All of a sudden, I saw Lord Īśāna asleep in the ocean-like

expanse of water.[1] He resembled a flower of Atasī, split collyrium and was free from impurities like the sky. He was dark like petals of a blue lotus. The immutable Lord was clad in yellow robes. His head was shining with a crown having the colour of the sun and dazzling like lightning. He had excellent features like the sky. His cheeks were being brushed by the earrings and the chest illuminated by the necklace. He was rendered splendid by the divine golden ornaments. He was lying on a couch of the serpent. The serpent served as pillow too. He had the splendour of a thousand suns. He had many arms and thighs.[2] He had innumerable faces. He was charming. He had a thousand eyes and necks. The heroic Lord was asleep in the ocean-like expanse (of water).

He had a great mass of matted hairs having the sparkling lustre of lightning. The Lord was stationed thus pervading the entire universe merged in a single expanse of water. The Lord had swallowed everything including Devas, Asuras and human beings. The omnipresent, unmanifest, infinite Lord had faces all round.

Near the soles of his feet, there was Umā Viśvarūpā, the highly fortunate one embellished with golden bracelets.

The goddess identical with Śrī, Hrī, Dhī (intellect), Vāk (speech), wielding the Viśvamāyā (Universal Māyā), Śivā, the goddess was identical with Siddhi, Kīrti (renown), Rati (goddess of love), Brāhmī, Kālarātri. She was not born of a womb. I saw her sitting very close to Īśvara. I saw the moon-faced goddess of all, Umā identical with Dhṛti (fortitude).[3]

33-43. I circumambulated Lord Īśa who was quiescent and asleep. He had the colour of fresh gold. He was associated with Umā. He was meritorious and excellent but was enveloped by darkness.

I then bowed down to him.

At the close of the night, the excellent Lord who was asleep, naturally woke up. When he woke, he stirred up the waters of the ocean with his arms. Reflecting on the destruction of the universe in the water, he began to consider what should be

---

1. Here Śiva is identified with Viṣṇu—a syncretism.
2. An echo of the Puruṣa-sūkta (RV X. 90).
3. Umā and Lakṣmī (all great female deities like Śrī, Vāk etc.) are treated as non-different.

done. The Lord of miraculous limbs assumed the form of a Boar.[1]

His splendour was like that of a huge rain-bearing cloud. His garland consisting of gold coins (golden-coloured stars), was hanging down. Adorned with a crown, the Lord held the conch, the discus and the sword. The noble-souled Lord identified himself with the Vedas and Vedāṅgas. The ancient Lord causing the origin of the three worlds holds the form of the three Vedas.

The very same Rudra who annihilated became Prapitāmaha for the purpose of creation. For the purpose of protection, he himself becomes Hari with the excellent discus, sword, club and lotus in his hands.

Distinction among them is unbecoming.[2] They are all noble-souled ones having the same physical form. An ignorant person who brings in distinction among them, albeit by means of apparently cogent reasons and arguments based on principles of reasoning, falls into terrible hell gradually. He who creates distinction (between these—Śiva and Viṣṇu) is a wicked soul with a hostile motive.

One may be devoted to any of these. After casting off the physical body, one certainly attains immortality through that devotion itself.

The same Lord, the creator, the protector and the annihilator presumably enchants the world by means of these physical forms. Hence one should avoid falling into delusion and entertain hatred in view of the different forms.

For the same reason the excellent Īśāna, the creator of the universe, assumed the form of the Boar. When the three worlds became immersed in the waters of the ocean, the immanent soul was sought within the vortex of the waters.

The Lord pierced through the water within the ocean and entered Pātāla in a moment. He touched the entire Earth sunk under water. By one of his curved fangs, Lord Viṣṇu of inimitable daring lifting up the Earth, the divine lady of lotus-petal-like eyes, who had got submerged in the water at the time of

1. Viṣṇu's Boar-incarnation is attributed to Śiva here.
2. Strong condemnation of treating Śiva and Viṣṇu as different—a syncretic trend of that (Purāṇic) age.

Pralaya when the peaks of mountains and the rocks therein got shattered.

44-53. With her body hanging, suspended at the tip of the curved fang (of the divine Boar) she shone like the moonlight sticking to the peak of Kailāsa. Of uneven form, she resembled the lightning sticking to the cusp or horn of the moon.

The Lord of manifested Sattva quality (or power) and of incomparable prowess lifted up from the middle of the water, the Earth sunk within the waters of the sea in the same manner as an elephant lifting the sinking she-elephant with force or (like a sailor) lifting the boat that has been shattered.

The noble Lord raised up the Earth from the great mass of watery expanse and then divided the whole range of the ocean as well. He deposited, as it were, the waters of the great ocean into the oceans and then into the rivers (also).

He re-created the mountains that had been shattered earlier. He created all the continents and seas. In the Kalpa he created the ranges of rocky mountains that had been arranged with the boulders.

After having assumed physical forms of various features he created groups of Devas and of Indras. Suddenly issued forth the Fire-god from his mouth, the Moon from the mind and the Sun from the eye.

As that Yogeśvara (Yoga personified) began to meditate, the group of Suras and Indra, the Vedas, the different Varṇas, all the medicinal herbs, juices, everything issued forth. From his mind was evolved the entire universe consisting of immobile beings, oviparous beings, viviparous beings, sweat-born beings, plants etc. that split the ground and grow up, in fact everything including insects, ants etc.

Then the great Lord mentally transformed himself into a multiformed being. The Lord of immutable soul pervaded everything by means of his eight Mūrtis (Cosmic forms) and thereafter sported about gracefully. He had richly flourishing splendour even as I was witnessing everything. He sported gracefully, O Brāhmaṇas(?). O king, I witnessed everything for the period of a Muhūrta.

After creating everything sportingly, the Lord of Devas, the creator of the Cosmos, omnipresent and having eyes all round, the primordial creator, vanished.

54-61. (In that short span of time) All those things consisting of names and forms, the entire universe was witnessed by me. They were surrounded by oceans and continents. Everything was overspread by the stars and constellations. Everything appeared wonderful with the sky, clouds and the system of planets full of different kinds of living beings. Yet I could not see the Sarvasureśvarī (the goddess of all Suras) in the form of the cow, the divinity of great esteem.

My mind became agitated thinking, 'Where can she be now?' I surveyed the various parts of the quarters. Excepting that Īśvarāṅgī (born of the limbs of the Lord) how was it that I could see all?

Thereafter I saw the splendid river here with crystal-clear waters. She had the blue hue of a big cloud. Her limbs were rendered splendid by many trees and she was surrounded by elephants, horses and birds. As before, I resorted to the banks of the divine river. I stationed myself in Amarakaṇṭaka and found myself happily resting. My soul was rid of excitement. It attained happiness. After having seen the river full of meritorious water, free from impurities even at the close of the Kalpa, I felt as though I was seeing my own mother looking at me compassionately. I was free from ailment and sorrow.

Those leading Brāhmaṇas who read and listen to this meritorious narrative of the Mahāvārāha Kalpa everyday become pure. They will get rid of all inauspiciousness and go to heaven inhabited by Amaras, Siddhas and Gandharvas. They will attain heavenly pleasures in the company of the celestial damsels resembling the pure moon and endowed with different kinds of charms.

CHAPTER TWENTY

Vārāhakalpa (continued)

Yudhiṣṭhira said:

1-2. Various acts and destructions have been heard by me, with your favour, O sinless one, that were done by Lord Śarva and seen by you. Now I wish to hear about the prowess of the

Lord wielding the Śārṅga bow. O eminent Brāhmaṇa, it behoves you to tell me whatever has been seen by you (about Viṣṇu).

Śrī Mārkaṇḍeya said:

3. Hereafter, I shall recount the characteristic (prognostic) features of the destruction of the subjects, the significant (portentious) mark that is seen and how the Kalpa is recycled.

4. There are falls of firebrands and meteors along with thunder. There is earthquake; a dust-storm as well as terrible loud report.

5. Yakṣas, Kinnaras and Gandharvas, Piśācas, Uragas and Rākṣasas—all these undergo annihilation when the close of the Yuga is imminent.

6. Mountains, oceans, rivers, different types of lakes, trees, creepers and grasses—all get dried up.

7-8. Thus when everything was under turmoil, when all regions were bereft of all medicinal herbs and water, when the three worlds consisting of mobile and immobile beings resembled a dry log of wood, at midday, when the time for ablution arrived, I saw the three worlds becoming inaccessible and in a form of fire too dazzling to be viewed.

9. Two Suns were seen in the east, O dear one. So also in the north and in the west. Similarly in the south too, two radiant Suns were seen.

10. Two Suns were stationed in Nāgaloka and two in the middle of the sky. Thus twelve Ādityas began to blaze in all the quarters.

11. They burnt the entire earth including mountains, parks and forests. Nothing was seen unburnt except Revā and myself.

12. When the earth was being burnt, the smell of ghee and sacrificial offerings issued forth. Thereupon my body became parched. Unbearable thirst too overwhelmed me.

13. I did not find water. Everything was dried up by the Suns. I looked into the Kamaṇḍalu (waterpot). That too was dry.

14. Then I was distressed with grief, particularly overwhelmed by thirst. I jumped up into the sky from the earth looking around.

15-16. Then I espied a house in the firmament beautifully furnished. O excellent king, desirous of seeing it, I passed through the ramparts of diverse types and wonderful features and reached the portals embellished with panels with bolts. The turrets and their tops were quaint and amusing.

17. Its height was eighty-six thousand Yojanas. Half thereof was separately embellished with gold and jewels.

18. O excellent king, in the centre thereof I saw a huge bed. A Being of divine tresses of hairs was lying on the bed.

19. He was lying down stretching a full Yojana long with curly hairs. His splendour was heightened by a wonderful crown of refulgent lustre.

20-21a. He was dark in complexion and had the lustre of lotus petals. His nose was excellent. His face was majestic like that of a lion. His arms were long. Excellent moustache and beard marked his cheeks. He was handsome with *Trivalī* (curly hairs near the navel) and his ears were adorned with earrings.

21b-23. He appeared to be stout with chubby fleshy limbs. His sides were embellished with Āvarta (eddy-like curves). His hips were extremely splendid. The knees and calves were well rounded. His palms were marked with the outline of a lotus. His excellent nails and fingers were slightly reddish. His voice appeared to resemble the thunder of clouds. He was handsome in every limb. Thus I saw Lord Puruṣottama in the middle of the bed.

24-25a He had a conch, a discus and a club in his hands. He was lying on his right side. His hand was lifted up with the rosary string suspended therefrom. His brilliance was like that of ten thousand Suns. On seeing him I became devoted to him and got ready to eulogize him.

[*Prayer*[1]]

25b-29. "Be victorious, O Īśa; be victorious, O Vāgīśa (Lord of Speech); be victorious, O Lord bedecked with divine ornaments of the limbs. Be victorious, O Lord of Devas. O glorious one, O eternal one, you are Brahman itself. All the worlds are stationed in your body, O Parameśvara. You are our goal.

Indeed, O Lord of Devas, all the worlds have you as the support as they are stationed.

1. This eulogy emphasizes the identity of Śiva and Viṣṇu.

You are the most excellent one of all beings. You are the creator and the support of the Earth. You are the Hautra (function of the Hotṛ Priest) of the Agnihotras. You alone are the Sūtra Mantra. You are the Gokarṇa (shrine), Bhadra Karṇa (a Śiva shrine Karnāli on Narmadā). You are the Maheśvara region.

You are the Kīrti (fame) of all the Kīrtis, the destroyer of wretchedness and sins. You are (the sacred place) Naimiṣa, Kurukṣetra and the great Viṣṇupada at Gayā

30. O Lord, the earth was sportingly covered with (one) foot (by you). O Lord, Bali was bound by you. Indra was reinstated in his position by you.

31-34. O Lord, you are the Yugas like Kali, Dvāpara, Tretā and Kṛta. You are the suppressor of Pralamba. You are the creator. You are the destroyer. You support the worlds. You are Kāla, the destroyer of all. All the clans of Devas were created by you alone, O God. You are the path of all the worlds. You are salvation, the greatest goal. Brahmā, the eternal one of the Rajas form is the Lord born from you. Rudra originating from (your) *Krodha* (Anger) is also so (born from you). You are established in Sattva. O Lord, the mobile and immobile beings have been created by you for the sake of sport."

Thus the Lord was eulogized by me, when my entire body was scorched.

35. O king, the Lord of all living beings was thus eulogized by me with great devotion. Even as I was eulogizing the Lord, I saw there pots filled with water.

36. Thereupon the thirst that had been forgotten by me became increased. I approached the side of that Puruṣa.

37-38. I thought thus when I was desirous of drinking water: 'He never saw me. He was asleep. He never woke up. He who is deluded by sin and tries to wake up a sleeping person incurs the great sin of Brāhmaṇa's slaughter.'

39-40. Even as this was being thought by me, a second being came there. He did not utter anything. He did not see anyone. He had worn an antelope skin on his left shoulder. He had matted hairs. He held a Kamaṇḍalu (waterpot) and a staff. A girdle encircled him. He was three-eyed. He had smeared ash all over the body. He was of great lustre.

41-42. Even as I was desirous of eulogizing him and gazed

at him with clear eyes, a woman embellished in all ornaments was seen. She was of excellent beauty in every limb. On seeing her I prostrated on the ground saying "Be victorious".

43–44. Be victorious, O goddess originating from the limbs of Rudra. Be victorious, O eternal Brāhmī. Be victorious, O Kaumārī, O Māhendrī, O Vaiṣṇavī, O Vāruṇī, be victorious, O Kauberī, O Sāvitrī; be victorious, O Dhātrī of excellent countenance. In this world consisting of mobile and immobile beings protect my body that has become scorched with thirst."

Śrī Devī said:

45. O tiger among Brahmaṇas, I am delighted by your splendid speech. O excellent Brahmaṇa, what is in your mind has been understood by me.

46. Listen, O Brāhmaṇa, I too have adopted this severe vow. Due to the levity common to all women, an austere vow has been adopted by me who am deficient in intellect.

47-48. If a righteous son well-known all over the world is to be born to me, I will first breast-feed a Brāhmaṇa and then alone my son. O great sage, such a son has been born to me. O eminent Brāhmaṇa, if you wish to be alive suck the breasts.

Śrī Mārkaṇḍeya said:

49-51. In the case of Brāhmaṇas this (namely sucking the breasts) is something not to be done.[1] Again a boy has to be invested with a sacred thread. Otherwise the Vrata cannot be fulfilled. O lotus-eyed one, Brāhmaṇa-hood is difficult to obtain in all the three worlds. Listen now how one becomes a Brāhmaṇa and by means of which Saṁskāras (consecratory rites). First there is the rite of Bījavāpana ('sowing of the seed') in women through sacred rites. It is called Bījakṣepa too since the seed is thrown (sown).

52-59. O lady of high esteem, at the end thereof the second one, Garbhādhāna (impregnation), takes place. Puṁsavana rite is the third. Śīmanta is the fourth one. The fifth one is

1. VV 49-58 give a list of 48 Saṁskāras. The list contians the names of sacrifices like Agniṣṭoma, Sautrāmaṇi etc., which can hardly be called 'Saṁskāras'. Old Smṛtis like Manu or Yājñavalkya do not specify the number of Saṁskāras. P.V. Kane in HD II.i deals with 16 Saṁskāras which are regarded as essential.

Jātakarma (post-natal rite). Nāmakarma (Naming) is called the sixth rite. Niṣkrāma (taking out the baby in open air for the first time) is the seventh rite. Annaprāśana (formal feeding with food) is the eighth rite. Cūḍākarma (cutting the lock of hair) is the ninth rite. The tenth one is Mauñjībandhana (investiture with the sacred thread). Thereafter the rites of Aiṣika, Dārvika, Saumika, Bhaumika, Patnīsaṁyojana (marriage) are performed. Then follows Daivakarma (offering oblations to gods). Then come Mānuṣyaka (rites in regard to human beings) and Pitṛkarma (propitiation of the ancestors). O splendid lady, these rites are performed on the tenth or eighth lunar days. Then follow the rites of Bhūta, Bhavya, Iṣṭa, Pārvaṇa, Śrāddha, Āgrayaṇa on the Śrāvaṇī day, during the Darśa and Paurṇamāsī of the months of Caitra and Aśvayuj, Nirūḍhapaśusavana, Sautrāmaṇi, Agniṣṭoma, Atyagniṣṭoma, Ṣoḍaśī, Vājapeya, Atirātra, Āptoryāma, Daśavājapeyas, forbearance towards all living beings, Anasūyā (absence of jealousy), Śauca (purity), Maṅgala, (auspiciousness), Akārpaṇya (absence of miserliness) and Aspṛhā (absence of desire). One becomes a Brāhmaṇa by consecration through these forty-eight Saṁskāras.

60. After realizing this, O highly esteemed lady, it does not behove you to compel me to drink breast-milk. O gentle lady, how can one like me drink breast-milk?

61-70. On hearing these words of mine, the lady spoke these words: "If you do not drink the breast-milk, the boy will die. It is heard in the three worlds, in the Vedas and in the Smṛtis that one is rid of all sins but cannot be rid of the sin of infanticide. The sin of killing will be incurred by you. Even a great devotee of the Lord has to suffer the consequences of infanticide in a hundred births. On death he incurs the state of a dog extending to three hundred years. At the close thereof he is born in the womb of a crow. There too he suffers the consequences of the sinful act during eight hundred births. He becomes a pig during ten births, at the close of which he is born as a worm. Then he has a gradual rise in the births of cow, elephant, horse and human being. Thus it is heard in Śrutis, Śāstras and the Vedas. O scorcher of enemies, O excellent Brāhmaṇa, the killing of a child brings about a sin more heinous than all other sins. A Brāhmaṇa committing the slaughter of a boy, is certainly cooked in Naraka. He undergoes torture at the hands of Yama for eight hundred years. If you drink my breast-milk, the fault is less severe. If you do not drink the sin shall extend to many years. In case you drink the milk there will be much merit besides the alleviation of hunger and thirst. Hence do not entertain in your mind any doubt. Do come, O Brāhmaṇa; for the sake of the boy drink the milk from my breasts."

71-74. On hearing those words I became ready to drink the milk from the breasts. I was never satisfied in the course of drinking the excellent breast-milk. O descendant of Bharata, thirty-three thousand years thus elapsed. Deluded by the deceptive slumber for a long time I woke up in the lap. After the delusion of sleep had vanished, O son of Pāṇḍu, I looked around and could not see the sleeping being or the boy. O descendant of Bharata, I saw those four waterpots. Nor was that goddess to be seen. All of them had gone somewhere.

75. While I was reflecting thus and standing there pondering over everything, the goddess spoke these words with slight laughter.

Śrī Devī said:

76-80. That sleeping person was Kṛṣṇa. The second being that came was Hara. The four pitchers were the oceans, O excellent Brāhmaṇa. The boy seen by you was Brahmā, the grandfather of the worlds. I should be known as Pṛthivī consisting of the seven continents and mountains. Here, O Brāhmaṇa, you see the excellent river Narmadā who left you on the ground where she is well-established. She of auspicious features flows for the good of all living beings. She is well-known as River Revā. Hence Narmadā has not become defunct. After realizing this be calm and normal, O great sage.

After saying this to me that Divinity vanished there itself.

81. It is thus that the Lord stationed in Sattva used to lie always during Pralaya—the great Lord in the form of Sattva on whose support the universe is sustained.

82. Thus the great and excellent miracle was seen and experienced by me. It is meritorious and destructive of all sins.

83. O excellent one among men, it has thus been narrated and it was this that you had asked for. O king of mighty arms, what else do you wish to hear?

CHAPTER TWENTYONE

The Origin of the River Kapilā

Yudhiṣṭhira said:

1-2. O excellent Brāhmaṇa, with your favour different narratives of miraculous import have been heard by me. I wish to hear further, O Brāhmaṇa, about good holy vows. Do tell me. How did this meritorious river named Narmadā, the most excellent one among all the rivers, become well-known? Tell me again, O sinless one.

Śrī Mārkaṇḍeya said:

3. Narmadā is the most excellent one among all rivers. It is destructive of all sins. It shall redeem all living beings, both mobile and immobile.

4-5. I shall recount to you the greatness of Narmadā which has been heard by me from my predecessors. O king, listen with concentration of mind. Gaṅgā is auspicious in Kanakhala; Sarasvatī in Kurukṣetra; but Narmadā is auspicious everywhere, whether it be a village or a forest.

6. The water of Sarasvatī sanctifies one in three days; the water of Yamunā in seven days; the water of Gaṅgā sanctifies one immediately; but the water of Narmadā does so through the very sight.

7-8. It is meritorious and beautiful at every step, in all the three worlds. In the region to the west of Kaliṅgadeśa on the mountain Amarakaṇṭaka, O great king, Devas, Gandharvas, sages and ascetics have performed penance and attained great Siddhis.

9. After taking his holy bath there, strictly controlling the sense-organs and scrupulously observing restraints and observing fast for a night, a man shall redeem a hundred members of his family.

10. O dear one, since the mountain Amarakaṇṭaka is a great Siddhi-kṣetra, it has been resorted to by all the Devas and served by sages.

11. Siddhas, Vidyādharas, Bhūtas and Gandharvas both visible and invisible, desirous of Siddhi, serve and resort to this excellent holy place.

12. Ever since then I too have resorted to the great holy spot. Indeed in this holy spot the Consort of Umā is stationed in the form of Praṇava.

13. Śrīkaṇṭha (Śiva) and his Gaṇas have been served by groups of all living beings. O king, I shall recount the details of this Tīrtha extending from this excellent mountain.

14-15a. O excellent king, even Brahmā is not competent to fully extol all the meritorious Tīrthas situated on either side of Narmadā.

15b. O leading king, it is heard that the excellent river is more than a hundred Yojanas long.

16-17. It is half a Yojana in width. There are sixty crore sixty thousand Tīrthas undoubtedly on both the banks of the river from the mountain upto the sea.

18. The Wind-god has mentioned that the Tīrthas number sixty-seven crore sixty-seven thousand sixty-seven hundred.

19. But, only in Kṛtayuga they become visible, O king. All pious-minded men see them always.

20. As Kali becomes severe and terrible, men become short in stature and deficient in intrinsic strength.

21. They say, O king, that Jāleśvara and other Tīrthas on this mountain accord satisfaction to the Pitṛs on whom they as well bestow heavenly pleasures and salvation.

22. The holy spot Dāruvana[1] is very excellent. There the confluence of Carukā is auspicious. On the north (bank) of Narmadā the holy spot of Carukeśvara is the most excellent.

23-25. Dārukeśvara Tīrtha, Vyatīpāteśvara, Pātāleśvara Tīrtha, Koṭiyajña—these, O excellent king, are on the northern bank of Revā. Near the side of Amareśvara there are one hundred eight Liṅgas, the chief whereof is Varuṇeśvara. They dispel all sins.

26. Near Māndhātṛpura are Siddheśvara and Yameśvara. To the east of Oṁkāra is the excellent Tīrtha of Kedāra.

27-28. Near it, O great king, is Svargadvāra ('Gateway to Heaven') that dispels sins. It is the meritorious Tīrtha named Brahmeśvara. In front of it is Saptasārasvata.

---

1. It is some local spot on the bank of Narmadā. It is different from Dāruvana (area round the famous Jyotirliṅga Āvanḍhyā Nāganātha) in Marathwada region of Maharashtra.

Then there are the Rudrāṣṭaka, Sāvitra and Somatīrtha. These are the Liṅgas, O Bull among the descendants of Bharata, on the southern bank of Revā.

29. O dear one, crores of Rudras are stationed on this mountain. They can be propitiated through ablutions, scents, garlands and unguents.

30. O king, the Rudras shall undoubtedly become pleased here. Sins can be wiped off by means of Japa. One attains infiniteness (Mokṣa) through meditation.

31. One obtains worldly pleasures through Dāna: So said Śaṅkara. In the region towards the west of the mountain, Lord Maheśvara himself, the eternal Lord, the primordial cause of the Cosmos, is stationed in the form of Praṇava.

32. A devotee should control his sense-organs and remain celibate. After taking his holy bath, he shall remain pure and perform the libation and other rites of the Pitṛs as enjoined by scriptures.

33. He should propitiate Pitṛ-gods with the water mixed with gingelly seeds. O son of Pāṇḍu, members of his family up to seven generations including himself rejoice in heaven.

34. He remains happy and enjoys different kinds of worldly pleasures. He rejoices for sixty thousand years (in heaven) duly adored by Suras.

35-36. He rejoices for a long period. After coming down from heaven, he is reborn in a family devoid of impurities, when he shall be rich, liberal in gifts, devoid of ailments and honoured by laymen. Again he remembers the holy spot and makes pilgrimage thereto.

37. During the second birth he will be very enthusiastic (in eagerly resorting to the eddy) in the performance of the Vrata with celibacy, observance of fasts and subduing of sense-organs.

38-46a. Withdrawing from all forms of violence he attains excellent merit. O king, know the meritorious benefit of the devotee who practises piety in this manner and gives up life. O son of Pāṇḍu, he rejoices in heaven for a hundred thousand years full of groups of Apsarās and reverberating with divine words and sounds. He shall be smeared with divine scents and unguents and adorned with divine ornaments. He plays about along with gods. He will be eulogized by Siddhas and Gandharvas.

After coming down (again) from heaven he becomes (is born as) a very powerful king possessing elephants, horses, chariots and other vehicles. He shall be conversant with holy rites and eagerly devoted to scriptural texts. He will dwell in a house full of gold and silver supported by hundreds of columns. It will have seven or eight storeys with excellent doorways and abounding in male and female servants and slaves.

Like the world of Indra, his abode shall be astir with the sighs and deep breaths of elephants in rut and the neighing sounds of horses. He shall be a glorious leader of kings of kings and a dear lover of all womenfolk. He shall stay in such a house for more than a hundred years enjoying pleasures and amusements. He shall be devoid of all ailments.

This is what will happen in case of those who die in Amareśvara.

46b-47a. He who devoutly enters into funeral pyre on Amarakaṇṭaka shall attain heaven after death (ultimately) reaching the greatest goal.

47b-49 It is known from the Purāṇa that everything regarding holy ablution, Dāna, Japa and Homa, whether auspicious or inauspicious, shall have a crore of times more of its benefit. The trees also growing on her banks and falling down after a lapse of time attain the greatest goal on being touched by the waters of Narmadā. His departure (death) thereto is without return (to Saṁsāra) like that of the wind in the firmament.

50-52. O king, if the devotee falls down (offers his body) into the Tīrtha, he will enjoy pleasures in Pātāla. Three thousand maidens stand in waiting in his abode seeking errands from him. Richly endowed with divine enjoyment of pleasures, he amuses himself for as long as he wishes (to do). On the whole of the earth stretching upto the sea, O excellent one among men, there is nothing like mountain Amarakaṇṭaka.

53. To the west of the mountain, it should be known that there is a Tīrtha, the eddy named Jāleśvara well-known in all the three worlds.

54. By offering balls of rice there and performing Sandhyā prayers, the Pitṛs become propitiated and satisfied for a period of twelve years.

55-57a. On the southern bank of Narmadā there is the

great river Kapilā[1] overgrown with Sarala (pine) and Arjuna trees, rendered beautiful by Khadiras and adorned by the creepers of Mādhavī and Sallakī. O king, it is always delightful with roaring beasts of prey, other beasts like jackals, monkeys etc., and chirping of different kinds of birds.

57b-58a. We have heard that there are more than a hundred crores of sages there. After performing penance there they have attained liberation. They have no rebirth. They never came back (to Saṁsāra).

58b-60a. Since the noble-souled Kapila performed penance there, a meritorious Tīrtha has sprung up there. It was resorted to formerly by the sages following Kapila; it has been praised by the name of Kapilā. It is destructive of all sins.

60b-62a. There in Amareśvara there are more than hundred crores of Tīrthas. One who stays for a night and day there, is rid of all sins after offering Dāna duly to an excellent Brāhmaṇa in accordance with one's capacity. Due to the favour of Īśvara everything shall become a crore of times more meritorious.

62b-64a. O descendant of Bharata, here the form of Praṇava is Anakṣara (not in the form of a syllable). It is in the form of Śiva himself. It will be one made with syllables and Mātrās(?). Creatures and animals, trees, hedges, creepers etc. meeting with death there undoubtedly attain heaven.

64b-65a. There itself is a great river named Viśalyā. By taking holy bath and offering Dāna duly there also, one will become meritorious.

65b-66. All the groups of Devas along with Kinnaras, great serpents, Yakṣas, Rākṣasas, Gandharvas, sages and ascetics come there and visit her in Amareśvara.

67a. Those two auspicious Kaṭas (ridges) were bowed down to by all of them after coming there.

67b-68. In the earlier awful Yuga that terrifies all the worlds, the son of Narmadā, who had been *Saśalya* (one with a dart within, i.e. one who suffers from pain) was rendered *Viśalya* (free from Śalya) by all the Devas and sages. Hence it is remembered as Viśalyā.[2]

1. De (p.4) states that Kapilā is an affluent (tributary) of Narmadā. This Purāṇa traces the name to Sage Kapila who is said to have performed penance on the banks of Narmadā.
2. A popular etymology. Another such etymological episode is given in vv 71-77 below:

Yudhiṣṭhira said:

69-70 How did Viśalyā rise up, O dear one. How did Kapilā? O sage, how did the son of Narmadā become one with Śalya? This is something mysterious to the people. O sage of good holy rites, I wish to hear.

Śrī Mārkaṇḍeya said:

71. Formerly, O king, the daughter of Dakṣa i.e. Dākṣāyaṇī (Gaurī) sported about in the waters of Narmadā with great joy along with the Trident-bearing One.

72. After rising up suddenly from the water she changed her clothes. The wet clothes of the goddess were sportingly squeezed and pressed by the attendants.

73-74a. When the clothes were being squeezed dry, drops of coloured water resembling a rainbow fell down. Hence the great river named Kapilā issued forth.

74b-77. The tawny-coloured water issuing from the clothes got mixed with the unguents. Due to the Kapila colour the river became Kapilā by name too. The water was mixed with the scented Rasas (unguents) of different kinds of flowers and rendered fragrant. Splendid hands as tender as sprouts squeezed the clothes and the water that issued forth became tawny-coloured with mixtures of different colours.

78. Hence the excellent river is called Kapilā by persons conversant with the topics of the Purāṇas. This excellent river Kapilā originating from the waters of Narmadā dropping from the clothes should be considered highly meritorious.

CHAPTER TWENTYTWO

The Origiṅ of Viśalyā

Śrī Mārkaṇḍeya said:

1-8. Henceforth I shall recount how it came to be Viśalyā,[1] one that is miraculous unto the people, the destroyer of all sins.

Agni, a mental son of Brahmā, was born. He was Mukhya Vahni. He was a highly righteous sage.

Svāhā who is remembered as a daughter of Dakṣa became his wife. O great king, three sons were born to her: (1) Āhavanīya Agni, (2) Dakṣiṇāgni, and (3) the third Gārhapatya. All the three worlds are sustained by these three.

This Gārhapatya Agni begot two splendid sons named Padmaka and Śaṅku. Both of them were excellent Agnis.

Gārhapatya Agni stayed on the banks of Narmadā and performed great penance and propitiated Rudra. He had great concentration and self-control.

He thus performed severe austerities for ten thousand years. The delighted Bull-emblemed great Lord spoke to him: "O highly esteemed one, tell me what you have in your mind. Even if what you desire is something very difficult to get, I shall undoubtedly bestow it on you."

The Agni said:

9-10. O Maheśvara, may this highly esteemed Narmadā and the sixteen other rivers be my wives with your favour.

I shall beget excellent sons of them in accordance with my desire. O Maheśvara, let this boon alone be granted to me.

Īśvara said:

11-20. These excellent rivers named Dhiṣṇi, of large eyes,

1. *Kāpila Hrada* removed the darts from the body of Dhīṣṇīndra, the son of Narmadā born from Gārhapatya Agni.
This episode is not found in any other Purāṇa and as such it is a special contribution of this author.
The main emphasis is on the efficacy of Narmadā in removing darts in the form of sins from human bodies by mere bath in Kapilā.

shall be your wives. Undoubtedly they are well-known in the Vedas.

The Agnis remembered in Adhvara (sacrifice) shall become their sons. They will become very famous by the name of Dhiṣṇya until the annihilation of all living beings.

After saying this Mahādeva vanished there itself. The excellent river Narmadā became his wife.

The following sixteen rivers too were duly declared as his wives: Kāverī, Kṛṣṇaveṇī, Revā, Yamunā, Godāvarī, Vitastā, Candrabhāgā, Irāvatī, Vipāśā, Kauśikī, Sarayū, Śatarudrikā, Śiprā, Sarasvatī, Hrādinī and Pāvanī.

That highly lustrous (Fire-god) divided himself among those Dhiṣṇis. Due to the transgression of the husband Śucis (fires, called Śucis) were born as the sons of Narmadā and other Dhiṣṇis. All these are remembered as Dhiṣṇyapas.

The well-known one named Dhiṣṇīndra became the son of Narmadā. He was powerful and unequalled in beauty of form, O king.

Thereafter a fight between Devas and Asuras broke out causing horripilation. It became famous in the three worlds as Mayatāraka.

The Suraș were attacked by the extremely terrible Daityas, the chief of whom were Maya and Tāra. They became terrified and they sought refuge in Viṣṇu.

21-30. "Save us, O Hṛṣīkeśa, from this awful calamity. Annihilate all the Daityas, the leaders whereof are Maya and Tāra." On being told thus, the Lord surveyed the ten directions. At that time Pāvaka (Fire) and Māruta (Wind) were seen in the battle by the Lord.

On being summoned by Viṣṇu both of them went near him instantly. They stood bowing down before the intelligent Lord of Devas.

Then the leading Pāvaka (Fire) Dhiṣṇi was told by the noble-souled Lord: "O son of Narmadā, burn down these extremely terrible Asuras."

On being told thus, those two gods, Pāvaka and Māruta, burned down all the Daityas, the leaders of whom were Maya and Tāra.

While being burnt they surrounded Agni by means of divine weapons resembling fire and sun. They were hundreds and thousands in number.

Along with groups of weapons Agni too burnt those great Asuras. Everything was enveloped in circles of flames by the wind.

Thus scorched and enveloped by flames of fire, the Daityas entered Pātāla and concealed themselves under water in thousands.

Thereafter all the Suras adored and honoured Agni, the immutable young son of Narmadā, and returned to heaven.

The son of Revā of excessive splendour and surrounded by fire (gods), full of darts as he was, hurriedly came to Narmadā eagerly to visit her.

31-36. On seeing her son, extremely wounded by a mass of weapons, Narmadā of meritorious waters got up struck with a shock. With her breasts excited due to the secretion of milk, she embraced him with both the arms. Taking the weapon-wounded son with her, she entered the Kāpila Hrada.

Immediately after the entry into the Kāpila Hrada that destroys sins, she instantly made the Saśalya one Viśalya (with darts removed).

Since he became Viśalya (dartless) after entering her auspicious water, the river Kapilā is called Viśalyā too by learned men.

Others too who are pure, clean and have concentration of mind are rid of *Pāpa-Śalyas* (darts in the form of sins). On death, they go to heaven.

Thus everything that was asked earlier by you as to the cause of the origin of Viśalyā has been recounted, O Lord of men.

CHAPTER TWENTYTHREE

The Greatness of the Confluence of Viśalyā

Mārkaṇḍeya said:

1-6. O king, those mortals with great devotion who cast off their lives at the confluence, attain the highest state.

He who goes to Amareśvara, abandons all cherished desires and gives up his life there shall invariably dwell in heaven.

A man who goes to the great mountain and gives us his life, shall go to Amarāvatī by means of an aerial chariot resembling the sun.

On seeing the man falling down from the mountain Amarakaṇṭaka, all the Apsarās say, "He shall be my husband."

Those conversant with piety say that the water of Sarasvatī is on a par with that of Gaṅgā. Men of enlightenment who know these things better, say that the water of Revā is far superior to it (i.e. the water of Gaṅgā). There is no doubt in it.

The place of one who keeps the water of Revā upon his head, is near the Lord of the leading Suras, because it is occupied for residence by many Vidyādharas, Kinnaras and others and is the abode of the greatest of merits.

7-15. O king, of what avail is the verbose talk? If one does not wish to see again the terrible ocean of worldly existence, one should always resort to Narmadā.

It is remembered as one that sanctifies all the three worlds. Even if one dies elsewhere he attains the goal of Gaṇeśvara.

This river is surrounded everywhere by many places of Yajñas. There is nothing here which is not a Tīrtha. As has been spoken by you, sinning men, whether they have performed penance or not, who die on her banks, go to Svarga like leading Amaras.

Thus, O excellent king, it is with a desire for the welfare of all the worlds that Kapilā and Viśalyā were created formerly by Īśvara.

By taking his holy bath there along with the observance of fast and control of the sense-organs, a man shall undoubtedly attain the benefit of a great Aśvamedha.

He who refrains from eating at this Tīrtha shall be rid of all sins and attain Śiva's place.

By taking the holy bath once in the confluence of Viśalyā, one attains that benefit which one attains through Snāna and Dāna done all over the earth extending to the seas.

Thus, O king, the meritorious and sacred river has been extolled to you. I shall narrate again whatever you may ask.

CHAPTER TWENTYFOUR

The Greatness of the Confluence of Karanarmadā

Śrī Mārkaṇḍeya said:

1-3. The confluence of Kara[1] and Narmadā in Māndhātṛpura shall take the Pitṛs to Viṣṇupura if one goes to the place, takes bath and propitiates the Pitṛs.

With a desire to kill the Daityas, Viṣṇu formerly rubbed his hands and took up the discus. From his perspiration the excellent river began to flow and joined Revā. By taking the holy ablution there, one is rid of all sins.

CHAPTER TWENTYFIVE

The Greatness of the Confluence of Nīlagaṅgā

Śrī Mārkaṇḍeya said:

1-3. O excellent king, to the eastern side of Oṁkāra is the confluence, well-known all over the world, where Nīlagaṅgā meets Revā.

By taking the holy bath there and performing Japa, what objective in the world will be impossible to get? One shall stay in the city of Nīlakaṇṭha for sixty thousand years.

By propitiating the Pitṛs in Śrāddha through water mixed with gingelly seeds, one shall redeem twenty-one generations including oneself.

1. The rivulet Kara, a tributary of Narmadā, is so named as it issued from the perspiration of Viṣṇu's hand.

CHAPTER TWENTYSIX

The Observance Called Madhūka Tṛtīyā[1]

Yudhiṣṭhira said:

1-7 O excellent Brāhmaṇa, Jāleśvara too has been mentioned earlier by you. How is it meritorious? How is it resorted to by Ṛṣis and Siddhas?

Śrī Mārkaṇḍeya said:

A greater Tirtha than Jāleśvara was never there before nor will there ever be (in future). O son of Pāṇḍu, listen as I recount its origin.

Formerly all the groups of sages along with groups of Maruts and Indra were extremely tormented by all the Asuras and were led to destruction in many ways.

On being killed and assailed by many Asuras headed by Bāṇāsura and having Jaṁbha and Śuṁbha as their leaders, they sought refuge in Brahmā.

They went by means of aerial chariots as huge as mountains, horses comparable (in bigness) to elephants, chariots of the size of cities drawn by lions and tigers and also by tortoises and crocodiles. Others went on foot.

After reaching the great region inaccessible to unrighteous persons, they saw the Lotus-born Lord, the benefactor of all the world. All of them went there and eulogized with concentration and mental purity.

---

1. This Vrata is observed on the 3rd day in the bright half of Phālguna. It is meant for women. It grants conjugal felicity and sons and is an insurance against widowhood. An observer of the Vrata is to fast on this day. The next day she is to worship Goddess Gaurī on a Madhūka tree and pray for *Saubhāgya* (conjugal felicity). Brāhmaṇa women whose husbands are alive are honoured with flowers, garments and edibles (Hemādri, *Vrata* I. 413-415). According to Bhaviṣya Purāṇa, the Vrata is to be observed on the 3rd day in the dark half of Phālguna. Our text prescribes this Vrata on the 3rd day of bright half of Caitra and also the rites to be observed throughout the fortnight.
Madhūka (*Cinometra ramiflora*, Moh in Marathi) is useful for distilling intoxicating liquor.

The Devas prayed:

8-15. Be victorious, O immeasurable Lotus-born One. Be victorious, O cause of creation. O most excellent one among Suras, we have sought refuge in you.

On hearing the words of the Devas of purified souls, the Grandfather replied in words as deep-sounding and resonant as the rumbling of clouds: "Wherefore have you come, O Devas? Why this paleness in everyone? By whom have you all been insulted? O immortal ones, do tell me quickly."

The Devas said:

There is a Dānava of great vigour and prowess named Bāṇa. He is arrogant on account of his strength. Everything belonging to us has been taken away by him. We have been deprived of all our wealth and jewels.

On hearing the words of the Devas, Brahmā, the grandfather of the worlds, the Lord of Devas, pondered: "What is the means for his destruction? The sinful Dānava cannot be killed by any of the heaven-dwellers excepting Lord Śaṅkara. He cannot be killed by me or Viṣṇu. We shall go there alone where Lord Maheśvara is present. He is the resort unto all. There is no one else."

After saying this, Brahmā, the most excellent one among the knowers of the Vedas, went to the place where Maheśvara was present. He was accompanied by learned Brāhmaṇas.

16-23. He eulogized Parameśvara through richly-worded prayers.

The Devas said:

Be victorious, O Lord of the chiefs of Devas. Be victorious, O one half of whose body is shared by Umā, O bull-seated one, O mighty-armed one having the Moon as the ornament.

Obeisance to the one holding in his front hand the trident. Obeisance to the wielder of Khaṭvāṅga. Be victorious, O Lord of goblins, O destroyer of Dakṣa's Yajña.

Obeisance, O Lord having (i.e. worshipped with) the five-syllabled (*namaḥ śivāya*) Mantra, O Lord having the five elements for physical form, O Īśāna having five faces. You are being sung about by the Vedas.

Obeisance to you who are always engaged in the activities of creation, sustenance and annihilation. O Aṣṭamūrti (one having eight cosmic forms), O destroyer of Smara! Remember the truth as eulogized.

O Lord, your person is praised by the Brāhmaṇas as being constituted of five bodies, viz. Sadyojāta, Vāmadeva, Aghora, Īśa and Tatpuruṣa. (These are the opening words of Mantras from 17. 1-5 *Mahānārāyaṇa Upaniṣad.*) In an extensive expanse of gold, O Hara, you coo like a swan.

On being eulogized thus by the groups of sages beginning with Brahmā and by the Suras and Asuras(?) the Lord became delighted in his mind and said to the groups of Devas:

Īśvara said:

24-34. Welcome unto the Devas and Vipras (Brāhmaṇas). The night has dawned well today. What shall we do? Tell me quickly. Who else is to be resorted to by Suras and Asuras?

What is the misery? What is the distress? Whence has fright arisen? Do tell me, O blessed ones, the cause thereof which you have been thinking of.

On being told thus by Rudra, the leading Suras replied displaying their respective bodies shyly with faces turned downwards: "There is a terrible Dānava of great virility and arrogant of his strength. He is well known by the name Bāṇa. He has three great cities.[1]

He has performed severe penance for a thousand years. Brahmā was delighted by his *Dama* (control over the sense-organs) and *Niyama* (restraints).

---

1. The Purāṇa regards Bāṇa as the king of Tripuras (three cities made of three metals). But Mbh, *Karṇa,* Ch. 33 names Kamalākṣa, Tārākṣa and Vidyaunmālī as the masters of these three cities. Those cities were created by Maya, the architect of Asuras and not by Brahmā as in this text. The capital of Bāṇa was Śoṇitapura (in Kumaun).

He granted him three impenetrable cities that can go wherever he wishes to go. They are made of steel, silver and gold.

The set of three cities has been created by Brahmā. It can move and go wherever one wishes to go. The Dānavas highly powerful due to it, stationed themselves in the three cities.

The great Asuras harass the entire region of the three worlds. Staff, noose, sword and other weapons are used to harass unagitating persons. The set of the three cities occupied by the Dānavas moves about like a wheel. As in the case of a mirage, it is visible at some places and invisible at others.

Wherever that great set of cities of the arrogant Dānava descends neither Brāhmaṇas nor Devas, neither cows nor other creatures are seen there. Nothing is seen where the three citie fall. Rivers, villages and many countries have been reduced to ash.

35-45. Gold, silver, jewels, pearls, the beautiful jewel-like women—all these he seizes forcibly.

O Hara, it is not possible for the groups of Devas to slay him with any weapon or missile either during day or at night. Hence, O Mahādeva, do burn him down. You alone are our last resort. Thus, O Lord of Devas, it behoves you to do this favour unto all of us.

O Lord, it behoves you to do everything whereby Devas, Gandharvas, sages and ascetics attain utmost courage."

Īśvara said:

I shall do all these things. Do not get dejected. Ere long I shall do what is conducive to your happiness.

After consoling all those Devas with Indra as their leader, the Lord of Devas thought about the means of the destruction of the three cities.

'How, in what manner, should the set of cities be destroyed by me? Excepting Nārada no other remedy is possible.'

After steadying himself thus, he meditated upon Nārada. At the very instant, the sage of excessive penance came like wind. The holy Lord had a Kamaṇḍalu (water-pot) held in his hand and three staffs tied together. He was endowed with perfect knowledge. He was resplendent with the Yogapaṭṭa (upper cloth) and rosary of beads as well as an umbrella. The matted hairs were kept tied upon his head. He had the splendour resembling that of fire and the Sun. He circumambulated the Lord three times and prostrated on the ground like a log of wood.

Nārada, the holy sage, joined his palms in veneration. He then eulogized Śarva, the lofty-minded Lord, with a great prayer.

Nārada said:

46-55. Be victorious, O Śaṁbhu, O Virūpākṣa (odd-eyed that is three-eyed one). Be victorious, O three-eyed Lord; be victorious, O Śaṅkara, O Īśāna, O Rudra, O Īśvara. Obeisance to you.

You are the Lord protector. You are the creator of the universe. O Lord, you alone are the annihilator. You are the protector of the worlds, the slayer of the wicked god of Death.

O Sureśāna, save us, O eternal Lord with the Vedas for your form, O eternal Bhava-mūrti, O enemy of worldly existence; be the bestower of freedom from fear on those who resort to you.

For the sake of the destruction of the possibility of being (born) in the world, I seek refuge in you.

Why have I been thought of, O Lord? May the command be given, O Lord.

Whose mind am I to agitate and excite? Who should tumble down on to the ground? Whom shall I instigate for a quarrel, O Lord, O foremost one among the victorious ones?

On hearing the words of Nārada, Mahādeva, the Lord of Devas, became glad with eyes in full bloom and spoke these words: "Welcome unto you, O sage par excellence, always fond of quarrels. O eternal son of Brahmā, conversant with the principles of playing on the Vīṇā, O Nārada, hasten to the great set of three cities of Bāṇa, the Lord of Dānavas. It causes great fright among all the worlds. The husbands there are on a par with the Devas and the wives are equal to the Apsarās. The great set of the three cities moves by the refulgence of those ladies. It cannot be split up by any means, O excellent Brāhmaṇa. You do go there quickly and enchant everyone by means of several rites of diverse characteristics."

Nārada said:

56-67. At your behest, O Lord of Devas, I shall get the excellent city broken up (by dissension) though it is impenetrable by diverse means on the part of the Devas including Vāsava (Indra).

After saying this, O king, the sage went to that excellent city of Bāṇa endowed with increasing prosperity and extending to a hundred Yojanas. All fanciful things had been stacked there. Different kinds of minerals gave it variegated, wonderful features. It was teeming with many mansions. It is (was) rendered brilliant with many buildings. It was equipped with ornamental gateways. It was rendered beautiful with panels with sliding bolts. It was equipped with many mechanical contrivances. It was sparkling with ramparts and moats. It abounded in tanks, wells and lakes as well as shrines of deities. It was embellished with lotus-ponds teeming with swans and Kāraṇḍavas. It was rich with many birds. The excellent city of Bāṇa had all these features.

Bāṇa's huge palatial residence was in its centre. It had seven storeys and was resplendent. It was embellished in gold with divine workmanship. It was rendered beautiful with pearl strings, diamonds and lapis lazuli. The ground was paved with gold plates and made splendid with jewels. Various sounds such as the breaths (trumpetings?) of elephants in rut, chariots, the neighing sounds of horses, the jingling sound of the anklets of women etc. made the atmosphere resonant.

The palace was guarded by Dānavas of awful features, arrogant due to their strength. They were armed with Khaḍgas (swords) and Tomaras. They had various weapons such as thunderbolts, goads and arrows. The excellent palatial residence of Bāṇa had these characteristic features. It was famous like the peak of Kailāsa and was comparable to the abode of Mahendra.

Nārada hurriedly proceeded towards that city by the way of sky. After going up to the gate he spoke these words to the Kṣattṛ (the officer in-charge): "O gatekeeper, O very wise one, O one expert in discharging royal duties! Be quick and inform Bāṇa that Nārada is waiting at the gate."

68-77. He bowed down to the feet of Nārada quickly. Then he began to submit to Bāṇa who was in the centre of the Royal Court. All his limbs began to tremble. He covered his face with the hand. Even as all the soldiers were listening he spoke these words: "There stands at the threshold, Nārada who is honoured and adored by Devas, Gandharvas, Yakṣas, Kinnaras and Dānavas. He is fond of (instigating) quarrels and is very difficult to pacify."

Bāṇa said:

Usher in the blessed son of Brahmā, the brilliant one who cannot be transgressed and who is unbearable. Why has he been stopped outside?

On hearing these words uttered by the Lord, he went there in great hurry and made Nārada step in.

On seeing the celestial sage Nārada adored by Suras, entering, the delighted Daitya got up at once and saluted the feet of the sage. He offered the sage a seat, formal Arghyapādya and adoration duly. Then he dedicated to him his kingdom and himself along with the kinsmen. Bāṇāsura himself enquired of the sage about his welfare.

Nārada said:

78-89. Excellent! Excellent! O mighty-armed one causing Danu's race to flourish! Who else excepting you is praise-worthy in the whole range of the three worlds? O leading scion of the family of Danu, O most excellent one among the descendants of Danu! I have been honoured with wealth and jewels of very excellent qualities; also by the offer of your kingdom as well as your own self. Who else will adore (me)?

I have nothing to do with the enjoyment of worldly pleasures. Enjoy your own unimperilled kingdom. I have come here after visiting Maheśvara only with an eagerness to see you.

I have heard that the set of your three cities moves about due to the chastity of your wife. O Lord of Dānavas, I have come here to see that celebrated wife of yours. If you consider it proper, do not delay; let me see her.

* * *

On hearing the words of Nārada, he looked at the Kañcukin, the elderly staff-bearing officer of the womens' inner apartment, endowed with good qualities. Delighted in his heart, the king made the quarters reverberate with his voice and told him: "O Kañcukin, may the chief queen accompanied by all the attendants of the inner apartment unhesitatingly grant an audience to Nārada." In view of the command of his master, he grasped the hand of Nārada, entered the apartment and said to the queen: "This is Nārada who has come to see you." On seeing the excellent sage, she bowed down to his feet and offered an excellent golden seat, Arghyapādya and other things. The holy sage who was pleased offered her the greatest blessing and said: "O queen, in the entire range of the three worlds, no other woman like you is seen, who is chaste, well-behaved and endowed with truthfulness and cleanliness. It is by your power that the set of the three cities always whirls like a wheel."

On hearing those words joyously uttered by Nārada, the queen who was the most excellent one among righteous and pious ladies, devoutly asked the sage about the sacred rites:

Rājñī (the queen) said:

90-92. O holy Sir, what are those Vratas in the world whereby Devas become pleased? What are the Dānas (religious gifts) offered which yield great benefits? What are those holy observances of fasts included by learned ones among the holy rites meant for women, by the performance whereof virtuous ladies go to heaven? O highly esteemed one, mention all these things truthfully. I wish to know everything. Do speak unhesitatingly.

Nārada said:

93. Excellent! Excellent! O highly blessed lady, you have put such a question as will enable all ladies to get their piety increased by paying heed to it.

94. By fasts and Dānas husband and sons come under control. I shall tell you those rites which when performed always bring about honour from kinsmen.

95-96. O beautiful lady, I shall mention those rites which bring good results if performed and bad results if not performed. If they are performed a *Durbhagā* (unfortunate woman) becomes *Subhagā* (fortunate). If they are not performed a *Subhagā* becomes *Durbhagā.* A woman without a son shall be blessed with a son if performed and cursed (on non-performance). A virgin obtains a husband and another becomes deprived of the husband (when not performed).

97-99a. Those who offer these things do not go near Yama: *Tiladhenu* (a cow made of gingelly seeds), gold, silver, cows, clothes, beverage, plot of land, scents, incense, unguents, sandals of wood or leather, umbrella, meritorious fans, oil for foot massage, oil for head, bathing requisites, beds and seats. Those who give these (as Dāna) do not go to Yama (- loka).

99b-100. If the following are offered to couples on Lalitādina (the day of Lalitā, probably 5th day in the bright half of Āśvina), there shall be conjugal felicity in this world and hereafter; Honey, black gram, milk, ghee, salt, jaggery, medicine, beverage, plot of land, paddy, sugarcane juice and smooth red clothes.

101-102a. The following things should be offered to a meritorious and handsome Brāhmaṇa of good conduct: I shall tell you, O queen, how these things should be given and on what *Tithis*:

[*Tithis and Dānas:*]

102b-104a. *I Lunar day*: A woman should observe the Vrata of purity on the Pratipadā day and offer fuel to a Brāhmaṇa in the forenoon, reciting the Mantra: "May Hutāśana (fire) be pleased with me." O beloved one of the king, in the course of her twenty-six births she will never experience either ailment or distress in her limbs and joints.

104b-105a. *II Lunar day*: A woman who joyously offers butter to an important Brāhmaṇa on the second lunar day, shall become one endowed with a smooth, stender body.

105b-107a. *III Lunar day*: Listen to the meritorious benefit of the woman who, on the third lunar day, offers salt to an excellent Brāhmaṇa, uttering the Mantra: "May Goddess Gaurī be pleased with me." A virgin will attain a husband and will sport about with him like Umā (with Śiva). She will never be a widow. She will obtain great fame.

107b-109a. *IV Lunar day*: After observing the Vrata of *Naktam* (i.e. taking food only at night) on the fourth lunar day she should offer sweetmeats (*Modakas*) to a Brāhmaṇa. She should utter the Mantra: "May the Lord of Devas, Gaṇanātha, Vināyaka be pleased." As a result of her act, O beautiful lady, there will never be any obstacle in any rite. So says the Grandfather (i.e. Brahmā.)

109b-110a. *V Lunar day*: A woman who offers gingelly seeds to a Brāhmaṇa on the fifth lunar day shall become endowed with beauty like Tilottamā.

110b-112a. *VI Lunar day*: A devout lady shall always offer a fruit of Madhūka on the sixth lunar day with the Agni-born Lord (i.e. Kārttikeya) in view to a Brāhmaṇa who has mastered the Vedas. Her son will become a great king like Skanda who is the most excellent one among the groups of Devas. He will be adored in all the worlds.

112b-115a. *VII Lunar day*: With the Lord of the Cosmos, the Lord of Devas, Divākara (Sun-god) in view, a devout lady should honour an excellent Brāhmaṇa with gold. The meritorious benefit of that sacred rite has been extolled by excellent Brāhmaṇas. O queen, I shall mention it to you. Listen with concentration of mind, O chaste lady. None of these skin diseases will occur in (affect) her limbs even if the sins of prior births happen to be in force: Scabies, leprosy, (leucoderma, white patches, pachydermia etc.

115b-117a. *VIII Lunar day*: On the eighth lunar day a devout, beautiful lady should offer a black cow to a Brāhmaṇa with good conduct, uttering the Mantra, "May Maheśvara be pleased." Her sin incurred in the course of many births perishes. She will become endowed with riches. There is no doubt about this because the Dāna is very excellent.

117b-119a. *IX Lunar day*: A woman should devoutly offer to a Brāhmaṇa, scents and incense with Kātyāyanī in view on the ninth lunar day. Listen to its benefit. If her brother, father, son or husband were to enter the battlefield, they shall never become overwhelmed because they are protected by that Dāna rite.

119b-121a. X *Lunar day*: O queen, a woman should offer sugarcane juice on the tenth lunar day to a Brāhmaṇa other than one with deficient limbs, with the Lokapālas (guardians of the worlds) in view. Due to that Dāna, she becomes the most endearing one for all the worlds. There is no doubt about this: So said Śaṅkara.

121b-123a. *XI* and *XII Lunar days*: On the eleventh day, a woman should observe fast and should offer water to a Brāhmaṇa devoted to Viṣṇu on the twelfth day with Nārāyaṇa in view. She will make people delighted with her touch and talk. She should purify people too. Since the gift of water will be of infinite benefit, it is considered great.

123b-125a. *XIII Lunar day*: With great devotion, a woman should offer to a Brāhmaṇa oil for foot-massage and oil for the head with Kāma (god of love) in view on the thirteenth lunar day. After death she may be born in any womb. In all those, she will never be separated from her husband.

125b-126a. *XIV Lunar day*: A woman should offer to a Brāhmaṇa on the fourteenth lunar day, with Dharma in view, a utensil and sandals. In regard to her all the worlds are never imperilled.

126b-127. *XV Lunar day*: Thus in the course of Śrāddha at the close of every fortnight, she shall propitiate excellent Brāhmaṇas. O queen, her line of progeny shall always be unbroken. Thus the efficacy of the Tīrthas and Dāna offerings has been recounted to you.

[*Propitiation of Plants and Herbs:*]

128-130. Also, listen to the propitiation of *Vanaspatis* (plants and herbs). One will attain heaven by approaching (devoutly) the following trees: Jambū, Nimba, Tinduka, Madhūka, Āmra, Āmalaka, Śālmalī, Vaṭa, Pippala, Śamī, Bilva, Amalivṛkṣa, Kadalī, Pāṭalī and other meritorious trees.

Nārada said:

131-134a. If a Vrata is performed in the month of Caitra by a woman, other Vratas are not on a par with even the sixteenth fraction thereof.

If it is listened to, O lady of good fortune, one will never see misfortune. Just as snow disappears when sunlight falls on it, so also misery and misfortune become dispelled due to this Vrata.

Listen now to the procedure of propitiation of Lalitā called Madhukā,[1] O lady of good fortune. Even as it is being recounted it is conducive to happiness.

134b-139. On the third lunar day of the bright half of Caitra a woman takes holy bath and keeps her mind pure. The image of Śaṅkara along with that of Umā is to be made out of the trunk of a Madhūka tree. They have to be duly installed by an excellent Brāhmaṇa. With scented flowers, incense, camphor and saffron, she adores the Lord with due utterance of the Mantras. The feet are adored uttering the Mantra: "Obeisance to Śiva." The penis is worshipped uttering "Obeisance to Manmatha." The belly is worshipped by uttering "Obeisance to Kālodara." The neck is worshipped by uttering "Obeisance to Nīlakaṇṭha." The head is worshipped by uttering "Obeisance to Sarvātman (one identical with all, one who is the soul of all)."

She then adores Umā. The belly is worshipped with the utterance "Obeisance to Kṣāmodarā ('one who has a lean belly'). The neck is worshipped by uttering the Mantra "Obeisance to Sukaṇṭhā ('one with excellent neck'). The head is worshipped by uttering "Obeisance to Saubhāgyadāyinī ('One who grants conjugal felicity')." The Arghya is offered later.

[*Arghya Mantra:*]

140. "Obeisance to you, O Lord of the chiefs of Devas, O consort of Umā, O Lord of the cosmos. O Lord, accept this Arghya and destroy all my misfortunes."

141. After the offering of Arghya, the *Karaka* (waterpot) is offered. It is filled with water and it is covered with a leaf of Madhūka and is offered along with a gold piece in accordance with the capacity of the devotee.

[*The Mantra for offering the Karaka:*]

142. "O Lalitā, the *Karaka* filled with water and endowed

1. VV 134-150 give details of a different variety of Madhūka Tṛtīyā. Goddess Lalitā is identified with Madhūka tree. The Vrata begins on the 3rd day of the bright half of Caitra and is to be continued every month and is to be concluded on 3rd day of the bright half of Phālguna.

with Saubhāgya (conjugal felicity) is offered to you. It should increase conjugal felicity etc."

143-152. Uttering this Mantra, the excellent Karaka is offered to a Brāhmaṇa. Till the next third lunar day of the bright half of the month the devotee should avoid salt. After praying for the forgiveness of the Goddess and the Lord of Devas the devotee should eat only the *Havis* at night. This procedure should be adopted every month. The Vrata is concluded on the third day of the bright half of Phālguna.

Salt is to be offered in the month of Vaiśākha and Ghee should be offered in the month of Jyeṣṭha. In the month of Āṣāḍha Niṣpāva (variety of rice) is to be offered. Milk is to be offered in Śrāvaṇa. *Mudgas* (green gram) are to be offered in the month of Nabhasya (Bhādrapada). Paddy is offered in Aśvayuja. A vessel of Śarkarā (sugar) is offered in Kārttika and also a *Karaka* filled with juice. In the month of Mārgaśīrṣa, Kārpāsa (cotton) is offered along with a *Karaka* filled with ghee. *Kuṁkuma* (saffron) is offered in the month of Pauṣa and in the month of Māgha a vessel filled with gingelly seeds is offered. In the month of Phālguna a vessel filled with sweetmeats is to be given. What is to be offered in the succeeding Tṛtīyā should be avoided in the course of the current month. The procedure in the case of these later rites is the same as before, O beloved one to mind. The same image made of Madhuvṛkṣa is to be worshipped regularly. Ultimately everything is handed over to the Brāhmaṇa preceptor.

Listen to the rite of Udyāpana[1] (ritualistic conclusion of a Vrata). The devotee goes to the Madhuvṛkṣa with all requisites kept ready. The image is fixed in the centre of Madhūka and Śarva stationed there as Umā sharing half of his body is to be worshipped.

153-159. Śarva is to be worshipped with profuse offerings of the adoration and repeatedly with Kuṁkuma, and garlands of very tender flowers as well as Kusuṁbha flowers and Kesara. Twelve couples should be offered pairs of Kausumbha (red in hue) cloths resembling the flowers of Atasī for wearing. Each of these pairs should be given pairs of sandals, umbrellas, necklaces,

1. The Udyāpana (concluding procedure of the Vrata) is described in vv 150–169.

chains, bangles, rings and beds with splendid sheets covering them. They should be smeared with Kuṁkuma and adored with many flowers. They are made to stay in the Madhūkāvāsaka (grove of Madhūka trees) and offered various jewels and fed duly. After they have taken food, they are to be made to rest on the beds and forgiveness is requested for since everything is rooted in the Guru. The Guru should be known as Maheśvara. If the Guru is pleased, the entire world consisting of Suras and Asuras is pleased. If one wishes for one's welfare, one should offer unto the Guru whatever one likes the most in the world, whatever endearing thing one has in the house. These things are to be offered by the rich, well-to-do people. What should be given by others is as mentioned below:

160-169. Others should worship two couples duly, the first couple being any and the second that of Guru and his wife. In adoring them, one should avoid *Vittaśāṭhya* (over-scrupulousness in the expenditure). Then forgiveness is craved from the Goddess, the Lord, the Brāhmaṇa and the Guru: "O Goddess Lalitā, just as you are never separated from Śaṁbhu, so also grant me non-separation from my husband and sons."

It is by performing the observance of Madhūkatṛtīyā in accordance with this procedure that Indrāṇī attained the status of the wife of Indra and also an excellent son. She attained conjugal felicity and good fortune in all the worlds and also excellent happiness with all prosperity.

A virgin who performs this Vrata in accordance with this procedure attains an excellent husband like Indrāṇī who got Indra.

An unfortunate one attains good fortune; a fortunate one begets a son. A lady with a son gains everlasting happiness. She never sees grief anywhere.

Misfortune accumulated in the course of many births certainly perishes. The lady after death goes to heaven and rejoices along with Umā.

After enjoying the worldly pleasures for more than hundreds of crores of years she is born into the world again when she gets a king as her husband.

The lady of good fortune then becomes richly endowed with beauty and bears a son destined to become a king.

Thus the Vrata that is the most excellent one of all Vratas

has been narrated to you completely. O lady of good fortune, whatever desire you have within your heart do ask for it.

CHAPTER TWENTYSEVEN

Creating Agitation in Tripura

Śrī Mārkaṇḍeya said:

1-6. On hearing the words of Nārada, the queen said: "Be pleased, O eminent Brāhmaṇa. Accept whatever Dānas you wish. I shall offer you gold, jewels as well as different kinds of garments. Other rare and valuable things too I shall offer to you."

On hearing the words of the queen, Nārada spoke thus: "O fair lady, let it be given to others, to the Brāhmaṇas who lack means of sustenance. We are richly endowed with everything acceptable and accessible always through devotion."

On being told thus the queen invited poor Brāhmaṇas who were masters of the Vedas and Vedāṅgas and began distributing gifts as would be conducive to Saubhāgya (conjugal bliss and fortune). "May Hari and Śaṅkara be always pleased with me due to this Dāna rite that increases *Saubhāgya* (conjugal felicity) as instructed by Nārada."

Thereafter the queen said to the great sage Nārada:

The Queen said:

7-13. Dāna has been made as instructed by you. It is done with my husband in view. O excellent Brāhmaṇa, in every birth of mine may Bāṇa alone be my husband. O dear excellent Brāhmaṇa, I don't have any other deity excepting Bāṇa. On the strength of this truth, may my husband live for a hundred years. Women need not perform any other holy rite as the husband alone is their deity. Still at your instance the Dāna has been duly offered. O honourable Sir, now let us do our duty. I to my husband, O Brāhmaṇa Sage, go now. May blessing be granted (to me).

* * *

Then, O excellent king, Nārada took leave of her saying "So be it," captivated the hearts of all and vanished from there with his mind dwelling on another matter. The Brāhmaṇa was duly adored by sky-walkers.

Then, O descendant of Bharata, all of them (the wives of Bāṇa) turned their minds towards their husband. Deluded and enchanted by Nārada all of them became pallid and devoid of lustre.

CHAPTER TWENTYEIGHT

Destruction of Tripura: Glorification of Jvāleśvara and Amareśvara Tīrthas

Mārkaṇḍeya said:

1. In the meantime Rudra occupied the banks of Narmadā. While he was sporting in the company of Umā, Nārada arrived there.

2. After bowing down to the Lord of the chiefs of Devas, Śaṅkara along with Umā, he submitted to the Lord the details of what happened then at Tripura:

3-4. "At the behest of my Lord (you), I went to the place where Bāṇa's palace was situated. After meeting Bāṇa as per formalities, I went to the great Antaḥpura. There I saw thousands of the queens of Bāṇa, the intelligent one. Then I stirred up that city in a befitting manner and in the way it had been desired and have now returned."

5. On hearing the words of Nārada, the Lord gave his approval saying, "Well done! Well done!" Then the Lord of Devas pondered over the whirling of Tripura.

6-7. He thought: 'Tripura moves like the discus whirled from his hand by Viṣṇu, the powerful one. It has great velocity and it is extensive. It has been preserved by my splendour. Bāṇa is reputed all over the world as one devoted to me. Word has been already given by me particularly to the Brāhmaṇas.'

8-12. Thus Maheśvara, the Lord of Devas, the Lord of the people, thought for a long time regarding the successful completion of the task.[1] The Three-eyed Lord meditated upon Mandara as the bow, the earth as the bow-string, the eternal Lord Viṣṇu as an arrow with the blazing Fire-god with faces (mouths) on all sides as the sharp arrowhead, the excellent-feathered Garuḍa in the centre of the two feathers at the tail-end. Then he made the Earth as the chariot and the two Aśvins as the yoke. (He fixed) god Indra as axel, Kubera (the Lord of wealth) at the front. Yama (was posted) at the right side, while terrible Kāla on the left; the Sun and the Moon were the wheels and Gandharvas spokes.

13-20. Surajyeṣṭha (Brahmā) was made the charioteer; the Vedas were made the excellent horses. The Vedāṅgas were turned into the iron bits in the mouth and the Chandas-s (Metres) were made the reins. The orally uttered Oṁkāra was made the whip by Maheśvara. Dhātā was placed at the head and Vidhātā behind. The Mārutas (Winds) gathered from all the quarters were placed in the Ūrdhva Yantra (the overhead mechanical device). All the following ones were fixed to all the joints: great Serpents, Piśācas, Siddhas, Vidyādharas, Gaṇas and groups of Bhūtas. Meru was stationed in the centre of the pole; the great mountain (Mahāgiri) was beneath the pole. The terrible serpents were stationed in the mechanical device; Varuṇa and Nairṛta in the Śamya (part of the chariot). Gāyatrī and Sāvitrī were stationed at the place where the rein was fastened. All round in the flagstaff of the chariot were placed Satya (truth), Śauca (cleanliness), Dama (control of the senses) and Rakṣā (protection). After making the chariot (embellished with) all the Devas, Maheśvara, the Lord of Devas, stood ready (for battle) wearing the coat of mail and holding the sword with the fingers having protectors made of leather of Godhā (mountain lizard). After adjusting his garments and binding the matted tresses of hair, he got his divine bow ready and fitted his excellent chariot. Stationed in the centre of the chariot, O Yudhiṣṭhira, the Lord shone brilliantly.

21-34. With the twang of the bow, he made the three worlds quake. After making the Vaiśākha-Sthāna (? special warrior posture), Hara remained steady there. After surveying for a

---

1. The description of the Chariot and other preparations against Tripura are reminiscent of similar preparations given in Mbh, *Karṇa*, Chs. 33-34. Here the enemy is Bāṇa, a devotee of Śiva.

long time, the Lord became angry with the eyes turning red. He then controlled himself and meditated on the great Mantra. With a desire to destroy the set of three cities, he released (shot) the arrow when all the three of them stood together in the space. For the period of a split half of a moment, he saw the group of the three cities and smote them with an arrow having three joints and three blades.

In regard to the set of the three cities, O most excellent one among the descendants of Bharata, all the people became highly frightened. The terrible ones in the form of Kāla began to laugh boisterously for the destruction of all Asuras. The men experienced pain and distress. They remained motionless with eyes not at all winking as though they were drawn in a picture. The Devas in their abodes prattled and laughed loudly. They (Asuras?) saw themselves adorned in red garments in dreams. With the red garlands round their heads, they fell into muddy whirlpools. They saw themselves with oil smeared on the heads. O excellent king, they saw themselves riding in the vehicles drawn by donkeys. The great Saṁvartaka wind, resembling the final destruction of the Yugas, uprooted many of the houses and groups of trees. There were earthquakes with loud thunder-like reports. Thousands of meteors fell down. The Lord showered blood mixed with much rough gravel. In the sacrificial fire-pits of the Brāhmaṇas, the fire, though properly oblated, burned with smoke and sparks. The elephants were rid of the stage of rut. The horses became deprived of their Sattva (intrinsic strength). Even when not played upon, there came sound from thousands of instruments. Though not shaken, the flagstaffs and various kinds of umbrellas fell down. The trees and the leaves began to burn. Everything was upset and there was much of hue and cry.

35-44. The violent gust of wind demolished the gardens of various kinds. Induced by it, all the flames and sparks blazed. The trees, hedges, creepers and houses all round were enveloped by the fire that blazed in all the directions. Everything that burned was seen blazing with the lustre of a Kiṁśuka leaf. On account of the smoke, it was impossible to go from house to house. All the people in Tripura began to wail and lament on being completely burned by the fire of the anger of Hara. The whole city of Tripura enkindled in all the quarters, began to burn. The tops and peaks were shattered in thousands and they fell down. The smoke-enveloped fire was seen blazing all round. It spread from quarter to quarter, dancing as it were. It rushed through forests, temples, all the houses and turrets. Urged by Kāla himself, the fire blazed everywhere in the city. Burning furiously as though enkindled by the anger of Hara, it burned everything in the worlds. The whole region around the three cities consisting of children and old people burnt along with the vehicles, forests and doorways of the houses. Some were engaged in taking food. Others were engaged in drinking liquor. The courtezans were engaged in dancing and singing. Distressed by the flames of fire, they embraced one another. O excellent king, all those who were being burnt became senseless.

45-60a. Other Dānavas there were burned and deluded by the fire. With their faces overwhelmed with the smoke, they could not go elsewhere. The lotus ponds abounding in golden lotuses and stirred up by the swans and Kāraṇḍava birds and the different kinds of tanks and wells blazed there. The parks in the cities and the lakes were seen burnt by fire. They were covered by faded lotuses. The extensive buildings and palaces over a range of eight Yojanas, resembling huge peaks of mountains, originally rendered splendid by jewels, were seen now completely burnt down and shattered on the ground. When the men, women, children and old people were being burnt everywhere, the ruthless fire went on burning. There was loud lamentation and wailing. O excellent king, some woman was sleeping soundly. Another was in intoxicated state. One lady of distinction had been sporting about and lying on her large bed. A woman of large eyes bedecked in a number of necklaces, who had been asleep, became distressed due to the smoke. The wretched woman too fell into the fire. A certain woman fond of her son had been closely embracing her son. She too was burnt by the blazing fire in Tripura. A certain golden-complexioned lady bedecked in sapphire saw her husband fallen. She too fell over him. A certain lady of solar lustre was lying asleep on her lover. When distressed by fire, O king, she embraced his neck still more closely. Another lady of cloud-like complexion had a loose girdle of gold and white upper cloth. She fell down on the ground. A certain lady had the lustre of the moon and a Kunda flower. She was adorned in sapphires. She was found praying to the fire with palms joined in reverence and kept over her head. While the clothes of a certain woman were burning the tresses of hair of another woman were seen blazing, O descendant of Bharata. All were frightened by even golden vessels, that resembled the blazing fire. A certain excellent lady distressed by too much of misery, lamented like a female osprey on seeing the husband reduced to ashes. She fell down on his head and embraced him closely. Another woman saw her husband reduced to ashes in her own house. She was distressed very much and lamented like a female osprey. A certain woman saw her mother and father senseless. She trembled and fell down on the ground in utter distress like an exhausted mare. A certain excellent woman on being burned ran about here and there. When a woman turned her face she could not see her son who had been in her lap.

60b-64a. Kuṁbhila's house was burnt and it fell on the ground. So also the ruthless fire burnt the houses of Kūṣmāṇḍa, Dhūmra, Kuhaka, Baka, Virūpanayana, Virūpākṣa, Śuṁbha, Ḍiṁbha, Raudra, the excellent Asura Prahlāda, Daṇḍapāṇi, Vipāṇi, Siṁhavaktra, Dundubha, Saṁhrāda, Ḍiṇḍi, Muṇḍi, Kravyāda, Vyāghravaktra, Bāṇa's brother and Bāṇa. So also the houses of other Dānavas, arrogant due to their strength.

64b-70. In every house the women who were being burnt began to lament uttering piteous words. They found themselves without support. They approached Śiva: "O Pāvaka, if you have any enmity towards the menfolk of the demon, what offence has been committed by the women who are like a cuckoo in the cage of domesticity. You are not ruthless. You are not too wicked. What anger do you cherish towards the womenfolk? Have you not heard this in the world that women should not be killed at any cost? But in your case you have the additional power in burning when you are induced by the wind. Mercy has not been shown by you. You do not have any chivalry towards women. Even barbarians (Mlecchas) show mercy on hearing the words of women. But a barbarian of barbarians is insensitive. He can not be restrained." Even as the women were lamenting thus, there, O descendant of Bharata, the fire continued to blaze with profuse flames and sparks. On seeing all these, Bāṇa who also felt scorched said:

71-79a. "I have been a sinful soul in having slighted Hara

and so I am doomed. Sinful and foolish that I have been, my (future) worlds have been destroyed.

Cows and Brāhmaṇas in this world as well as hereafter have been slain. Foodstuffs and beverages have been destroyed, so also Maṭhas (religious institutions), parks and penance-groves. The hermitages of the sages, the parks of deities, the abodes of Gaṇas etc. have been demolished. Due to that sin my penance and power have been upset. What shall I do with my wealth? With my kingdom? With my Antaḥpura? I had been of deluded intellect. I would rather seek refuge in the feet of Śaṅkara. Neither mother nor father, neither kinsmen nor other people excepting Maheśāna can be the dispeller of the greatest distress. The fruit of the sin committed by oneself is to be tasted by oneself. I shall also get burned along with all those good men." After saying thus he kept the Śivaliṅga on the head and hurriedly went out of the house. He was enveloped by fire. Utterly distressed, with all the limbs sweating profusely, faltering frequently he began to eulogize Hara with words choked and sought refuge in him.

79b-82. "O Śaṅkara, if I am to be killed, I have already been completely burned by the fire of your anger. O Mahādeva, let not this Liṅga be destroyed by you with your favour, O Great Lord. I have adored, O most excellent one among Suras, I have meditated with devotion, O Lord. Hence it behoves you to guard this which is dearer to me than my life. If I am to be blessed by you, O most excellent one among Suras, or if I am to be killed, O Mahādeva, let my devotion to you be constant in every birth, whether among animals, insects or birds, in any of the brutish creatures as a result of my own Karma; let my devotion to you be firm and unshakeable."

83. After saying thus the highly esteemed Bāṇa, the most excellent one among devout persons, propitiated the Lord of the chiefs of Devas by means of a hymn as follows:

[*Eulogy of Śiva:*]

Bāṇa said:

84-100. O Śiva, O Śaṅkara, obeisance to the annihilator of everything. Obeisance to the one that dispels the distress of those who are afraid of the worldly existence. Obeisance, O Lord, O destroyer of the body of the Flower-weaponed One

(Manmatha), the person who likes to please young women. Be victorious, O Lord of Pārvatī; be victorious, O essence of the ultimate truth. O Lord who have made a necklace of terrible serpents, be victorious, O Lord who have applied pure ashes on his limbs. Be victorious, O root-cause of all Mantras, the sole deserving person in the universe. Be victorious, O Lord with clusters of matted hairs rendered tawny by the venomous serpents. Be victorious, O Lord whose bow Pināka is held (ready) by Bhairava. Be victorious, O odd-eyed one, O Lord without attachment. Be victorious, O Śaṅkara wearing the waves of Gaṅgā. Be victorious, O Lord with terrible forms, with the Khaṭvāṅga in the hand, O moon-crested one. Be victorious, O most praise-worthy one in all the worlds. Be victorious, O Lord of the most excellent ones among Ṣuras, O essence of the world of Suras. Be victorious, O Śarva, who have burnt down all essential things. Be victorious, O Lord worthy of being glorified, the purest one of all the worlds. Be victorious, O Bull-emblemed One, with conducts of diverse kinds. Be victorious, O Lord with well-arranged garland of human skeletons, O Lord, O Kāla unto the skeleton of the body of Aghāsura. Be victorious, O blue-throated one, O Lord with the gait of an excellent bull. Be victorious, O suppressor of the sins of all the worlds. Be victorious, O Lord whose feet have been bowed to by Siddhas, Suras and Asuras. Be victorious, O Rudra who take one across the terrible ocean of worldly existence. Be victorious, O Giriśa worthy of being honoured by the Lord of Suras. Be victorious, O Lord of subtle form, O Lord worthy of being pondered over. Be victorious, O Lord by whom the Tripura has been burned, O intrinsic strength of the universe. Be victorious, O truth of all scriptures. Be victorious, O Lord difficult to be comprehended. O redeemer from worldly existence, O redeemer of devotees from the terrible, big ocean of worldly existence full of the sins of Kali. Be victorious, O Lord of the groups of Suras, Asuras and Devas. Obeisance, O Lord with faces of horse, monkey, lion and lordly elephant. O Lord of great shortness, stoutness and great length! It is impossible for Amaras to perceive you, O Nirañjana (one devoid of afflicting attachment). I bow down to your feet. Be victorious, O Lord accompanied by Aṁbā (Mother goddess), O Lord Hara having the splendour of excellent eyes. What is it that one who reaches the greatest height does not destroy by not attaining you? Then, even penance will be one that disturbs mostly; though great, it is very terrible. Neither sons nor kinsmen, neither wives nor all the friends of the world will approach one in difficulties, one who moves about alone. Whatever has been done by one, auspicious or inauspicious, that alone will accompany him like a caravan when he goes ahead. There is no fear unto a person who moves about without much wealth about him. A rich man will not be rid of fear. Hence I shall forsake wealth. Greedy persons commit sins. Even after hearing all about righteousness, after having comprehended it, men are not pure in every detail.

You are Viṣṇu, the Lord of the universe. You are the eternal Lord in the form of Brahmā, O Lord of the chiefs of Devas. You are Indra, O Lord of Suras. Obeisance to you. You are the Earth; you are Varuṇa; you are the wind; you are the Fire-god; you are the initiation; you are the householder performing the sacrifice; you are the firmament; you are Soma (the Moon, the Soma juice); you are the Sun; you are the Lord of wealth; you are Yama; you are Guru (Jupiter); the entire universe is pervaded by you in the same manner as the three worlds are enveloped by the refulgent splendour of the Sun.

101. On hearing this hymn composed by Bāṇa, Lord Maheśvara eschewed his anger. Delighted within himself he spoke these words:

Īśvara said:

102-103. From now onwards, O Dānava, you need not be afraid. Stay in your golden abode or by my side along with your sons, grandsons, kinsmen and wife. From now onwards, O dear one, you are one who cannot be killed by any enemy.

Mārkaṇḍeya said:

104-105a. O descendant of Bharata, again a boon was granted by the Lord of Devas: "Honoured and adored by Suras and Asuras, do reside happily at your pleasure in heaven, mortal world and the nether regions, without perishing and without changing."

105b-112. Thereafter, Rudra restrained the fire. His third Pura was saved by Lord Śaṁbhu. The other two engulfed by the clusters of flames fell down on the ground. Rising half above the flames reached heaven(?). The sound *Hā-Hā* uttered by the groups of sages was great and loud. So also the lamentations of the gods of great esteem, Siddhas, Vidyādharas and others. One piece fell on Śrīśaila. O king, the second one fell on the mountain Amarakaṇṭaka. Since it fell down blazing it is remembered as Jvāleśvara[1]. When the Tripura was burnt down, O king, when the excellent piece fell down, Lord Rudra stayed there as the person restraining the clusters of flames for the sake of protecting the sages continuing lamentations of *Hā-Hā*. Maheśāna stood there accompanied by Umā and Vṛṣabha, his own form. He who at least remembers mentally Amarakaṇṭaka with devotion, shall undoubtedly attain more merit than that of Cāndrāyaṇa.

113-120. Since, O most excellent one among the descendants of Bharata, the excellent mountain is highly meritorious, it shall always be destructive of all sins. It is overgrown with various kinds of trees and creepers. It is rendered splendid by different kinds of flowers. Various kinds of hedges and creepers abound therein. It is overspread by various creepers. It is infested by lions and tigers. It is adorned by herds of deer. It is always joyously filled with the roaring sound of the beasts of prey. There on that mountain Śaṅkara, the Lord of the chiefs of Devas, is served by thousands of gods, the chiefs of whom are Brahmā, Indra and Viṣṇu. He who falls off the precipices of this mountain Amarakaṇṭaka, sports about successively in all the fourteen worlds, O king, i.e. the worlds[2] of Indra, Vahni, Kubera, Vāyu, Yama, Nirṛti, Varuṇa, Soma, Sūrya, Brahmā (whose region is devoid of pain), Viṣṇu, Umārudra and thereafter that of Īśvara. The greatest world is that of Sadāśiva. It is quiescent, subtle, the luminosity that is beyond all sense-organs. An intelligent devotee gets merged into it undoubtedly in accordance with this procedure.

Yudhiṣṭhira said:

121. O excellent sage, is there any special procedure envisaged

1. The Tīrtha Jvāleśvara is etymologically connected with the burning of the second city out of Tripuras.
2. A list of 14 Bhuvanas.

in regard to falling down the precipice? O great sage, I have a great doubt in this regard; do tell me everything.

Śrī Mārkaṇḍeya said:

122-132. Listen, O son of Pāṇḍu, I shall tell you that procedure. After performing a rite at the outset, a devotee shall fall down the precipice. He shall at first perform three Kṛcchra rites after performing the Japa a million times. He should take in only vegetables (greens) and barley water. He should take ablutions three times (a day) and remain clean. He should worship Īśa, the three-eyed Lord of Devas, three times. O great king, the number of Homas shall be one-tenth thereof(?) He should perform the Japa of the Lord a hundred thousand times and worship with scents and garlands. At night he shall in dream see himself seated in an aerial chariot. Thereafter he should hurl himself. One who hurls himself in accordance with this procedure shall attain the heavenly world and sport about along with Devas. After enjoying soul-stirring pleasures for thirty crore thirty thousand years, he shall return to the earth and enjoy the whole earth under his single umbrella. He will be adored by the people. Freed from ailments and grief he will live for a hundred years. That Tīrtha is well-known in all the three worlds as Jvāleśvara. O son of Kuntī, the river Jvālā created by Śiva flows there. After extinguishing the fire in the city of Bāṇa, it joins Revā, O great king. The devotee should take his holy bath there in accordance with the injunctions. Duly uttering the Mantras he shall propitiate the Pitṛs and deities with water mixed with gingelly seeds and offerings of balls of rice. He shall attain the benefit of Pauṇḍarīka sacrifice. O king, he who performs Anāśaka ('no destruction', 'not taking food') in that Tīrtha is rid of all sins. He goes to Rudraloka.

133-142. He shall become the Lord of Amaras (Devas) served by hundreds of Devas and attended upon by groups of sages. So he shall be excessively meritorious. The Amarakaṇṭaka Tīrtha extending to a Yojana all round is very meritorious. It is excellent and meritorious, because there are crores of Rudras. If a devotee circumambulates that lofty mountain, it is undoubtedly as good as though the entire earth has been circumambulated. The three kinds of sins incurred through mind, words and deeds become destroyed: So said Śaṅkara.

O king, by the side of Amareśvara is the Tīrtha Śakreśvara. Formerly it was installed by Śakra after performing penance.

The auspicious Tīrtha named Kuśāvarta has been created by Brahmā. It is well known as Brahmakuṇḍa. Beyond that is Haṁsatīrtha. So also Aṁbarīṣa Tīrtha and Mahākāleśvara. To the east of Kāverī is the Tīrtha Mātṛkeśvara. These are on the southern bank of Revā, O great scion of the family of Bharata. They dispel sins if they are resorted to, bathed in or if the Dāna rite is performed. Śiva is famous as Bhairava on Bhṛgutuṅga, O great king. To the south thereof is the Tīrtha Capaleśvara. These are situated on the northern bank of Revā. They dispel misery. By worshipping them and bowing to them, one shall attain the benefit of the pilgrimage. They cause obstacles to men, if they are not visited or adored.

CHAPTER TWENTYNINE

The Greatness of the Confluence of Kāverī and Narmadā

Yudhiṣṭhira said:

1-5. O excellent one, Kāveri[1] is well known in the three worlds. O Mārkaṇḍa, I wish to listen to her real greatness. What is the mode of visiting that river? O Lord, what is the benefit of the touch thereof? O Sage, what benefit accrues from ablution, Japa, Dāna and Upavāsa (observance of fast there at the confluence of Kāverī)? Do narrate, O highly esteemed one. I have heard that any holy rite heard, seen, narrated, performed or approved of does sanctify one. It is the Vedic statement, O sage, that as in the case of Dharma, so in that of heaven and hell too.

Śrī Mārkaṇḍeya said:

6-14. Excellent! Excellent! O highly esteemed one, since

1. This is a small tributary of Narmadā and not the famous river of Karnatak. The attainment of the Kingship of Yakṣas is attributed to the sacred efficacy of the confluence of Kāverī and Narmadā.

you have asked me, listen with concentration to the excellent benefit of Kāverī. There is a Yakṣa of great intrinsic strength, well-known by the name Kubera. By the power of the Tīrtha, O king, he became the king of Yakṣas.

Hence listen to it along with the proper procedure (of bath etc.) with great devotion, O king of great esteem. He attained Siddhi through (the merit accrued from bath in) the confluence of Kāverī.

In the confluence, well-known in the world, of Kāverī and Narmadā, Kubera who was really valourous, took his holy bath and became clean. He duly observed all the restraints (and instructions) based on the injunctions of the sacred scriptures, O excellent one among men. He propitiated the eternal Mahādeva with single-minded concentration. He spent a month taking food once a day. Then he spent some time taking food on the sixth day only? Then he spent some time, O excellent king, by observing fast for a fortnight. The sensible one, thereafter, spent some time by taking in only roots, greens and fruits. Then for some time he stayed in the Tīrtha with moss for his food. He spent some time with the observance of expiations called Parāka and Kṛcchra, O honoured one. Then (he spent) some time with the observance of Cāndrāyaṇa and then some time with wind and water as food. Thus, O excellent one among men, eschewing lust and attachment, he stayed there for more than a hundred years torturing his body and making it emaciated.

15-25. At the end of a hundred years, Maheśvara, the Lord of Devas, became pleased with his great devotion and spoke to him smilingly: "O Yakṣa of great strength and excellent holy rites, choose a boon. I have become pleased with your devotion. I shall grant you what you wish."

The Yakṣa said:

If you are pleased, O Lord of Devas along with Umā, O Śaṅkara, let me be the Lord of all the Yakṣas from to-day without an end and free from any change and reduction, with devotion unto you duly kept before me. O Parameśvara, grant unto me the inclination for righteous actions.

Īśvara said:

What has been requested for by you is the fruit of your own righteousness? The same is granted.

After saying this Hara vanished.

He too had his holy ablution in accordance with the injunctions. He propitiated the Pitṛs and deities. Taking leave of the Tīrtha, he went home with his objects achieved. Honoured by Yakṣas, he had his coronation in accordance with the injunctions. He ruled over the extensive excellent kingdom.

O sinless one, there many other Suras, Siddhas, Yakṣas, Gandharvas, Kinnaras, groups of celestial damsels and sages have attained spiritual perfection. Hence they know that the confluence of Kāverī is destructive of all sins. It is the gateway unto all heavenly worlds, O Yudhiṣṭhira. If people take their holy bath in the Kāverī confluence and offer libations with gingelly seeds, they are blessed. They are noble-souled and they have led their life excellently, O dear one. Ten earlier and ten later generations on the mother's side as well as those on the father's side of the devotee are redeemed by him from the hellish ocean.

26-37. Hence, a man must make every effort to have his holy ablution there. He should worship Lord Īśvara if he seeks the eternal state (i.e. Mokṣa). O king, *Snāna, Dāna* and *Arcana* (adoration) performed devoutly by men (there) have more benefit than a horse-sacrifice, O excellent one among men. Everlasting heavenly pleasure is obtained through Homa; the life-span gets increased due to *Japa*; one attains the eternal region characterised by Śivakalā(?) through meditation.

O Lord of men, one who enters fire in that Tīrtha, shall stay in Agniloka until the annihilation of all living beings.

O excellent one among men, listen to the meritorious benefit of that person who observes the rite of fasting in the Tīrtha. He will rejoice with deities in an aerial chariot resembling the sun and fully occupied by Gandharvas and Apsarās. He will be fanned by excellent women.

For sixty thousand years and sixty centuries he sports about stationed in Rudraloka. At the end he comes to the earth born as a king enjoying all pleasures and engaged in munificent gifts. Freed from anguish and grief, he shall live for a hundred years.

O king, River Kāverī has all these good qualities. She is well-known in all the three worlds at the confluence of Narmadā. Those who have controlled their speech, body and mind and those who are engaged in the meditation on one worthy of being meditated upon, at the confluence of Kāverī, O dear one, shall also attain salvation.

Listen, O excellent king, I shall recount another miraculous thing. What other (river) is on a par with the river in all the three worlds?

There is no doubt about this that those who have reached Narmadā, those who circumambulate her, and those who drink her water are meritorious.

38-43. For another fifteen births there will not be any break in the line of their succession. Their sin gets dissolved like snow at the time of sunrise. A man who takes his holy ablution in Kāverī obtains the benefit usually attained at the confluence of Gaṅgā and Yamunā. It is remembered as eight times more beneficial when Tuesday coincides with the fourteenth lunar day, during Vyatīpāta, during the transit of the Sun and when Rāhu and the Moon come in conjunction (lunar eclipse).

If at the confluence of Gaṅgā and Yamunā the merit of ablution is equal to the weight of Yavas (barley grains) eighty in number, at the confluence of Kāverī and Narmadā the same is remembered as eight times more. Gaṅgā is honoured by sixty thousand Kṣetrapālas (Guardians of holy shrines). Other Tīrthas are guarded by half that number. There is no doubt about it. The confluences of the rivers mentioned in Amareśvara are guarded by eighty thousand Kṣetrapālas.

44-48. So also to the south of Amareśvara, two Liṅgas guard the Tīrtha, one being Liṅga Capaleśvara and the second Caṇḍahasta. They were formerly installed by Śiva as the guardians of Kāverī etc. The divine Narmadā existing over many Kalpas, is guarded by a hundred thousand (Kṣetrapālas). The mountain is guarded by a hundred thousand Oṁkāras, the persons engaged by Īśa and equipped with sixty bows. A sin committed in other places perishes in this holy spot. A sin committed in this Tīrtha becomes fixed forever.

Thus O dear one, Kāverī, the most excellent one among rivers, has been recounted to you. She has originated from Rudra's body. Hence this most excellent river is meritorious.

CHAPTER THIRTY

The Glory of Dāru Tīrtha

Śrī Mārkaṇḍeya said:

1-5. On the northern bank of Narmadā, there is the excellent Dārutīrtha where an excellent Brāhmaṇa performed penance, O highly esteemed one, and became a Siddha.

Yudhiṣṭhira said:

Who is this most excellent Brāhmaṇa Dāruka who became a Siddha there, O great sage? Whose son was he? It behoves you to recount this to me.

Śrī Mārkaṇḍeya said:

In the great Bhārgava family was born a highly fortunate Brāhmaṇa named Dāru as the son of the intelligent Devaśarman. He was a master of the Vedas and Vedāṅgas. He became a celibate student, a householder and a forest-dwelling hermit consecutively. (Ultimately) as a world-renouncing ascetic he performed severe austerities in accordance with the injunctions in regard to the sacred rites of Sannyāsa. O Yudhiṣṭhira, he meditated on Mahādeva, abstaining from food intake. He stayed at that Tīrtha till the end of his life.

6-10. That Tīrtha became well-known in all the three worlds after his name. One should take the holy bath there, in accordance with the injunctions and adore the Pitṛs and deities. He should be truthful in speech and subdue anger. He should be engaged in what is beneficial to all living beings. O king, here itself he will obtain all desires in every respect. If one is engrossed in truth and purity and performs the rite of *Upavāsa* (fast), he shall undoubtedly attain the benefit of the Sautrāmaṇi sacrifice. A follower of Ṛgveda should recite Ṛk passages; a master of Sāmaveda Sāman hymns; and a follower of Yajurveda should perform the *Japa* of Yajur Mantras. They will obtain excellent benefit. Śaṅkara said that if a person abandons his life in that Tīrtha in accordance with the injunctions, he will attain the ultimate state from which there is no return.

CHAPTER THIRTYONE

The Greatness of Brahmāvarta

Śrī Mārkaṇḍeya said:

1-6a. Thereafter one should proceed to the Tīrtha well-known in all the three worlds as Brahmāvarta[1]. It is destructive of all sins. There, O Yudhiṣṭhira, Brahmā is always present as a perpetual worshipper. With the arms lifted up and without any support he continues to move around perpetually. For twelve years he remained as a Mahāvratī (observer of great holy vows), taking food only once (a day). He remained in this Tīrtha meditating on Maheśvara in accordance with the injunctions. Hence, O Lord, that meritorious Tīrtha came to be called Brahmāvarta. One should take one's ablution there in accordance with the injunctions and propitiate the Pitṛs and deities. He should worship Īśāna, the Lord, or Viṣṇu, the great Lord. By the power of that Tīrtha he obtains that benefit which usually accrues from all Yajñas performed with due monetary gifts.

6b-10. Every Tīrtha becomes well known in the world after the name of a Deva, Dānava or Dvija who has attained spiritual enlightenment there. It is also great. Neither water nor ground, neither fertile field nor arid ground attain sanctity without the (spiritual) efforts of men. People achieve spiritual perfection through their power, resoluteness and fortitude, O king.
Due to blunders as well as covetousness people certainly fall into hell. Wherever a sage resides after restraining his sense-organs, there springs up a Kurukṣetra, Naimiṣa or Puṣkara.

1. This is not the famous Brahmāvarta, the region between Sarasvatī and Dṛṣadvatī, which later became known as Kurukṣetra. The author wants to bring all famous sacred places to the banks of Narmadā.

CHAPTER THIRTYTWO

The Greatness of Patreśvara Tīrtha

Śrī Mārkaṇḍeya said:

1-8. From there a pilgrim should go to Patreśvara that is destructive of all sins. It is there that the highly esteemed, powerful son of Citrasena became a Siddha (spiritually perfect).

Yudhiṣṭhira said:

O holy Sir, I wish to know who was this Siddha of great austerities, who attained spiritual perfection in that Tīrtha? Whose son was he and what was the cause (of his perfection)?

Śrī Mārkaṇḍeya said:

O excellent king, there was a former intimate friend of Indra called Citra. He had great splendour. His son was well-known as Patreśvara. He was handsome and fortunate. He was a terror unto all enemies. He was so close a friend of Indra as though he was another Jaya (Jayanta).

Once in the middle of the Royal Assembly where all the Devas had gathered together, he became much infatuated by the dance and songs of Menakā for a long time. He transgressed all bounds of decency. It was as though his life had become extinct. The Lord of Suras cursed him who had no control over his senses: "Though you are staying in Svarga, yet you have succumbed to weaknesses like a mortal. Hence you will certainly spend a long time in the mortal world."

On being cursed thus by the Lord of Suras, the youthful son of Citrasena began to tremble. With palms joined in reverence, he spoke to the excellent one among Suras:

Patreśvara said:

9-15. I have been sinful, infatuated and lost control of the mind and senses. I, therefore, reaped the fruit thereof. But it behoves you to be pleased.

Śakra said:

Resort to the banks of Narmadā and propitiate the quiescent Śiva for twelve years with the senses under control. You will attain a good state. The scriptures declare that this world (i.e. Svarga) belongs to pious persons having self-control, truthfulness and purity, and not to people who are sinners.

When this was told by the intelligent Thousand-eyed One, the sensible son of the Gandharva bowed down to him and went to the earth.

He took his holy bath in the pure waters of Revā near Brahmāvarta. After performing Japa in accordance with the injunctions, he adored Śaṅkara by means of air, water, oilcake, fruits, flowers and leaves. He maintained himself by eating roots and drinking barley water. He performed severe austerities with five fires around him. Thereupon, the Lord became pleased.

He saw the Trident-bearing Consort of Umā, the bestower of boons. He had the Pināka bow in his hand. The Destroyer of Andhaka (Śiva) had the crescent moon for his crest-jewel and elephant hide as his cloth. On seeing the Lord in front, he fell down (at his feet).

Īśvara said:

16-25. Welfare unto you. Choose your boon. O sinless one, I shall grant you the boon. Whatever you wish, I shall give you. No doubt need be entertained in this.

Patreśvara said:

If you are pleased, O Lord of Devas, if a boon has to be granted to me, O Lord, be stationed here for ever in the Tīrtha after my name.

On hearing this, Mahādeva in words choked with joy said: "So be it". Then the delighted Lord Śaṅkara went away along with Umā.

When the Lord went to heaven, he took his holy plunge in the Tīrtha, propitiated the Pitṛs in accordance with the injunctions regarding the Japa and installed the Lord of Devas duly,

O descendant of Bharata. It became well known in all the three worlds as Patreśvara.

After being rid of his curse, O king, he went to the beautiful Indraloka. He was received with the utterances of "Be victorious" etc., and was highly delighted thereby. Thus, O Yudhiṣṭhira, the question you had put has been clarified. One is rid of all sins by a single holy ablution there. He who after holy ablution and adoration of the Pitṛs and Devas shall worship Mahādeva in that Tīrtha, O Yudhiṣṭhira, obtains the benefit of a horse-sacrifice. After death he will sport about in the city of Śiva for more than a hundred years and then be born among mortals as a king or someone of the same status as that of a king. He will be conversant with the truth of the Vedas and Vedāṅgas and live a hundred years without sickness or grief. Again he shall remember that water (the Tirtha i.e. Revā).

CHAPTER THIRTYTHREE

The Greatness of Agni Tīrtha

Śrī Mārkaṇḍeya said:

1-7. Thereafter one should go to the excellent Agnitīrtha, O great king. It is there that Agni went on being enchanted by Kāma.

Yudhiṣṭhira said:

How was the Lord (Agni), the sustainer of the universe, defiled by Kāma? How can there be perpetual residence (of Agni) in single places? This is unparalleled and mysterious, the most excellent in all the worlds. Do tell me, O highly esteemed one, I have very great curiosity.

Śrī Mārkaṇḍeya said:

Excellent! Excellent! O highly intelligent one! An excellent question has been put by you, O sinless one. I shall mention (the answer to it) as was heard from Maheśvara.

There was a great king named Duryodhana[1] in Kṛtayuga. He was fully equipped with elephants, horses and chariots and he duly protected the earth. On seeing the king richly endowed with handsome features and youthful figure and enjoying rich and divine pleasures, Narmadā sought him.[2] The highly delighted king of Māhiṣmatī abandoned other young maidens and loved that girl.

8-14. O excellent king, he (that king) sported with her and at the proper time Narmadā gave birth to a lotus-eyed girl. Richly endowed with beauty in every limb and joint, she became well-known in all the worlds. The father and the mother had affectionate attachment to her. After a long time the excellent girl reached the prime of her youth, O king, but even when wooed she never wished to offer herself.

On another day, Vahni (Fire-god) assumed the form of a Brāhmaṇa of great austerities, slowly approached the king and requested him secretly: "O excellent scion of the family of Raghu, I am a Brāhmaṇa deficient in progeny, poor and helpless. I woo her (your daughter) to become my wife. Your daughter named Sudarśanā is unrivalled all over the earth in her physical beauty. She lives (grows) in your palace; O highly esteemed one, do give her to me. I am alone. I have become disgusted with long celibacy. I am now afflicted with love. O dear one, it behoves you to do me this favour, since I earnestly beg for it."

Rājā (*The King*) *said:*

15-23. O excellent Brāhmaṇa, I will never give my splendid daughter to one who belongs to another caste and is also devoid of wealth; you may go.

On being told this, Vahni (Fire-god) became excessively afflicted. Without saying anything further to the king, he vanished there itself.

1. The story is borrowed from Mbh, *Anuśāsana* Ch. 3. This king Duryodhana is different from the Mahābhārata hero, Duryodhana, son of Dhṛtarāṣṭra. This Purāṇa utilises the episode for the glorification of Agni Tirtha on Narmadā.
2. Narmadā seems to be enamoured of even human beings. Before meeting her consort, the Sea, she married Agni (domestic fire) and got a son. Now she marries King Duryodhana and gave birth to a daughter who was given to Agni in marriage.

After the Brāhmaṇa had gone away, the king took counsel with his ministers and priests. Highly delighted, he occupied his seat in front of the sacrificial pit. Even as he was devoutly performing the sacrifice in the company of the Brāhmaṇas, O descendant of Bharata, Vahni vanished from the place even as all of them were watching. The Brāhmaṇas became disappointed. They went to the palace of the king with disappointment in their minds and spoke to the king:

The Brāhmaṇas said:

O great king Duryodhana, may this mysterious event be heard. This miraculous thing has not been heard or seen before, O excellent king. O king, all of us began duly our sacrificial rites in the fire. For some reason the fire is neither seen nor does it burn.

On hearing this terribly unpleasant thing issuing from the mouths of the Brāhmaṇas, the king fell down from his seat on the ground like a tree, the root of which has been cut. He soon recovered and became composed in a short while, but looked all round as though he had become mad and spoke these words:

24-34. "O excellent Brāhmaṇas, what is this mysterious incident? Consider this from the standpoint of the scriptures and do tell me the reason hereof. What is the reason for the disappearance of fire? Is it any of my sins or yours, whereby the Fire-god has vanished from the hall of sacred fire. Was there any loophole in the course of the recitation of the Mantras? Was any rite performed without the requisite Dakṣiṇā? Was there any omission of the due rites? Why is Vahni not to be seen? There is no enemy like Yajña. If there is any fault in the cooked food served, it will burn the nation. If it is without the utterance of the requisite Mantras it will burn the Ṛtviks. If it is deficient in Dakṣiṇās it will destroy the Dātṛ (donor)."

The Brāhmaṇas said:

We are not guilty of the omission of the Mantras. Nor, O king, are we negligent in our Vratas. You are not short of the *Dravyas* (money, sacrificial requisites). Please reflect whether there is any other fault.

The King said:

Yet, all of you join together and think about the means of remedy whereby there will be all-round welfare always in this world as well as hereafter.

On being told thus, all those Brāhmaṇas came to a final decision. They, observing fast, stationed themselves at the place where the fire had vanished. Then in their dream the excessively refulgent Fire-god said to the Brāhmaṇas: "May ye all hear the cause of my disappearance. The king was requested by me to give his daughter to me, but he does not wish to give. Therefore, I have vanished from the sacrificial hall, O excellent Brāhmaṇas. If only the king is prepared to offer his highly honoured daughter to me, then will I be present burning brightly in his abode. Not otherwise."

On listening to these words issued from the mouth of the Fire-god, those Brāhmaṇas, struck with wonder causing their eyes to glisten, spoke these words to the king:

35-46. "After knowing your view all of us went to the sacrificial chamber, observed fast and stayed there for the night. Then we saw the Fire-god. We were told by him: 'If the king is prepared to give his daughter to me, I shall continue to stay in his palace and blaze; not otherwise, O Brāhmaṇas.' After coming to know of this, it behoves you to give your daughter, O great king."

The King said:

Your words and those of that god should be kept in mind by me. I wish to stipulate an excellent condition in regard to the offer of my daughter. May the Fire-god be present always in my abode. I shall give my daughter of charming side-glances; not otherwise.

On hearing this, the Brāhmaṇas hurriedly approached the Fire-god and got the marriage performed. Hutāśana (Fire-god) became delighted on getting Sudarśanā. O Yudhiṣṭhira, thereafter he remained ever present in Māhiṣmatī and continued to blaze. Ever since then the people call that Tīrtha 'Agnitīrtha'. Those who became purified by means of holy ablutions and Dāna at the juncture of the two halves of the month and propitiate the Pitṛs and Devas became possessed of the benefits of a horse-sacrifice.

If gold is offered as gift at that Tīrtha, O king, one acquires the merit of gifting plots of land. There is no doubt about this.

If one observes the vow of non-intake of food in that Tīrtha, one becomes able to sport about in Agniloka after death and is honoured by Suras.

Thus the origin of Agnitīrtha has been recounted to you by me. It is conducive to the destruction of all sins. Merely on being listened to, it is meritorious, O most excellent one among men. It is conducive to wealth and destructive of sins for ever. So said Śaṅkara.

CHAPTER THIRTYFOUR

Description of Ravi Tīrtha

Śrī Mārkaṇḍeya said:

1-9. There itself is another Tīrtha of the noble-souled Āditya (Sun-god). I shall glorify it, O excellent one among men, if you are interested in listening.

Yudhiṣṭhira said:

On hearing this incomparable mystery coming out of your mouth, I am struck with wonder and I experience horripilation, O excellent sage.

The Thousand-rayed Lord is the annihilator, creator and free from any contamination. He caused the uplift of the worlds through his incarnation on the bank of Narmadā. Is the Lord in the form of a man? Or does he redeem as a result of penance? In whose family did he take his birth? Under whose control did he come to be?

Śrī Mārkaṇḍeya said:

A devout, pure Brāhmaṇa born in the family of Kulika made preparation for pilgrimage to that Tīrtha thinking, 'I shall visit the Sun-god'.

He made the journey of more than a hundred Yojanas without taking food and without drinking water. He was verily prevented from the journey in a dream: "O sage of great Sattva quality, enough of your Vrata of this sort. Look at me, I have pervaded everything, the mobile and immobile beings. I blaze. I withhold rain and I then release it too. He who sees me not dead but as Mṛtyu (cause of death) sees reality. Choose any fair boon whatever has been desired by you."

The Brāhmaṇa said:

10-17. If you are pleased, O Lord, if the boon is to be given to me, be present for ever on the northern bank of Narmadā. O Lord, be the bestower of boons to those persons who are self-controlled and remember you with great devotion, though staying a hundred Yojanas away.

Be the bestower of boons to those who are hunchbacked, blind, deaf and dumb, or those who have some defect in some limb or sense-organ and bow unto your feet. Without delay, O Lord, show mercy to those whose noses are shattered, whose intellects are retarded and of whom there remain only bones and skin.

Be the bestower of boons, O Lord of the universe, to those who worship you everyday after taking the holy bath in Narmadā water.

O unswerving Lord, grant the desired boons to those who eulogize you in the morning through Vedic and secular prayers. O Lord, this is my final boon that boons should be granted to those men on the earth who get their haircut or shaving when you are in full view.

Out of pity the Lord thereupon told the sage, "Let it be so". O great king, he stationed himself there with a hundredth part and then vanished.

18-24. A man should go to that Tīrtha with great devotion and perform the holy ablution. He should propitiate the Pitṛs and Devas. He shall thereby derive the benefit of Agniṣṭoma.

He who immolates himself by entering fire at that Tīrtha, O king, goes to Agniloka brightening all the quarters.

He who gives up his body after reaching that Tīrtha, shall go to the world of Varuṇa. So said Śaṅkara.

He who abandons worldly life by adopting Sannyāsa at that Tīrtha and quits life, is honoured in the heavenly world where groups of Apsarās are (in attendance) and divine (musical) sounds reverberate. After staying there he returns to the mortal world and becomes well-conversant with the Vedas and Vedāṅgas. He shall be rid of ailments and grief and shall be the Lord of crores and crores. Accompanied by sons and wife he shall live a hundred years.

He who gets up early in the morning and remembers the Sun-god there becomes undoubtedly rid of the sins committed throughout the life.

CHAPTER THIRTYFIVE

Glorification of Meghanāda Tīrtha

Yudhiṣṭhira said:

1-7. What is the reason for which Mahādeva stands in the middle of water, O excellent Brāhmaṇa, after avoiding the northern and southern banks?

Śrī Mārkaṇḍeya said:

This narrative, O dear one, is unparalleled, meritorious and pleasing to the ears. I shall recount to you entirely what has been heard in the Purāṇas.

O highly esteemed one, in Tretā Yuga Rāvaṇa who was an enemy of Devas, conqueror of the three worlds, terrible, frightening to both Suras and Asuras, impossible of being killed by Devas, Dānavas, Gandharvas, sages and ascetics, was going around the earth by means of his aerial chariot.

At that time, a haughty Dānava named Maya staying within a cave was performing penance in the middle of the Vindhya range of mountains. The Rākṣasa (i.e. Rāvaṇa) approached him humbly on the ground. He was adored and honoured with reverence, Dānas etc. (Rāvaṇa) asked: "To whom does this girl with eyes resembling lotus petals and countenance like the full moon belong? What is her name? O Sir, why does she perform the severe penance?"

Maya said:

8-11. I am the excellent Lord of Dānavas and am called Maya. The name of my wife is Tejovatī. Her splendid daughter is well known as Mandodarī. She is engaged in penance for the sake of a husband and hence she is adoring the splendid Husband of Umā.

On hearing those words Rāvaṇa who had been deluded due to arrogance, became humble and spoke to Maya:

"I am born of the family of Pulastya. I have humiliated the pride of Devas and Dānavas, O highly esteemed one. I request you. It behoves you to offer your daughter."

12-16. After realizing his connexion with Pitāmaha (Brahmā) the noble-souled Maya honoured Rāvaṇa duly and offered his daughter. The Rākṣasa was duly honoured by the night-stalkers (i.e. demons). He took her in an aerial chariot and began to sport about in the celestial garden with her.

After some time, O descendant of Bharata, Rāvaṇa who could make people cry, begot a son and became the most excellent one among those who had sons.

Even as he was born, the child of huge body gave out a loud cry (sound) like that of the Saṁvartaka cloud, whereby the worlds became benumbed. After hearing that terrible roar, Brahmā, the grandfather of the worlds, named him Meghanāda.

17-25. Having been named thus he took up a great Vrata and propitiated Śaṅkara, the Lord of Devas, along with Umā. He made his body lean through *Vrata, Niyama, Dāna,* observances, *Homa, Japa* in accordance with the injunctions and by performing Kṛcchra and Cāndrāyaṇa. On a certain day he went to Mountain Kailāsa, took up two Liṅgas and proceeded towards the South. After coming to the banks of Narmadā, the mighty Dānava became desirous of taking a holy bath. He placed the Liṅgas down and performed Japa and adored the Lord, O king. The night-stalker became contented by the stay in the shrine, holy ablution and Homa in the fire. When he wished to go back to Laṅkā, O excellent king, he took up one of the Liṅgas with his left hand and the other one with the other hand with due devotion. By the time the son of Rāvaṇa could take up the Mahāliṅga it fell down in the waters of Narmadā. He uttered "Go, Go" and installed it in the middle of the water. After bowing down to Lord Parameṣṭhin, the son of Rāvaṇa went away by the aerial path duly honoured by the demons. Ever since then the Tīrtha became well known as Meghanāda.

26-31. The roar had been heard before and it was the cause of the destruction of all sins, O great king. One who takes his holy bath in that Tīrtha well-known as *Garjana* and stays there for a day and a night shall obtain the merit of performing a horse-sacrifice.

If a person performs the rite of offering balls of rice in that Tīrtha, O king, there is no doubt about this that the merit that accrues from a Sattrayajña will accrue to him. He has propitiated the Piṭrs for twelve years. If a person feeds a Brāhmaṇa with the food of all six tastes, O descendant of Bharata, at that Tīrtha, O excellent one among men, the devotee obtains everlasting merit.

He who brings his life to an end with a purified soul shall stay in Śaṅkara's world until the destruction of all living beings.

Thus, O tiger among men, the excellent origin of Garjana Tīrtha has been recounted to you due to ties of affection. It causes the destruction of all sins.

CHAPTER THIRTYSIX

The Glory of Dāruka Tīrtha

Śrī Mārkaṇḍeya said:

1-6. Thereafter, O great king, one should go to the excellent Dāru Tīrtha[1] where Indra's friend Dāruka became a Siddha formerly.

Yudhiṣṭhira said:

O sinless one, how was the penance performed formerly by Dāruka? I wish to hear the procedure thereof from you, O excellent Brāhmaṇa.

1. As noted in Chapter 231 *infra.* Dāruka Tīrtha is repeated four times (*catvāro dārukeśvarāḥ*) in this text.

Śrī Mārkaṇḍeya said:

Well, I shall recount to you the wonderful incident that occurred long back in the celestial assembly of the sages of purified souls. The name of the favourite charioteer of Indra was Mātali. Once for some reason he cursed his son. The son affected by the curse quaked and fell at the splendid feet of Indra with his head touching them. He submitted to the Lord of Devas (the full details). The Lord of Suras told the accursed one how and by means of what rite could the terrible curse come to an end:

7-13. "Go to the banks of Narmadā and stay there till the end of the Yuga propitiating Maheśvara. Then you will have a rebirth. In this birth you will be well known by the name Dāruka[1] in the form of a human being. After serving the great Lord holding the conch, discus and club you will attain Siddhi."

On being told thus by the intelligent thousand-eyed Indra, (the son of Mātali) who had lost his senses, bowed down to him and came to the banks of Narmadā. By means of Vratas and fasts he mortified his body. He was always engaged in Japa and Homa and propitiated the trident-bearing, noble-souled Mahādeva, the bestower of boons. He adored with great devotion, O king, till the ultimate annihilation of all living beings. The excessively wise son of Mātali became a charioteer of a partial incarnation of Viṣṇu. Propitiating the Lord of the Cosmos he attained the good state (i.e. Mokṣa).

14-19. Thus, O dear one of good holy Vratas, the origin of Dārutīrtha has been recounted in the manner it was narrated to me by Śaṅkara.

On hearing it, Yudhiṣṭhira was struck with great wonder. He saw his brothers with hairs standing on end repeatedly.

Śrī Mārkaṇḍeya said:

A man who takes his holy ablution there duly, says the Sandhyā

1. Dāruka was a trusted charioteer of Kṛṣṇa and is mentioned many times in Mbh. Before his death, Kṛṣṇa sent Dāruka to Pāṇḍavas with the news of the catastrophic destruction of Yādavas (Mbh, *Mausala* 4.2-3). This Purāṇa writer claims the greatness of Dāruka's career to this Tīrtha by naming it Dāruka Tīrtha.

prayers, worships Śaṅkara, the Lord of Devas, and begins the repeated recitation of the Vedas with concentration, shall undoubtedly attain the merit of a horse-sacrifice. One who devoutly feeds Brāhmaṇas at that Tīrtha with great purity attains the merit of feeding a thousand Brāhmaṇas (elsewhere). Whatever has been performed with pure intention, viz. Snāna (holy bath), Dāna (offering gifts), Japa, Homa, self-study of the Vedas, adoration of the deities etc. shall be fruitful.

CHAPTER THIRTYSEVEN

Glorification of Deva Tīrtha

Śrī Mārkaṇḍeya said:

1-8. Therefrom, O eminent king, one should go to the excellent Tīrtha called Devatīrtha where thirty-three Devas took their holy bath and attained great Siddhi.

Yudhiṣṭhira asked:

How did all the Suras attain the great Siddhi, O dear one? All of them had been conquered by the powerful Dānavas. How did they get highest salvation by taking the holy bath in the Tīrtha?

Śrī Mārkaṇḍeya said:

Formerly, O king, Indra along with the groups of Devas, was ousted from his kingdom by the awful hordes of Daityas of great might in the course of a battle.

Their army was shattered by the divisions of elephants, horses and chariots. On being annihilated and smashed and dissipated by the onslaughts they fled along the roads. Assailed by Jambha, Śumbha and Niśumbha, Kūṣmāṇḍa, Kuhaka and others, they trembled with fear and all of them approached God Brahmā. The Devas with Vahni as their leader bowed down their heads to Brahmā Parameṣṭhin and submitted thus : "See, see, O highly esteemed one, we have been smashed to smithereens by the Dānavas. We have been separated from our sons and wives. Hence we have sought refuge in you. Save us, O Lord of Devas, O grandfather of all the worlds. O Lord of Suras, O Parameśvara, barring you we have no other refuge."

Brahmā said:

9-17. For the sake of the destruction of the Dānavas, station yourselves on the banks of Narmadā and perform penance in the place with composure. Penance is the greatest strength.

There is no other means of remedy; there is no Mantra or rite excepting the meritorious waters of Revā, the cause of the destruction of all sins. It is my opinion that poverty, ailment, death, imprisonment and other difficulties are the results of sin. After realizing this, perform severe penance.

On hearing those truthful words of Brahmā Parameṣṭhin, all the Suras with Agni as their leader came to Narmadā.

There they performed severe penance and attained Siddhi. Ever since then that Tīrtha is being sung about as the excellent Devatīrtha in all the three worlds. It is conducive to the destruction of all sins.

A man who has controlled his sense-organs duly and goes there and devoutly takes the holy bath, shall obtain *Mauktika* (pearl, salvation).

He who feeds a few Brāhmaṇas at that Tīrtha shall obtain, O king, the merit as though he has fed a thousand Brāhmaṇas. Devaśilā ('the Rock of Gods') there is very beautiful and is conducive to the increase of great merit.

18-22. Those who die after renunciation shall obtain everlasting state (i.e. Mokṣa). He who enters burning fire there at that Tīrtha, O Lord of men, shall stay in Rudraloka until the annihilation of all living beings.

Thus Snāna, Japa, Homa, self-study of the Vedas, adoration of the deities, good and evil deeds done at that Tīrtha shall be everlasting.

Thus the origin and procedure of the pilgrimage to Devatīrtha has been entirely recounted to you as was heard from Śaṅkara.

Those who read this story of Devatīrtha that destroys sins and redeems devotees from all miseries do go to Devaloka.

CHAPTER THIRTYEIGHT

The Greatness of Narmadeśvara Tīrtha

Śrī Mārkaṇḍeya said:

1-12. Therefrom, O great king, one should go to the excellent Tīrtha named Guhāvāsī where Mahādeva spent millions of years as a Siddha staying in a cave.

Yudhiṣṭhira said:

For what reason, O dear one, did Mahādeva, the preceptor of the universe, spend so long a period in the cave, O excellent Brāhmaṇa? O sinless one, narrate this completely in detail to me. I wish to hear everything in full. I am extremely interested.

Śrī Mārkaṇḍeya said:

Excellent! O great king, an excellent question has been put by you. This is fully explained in the Purāṇa. Now that I am pretty old, it is difficult for me to expatiate upon it. It occurred pretty long back. It is a matter of hoary antiquity. Hence I shall succinctly tell you, O dear one. Know it from me.

Formerly, O king, in Kṛtayuga, there was a great forest named Dāruvana. It was overgrown with many trees and creepers. It was splendidly beautified by various tender creepers. It was resorted to by lions, tigers, boars, elephants and rhinoceroses. There were many birds there. It was like the divine park Caitraratha.

There some highly wise men of very severe austerities lived devoutly, strictly adhering to the system of four Āśramas (stages of life), viz. celibate student, householder, retired hermit and recluse. All of them desired the greatest state (Mokṣa). They strictly practised their own respective duties.

Once, during spring, for some undisclosed reason, Mahādeva was proceeding in an aerial chariot along with Umā. There he saw a hermitage in water reverberating with the Ṛk, Sāman and Yajus hymns. The way in and out could not be seen. It was conducive to the destruction of all sins. On seeing it, the goddess was delighted. She asked the Lord of the chiefs of Devas with the moon for his crest jewel, in words choked with excessive delight:

The Devī said:

13-22. O Lord, whose is this hermitage echoing with the sounds of the Vedic texts? On seeing this one becomes rid of all tiresome feelings of hunger, thirst etc.

Maheśvara said:

O goddess, have you not heard about this great Dāruvana? Many Brāhmaṇas dwell here as householders. All the women-folk there are engaged solely in attending on their husbands. O Daughter of the Mountain, no other deity is known to them. No other sacred duty is practised by them.

On hearing this excellent statement uttered by the Lord of Devas, she became overcome by curiosity and said to Śaṅkara again: "O Lord, O Mahādeva, it has been stated by you that the women are engaged in the sacred duty of attending on their husbands. Be like Madana (god of love) and upset their fidelity."

Īśvara said:

O my beloved, I do not approve of what has been spoken by you. Indeed the Brāhmaṇas are great beings. One should not act antagonistically to them or displease them. Anger is the striking weapon of Brāhmaṇas. Discus is the striking weapon of Hari. (Their) Anger is more ruthless than the discus. Hence one should not infuriate a Brāhmaṇa.

Neither Devas nor common people, neither Nāgas nor Asuras in all the three worlds, have survived from being destroyed after being (angrily) looked at by them.

Salvation, Svarga (heavenly pleasure), earthly benefit and welfare in the mortal world all come only to those towards whom the highly esteemed Brāhmaṇas, the deities of the earth, are well-disposed.

By realizing this, O highly esteemed lady, leave your improper insistence on the proposed act. That wherewith Brāhmaṇas become angry is antagonistic to the other world as well.

The goddess said:

23-38. O Lord, the honour of those ladies is highly esteemed by the Suras unless you suppress it and keep it low. I am not your beloved nor am I subservient to you. O Mahādeva, in the Lokāloka there is nothing which cannot be accomplished by you. O most excellent one among Suras, may at least this single task (request) of mine be carried out.

On being told thus by the goddess, Mahādeva who is favourably disposed towards the inclinations and behests of the goddess, adopted the form of a Kāpālika and went to Dāruvaṇa. He adjusted the dishevelled matted hairs and retained only the moon as his crest-jewel and a chain round the neck along with the earrings. He wore the hide of a tiger and was bedecked in girdle and necklaces. He seemed to cause tremor in the earth through the loud jingling sounds of the anklets. The matted hairs were tied up and the great Lord had smeared his body with holy ash. In his hand he retained the skull of the noble-souled Brahmā. He played on his big Ḍamaru (drum) causing the earth to quake. He reached Dāruvana in the morning.

By that time all those meritorious people who desired (to collect) flowers, leaves and fruits went with others. The wind was blowing. On seeing the miraculous form of the Lord, O descendant of Bharata, the minds of those young women became defiled by Kāma (God of Love).

On seeing the splendid male, all those excellent ladies, the womenfolk of Dāruvana, experienced exudation of perspiration in their bodies due to exhilaration.

On seeing the miraculous Lord, there were various types of outbursts of emotional excitement among those ladies, O best of men. (Those wives of the Brāhmaṇas were upset emotionally.) Some of them could not know where their garments were. Others lost their upper garment on seeing the wonderful form of the Lord. They were extremely enchanted and fascinated. The tresses of hairs of some of them got dishevelled. Some stood up from their seats desirous of offering alms but could not even stir. One lady who was overproud of her beauty and youthful form forgot to breast-feed her son lying on her lap. On seeing Mahādeva, another lady became struck by the arrows of Kāma. She pressed down her protruding breasts with her arms. Sighing and expelling hot breaths, she ceased to talk. Thus Parameśvara made all those womenfolk excited in a wonderful way and went off.

39-46. By that time, all those Brāhmaṇas after wandering all over the great forest came back to their abodes and saw their wives weak and for splendour. Those ladies who had great devotion towards their husbands formerly had now slipped down from chastity. On coming to know of this, those excellent Brāhmaṇas came out. They consulted one another and understood that Lord Maheśvara had vanished after upsetting the minds of their ladies. One infuriated Brāhmaṇa lifted a stick and ran. Another raised up a Kalmāṣayaṣṭi (spotted stick?) and still others a handful of Darbha grass. They ran about here and there in the forest, O king; the noble-souled ones gathered together and said in anger:

"If we have performed any Homas, if we have propitiated our preceptors, then, by the strength of that truth let the excellent Liṅga (Penis) of the Lord fall down. If we have gone from one Āśrama (stage of life) to another in the due order as laid down in the scriptures, then by the strength of that truth, let the Liṅga of the Lord fall on the ground. Thus, by the power of the truth of the Brāhmaṇas repeated thrice, even as Śiva stood seeing, his Liṅga fell down on the ground.[1]

47-54. In Lokāloka there was a great lamentation, O descendant of Bharata, when the Liṅga of the Lord fell down and the great destruction of the whole universe became imminent.

The sound of the Liṅga falling down was extremely terrible. There were terrible earthquakes and falling of comets and

1. After the Vedic period, people seem to have forgotten the identity of Rudra and Agni. They forgot that the *Liṅga* is a symbol of blazing flame of sacrificial fire. Though the procedure of Liṅga-worship and Fire-worship was the same (G.B. Dandage, *Yajña, Rudra* and *Śivaliṅga*) people in the Purāṇic period identified the Piṇḍī of Śiva with phallus. And to explain separateness of the Liṅga from Śiva's body a story for its fall was created.

There are different versions of the fall of Śiva's penis:

i. Pārvatī instigates Śiva to tempt the wives of sages in Dāruvana—an indecent act for which sages forced him to drop his penis.

ii. After self-immolation of Satī (Śiva's first wife) Śiva in his bereavement went a-begging in Dāruvana—a colony of sages. Wives of sages went after him and as a penalty Śiva was made to drop his penis.

iii. Śiva of his own accord cut down his own penis (Mbh, *Sauptika* 7.21). As Śiva is adorable, his penis too was regarded adorable. Versions (i) and (ii) above hint at the superiority of sages over Śiva.

meteors when the Liṅga of the Lord fell down. The tops of mountains fell down and the seas became dried up. The Devas became moody and dispirited.

All of them collected together and approached Brahmā Parameṣṭhin. With their palms joined in reverence they eulogized him with different kinds of hymns. The Lord of the universe with four lotus-like faces became delighted. He said to the distressed Suras: "Do not be grief-stricken. The Three-eyed Lord of Devas has been affected by the curse of Brāhmaṇas. When those Brāhmaṇas endowed with penance are pleased, he will become free (from the effect of the curse) again." O suppressor of enemies, on hearing this the Devas went back. All of them and the sages thought together, O descendant of Bharata. Along with Viśvāmitra, Vasiṣṭha, Jābāli, Kaśyapa and others they said to the Slayer of Tripura:

55-59. "O Lord of Suras, the spiritual splendour of the twice-born is extremely powerful. Endowed with forbearance and performing the penance, you shall become devoid of fatigue. Since it was due to the resentment of the sages that the excellent Liṅga of yours, O Mahādeva, fell down, it will not become worthy of being worshipped. The merit that men attain by worshipping the Liṅga cannot be obtained either by performing Agnihotra or Agniṣṭoma. By the words of Devas, Dānavas, Yakṣas, Gandharvas, Uragas, Rākṣasas and the Brāhmaṇas it will be worthy of being worshipped. It will be worthy of being worshipped by Brahmā, Viṣṇu, Indra and Candra. It is the benefit of your Liṅga in this world as well as in the other."

60-68. On being told thus, the Lord of the cosmos bowed down to the excellent Brāhmaṇas. Endowed with great delight he joined his palms in reverence and spoke: "Brāhmaṇas are mobile Tīrthas bereft of water. They can be desired by all. Dirty (sinful) people become purified by the water of the words of these Brāhmaṇas. There is no holy spot, no Tīrtha where after causing the anger of a Brāhmaṇa one can go and get purified. Even Puṣkaras (holy places) are Ūṣaras (arid lands). That which is not composed by Brāhmaṇas is no Śāstra; that which is not offered to a Brāhmaṇa is no Dāna; that which is no outcome of the favour of a Brāhmaṇa is no happiness; and that which is not caused by the anger of a Brāhmaṇa is no misery. All the Tīrthas throughout the earth and also Gaṅgā and other rivers do not deserve even a sixteenth part of one sentence of a Brāhmaṇa."

After duly honouring all the Brāhmaṇas, after being permitted by the great sages, the Lord went to the excellent bank of Narmadā.

The Lord observed the great Vrata, became engaged in Japa and Snāna and performed the penance for an Arbuda (many millions) of years residing in a Guhā (cave). When the observance was concluded, the Lord installed Maheśvara. Being saluted by the Suras, the Lord went to Kailāsa along with them.

Since Parameśvara had been installed on the banks of Narmadā by him, for that reason he is called Narmadeśvara.[1]

69-75. A Yati who has conquered all the sense-organs, who takes his holy bath and worships Mahādeva, Narmadeśvara (Lord of Narmadā), shall obtain the merit of a horse-sacrifice.

If anyone offers to the Pitṛs gingelly seeds, water, Kuśa grass and flowers, O son of Pāṇḍu, his ancestors of twenty-one generations rejoice in Svarga.

He who feeds Brāhmaṇas in that Tīrtha with milk pudding mixed with ghee, O king, obtains the merit accruing from a crore (i.e. feeding a crore of Brāhmaṇas elsewhere).

O Yudhiṣṭhira, he who stands in the middle of the water and offers gold or silver to Brāhmaṇas shall obtain the merit of Agniṣṭoma. He who approaches Narmadeśvara and stays there without food on the eighth or fourteenth lunar day shall attain the fruit of the (fulfilment of) birth.

He who enters burning fire in that Tīrtha, O king, shall be free from the fear of ailments for seven births, O descendant of Bharata.

He who abstains from food intake in that Tīrtha his goal shall be Rudraloka from where he will never return.

76-77. Thus the procedure of the pilgrimage and the origin thereof have been recounted to you, O excellent one among men. In the Purāṇa it has been laid down in detail. A man who glorifies the origin of Narmadeśvara and who listens to it with devotion shall obtain the merit of the holy ablution.

---

1. The Liṅga was installed by Lord Śiva himself on Narmadā and came to be called Narmadeśvara.

CHAPTER THIRTYNINE

The Greatness of Kapilā Tīrtha

Śrī Mārkaṇḍeya said:

1-9. From there, one should go to the excellent Tīrtha called Kapilā Tīrtha. By the holy ablution alone with devotion (in it), a man is liberated from all sins.

Yudhiṣṭhira said:

O excellent Brāhmaṇa, the greatness of Narmadeśvara, the cause of great wonder in all the worlds, has been recounted. Now do narrate to me Kapilā Tīrtha. At what time, in what connection did that excellent Tīrtha originate? O holy Lord, how was the meritorious Tīrtha that destroys all sins, originated?

Śrī Mārkaṇḍeya said:

Listen, O king, O descendant of Bharata, I shall extol the excellent Kapilā Tīrtha, on hearing which your surprise shall vanish entirely. Formerly in the beginning of Kṛtayuga, Brahmā, the grandfather of the worlds, created the entire range of living beings of four types. He was engaged in Japa and Homa thereafter devoutly. He meditated for a short while and stayed there at the sacrificial pit. From the blazing sacrificial pit, Kapilā (a tawny-coloured cow) rose up. Her horns were as refulgent as the flames of fire. The cow yielding good milk had three eyes. She was entirely fiery (in form) with a fiery back with all the limbs fiery. She had all the (good) characteristics. Her voice was as sweet as the jingling sound of a bell. On seeing that highly esteemed Kapilā in the centre of the sacrificial pit, Brahmā, the preceptor of the worlds, bowed down and spoke thus:

10-19. "O meritorious Kapilā, obeisance to you. O auspicious one bowed down to by all the worlds, O divine one, you are conducive to all auspiciousness, inimitable and incomparable in all the three worlds. You are Lakṣmī; you are Smṛti; you are intellect; you are fortitude. O lady of excellent countenance, you are well-known as Goddess Umā. You are Satī.

There is no doubt in this. You are the great Goddess Vaiṣṇavī; you are Mahādevī. O lady of excellent countenance, you are Brahmāṇī. O highly esteemed one, you are Kumārī. You are Bhakti (devotion) as well as Śraddhā (faith). You are Kālarātri unto living beings. You are the maiden Parameśvarī. You are the units of time: Lava, Truṭi, Muhūrta, Lakṣa, year, month, Kṣaṇa, entire Kāla. In the whole range of the three worlds consisting of mobile and immobile beings, there is nothing without you."

On being eulogized thus with honour by Parameṣṭhin, Kapilā said to the highly esteemed Lotus-born Lord: "O Lord of Devas, O preceptor of the universe, I am pleased with your words (Eulogy). What should I do to please you? (Lit 'what task tleasant to you can I do for you today?). Tell me everything, O Grandfather."

Brahmā said:

O Parameśvarī, you have been created by me for the sake of the welfare of the world. Hence, go to the mortal world from heaven with a desire for the welfare of all the worlds. You contain within you all the Devas. You are identical with all the worlds. If people offer (you) in accordance with the injunctions, they will have their residence in heaven.

After saying this[1] to Brahmā Goddess Parameśvarī came to the surface of the earth, duly venerated by Suras and Siddhas.

Yudhiṣṭhira said:

20-26. When, O dear one, at the instance of Brahmā, the splendid one came here, how were the Devas and the worlds stationed in her limbs? O excellent Brāhmaṇa, how did Kapilā settle herself in the Ūṣara (arid) Kṣetra? Tell me this.

Śrī Mārkaṇḍeya said:

On being told by Brahmā, the creator of the world, from

1. *'evam uktvā' tato devī brahmāṇam,'*: This text is corrupt. If emended as *'evam uktā tato devī brahmaṇā parameśvarī* 'When addressed thus by God Brahmā etc', the meaning becomes clear.

Brahmaloka she went to the meritorious Narmadā, the sanctifier of the worlds. She performed extensive austerities on Narmadā resorting to the banks. Then she wandered all over the earth, including the mountains, forests and parks. Ever since then, O great king, it became well known as the excellent Kapilā Tīrtha, destructive of all sins and resorted to by the groups of sages.

If one takes the holy bath in that Tīrtha in accordance with the injunctions and offers a Kapilā (tawny-coloured) cow, it is as good as the entire earth along with mountains, forests and parks has been gifted by him.

He who devoutly watches that cow being gifted to an excellent Brāhmaṇa, finds his sins accumulated in the course of a hundred years, perished. There is no doubt about this.

27-33a. Those Lokas, viz. Bhūḥ, Bhuvaḥ, Svaḥ, Mahaḥ, Jana, Satya and Tapas are stationed on her back, O excellent king.[1]

The Fire-god is stationed in the mouth; the serpents in the teeth; Dhātā and Vidhātā on the lips; Sarasvatī on the tongue; the thousand-rayed Lords, the Sun and the Moon, in the eyes; the Wind-god is stationed, O excellent king, at the centre of the nostrils. Mahādeva is on the forehead; Aśvins in the ears; Nara and Nārāyaṇa in the horns; the Grandfather in the middle of the horns; Kaṁbala and the noose-holding Varuṇa are stationed beneath. Yama, the holy Lord, has resorted to the belly and stationed there. The serpents are stationed in the hoofs; the rays of the Sun at the tip of the tail. Those who keep such a Kapilā in their houses, the Kapilā identical with all the Devas, are really blessed. There is no doubt about this.

33b-38. If anyone circumambulates a Kapilā after getting up early in the morning, it is as good as circumambulating the earth including mountains, forests and parks. One should bathe Śaṅkara with Kapilā-Pañcagavya (five milk-products from a tawny-coloured cow); he should observe fast at that Tīrtha. After taking the holy bath in accordance with the injunctions he should propitiate the Pitṛs and deities. All the members of his family including ten ancestors and ten successors become satisfied and ascend to heaven with his wishes in mind.

---

1. VV 27-37a describe how various parts of cow's body are occupied by Devas. Hence she is said to be "Constituted of Devas".

Thus the procedure (of pilgrimage) and the origin of Kapilā Tīrtha has been narrated to you as well as the benefit or the merit thereof, O excellent king. It is conducive to the attainment of wealth, fame and long span of life. It is an excellent one destroying all miseries. On listening to it, one is liberated from all sins. There is no doubt about it.

CHAPTER FORTY

The Greatness of Karañjeśvara Tīrtha

Śrī Mārkaṇḍeya said:

1-9. Therefrom a person should go to the excellent Tīrtha Karañjeśvara, O great king, where a Daitya became a Siddha and well-known in all the worlds.

Yudhiṣṭhira said:

O highly esteemed one, a person of great penance became a Śiddha in that Tīrtha. Whose son was he? How and at what time did he become a Siddha? Tell me, O Brāhmaṇa.

Śrī Mārkaṇḍeya said:

Formerly in Kṛtayuga, O king, a mental son of Brahmā named Marīci was born. He was conversant with the principles of the Vedas and Vedāṅgas.

He was a storehouse of penance. He too had a mental son after a great deal of time. His mental son was like another Brahmā.

Marīci had these qualities: forbearance, self-control, compassion, munificence, truthfulness, cleanliness and straightforwardness. O descendant of Bharata, the son too had all these qualities.

On seeing Kaśyapa, the excellent Brāhmaṇa endowed with all these good qualities, Dakṣa, the Prajāpati, gave him his daughters as wives. They were Aditi, Diti, Danu and ten others. They had sons and grandsons, O eminent descendant of Bharata.

Aditi gave birth to sons, the leader of whom was Indra. They were born of Kaśyapa, the Prajāpati, O mighty-armed one.

All the three great worlds including the mobile and immobile beings were pervaded by them. A highly esteemed son was born to Danu. He was named Karañja.

10-18. He was richly endowed with all good features. Even as a boy, he performed great penance after resorting to the banks of Narmadā. His penance was excellent and very severe. It continued for a thousand divine years. It consisted of Kṛcchra, Cāndrāyaṇa etc., O king.

His diet consisted of greens, roots and fruits. He regularly had holy bath and performed Homa. Mahādeva was pleased thereat and (came there) along with Umā.

The Lord, the Slayer of the Tripuras, offered him boons as he pleased: "O Karañja of great strength, I am pleased with you. O sinless one, choose a boon. I shall grant it except that of immortality."

Karañja said:

O Mahādeva, if you are pleased, if I am to be given a boon, then let my sons and grandsons be inclined towards righteousness.

Saying "So be it" and accompanied by Umā, the bull-vehicled Mahādeva vanished there itself along with his Gaṇas.

When the Lord had vanished, the Daitya installed Mahādeva after his name and joyously went home.

Ever since then that Tīrtha became the most excellent one of all the Tīrthas. Merely by taking his holy bath there a man is rid of all sins.

19-26. He who takes his bath in that Tīrtha and propitiates Pitṛs and deities shall undoubtedly attain the merit of Agniṣṭoma Yajña.

He who abstains from food-intake there in that Tīrtha, O king, goes to Rudraloka and never returns from there. O son of Dharma, he who abandons his life in its waters or in fire, dwells in the place of Śiva for twenty thousand years. When the merit is exhausted, he is born in a pure family. He becomes conversant with the Vedas and Vedāṅgas and efficient in all Śāstras. As a king or one of royal nobility he will live for a hundred years accompanied by sons and grandsons and devoid of all ailments.

Thus whatever was asked by you, O sinless one, has been recounted regarding the benefit of the Tīrtha as well as of the Snāna and Dāna there, O descendant of Bharata.

This story is meritorious, destructive of sins and evil dreams of those who read or listen to the excellent greatness of the Tīrtha. Śaṅkara has said that the merit is everlasting if a devotee reads this at the time of Śrāddha with devotion to the Pitṛs.

CHAPTER FORTYONE

The Greatness of Kuṇḍaleśvara Tīrtha

Śrī Mārkaṇḍeya said:

1-9. From there, a person should go to the excellent Kuṇḍaleśvara Tīrtha where the great Yakṣa Kuṇḍadhāra became a Siddha, O excellent king, after performing severe penance that caused fright to Suras and Asuras. He sported about in the palace of Paulastya, O excellent king.

Yudhiṣṭhira said:

In which Yuga was he born? Whose son was this highly intelligent one by whom Śaṅkara was propitiated by performing severe penance? O dear one, O sinless one, tell me this in detail. I don't feel satiated by listening to the excellent nectarine story.

Śrī Mārkaṇḍeya said:

Viśravas, son of Pulastya, was born in Tretā Yuga as son of Bharadvāja's daughter. He was on a par with Brahmā. He was much satisfied by his devout wife. He begot a son, Dhanada who (later on had lots of grandchildren) and was characterized by all good features.

As soon as he was born, Brahmā, the grandfather of the worlds, came to know of it and was delighted along with the sages and the Devas. He named the boy: "As you are born of Viśravas and became my grandson, O sinless one, the name

Vaiśravaṇa has been given to you. You will become the protector of the wealth of all the Devas. As the fourth guardian of quarters, you will be free from old age and death."

10-15. O great king, his wife was as well known as Īśvarī. The Yakṣa became the excellent Lord of Yakṣas. His son was Kuṇḍa.

He attained excellent physical form. With the permission of his parents, he went to the banks of Narmadā and performed severe penance. During summer he performed the penance in the centre of five fires; during rainy season he slept on bare ground; during Hemanta he stood in the middle of water; for a hundred years he took in only air (as food). When a hundred years were completed, he stood on a single toe, O king. Thereafter, as a mere skeleton, he raised his arms and stood thus. Kuṇḍala controlled his breath and performed the penance, O leader among the descendants of Bharata. In the fourth century of the years (of penance), the Bull-vehicled Lord became pleased (and said): "O dear one, choose a boon whatever you may wish for in your mind. I shall undoubtedly grant you the same."

Kuṇḍala said:

16-21. I should be invincible to all the enemies. Let me move about in the city of the Lord of Yakṣas with his favour. Let me move about as his attendant.

Saying "So be it", Mahādeva, venerated by all the worlds, went through the sky to Mountain Kailāsa.

When the Lord vanished, the Yakṣa installed the Lord of Devas, the excellent Kuṇḍaleśvara, joyously.

He adorned the Lord of the cosmos with flowers, unguents and incense, vehicles (*vimānaiḥ*), chowries and umbrellas and things causing satisfaction to the Liṅga[1].

After propitiating the Brāhmaṇas well with food, drink, ornaments etc., and pleasing Mahādeva he went to his abode.

Ever since then, that Tīrtha became well known in all the three worlds by the name Kuṇḍaleśvara. It is excellent and exceedingly meritorious.

---

1. *Pūraṇa* 'satisfaction' MW 642.

22-29. Anyone who is engaged in the observance of ritualistic fast at that Tīrtha and worships Īśāna, the Lord, becomes rid of all sins.

He who offers to Brāhmaṇas gold, silver, jewels or pearls and feeds them becomes happy. He rejoices in heaven.

One may belong to the Ṛk, Yajus or Sāma Śākhā of the Veda. If one takes the holy bath in the Tīrtha and recites a Ṛk Mantra, he enjoys the entire benefit (of reciting the Veda completely). Listen, O son of Pāṇḍu, to the benefit of one who offers a cow to Brāhmaṇas. He is honoured in Svarga Loka for as many thousands of years as there are hairs in it and in its progeny. He will attain residence in Svarga in the company of his sons and grandsons. The man of great esteem shall dwell in Svarga for so many years along with sons and grandsons.

A man who offers food there, goes to the world of Maheśa and dwells there for numerous years. There is no doubt about it. He becomes happy and rejoices in Svargaloka where Gandharvas, Siddhas and Apsarās sing.

Thus, O son of Dharma and Pṛthā, the whole of the power of the Tīrtha has been recounted to you. He who listens and eulogizes is rid of all sins and again comes back to these three worlds due to its prowess.

CHAPTER FORTYTWO

The Greatness of Pippalāda Tīrtha

Śrī Mārkaṇḍeya said:

1-7. Therefrom, one should go to the excellent Pippaleśvara where Pippalāda, a great Yogin of austere penance, became a Siddha.

Yudhiṣṭhira said:

O holy Sir, I wish to hear the story of Pippalāda[1] and the greatness of that Tīrtha where the great ascetic became a Siddha. Whose son was he? O highly esteemed one, why did he perform the penance? O sinless one, narrate this in full detail.

Mārkaṇḍeya said:

The highly venerable Yājñavalkya who had mastered the Vedas and Vedāṅgas performed an excellent penance while he was at Mithilā. The sister of the intelligent Yājñavalkya became a widow unfortunately in her seventh year itself. As a result of her previous Karma, she was also an orphan without her parents. In her husband's family too there was no one. Hence she was alone.

Wandering over the earth, she gradually came near her brother who was performing a penance with a desire for the other world and its happiness.

---

1. Pippalāda was an ancient sage who, according to *Praśna Upaniṣad*, imparted spiritual knowledge to sages such as Sukeśa, Śaibya and others. He visited Bhīṣma while the latter was on the bed of arrows (Mbh, *Śānti* 47.9).
The author of *Skanda* I.i.17 records him to be the son of Dadhīca and Suvarcas. When Dadhīca handed over his body to Devas Suvarcas placed the new-born baby under the shade of a Pippala tree which nursed it on its fruits. Hence the name.
The author of *Revākhaṇḍa*, in his enhusiasm to glorify a *Kṣetra* on Revā is insensitive to the reputation of the great sage Yājñavalkya, the court philosopher of Janaka of Mithilā.
He makes Pippalāda a bastard born of Yājñavalkya and his widowed sister. Pippalāda creates a Kṛtyā (Female Ogress) to kill Yājñavalkya who is shown to have run from Janaka and other gods.
Popular etymology of Pippalāda gave rise to such stories.

8-13. She attended to his needs and stayed there performing penance. On a certain occasion, she had her monthly course during the day when she took her bath. She saw a rag kept concealed and so wore it as her undergarment. In the meantime, at night Yājñavalkya had an erotic dream in a place where there was none. As a result of the dream, there was an emission of semen in his loin cloth. It resembled a drop of blood. Since he was refulgent with his austere penance, it had the lustre of fire. The poor Brāhmaṇa woke up and found the piece of cloth defiled. He thought it not worthy of being touched and so cast it off and washed himself clean in accordance with the injunctions in the Smṛti texts. Bath at night has been prohibited. So the Brāhmaṇa went to sleep again. At midnight the woman took this cloth and covered her vaginal aperture. In the morning the sage searched for his loin cloth here and there. Thereupon the Brāhmaṇa woman said: "Dear Sir, what are you searching for? What do you want? Tell me the fact."

Yājñavalkya said:

14-23. I had an unholy dream at night, O fair lady. My loin cloth became wet, which I kept aside. It is not to be seen now.

On hearing this statement, the Brāhmaṇa lady became excessively frightened, O king. She said: "O Brāhmaṇa, that piece of cloth was worn as an undergarment by me after my menstrual bath." On hearing her words the great sage burst out: "Alas! Alas!" and fell on the ground like a tree the root of which had been cut. Pure like the sky, the innocent lady asked: "What is this?" Consoling the Brāhmaṇa, she spoke thus: "Tell me the reason even if it were to be the uttermost secret, so that we shall ponder over it and get the remedy carried out." After reflecting for some time, he found it possible to speak. With a frightened mind, he spoke out. Listen to what he said, O king: "O lady of auspicious Vratas, it is none of your faults nor mine. Of the foetus in your womb, fate alone is the cause. It has to be carefully preserved by you forever. It should not be destroyed. It should be awaited till the whole period is over." The chaste lady was ashamed. Yet she said in distress, "So be it". She nurtured the child in the womb till the normal delivery.

As soon as the child was born, the Brāhmaṇa lady came to the root of a banyan tree. Abandoning the child there she spoke thus:

24-33. "May all those living beings in all the worlds, mobile and immobile, protect this child abandoned by me."

After saying this, the Brāhmaṇa lady went away, O excellent king.

The child in that plight lay still for a short while. Then it threw up the hands and legs winking the splendid eyes. Then it opened its eyes and cried making shockingly awful sounds. Due to the sound the mobile and immobile beings became frightened. The earth shook violently along with its mountains, forests and parks. On taking that hungry Brāhmaṇa child to be some great spirit, the tree continued to spread its shade over him. For the sake of drinking, the child had its nectarine exudation, O descendant of Bharata. Thus the boy grew up there. He delightedly pondered: 'What is the state of Planets in my case?' Thereupon the Planet of cruel movements (i.e. Saturn) was angrily looked at and Śanaiścara, the Planet of slow motion, fell suddenly on to the ground. Utterly frightened he joined his palms in veneration and said: "O Brāhmaṇa, O Pippalāda, O great sage! What is my offence, pray? I was moving in my orbit in the space. Why have I been caused to fall on the ground?" On being asked thus by the son of the Sun (i.e. Saturn), Pippalāda, the great sage, spoke these words angrily. Hear it, O king: "O Sauri (son of the Sun), O evil-minded one, why do you harass me, a child bereft of father and mother? Explain to me thoroughly."

Śanaiścara said:

34-45. Ruthlessness is my innate nature. My viewing is also likewise. Leave me free. I shall undoubtedly do what you ask me to do.

Pippalāda said:

From now onwards, children upto the age of sixteen should not be tormented by you. This condition has been stipulated, O Planet.

He said "Let it be so". After saying this, he went away and

returned. The Slow-moving One (Saturn) bowed down to the excellent sage and took the celestial path.

When he vanished, the boy of great tenacity thought of his father and was overwhelmed with anger. He concentrated his mind on fire and created fire there. He uttered Kṛtyā Mantras and performed Homa in the fire uttering "May the Kṛtyā issue forth". At once that girl adorned with clusters of flames and resembling fire came out and said: "What shall I do? Shall I dry up the seas? Shall I smash down the mountains? Shall I envelop the earth? Shall I make the firmament tumble down? On whose head shall I fall? O Brāhmaṇa, whom shall I slay? Let the task be mentioned quickly. Do not cause waste of time for me."

On hearing her words, Pippalāda of great austerity, got his eyes red in colour and spoke these words: "O auspicious lady, it was with great paroxysm of anger that you have been thought of by me. My father is Yājñavalkya. Fall on him. Do not delay." On being told thus, she went hurriedly exploding the firmament. Yājñavalkya, the noble-souled, highly intelligent, great sage was performing penance staying at Mithilā. The highly refulgent sage looked around at the various quarters when he saw the great spirit having the lustre of fire and the sun, present there.

46-58. On seeing it arriving suddenly, the great sage became very frightened. Pursued by the spirit he went to King Janaka. "Know that I, ordinarily a refuge to others, have come to you (for protection), O excellent king. If you are capable, O king, save me from the terror of the great spirit." The king spoke these words: "The spirit has originated from Brāhmaṇical splendour. It cannot be restrained. It is difficult to overcome. I cannot protect you."

Thereafter the great ascetic went to another excellent king, seeking refuge. Abandoned by him, he went to the abode of Indra out of fear. The trembling Brāhmaṇa repeatedly said: "O king of Devas, I offer obeisance to you. Save me from the fear of the great spirit."

On hearing his words, the King of Devas said this: "I am unable to save you from the fury of a Brāhmaṇa."

Then that Brāhmaṇa, the most excellent one among the knowers of Brahman, went to Brahmā's abode and then to

Viṣṇuloka. He was addressed by him too in the same way. Then, O king, the sage became distressed and lost hope of remaining alive. Pursued by the spirit he went to the abode of Śaṅkara. Yājñavalkya who was endowed with the power of Yoga, O son of Pāṇḍu, concealed himself in the middle of the flesh and nail (of Lord Śiva) so much so that even the Lord could not see.

At last the spirit arrived there blazing with the lustre of fire and the sun. It said to Maheśvara, the Lord of Devas: "Leave off, leave off the person." On being told thus by that spirit, O descendant of Bharata, Mahādeva showed the leading Yogin between the nail and the flesh. The Lord of goblins subdued the spirit and said to the sage who had been in great danger: "O great sage, O Brāhmaṇa, do not be afraid. Come out." Thereafter on seeing the spirit settled in a very subtle body, he asked thus: "O great spirit, what will you do with him? Tell me."

The Kṛtyā said:

59-66. O Lord of Devas, I have been thought of by Pippalāda overwhelmed with anger. I shall destroy his body. O Lord, I have been invoked for doing this act of violence.

On hearing these words that had escaped from the mouth of the spirit, Mahādeva, conversant with Mantras whispered some Mantras to Yājñavalkya who was stationed in his waist. O Yudhiṣṭhira, he gave the Brāhmaṇa the name Yogīśvara. The Lord of Devas discharged him and vanished there itself.

Pippalāda had sent away that spirit. But he was gloomy on account of his parents. He resorted to the bank of Narmadā and performed penance standing on a single toe and abstaining from food till his sixteenth year. O king, he thus propitiated the Lord of Devas, Śaṅkara along with Umā. Thereafter Śaṅkara who was pleased with him spoke these words:

Īśvara said:

O Brāhmaṇa of good holy rites, I am pleased with your penance. Choose a boon wished for by you mentally. I shall grant it.

Pippalāda said:

If the Lord is pleased with me, if a boon has to be granted to me, O Lord Maheśvara, be present in this Tīrtha here.

67-74. On being told thus, the Lord said to Pippalāda, the great sage, "So be it" and vanished along with the groups of goblins.

After the Lord had gone Pippalāda took his holy bath in the great waters, installed Mahādeva and went to Uttara Parvata (Northern Mountain). A person should take his holy bath devoutly in the Tīrtha there, uttering the relevant Mantras, O king, propitiate Pitṛs and Devas and worship Maheśvara. He shall get the excellent benefit of Aśvamedha Yajña (horse-sacrifice). On death he goes to the city of Rudra. No doubt should there be in this connection.

With the Pitṛs in view, the devotee should feed Brāhmaṇas, O descendant of Bharata. They will rejoice in heaven for twelve years.

If any one adopts Sannyāsa and abandons his body in the Tīrtha, his goal (destination) shall be Rudraloka from where he will never return.

Thus everything that was asked by you (i.e. the greatness and the origin of the Pippalāda Tīrtha), O sinless one, has been explained.

This is meritorious, destructive of sins, conducive to wealth, dispelling evil dreams and all the sins of those who read or listen to shall be dispelled.

CHAPTER FORTYTHREE

The Greatness of Vimaleśvara Tīrtha

Śrī Mārkaṇḍeya said:

1-8. From there, O great king, a pilgrim should go to the excellent Vimaleśvara. There the divine rock (Devaśilā, the divine slab) is beautiful, made by Devas themselves. The person should take his holy bath there with devotion and adore

Brāhmaṇas. O king, even with the least of Dāna he will gain much. There is no limit thereto.

Yudhiṣṭhira said:

O great Brāhmaṇa, what are those Dānas considered praiseworthy in the world, on offering which devoutly a man becomes liberated from all sins?

Śrī Mārkaṇḍeya said:

Gold, silver, copper, jewels, pearls, plots of land and cows gifted liberate a man from inauspiciousness.

He who abandons his life in that Tīrtha shall reside in Rudraloka as long as the ultimate destruction of all living beings.

From there he should go to Puṣkariṇī that is destructive of all sins. After taking the holy bath there, he should adore Lord Divākara (Sun-god), a mass of splendour.

He should recite a Ṛk or a Sāman hymn. He shall attain the benefit of reciting Sāmaveda.

By uttering a Mantra of Yajurveda or Ṛgveda he will attain the benefit of reciting (the whole of) Yajurveda or Ṛgveda similarly.

Meditating on Divākara he should recite the Mantra or even a syllable thereof. By the Japa of *Ādityahṛdaya* one is liberated from all sins.

9-18. The devotee should take his holy bath in that Tīrtha and duly adore Brāhmaṇas. His merit becomes a crore times more. There is no doubt about it.

One who dies in that Tīrtha through abstention from food-intake, or by entering fire, or falling into the waters or by jumping from the rocky precipice attains the great goal (Mokṣa). O excellent king, a Brāhmaṇa, or a Kṣatriya, or a Vaiśya or a Śūdra performing the duties laid down, shall attain the greatest goal (Mokṣa).

Yudhiṣṭhira said:

Tell me the means whereby all the different Varṇas (castes) become freed from all sins after knowíng ailments, loss of energy and delusion.

Śrī Mārkaṇḍeya said:

A Brāhmaṇa devoid of lust and anger, forsaking his life through fasts, obtains the goal of the good by making use of gingelly seeds mixed with water (for libation) and gingelly oil for head bath. A Kṣatriya shall attain the goal of the good by courting death in battle. In case there is no war, O highly intelligent one, he shall obtain the same through service. One suffering from a chronic illness or under the adverse influence of evil Planets or a very old man or one whose sense-organs have been impaired, should burn himself in fire duly and obtain the goal of the good.

A Vaiśya too abandoning his life in this manner shall attain auspiciousness. With purity of feelings, he should abandon himself into the waters and attain the status of Śiva.

A Śūdra too obtains good goal by serving Brāhmaṇas and propitiating Maheśvara. Otherwise he is not liberated. The sinner falls certainly into hell.

Or if he is unable to make use of Praṇava, or to offer gifts to Brāhmaṇas as well as the preceptor, he should dry up his body in the five fires after taking leave of excellent Brāhmaṇas.

19-26. He should take leave of Brāhmaṇas who are quiescent, have self-control, have controlled anger and who have mastered scriptures and are very efficient. He should prepare Karīṣāgni (fire of dry cowdung) with their advice (to burn himself).

Thus the Varṇas become deluded by arrogance, by following wrong methods(?) Just as a blind man falls into the cave of a mountain so also they fall into a terrible hell.

Those who eschew the injunctions of the scriptures and behave as they please, are born as worms. No balls of rice are offered to them nor need they be offered libation and other rites.

Those who resort to activities according to their whims and fancy, abandoning the pious rites mentioned in the Śruti and Smṛti do fall into hell. O Yudhiṣṭhira, there are twenty-eight crores of Narakas (Hells). They may fall into any or all of these hells. Human birth is rarely achieved, O king. It is acquired by means of many pious rites.

Being born as a man, one who eschews arrogance and malice,

controlling himself always, he alone can be called *Jñānacakṣuḥ* ('Knowledge-eyed' i.e. wise)

If one is blinded by the Timira (disease of the eye, darkness) of ignorance and one's eye is not opened by the application of collyrium of perfect knowledge, one should be known as congenitally blind.

O excellent king, thus everything that was asked by you has been explained.

27-33. As uttered by Rudra himself, Narmadā is the most excellent of all rivers and has issued forth from Rudra's body. She shall redeem all living beings, mobile and immobile. This highly meritorious river has been made to come down for the benefit of all the worlds, by the noble-souled Īśvara, the presiding deity of all the Devas.

The sins committed mentally, verbally and physically perish as a result of the holy bath. This river has come out of Rudra's body. Hence she is highly meritorious. Everyday a devotee should get up in the morning and step on the ground devoutly. Then he should recite this Mantra. O dear one, he attains the benefit of the holy bath: "Obeisance, O divine one of meritorious waters. Obeisance to one that flows towards the ocean. O redeemer from sins, I make obeisance to you. Obeisance, O excellent-countenanced divine one. Obeisance to you who are served by groups of excellent sages. Obeisance to you who have issued forth from the body of the Three-eyed Lord. Obeisance to you who are the most excellent one of those of holy activities. Obeisance to you who are the perpetual sanctifier of all holy ones."

CHAPTER FORTYFOUR

Eulogy of Śūlabheda

Śrī Mārkaṇḍeya said:

1-8. Listen, O king, to that Tīrtha which is the most excellent one of all the Tīrthas. It has been created by the Trident-bearing Lord on the southern bank of Revā. It has been created, O excellent king, for the salvation of all great men.

Yudhiṣṭhira said:

O excellent Brāhmaṇa, various pious rites have been heard by me with your favour. All the Dānadharmas and different kinds of Tīrthas also have been heard. I wish to hear about another thing whereby Saṁsāra (worldly existence) is cut off and salvation is attained and there is no rebirth. Do recount all these things. Please do me this favour, O excellent Brāhmaṇa.

Śrī Mārkaṇḍeya said:

Listen with single-minded attention to the Tīrtha greater than the other Tīrthas. On hearing its power, one is rid of the sins committed during a year, whether the sins be verbal or mental or particularly physical. By glorifying that Tīrtha one is liberated from all sins.

The Tīrtha extends to five Krośas, O king. It bestows worldly pleasures and salvation. It is divine and beneficent to the living beings that commit sinful deeds.

On the southern bank (of Revā) there is a mountain named Bhṛgu. It is on its top that the Tīrtha has been established by Śambhu.

9-20. It is well known as Śūlabheda in all the three worlds, O king. The trees that grow there in all the four quarters of the Tīrtha undoubtedly go to the abode of Rudra when they fall down.

The creatures and birds on the earth that die there in that Tīrtha go to the greatest world. There is no doubt about it.

The Gaṅgā that issues from Pātāla is called Bhogavatī. She has come out through Śūlabheda. She is destructive of all sins. There is another great meritorious river named Gīrvāṇa flowing there into the middle of the Kuṇḍa which has been dug up by the Trident-bearing Lord by piercing with it (i.e. his trident).

Then the ancient river Sarasvatī issued forth, O king, which redeems one from all sins.

In the place where these three including Bhāsvatī flow and where there is the rock called Gīrvāṇa there is a Tīrtha the like of which was never before nor will there ever be (hereafter).

Kedāra, Prayāga, Kurukṣetra, Gayā and other excellent Tīrthas do not merit even a sixteenth fraction of that Tīrtha. Five holy places are separate Tīrthas. I shall recount them in aggregate succinctly and then each one separately.

Just as Gayā is meritorious in Nābhī, Cakratīrtha is on a par with it. Just as Kūpa (Well) in Dharmāraṇya is meritorious, Śūlabheda is on a par with it. Just as Brahmayūpa is meritorious, the case of Devanadī is of that sort. Just as Gayāśiras is meritorious, so also is the Śilā (Rock) of the Suras; just as the Puṣkara shrine, so also is Mārkaṇḍahrada. Offering balls of rice and libation of water to Pitṛs there is everlasting to the Pitṛs. He who performs Śrāddha there and drinks the water everyday is liberated from all sins like a serpent which is liberated from its slough. The devotee should honour unblamable Brāhmaṇas bereft of arrogance and anger.

21-28. A Dāna rite extending to thirteen days shall be thirteen times more meritorious.

By visiting the venerated God Gaṇanātha with a countenance resembling that of an elephant, all obstacles perish after seeing the Lord of Kaṁbala Kṣetra. One should worship with great devotion, Maheśvara with the trident in his hand. Umā has to be carefully adored to the east of the Lord. Thereafter the person shall devoutly worship Mārkaṇḍeśa residing in the cave. He is liberated from all sins committed knowingly and unknowingly.

One who has entered the centre of the cave should recite the three-syllabled Sūkta (or Sūkta beginning with *tri-aṁbakam yajāmahe*). He will obtain a sixth fraction of the merit accruing from Nīlaparvata. Trinaras (? three men) stand there with the Ādityas and Maruts.

Excellent is the Koṭiliṅga Sthāna full of all the Devas. Just as all the rivers ultimately get merged in ocean, so also the sins perish by visiting Śūlabheda, the proof of which is directly perceived even today, O king.

29-34. Sparks appear in the centre of the Liṅga when bathed. The second proof there is that a drop of oil does not spread. This is the proof originating from the power of Śūlabheda.

He who remembers Śūlabheda everyday three times shall become purified internally and externally, O king.

Though I had been asked even by Suras, it was not mentioned to anyone by me. The Tīrtha has to be treated as the greatest secret of all secrets.

It should always be considered secret. It is destructive of all sins, of all defects. It is meritorious and excellent, O Lord of people. Śūlabheda is the Tīrtha full of all Tīrthas. When its power is heard one is rid of all sins.

O dear one, Śūlabheda has been succinctly narrated to you. A man who devoutly listens to it is rid of all sins.

CHAPTER FORTYFIVE

Andhaka Gets a Boon

Śrī Mārkaṇḍeya said:

1-8. This very question was put to Maheśvara formerly by King Uttānapāda in the assembly of sages and Devas.

Uttānapāda said:

This Tīrtha is extremely meritorious and full of all Devas. It is considered as more secret than others so much so that no other more secret place has been heard or seen. How did Śūlabheda come into being? By whom has it been created? O Lord, tell me in detail the greatness of that Tīrtha.

Īśvara said:

Formerly there was a Dānava of great vigour, arrogant of his strength. No man was great in strength like him. He was son of Brahmā's son. He was irrepressibly arrogant and his name was Andhaka. Staying in his own abode, he, the sinner, ruled his kingdom bereft of thorns (opponents). He was well nourished and highly delighted. He stayed in the mortal world but he could not be assailed by the Suras. The abode of that sinner was as though a garden of fire.

In the meanwhile, O descendant of Bharata, he thought thus on a certain occasion: 'I shall propitiate Mahādeva whereby he will bless me. I will request him for a divine boon which is in my mind.'

After resolving thus, Andhaka went out of his house.

9-17. He reached the bank of Revā. The Dānava performed

a fierce and severe penance that caused hairs to stand. He abstained from food for a thousand divine years. The second thousand of divine years, he spent taking in only water. In the third thousand, he was engaged in inhaling smoke. For the fourth space of thousand years, he practised Yoga. No one before had performed an extremely fierce penance of this sort. O descendant of Bharata, (his) only the bones and skin (in his body) remained.

A column of smoke rose from his head, O king, which went beyond Devaloka and remained pervading Kailāsa.

Then Umā who was seated near the Lord spoke these words: "Who is this engaged in fierce penance in the human world? O Parameśvara, four thousand years have elapsed. Such a penance has never been performed by anyone. A penance like this has not been seen or heard. O Lord, why are you indifferent in regard to this devotee endowed with regular observances. O Lord, you grant boons quickly to all others with less penance. O Maheśvara who are reputed to be a lover of devotees, until this Dānava is raised up (from penance) I would rather not play the game of dice with you."

Īśvara said:

18-26. Excellent! Excellent! O great goddess marked with all auspicious characteristics, I do not know that the great Dānava is undergoing sufferings. O fair lady, he has established himself in the Yogic practice meditating on the greatest position (Brahman). Come with me to the place where he is performing his penance.

After saying this, Lord Maheśvara went there accompanied by Umā. He was seen by Lord Śaṁbhu as one reduced to mere bones and skin. The delighted Maheśvara, the Lord of Devas, said: "Oh! A strenuous feat has been displayed by you, terrible, awe-inspiring and causing horripilation! Why have you, O dear one, performed such a terrible penance? I shall grant you the boon, O dear one, whatever may be in your mind."

Andhaka said:

If you are pleased with me, O Lord, if you wish to grant a

boon, O Śaṅkara, O Maheśvara, I shall vanquish all the Suras with your favour.

Īśvara said:

The Devas should never be fought with, even in dream. What is impossible should not be mentioned—what is not appealing to the mind. Request for something else which may be in your mind. You will enjoy different kinds of pleasures in the mortal worlds or Pātālas on a par with the pleasures of Svarga. Do rule the kingdom without impediments, like the Lord of Devas in Svarga.

27-33. On hearing the words of the Lord, Andhaka stood there disappointed and gloomy. He said: "My painful struggles and austerities have become futile. Nothing has been achieved by me." He took a deep sigh and fell on the ground like a tree the roots of which have been cut. He lay breathless.

On seeing him senseless, the Goddess spoke these words: "O Śaṅkara, grant this (Dānava) whatever he desires. If you neglect your devotees, it will result in your disrepute."

Īśvara said:

O goddess, if I grant him the boon in accordance with his wish, then he will never care for Viṣṇu, Brahmā, even for me and also other Suras. O goddess of Devas, having attained the height of power, he will slight and disregard all.

The Devī said:

O Maheśvara, lift him up by some means. Let a boon be granted like "Conquer all the Suras except Viṣṇu."

Īśvara said:

34-41. This is the same splendid way, O fair lady, as has occurred to my mind. I shall grant him the boon as has been suggested by you.

Then being sprinkled with nectar, he became normal and peaceful in a moment. He was refreshed with all the limbs having regained their splendour.

The Lord said:

Listen with concentrated mind. Accept the excellent boon. I shall grant you what pleases you excluding the operation thereof against Viṣṇu. Everything shall be successful in your case. Let not your righteousness be otherwise. O Asura, if you are inclined (to accept) I shall grant you the boon. You will conquer all the Suras, excluding Viṣṇu and me.

Andhaka said:

Let it be so. Relying on my strength alone, O Maheśvara, I shall conquer (all) excluding Viṣṇu. I have become contented. O Lord, do go along with Umā to the excellent peak of Kailāsa.

After this riding on his great bull, the Lord who had granted him the boon, vanished there itself along with Umā.

CHAPTER FORTYSIX

Abduction of Śacī

Śrī Mārkaṇḍeya said:

1-4. After getting the boon, the Dānava went to his city. It had quadrangles of diverse types. There were many gardens full of plantain groves, jackfruit trees, Bakulas, mangoes, Āmrātakas, Campakas, Aśokas, coconut trees, pomegranates, citrons and various other kinds of fine trees. There were many lakes beautifying the gardens. The temples of divine features were decorated with a series of banners and festoons. The whole place reverberated with the sounds of the chanting of the Vedas and other auspicious passages and musical notes.

5-13. He entered his divine abode made of gold and golden strings and saw his sons, wife, ministers, servants and slaves. Then he saw many persons shouting cries of victory and running about here and there. With ensigns and banners raised up, they revealed the radiance of their hearts. Some of them tied festoons and raised arched doorways. Some of them scattered flowers. Others rushed towards Andhaka to greet him with citrons in their hands. Some people in the city were seen holding vessels filled with cooked food. There itself many people were seen with hands full. There hundreds and thousands of women held pots filled with raw rice-grains. The Brāhmaṇas recited Mantras and the women (sang) auspicious songs. The Ministers and the servants brought elephants as presents. Everyone of the citizens felicitated him. He saw all including the cavalry and infantry in motion. He saw the treasuries filled with gold. He saw she-buffaloes, cows, bulls and umbrellas.

In this way Andhaka lived in the mortal world for some time with feelings of elation and satisfaction. He was never attacked by Suras.

14. After coming to know that he had secured great boons the heaven-dwellers began to feel apprehensive. They collected together and sought refuge in Indra.

Śakra said:

15-23. How is it that all the heaven-dwellers have come here? Wherefrom has fear arisen in your case? Why have you come seeking refuge?

Thereupon all the Devas spoke these words to Śakra:

The Devas said:

O Lord of Suras, there is a Daitya named Andhaka. He has become all the more powerful on account of the boons granted by Śaṁbhu. He is invincible unto all the Devas. What should be done now? O Lord of Devas, consider this yourself. What means should be employed?

Thus the Devas spoke to Śakra. Then they had mutual consultation. While they were doing so, the Dānava came to know of it through the reports made by the spies. On coming to know about the congregation of the Devas, the Dānava came out of his abode alone, seated in his chariot and equipped with many weapons. O king, he passed over the impassable upper ridge of Meru sportingly. It had been strengthened with golden ramparts. The upper surface of Meru was rendered splendid through different kinds of hermitages. It was very difficult for the hordes of enemies to gain access to that place, O excellent king. The Asura however entered that place sportingly (and without effort) as though it was his own abode. The Slayer of Vṛtra (i.e. Indra) became afraid and he offered his own seat. Andhaka sat there on the splendid seat of Śakra himself. He surveyed the entire place full of the Devas all round.

Śakra said:

24-33. What is the purpose of your visit to this place? Do tell me. O Dānava, whatever wealth we possess, I shall hand over to you.

Andhaka said:

I do not desire the wealth, nor elephants, O Lord of Suras; show me your great elephant Airāvata embellished with all heavenly ornaments. Show me the horse Uccaiḥśravas, the jewels (beauties) beginning with Urvaśī. O Lord of heaven, show me the flowers of Pārijātaka and the many varieties of trees. O Consort of Śacī, show me all the kinds of musical instruments.

On hearing these words of his, Śakra thought thus (in his mind): 'I don't see at all anyone who can kill this sinner. (If) the heavenly world is miserable, there is no one to accord it protection.' Frightened thus, he gave the musical instruments and other things. After making the Asura seated on the stage, he made the groups of Apsarās perform the Tāṇḍava dance. All the Suras including Yama, Māruta and Kinnaras also sat there. O king, one by one all the Apsarās beginning with Urvaśī danced before him to the accompaniment of songs and musical notes of the instruments. His mind was never at rest. (His mind was not satisfied) after witnessing the Apsarās, O king; his mind became enamoured of Śacī. He seized Śakra's wife and proceeded towards his city. Thereupon the war between Andhaka and the Suras ensued.

34-38. With different kinds of weapons such as discus, thunderbolt and other heavy means of fighting all the groups of the Devas were smashed, O excellent king, in the war. All the Suras became distressed. They were destroyed in many ways. All the Māruts were broken down at the war front. Just as a single lion walks (triumphantly) through the forest after killing all the elephants, so also he, single-handedly defeated all of them and routed them. Just as the immature lord of a village may harass all the people and seize wealth and garments and never feels the harassment of subjects for himself, so also that great Dānava seized Śakra's wife and went away.

CHAPTER FORTYSEVEN

Devas Return to Svarga

Śrī Mārkaṇḍeya said:

1-3. All the Gīrvāṇas (Devas) sought refuge in Brahmā. They reached the world of Brahmā, riding on their elephants having the size of excellent mountains, horses comparable to elephants, chariots having the size of a city fitted with lions and tigers, and also on tortoises, buffaloes and crocodiles. The Devas reached the world of Brahmā with Śakra as their leader. On seeing the Lotus-born Lord, the Suras prostrated themselves with the eight limbs touching the ground.

The Devas said:

4-6. Be victorious, O Lord worthy of being respected by the whole universe. Be victorious, O cause of the worldly existence. O most excellent one among Suras, O (Lord) having lotus as your source of origin, we have sought refuge in you alone.

On hearing the distressful words of Devas of purified souls, he (Brahmā) spoke to Devarāja (Indra) in a voice deep and majestic like the rumbling of clouds:

"Why have you come here, O Devas? Wherefore is this pallor seen on the face of everyone? By whom have all of you been insulted. May this be reported to me quickly."

The Devas said:

7-11. O Lotus-born Lord, the great Daitya named Andhaka is enormously powerful. By him all the groups of the Devas have been deprived of their wealth and jewels. After killing groups of Devas by means of sword, discus and axe, that Dānava abducted Śakra's wife forcibly and went away.

* * *

On hearing the words of the Devas, Brahmā, the grandfather of the worlds, began to ponder, O great king, about the means of slaying the Dānava: "The sinful Dānava cannot be killed by you all the heaven-dwellers. He (i.e. Viṣṇu) is the saviour of all the worlds. There is no one else."

Thus all the Suras were addressed by Brahmā. Thereafter, keeping Brahmā at the head, all of them went to the place where Keśava was present. They (Brahmā and others) eulogized the Discus-bearing Lord by means of hymns of prayer.

The Devas said:

12-19. O Lord of the chiefs of Devas, O Lord whose bosom has been resorted to by Lakṣmī, be victorious. O Lord of Devas, O destroyer of Asuras, we have sought refuge in you.

On being eulogized by all the Suras beginning with Brahmā, Janārdana became pleased in his mind and said to the groups of the Suras:

Śrī Vāsudeva said:

Welcome unto the Devas and Vipras. Today the night has dawned very well (by your arrival). What is your task on hand? Let it be mentioned quickly. With whom are the heaven-dwellers angry? What is your misery? What is your distress? Whence has terror originated? O highly blessed ones, mention the cause thereof and whatever lurks in your minds. Today let that person who has caused discomfiture (to you) go to the abode of Yama.

On being told thus by Kṛṣṇa, they all said, shyly pointing out their bodies and bowing down their heads: "O Lord, we have been deprived of our kingdom by Andhaka and hence rendered lustreless and lacking all radiance. O Lord, protect us like a father protecting the son. Slay the enemy of Indra along with his sons and grandsons." The Lotus-seated One (i.e. Brahmā) also said thus. Thereupon the great Lord whose lotus-like feet have been bowed down to by Suras and Asuras, and who was equipped with the conch, discus, club and bow, got up from the couch of serpent. He stood in front of the Devas.

Śrī Vāsudeva said:

20-22. I will kill that sinner by whom the Suras have been harassed, (wherever he happens to be) whether he stays in Pātāla, mortal world or in heaven itself. May the Devas go to their own abode contented with enhanced energy.

On hearing those words of Viṣṇu, all of them beginning with Brahmā and including Vāsava, bowed to Hari delightedly and went to heaven by means of their respective vehicles.

CHAPTER FORTYEIGHT

Andhaka Blessed

Uttānapāda said:

1-6. O Lord, in which place did that Andhaka, the great Daitya, stay? After conquering all the Devas which place did he resort to?

Śrī Maheśa said:

O king, I shall tell you the place which the Dānava resorted to after reaching Pātāla. He began to ravish girls. Keśava came to know that the Dānava was staying there. He took up the bow and discharged an Agni missile, intending, 'Let him (Andhaka) be burned.'

When he was scorched by fire, he (Andhaka) discharged a Vāruṇa missile. The Āgneya missile was subdued by the great Vāruṇa missile.

Then he began to think, 'By whom has this arrow been discharged? Whose is this manly power? Who will (hence) go to the abode of Yama?'

Thereupon the demon Andhaka, infuriated in the battle, set out along the path of the arrow and saw Janārdana with the bow kept ready in his hand.

Andhaka said:

7-14. You will not be happy any more, that you have been

seen by me. Just as an elephant cannot escape from the sight of a tiger, so you too cannot go. When a mouse falls a prey to a cat, it cannot get away. You are in a similar plight in front of me.

I am going to send you along the terrible path of Yama. I have been searching for you and was about to proceed towards your abode. But, O Keśava, you have been brought into a straight fight with me by Kāla. All those many Dānavas who were defeated earlier by you were not men, they were only women, O Keśava. But I will not fight with you by means of any weapon.

Even as the great Dānava spoke thus, Keśava did not become angry. On seeing him not caring to fight, the Dānava thought thus: 'I shall have a (wrestling) duel with him.' After resolving thus, O king, he fought. He was kicked down to the ground by Kṛṣṇa with his foot.

Within a short while he composed himself and got up. Realizing that he was incompetent for a full-fledged duel, he began to employ the expedient of Sāman (peaceful overtures). He brought together the palms with pure intentions and prostrated himself with eight limbs touching the ground.

Andhaka said:

15-24. Be victorious; obeisance to Kṛṣṇa, Hari, Viṣṇu, the victorious. Be victorious, O Hṛṣīkeśa. Obeisance to the creator of the universe, to the noble-souled Acyuta. Obeisance to the lotus-navelled one. Obeisance to the Lord having lotus garlands, to Śrīśa (Lord of Śrī), to Janārdana, to the yellow-robed one. O Śrīpati, be victorious. Perpetual obeisance to Govinda. Obeisance to the Lord lying down in the ocean. Obeisance to the roaring Narasiṁha of a hideous face. Obeisance to Śārṅgin, of dark complexion, holding the conch, discus and club. Obeisance to you, the Lord in the form of Vāmana, to the Lord in the form of Yajña. Obeisance to the Lord in the form of Varāha; to the Lord who measured the three worlds with (three) steps. Obeisance, obeisance to Keśava who has pervaded all the quarters. O Vāsudeva, obeisance to you. Obeisance to the destroyer of Kaiṭabha. Obeisance to you, O most excellent one among Suras, O leader of Suras, O resort of Lakṣmī. I bow unto all those who pay respects to Viṣṇu, the Lord of Devas, to Prajāpati, the creator of the universe. I bow unto all those who make obeisance to the intelligent Vāsudeva, the Lord of the entire range of living beings. I bow unto all those who make obeisance to Viṣṇu of immeasurable brilliance, the Yajñavarāha (the boar of sacrificial features). Again and again I make obeisance unto you, the storehouse of all Guṇas. O Lord, O ocean of mercy, O Lord fond of all devotees and all forms of devotion!

Śrī Bhagavān said:

25-28. O great Dānava, I am pleased with you. Choose any boon as desired. I shall grant you a boon even if it be something rare in all the three worlds.

Andhaka said:

O Lord, if you are pleased with me and are willing to grant me a desired boon, O Lord, then do grant me the favour of a fight with you that is extremely splendid. Thereupon, sanctified by your hands, I shall go to splendid worlds.

Śrī Bhagavān said:

How can I fight with you now that I have been propitiated by you? My anger cannot be aroused against you, O Andhaka. How will I then fight? You are undoubtedly inclined towards combat. If so, do go to fight with Lord Maheśvara.

Andhaka said:

29-36. There my objective is not achieved.

Śrī Bhagavān said:

Son, go and shake the peak (of Kailāsa) with all your might. When the peak is shaken the Lord of Devas shall become terribly infuriated. O Dānava, the enraged Śaṅkara shall grant you the favour of a terrible fight.

At the instance of Viṣṇu, the sinful Dānava went to the place where Maheśvara was present. After reaching the Kailāsa peak, he shook it frequently. When the peak was shaken, all the three worlds too shook. The many summits of the peaks shook and fell down. O king, soon the four oceans became one. Meteors fell and many trees tumbled down. In the company of Umā, the Lord became surprised. Goddess Girijā closely embraced the Lord and spoke these words: "O Lord, why does this mountain shake? Why does this earth quake? Why do the serpent Śeṣa, the mortal world and the nether worlds shake? Is this the utter annihilation of the Yuga? It behoves you to narrate it to me."

Īśvara said:

37-44. Whose mind has become wicked? Who has put his hand into the mouth of the serpent? On whose forehead Varman[1] (coat of mail?) has been put? He will go to the abode of Yama. I have been asleep after resorting to Kailāsa. Undoubtedly if anyone wakes me up and comes face to face with me I will kill him.

The Lord of Devas further thought, 'There is no doubt about this that this is Andhaka.' Thereafter he considered the means whereby he could be easily killed in an instant.

All the Suras headed by Brahmā came along with the Vasus. He made a chariot consisting of all the Devas.[2] Some of the Devas stationed themselves in the wheel; some at the tip and the sides of the snout. Some of the Devas stationed themselves on the navel and some on the *Dhuryas* (forepart of the poles of the chariot). Some remained steady on the *Dhuris* (foremost part on the chariot) and some on the *Yūpas*. Some of them were the supporting pillars of the *Syandana* (chariot). Some were *Syandanaveṣṭakas* (serving as cover of the chariot). Others stationed themselves on *Āmalasāraka* (a part of the chariot) and still others stationed themselves on its pot-like dome. Thus the divine chariot rendered splendid by the banners, garlands etc., became terrifying to the enemies. After making this chariot consisting of the Devas, Maheśvara, the preceptor of the uni-

1. Probably 'Karman' as *Va* (व) and *Ka* (क) are similar in Devanāgarī script. If emended thus it means 'On whose forehead is this act imprinted (i.e. to whom has this act been allotted by Destiny)?'
2. An echo of the chariot prepared for killing Tripurāsura. Here the names of gods so employed are not given.

verse, ascended it. With anger the Lord set out to the place where the Dānava was present.

45-58. He said, "Stop! Stop! O evil-minded one, where do you go?" Taking up the bow in his hand, he discharged arrows at the Dānava. When the Dānava stood firm in the battle, the Lord cut off his arrows. Andhaka was then covered (with a volley of arrows). Neither the sun nor the sky, nor the moon were to be seen there. The Dānava then discharged the Āgneya (pertaining to the Fire-god) missile on Śiva. All the Devas trembled with fear on being scorched by the smouldering charcoals dropping from the arrows. (They cried:) "O Mahādeva, save us, save us. We are being burnt by the Dānava."

Thereupon the Lord of Devas fitted a Vāruṇa missile on his bow. Within a moment the Āgneya missile was destroyed by the Vāruṇa missile. Thereupon in the battlefield a Vāyavya (pertaining to the Wind) missile was discharged by the Dānava. O dear one, the Vāruṇa missile vanished on being destroyed by the Vāyavya missile. With infuriated mind the Lord then discharged a Sārpa (serpentine) missile. Undoubtedly the Māruta (Vāyavya) missile was destroyed by the serpentine arrows. Thereat a Gāruḍa missile was sportingly discharged by the Dānava. On seeing the Gāruḍa missile the Sārpa missile disappeared. Thereupon a Nārasiṁha missile was discharged by the Lord of Devas. The Gāruḍa missile was destroyed by the Nārasiṁha missile. Thus one missile was suppressed by another missile. They did not affect either of them. O dear one, the great war became equally terrifying unto the Suras and the Asuras. Various weapons were employed such as discus, dart, arrow, Tomara, sword, Mudgara, Bhalla and the splendid Karṇikāra. Yet the Dānava could not be killed by those diverse kinds of weapons. Then swords, darts and Tomaras, all terrible with flames issuing forth were discharged by the Bull-emblemed Lord in the battle against the Dānava. But like a Gauḍa maiden the missile never touched the body (of the Dānava).

Thereupon Śiva and Andhaka abandoned the weapons and engaged themselves in hand-to-hand fight (wrestling). They caught hold of each other's hands and began to hit with fists. Thus Śiva and Andhaka fought employing all the means of a regular war.

Śrī Mārkaṇḍeya said:

59-65. The Lord of Devas began to think about the means of restraining Andhaka. "There is no doubt that I will kill the evil-minded one." O excellent king, when he was hurled by Śiva the Dānava fell on the ground face down and hands lifted up. Then the enemy of Devas became furious. The Lord of Devas was kept in the armpit, pressed and afflicted. Lord Maheśvara became motionless and he swooned. On seeing him senseless the Dānava thought thus: 'Alas, an evil action has been perpetrated by me, a sinner. What shall I do? Where can I get rid of the Karma?'

He carried the Lord in his arms (in the particular position called *Utsaṅga*) and went to the Kailāsa mountain. The king of Daityas placed Śaṅkara on the bed and went out. The Lord who fell on the bed began to feel the pain. He saw himself in his own abode.

66-74. "How was this discomfiture brought down upon me by that evil-minded wretch?" Saying this he was overwhelmed with anger and he rushed against the Dānava after seizing an iron bar weighing a thousand Bhāras. On seeing the Dānava, the Lord hurled it on to the head of the Dānava.

Then the Dānava laughingly cut it with his sword. Thereupon in the great battle the missile named Kaucchera was recollected by the Lord. Even as it blazed, it was hurled hitting the Dānava in his chest instantly. On being hit with that, the Dānava vomited blood. He fell face-down and was pierced with the trident. Again he was split into two by the Lord of Devas with his trident. Fixed at the tip of the trident the sinful wretch was whirled like a wheel. Every drop of blood that fell on the ground from his body gave rise to Dānavas with weapons in their hands. Thereupon the Lord became utterly afflicted on account of the energetic Dānava.

At that time Durgā, Cāmuṇḍā of terrifying countenance, was remembered by the Lord. Presently she came on the scene shining with different kinds of weapons and striking terror with her very appearance. She had long curved fangs, a huge body, tawny-coloured eyes and the earlobes hanging loose. She said, "O Lord, may the command be given. Who is to go to the abode of Yama?"

Īśvara said:

75-85. O fair lady, drink the blood of this Dānava as much as you please. O Durgā, lap up the blood that drops on to the ground. Do not delay. O fair lady, extend a helping hand so that I can kill the Dānava.

On being told thus, that Goddess Durgā drank the blood. All the Dānavas numbering many thousands were killed by the Lord of Devas. On seeing those Dānavas brought down to the ground Andhaka eulogized Maheśvara, the Lord of Devas:

Andhaka said:

Be victorious, O Lord of the chiefs of Devas having half of Umā's body as part of your own body. Obeisance to you, O Lord of the chiefs of Devas. Obeisance to Śarva, possessing three Guṇas within him.

O Lord seated on the bull! O Lord with the moon for your crest jewel! Be victorious, O Lord with the Khaṭvāṅga in the hand. Obeisance to you, O Gaṅgādhara.

Obeisance to you holding Ḍamaru in the hand. Obeisance to the Lord having the garland of skulls. Obeisance to Maheśa, the destroyer of Smara's body. Obeisance to you, to Maheśa.

Obeisance to the Lord who shattered the teeth of Pūṣan. Obeisance to you, the Lord of Gaṇas. Be victorious, O Lord with a handsome body. Obeisance to the Lord without form, to the multi-formed Lord.

O Śaṅkara, obeisance to the destroyer of the head of Viriñci. Obeisance to you, the Lord who reside in the cremation ground and have terrifying forms.

You are omnipresent. You are the creator. You are the destroyer. No one else. You are the earth. You are the quarters. You are Guru (Jupiter) and Bhārgava (Venus). O Lord of the chiefs of Devas, you are Sauri (Saturn) and also the son of the Earth (Mars). All those visible things, the stars, the planets etc., are you yourself.

After eulogizing the Lord thus, the Dānava bowed down to Maheśvara with palms joined together.

Īśvara said:

86-90. Well! Well! O Dānava of great intrinsic strength, request for a boon. I am the donor and you are the suppliant. I shall grant whatever is desired.

Andhaka said:

O Lord of Devas, if you are pleased, if a boon is to be granted to me, then I should be made one on a par with yourself. No other boon. I shall be *Bhasmī* (one smeared with ash), *Jaṭī* (one having matted hairs), *Trinetrī* (having three eyes), *Triśūlī* (having a trident), *Caturbhuja* (having four arms), having a tiger hide as the upper garment and serpents for Yajñopavīta. O Maheśvara, if you are pleased, I shall desire these.

Īśvara said:

I shall grant you the boon as requested by you, O sinless one. Dear son, stationed among my Gaṇas you shall become Bhṛṅgīśa.

CHAPTER FORTYNINE

Glorification of Śūlabheda

Śrī Mārkaṇḍeya said:

1-9. After subduing Andhaka, Maheśvara, the Lord of Devas, Rudra, went to Kailāsa mountain along with Umā.

Then the Devas too led by Brahmā and including Vāsava came there. Delighted and contented, all of them bowed down to the Consort of Pārvatī.

Īśvara said:

O Pitāmaha! May all those who have come, sit here. For the sake of the Devas, the Dānava has been killed. On account of his blood my trident cannot be free from impurities. O Brahmā, one engrossed in a splendid Vrata, penance and Japya (utterance of holy names) has been killed. O Four-faced Lord, I wish to perform an elaborate pilgrimage. All those of you who have assembled here may come along with me.

After saying thus, the Lord of the chiefs of Devas set out towards Prabhāsa. Beginning with Prabhāsa, he took bath in all the Tīrthas between Gaṅgā and the ocean. Still, O king, there was no clearance from impurity. Then the Lord went to Narmadā along with the Devas. He, fond of austerity as he was, took bath on the northern as well as southern bank. He then went to a spot named Bhṛgu on the mountain on the southern bank. O king, staying there along with the Devas, Mahādeva wandered over many places. Getting dejected ultimately he sat down.

10-16. Since that spot appeared fascinating to all the heaven-dwellers, Lord Maheśvara considered it a special Tīrtha (of unique features) and stayed there.

He pierced the mountain with his trident. Thereby Rasātala too got split then and the trident became free from impurities. No stain or pollution was seen anywhere.

The highly meritorious Bhāratī was invoked there by the Devas. The highly meritorious Sarasvatī issued forth from the mountain. Here, there is a second confluence like that of white and black (waters) at Veṇī (Prayāga). Brahmā himself installed the excellent Brahmeśa Liṅga. It is highly meritorious and destructive of all miseries. Lord Janārdana himself is stationed to the south thereof. The river is ever present there at the tip of the foot of Viṣṇu. There was no outlet to the water as it stood held up within the walls of the pit. With the tip of the trident, a line was drawn. Thereupon, O king, the water began to flow and it fell into the great river Revā.

17-28. The *Jalaliṅga* is the highly meritorious Cakratīrtha, O excellent king. The Lord of Devas himself duly performed the holy ablution at the spot Śūlabheda. He considered himself pure as if no sin had been committed. To the northern quarter thereof the Lord of Devas, the preceptor of the universe, the trident-bearing Lord of the chiefs of Devas established himself.

Among all the Tīrthas that alone was the holiest place and consisted of all Devas. It is meritorious and destructive of all sins and miseries. The preceptor of the universe installed the

Lord of Devas in that Tīrtha and released[1] (appointed) one hundred eight guardian-deities, the one hundred eight Vināyakas. Those one hundred eight Kṣetrapālas cautiously guard it.

Obstacles hinder one who wishes to stay there. Some people are engrossed in domestic worries; some, in agriculture; some organize meetings; some are engaged in earning money; some indulge in indirect allegations; some are always engaged in violence; some are infatuated with other men's wives; some destroy the means of sustenance of others. Others offer excuses like: "How can we go to the Tīrthas? The wife is afflicted with hunger and so the sons and servants and others." The men are kept entangled in the nets of illusion by the groups of Devas.

Men who are habitual sinners do not get the opportunity for the holy ablution (here). Groups of the servants of Devas always protect that Tīrtha. Men who are blessed and meritorious do get the opportunity for the holy ablution in Sarasvatī, Bhogavatī and especially in the celestial river (Gaṅgā). This confluence is meritorious like that of white (Gaṅgā) and black (Yamunā) currents at the Veṇī (Prayāga). On seeing the Tīrtha, all the Devas became delighted in their minds.

29-39. They went to the presence of the Lord and began to extol: "O Lord of Devas! This Tīrtha is on a par with your Gayātīrtha. Another Tīrtha, the most secret of all secret Tīrthas, like this was never there nor will there ever be." The Trident-bearing Lord was worshipped by Indra and others, the groups of Apsarās, Yakṣas, Kinnaras, Gandharvas, the Guardians of the Quarters and of the worlds. Through dances and songs and prayers, he was worshipped by all the Suras and Asuras, by Gaṇas and by all the Siddhas, Nāgas and others. Maheśvara was worshipped by them. O king, the spot was pierced by the Lord with the tip of his trident. Even today the eddy filled by the Suras is seen in three distinct ways. The group of three Kuṇḍas, O tiger among men, is great and is always full of confused noise. It is destructive of all sins. It dispels all miseries and it is excellent.

1. The reading *"rakṣapālān muktvā"* (releasing the guardians or guards) appears defective. If '*muktvā*' is emended as '*yuktvā*', "appointing guardians", it makes better sense. In Devanāgarī script '*yu*' (यु) and '*mu*' (मु) in MSS appear alike. Hence '*muktvā*' might have been read (composed) for '*yuktvā*'.

A person who takes his holy bath there after observing fast duly, is rid of a year's sins even if he has not received initiation (Dīkṣā) and knows no Mantras.

Those who duly take the holy ablution with (the utterance of) five Mantras mentioned in the Vedas along with auspicious pots filled with gold, or with ten syllables, six syllables or three syllables (they attain better fruit).

O king, twice-born ones should perform the requisite rituals separately in the Tīrtha. In the case of Brāhmaṇas, Kṣatriyas and Vaiśyas as well as of women and Śūdras (the mode is the same). They should duly perform the holy bath after meditating upon the three generations. Men who drink water uttering the ten-syllabled Mantra, go to the great world of Lord Maheśvara. Water drunk from Rudrakuṇḍa is like that drunk in Kedāra.

40-48. The syllable *Kṣa* used in conjunction with five Rephas (letter *Ra*) is honoured by Suras ("*Rakṣa, Rakṣa*" repeated five times) used along with Oṁkāra (ten-syllabled Mantra) should be known as praiseworthy.

A person who controls his sense-organs and duly performs the holy ablution and offers libations to the Pitṛs and the deities with water mixed with gingelly seeds, shall redeem the members of his family upto twenty generations, ten before and ten after him.

One who performs Śrāddha in the Śūlabheda Tīrtha shall undoubtedly obtain that merit which a man who performs Śrāddha in the five holy spots including Gayā gets.

If the devotee makes Dāna duly, the merit is everlasting. Even his *Duṣkṛta* (evil) turns to be *Sukṛta* (merit).

Just as Gayāśiras is always meritorious in regard to the rites unto the Pitṛs, so also Śūlabheda Tīrtha is meritorious by means of holy baths, libations and Dānas. A Kṣatriya should make the following thirteen gifts to a Brāhmaṇa who has mastered the Vedas, is of noble parentage, who has controlled his sense-organs, is clean, who is richly endowed with scholarship and mastery of the Vedas, is free from hypocrisy and who regularly performs his duties. The gifts shall be made on thirteen days and the merit thereof shall be thirteen times more. The gifts should be in the form of gold, cow, earth (plot of land), gingelly seeds, seat, a pair of shoes, bed, excellent horses, a pair of clothes, grains, a furnished house, a plough with the tie to the yoke and a cultivated field.

CHAPTER FIFTY

Rules about the Eligibility for Dāna

Uttānapāda asked:

1-5. O Lord, what type of Brāhmaṇas are worthy of being adored? What type are proclaimed as not worthy of being adored, especially in connection with Śrāddha rites, Dāna rites and rites connected with marriage celebration? Kindly let me know whether the faith in regard to Śrāddha and other rites arises by the intercession of divine beings or Destiny. O Lord, to whom is Dāna not offered?

Īśvara said:

An elephant made of wood, a deer made of hide and a Brāhmaṇa who has not studied the Vedas—all these three are so by name only. Just as a eunuch is useless (unproductive) for women, just as a cow is useless for a cow, just as a gift made to an ignorant person is useless (meritless), so also a Brāhmaṇa without the knowledge of Ṛk (Ṛgveda) is useless.

Just as a sower who sows seeds in an arid place, does not reap the fruit thereof, so also a donor making a gift unto one without the knowledge of Ṛk does not derive any merit.

6-8. The following Brāhmaṇas should always be avoided[1] after due consideration: a chronic patient; one deficient in organs or having extra limbs; one-eyed; a son (born) of a widow; one who violates the vow of continence; one with black teeth; a gluttonous one eating everything (pure, impure); a paramour of a Śūdra woman; one who betrays friends; a slanderer; one who sells Soma juice; one who censures others; one who abandons father, mother and the preceptor; one who always censures Brāhmaṇas etc. O king, a Brāhmaṇa who eats the cooked food of a Śūdra though consecrated with Mantras is a Karmacāṇḍāla (Cāṇḍāla by acts as against one born as a

1. Compare the lists of undeserving donees given in Mbh, *Vana*, 300.5-9. The list given here is similar to *infra* SkP VII.i.205.58-72. The list of undeserving donees is similar to that of ineligibles for invitation to Śrāddha. Manu III. 150-166 gives a long list of such persons, which has been adopted by this text.

Cāṇḍāla). If one touches him, one should take bath. He is not worthy of being even touched.

9-14. After a careful enquiry these Brāhmaṇas should be abandoned: one with defective nails; one associating with a Śūdra woman; a thief; a bastard; one who depends upon great gifts and one who indulges in self-destruction; one who teaches on wages; a eunuch; a ravisher of a virgin and an accursed one.

If a Brāhmaṇa accepts a gift and trades therewith, one should not offer him gifts. It shall be futile.

There are Brāhmaṇas well-endowed with learning and regular study of the Vedas. They are of excellent conduct as well. A gift given unto them becomes everlasting. O king, make gifts to poor people and not flourishing ones. A medicine gives relief to the sick. Of what avail are medicines given to one devoid of illness?

Uttānapāda said:

What is the procedure thereof? What are the rites regarding Tīrtha Śrāddha? How is a gift to be made? O Śaṅkara, describe this to me.

Īśvara said:

15-26. A person should control all his sense-organs with great purity and devoutly perform Śrāddha at home. He should circumambulate the preceptor after feeding him and silently follow him till he reaches the boundary (of the village) (and bid farewell to him). Then he should go to Śūlabheda and duly perform the holy ablution. If a devotee performs Śrāddha with Havya, Kavya etc., in due order in five holy spots and then offers balls of rice along with milk pudding, honey and ghee, the Pitṛs are propitiated for seventeen years.

If a devotee performs the Śrāddha with raw rice grains, Badaras, Iṅgudas, honey and ghee in this Tīrtha, he too shall obtain the merit thereof. There is no doubt about it. He who assiduously offers shoes to Brāhmaṇas shall undoubtedly attain heaven, riding on a horse.

He who offers a bed, a horse and especially an umbrella shall go seated on an aerial chariot, surrounded by groups of celestial damsels.

He who gives an excellent house along with seven kinds of grain shall reside in a golden house in my world as he pleases.

He who gives a Tiladhenu (a cow made of gingelly seeds) covered with a cloth and accompanied by a calf shall dwell in heaven until the ultimate annihilation of all living beings.

O king, if the person gives water and cooked food in his own house, or in a forest or on the path to a pilgrim-centre, he shall never see the world of Yama. He will attain the merit as though all the types of gifts have been given (by him).

One should make gift of water, cooked food and freedom from fear. There has never been a greater gift than cooked rice nor will there ever be any.

If a devotee makes the gift of a virgin, or that of a bull, his residence shall be there where I am present. It cannot be otherwise.

Uttānapāda said:

27-29. O Lord, how is the gift of a virgin to be made by righteous persons? How is a wife to be nourished (taken care of)? How is the marriage rite of a virgin to be performed? O Lord of Devas, I have one more thing to ask. To whom is a virgin not to be given? O Lord, where should she be offered? By giving to whom will it be of everlasting merit? What is the criterion for considering something as best, middling or base, O Lord? How can (a gift) be Rājasa or Tāmasa or one having no better (i.e. Sāttvika)?

Īśvara said:

30-36. Of all Dānas, *Kanyā Dāna* (gift of a virgin) is the best. A parent should give his daughter after approaching a boy of noble birth, handsome features, learning and discretion. The father should give his well-adorned daughter on an auspicious Lagna and Muhūrta. If he offers horses, elephants and garments in accordance with his capacity, his stay shall be in the region where there is no ailment.

If the daughter dearer than one's own life is given away, it is as though all the three worlds have been given away along with the mobile and immobile beings. If anyone begs for wealth for the sake of a virgin, he shall be a Karmacāṇḍāla (a Cāṇḍāla in action) and he shall become a woodworm after death. If, out of food-greediness, anyone takes food in his house, he will become pure only by means of the expiation called Cāndrāyaṇa or Taptakṛcchra.

Uttānapāda said:

If one has no wealth in one's house but has a daughter to be given away, how can he celebrate her marriage if he does not beg?

Īśvara said:

37-46. O king, one should celebrate the marriage of a daughter, even if one has no wealth, merely by repeating the name of the virgin. It does not bring about any defect.

Without begging if the Dāna is made after approaching (a groom), it is the most excellent Dāna. Even if the Yuga comes to a close this (benefit of Dāna) does not become ineffective. The Uttama (excellent) Dāna is after approaching (the groom). If the groom is invited (and given the daughter), it is proclaimed as middling; if he is begged of it is base; if (he) makes the request "Give! Give!" it is the meanest.

If a stone is tied to another and dropped into water, both of them (sink down and) perish. So also is the gift of cooked food given to one not deserving.

Hence a gift (Dāna) is not to be made to one who is incompetent. It brings down the donor and especially oneself. One who is competent takes both across like dry wood put in water. Just as a boat, so also a learned man takes one to the other shore.

If an *Āhitāgni* (a Brāhmaṇa maintaining perpetual sacrificial fire in the family) accepts gifts from Śūdras, he is no better than a Śūdra here in this birth. After death he becomes a dog.

Accepting gifts from indecent people secretly and despicably is a futile effort in regard to a Brāhmaṇa who is an *Agnihotrin*. That man is unworthy of being fed. He is burned with Kāriṣa fire (fire of cowdung cakes). Afterwards for seven births he is undoubtedly born as a mat-maker. The Dāna made through sense of shame or for the desire of being considered chivalrous or because of importunity or through restraint and the Dāna made to servants—all these are futile.

CHAPTER FIFTYONE

Glorification of Dānadharma

Uttānapāda said:

1-9. O Īśvara, at what time is Śrāddha and Dāna to be performed and on what lunar day should pilgrimage be done? Tell me quickly.

Īśvara said:

Just as Pitṛtīrtha (i.e. Gayā) is meritorious, excellent and conductive to the fulfilment of all desires, so also this Tīrtha is meritorious for the performance of holy bath, giving Dāna, offering libations etc. One should perform special Śrāddha in all the Yugādis (days on which Yugas began). O dear one here are the names etc. of the Manvantaras:

Month & Tithi on which a Manvantara started			Name of the Manvantara
Aśvayuj	Bright half,	Ninth day	Sūryasāvarṇi
Kārttika	Bright half,	Twelfth	Svāyaṁbhuva
Caitra	Bright half,	Third	Uttama
Bhādrapada	Bright half,	Third	Tāmasa
Āṣāḍha	Bright half,	Tenth	Cākṣuṣa
Māgha	Bright half,	Seventh	Vaivasvata
Śrāvaṇa	Dark half,	Eighth	Dakṣasāvarṇi
Āṣāḍha	Full Moon		Rudrasāvarṇi
Phālguna	New Moon		Svārociṣa
Pauṣa	Bright half,	Eleventh	Raivata
Kārttika	Full Moon		Indrasāvarṇi
Phālguna	Full Moon		Brahmasāvarṇi
Caitra	Full Moon		Raucya
Jyeṣṭha	Full Moon		Dharmasāvarṇi

The first days of the Manvantaras are proclaimed as those according infinite benefit. O king, Śrāddha is to be performed in the course of both the transits of the Sun viz. northern as well as southern. The following are the occasions for the performance of Śraddha: the third lunar day in the months of Kārttika, Māgha and Vaiśākha; the full-moon day in Caitra and

Jyeṣṭha; the Aṣṭakas (seventh, eighth and ninth lunar days); the Saṅkrānti day (transit of the Sun in the signs of zodiac); and the Vyatīpāta day. What is offered during these days is proclaimed as everlasting.

10-16. One should observe fast on the eleventh day in the bright half of the month of Madhu (Caitra). At night he should keep awake near the feet of Viṣṇu. Those who perform the adoration of Viṣṇu with incense, light, Naivedyas (food offerings), flower garlands, agallochum, sandal etc. and read the old legends (Purāṇas) and a Brāhmaṇa who repeats the Sūktas from the Ṛk, Yajus or Sāma Vedas shall be rid of all sins. He goes to the world of Viṣṇu.

In the morning after assiduously worshipping Brāhmaṇas, he should perform Śrāddha and should make gifts (within his capacity) of cow, gold, cloth etc. His Pitṛs become pleased until the annihilation of all the living beings. The performer of the Śrāddha shall go there where Lord Janārdana is present.

On the thirteenth lunar day he should start from there for the Liṅga stationed in the cave. By seeing Lord Īśāna named Mārkaṇḍa, he is rid of all sins.

Uttānapāda said:

O Mahādeva, by whom was the highly splendid Liṅga installed within the cave? O Lord, it behoves you to narrate it to me.

Īśvara said:

17-28. The eminent sage Mārkaṇḍeya is well-known in all the three worlds. He performed severe austerities for a period of one thousand divine years. He entered the cave and practised Yoga there. The Liṅga named Mārkaṇḍeśvara was installed by him. A pilgrim should take his holy ablution there devoutly, observe fast and control the sense-organs. Keeping awake at night, he should assiduously offer lamps. The Lord should be bathed in Pañcāmṛta in accordance with one's capacity. After anointing the Lord therewith, he should duly perform the adoration. Brāhmaṇas should perform Japa (chanting of Mantras) of the Mantras current in their Śākhās (branch of their particular Veda). They should also recite Sāvitrī Mantra one thousand eight or one hundred eight times. By doing this, O excellent king, the person shall attain the fruit of his birth. On the fourteenth day he should again take his holy bath and perform the adoration duly. Gifts should be made after testing the worth of the recipient, if one wishes for one's own welfare. Undoubtedly the Pitṛs are pleased with him for twelve years. The donor goes to that place where the enjoyment is eternal. After entering the middle of the cave the pilgrim should wallow on the ground as much as he can. The merit that is derived from the Nīla Mountain is entirely attained by them. Listen to the meritorious fruit of the person who performs Śrāddha at every Parva at Śūlabheda, especially at the end of the month of Caitra (on the New-Moon day). He shall obtain the Puṇya derived at Kedāra, at the confluence of Gaṅgā and the ocean, at the confluence of black and white (i.e. Gaṅgā and Yamunā) or in other Tīrthas, especially the Puṇya (Merit) that is derived from Arbuda and Amara mountain. One should propitiate the Pitṛs and deities in accordance with the injunction and with due utterance of the Mantras. The man thereby attains the fruit of all the Tīrthas beginning with Gayā.

29-43. He would redeem twenty generations of his family, ten before him and ten after him. Thereafter the person should remain pure and with a mind fully concentrated perform Nyāsa on the southern idol as mentioned before and offer eight flowers. These are the eight mental flowers mentioned in the scriptures: Listen. They are: (1) Vārija, (2) Saumya, (3) Āgneya, (4) Vāyavya, (5) Pārthiva, (6) Vānaspatya, (7) Prājāpatya, and (8) Śivapuṣpa. Now listen to the meaning of these: (1) *Vārija* should be known as water; (2) Saumya means honey, ghee and milk; (3) *Āgneya* means incense, light etc.; (4) *Vāyavya* means sandalpaste etc.; (5) *Pārthiva* means roots, bulbous roots etc.; (6) *Vānaspatya* means fruits; (7) *Prājāpatya* means reading and recitation; and (8) *Śivapuṣpa* is vāsanā (imagination, knowledge through intuition etc.).

(Alternatively:) Non-violence is the first Puṣpa. Control of sense-organs is the second. The third Puṣpa is *Dayā* (compassion). Kṣamā (forbearance) is the fourth Puṣpa; then *Dhyāna* (meditation) is a Puṣpa; then *Tapaḥ* (austerity) and the seventh is *Jñāna Puṣpa*. Truth is the eighth Puṣpa. The deities are pleased with these. Ascetics and wise ones should be pleased through devotion, O king. An umbrella, a covering cloth and a pair of sandals should be offered. If one is adored with these, three persons (generations) are adored. The person shall stay in the heavenly world until all the living beings are annihilated. Men should perform *Jāpya* with devotion to the Trident-bearing Lord. They should anoint the Lord of Devas with Pañcāmṛta, Pañcagavya, Yakṣakardama and Kuṅkuma as well as Śrīkhaṇḍa, agallochum and sandalpaste. They should perform the worship of the Trident-bearing Lord with different kinds of flowers, keep awake at night and offer lights assiduously. Incense and Naivedya should be offered and Purāṇic legends should be read. Men who stay there should perform Japa devoutly. *Śrīsūkta, Pauruṣasūkta, Pāvamāna, Vṛṣākapi* and other Vedic Mantras should be chanted. Then the *Rudrasūkta* of various sorts should be recited. He shall adore the Brāhmaṇas devoutly. The devotee adoring and bowing to them with various kinds of offerings is honoured in the world of Śiva.

44-55. A follower of Ṛgveda chants the Sūktas *agnimīle* etc. A follower of Yajurveda should chant *Rudra Sūkta, Puruṣa Sūkta, Ślokādhyāya, Śukriya,* the groups of Mantras beginning with *iṣetvā,* etc., *Jyotir Brāhmaṇa, Gāyatrya, Madhu* and *Maṇḍala Brāhmaṇas.*

A follower of Yajurveda should recite the Sūktas of *Devavrata, Vāmadevya, Puruṣarṣabha* and *Bṛhadrathantara.* These devotees shall proceed to that place where Lord Maheśvara is present.

If a devotee performs *Pādaśauca* (cleansing of the feet) and *Abhyaṅga* (oil bath) here with great devotion, he undoubtedly obtains the merit that accrues from the gift of a cow. He should feed Brāhmaṇas with honey and milk-pudding. If a single Brāhmaṇa is fed, it is as though ten millions have been fed. The devotee should with great devotion give to an excellent Brāhmaṇa, gold, silver or a garment. Thereby Devas, human beings and Pitṛs become propitiated.

At the time of a lunar or solar eclipse, men should take their holy bath with great devotion, worship the deity and perform Japa and Homa. They should make gifts in accordance with their capacity, to a Brāhmaṇa who has mastered the Vedas. The following gifts should be made to a deserving person: a horse, a chariot, an elephant, a vehicle, Tulāpuruṣa (things equal to one in weight), a cart filled with seven types of food-grains, a plough along with the tie of the yoke and mature bullocks bearing the yoke, cows, plots of lands, gingelly seeds, gold etc. The recipient should be duly adored.

Nothing should be given to an undeserving person by a sensible person desirous of prosperity. Since the earth holds all living beings, a plot of land producing all kinds of vegetation should be given to a Brāhmaṇa.

Now, O great king, listen to the benefit of gifting cows.

56-62. When two legs and the face of the calf are seen at the vaginal outlet of a cow, she should be known as the very earth, so long as she does not release the calf from the womb. Somehow the devotee should offer her to a Brāhmaṇa. The merit thereof is as though the earth consisting of mountains, forests and great parks has been gifted. On being gifted the cow shall redeem twenty-one generations of the family.

When the Sun or the Moon is eclipsed, then blessed ones shall give a milch cow with her hoofs covered with silver, along with a cloth and a brass vessel for milking.

I do not know the amount of the merit thereof even after the lapse of hundreds of years. O king, there is numerical limit to the merit earned for every gift made on other occasions but for a gift made at the time of lunar or solar eclipse there is no such limit.

Where a cow is seen, O king, all the Tīrthas are there. One should understand that Parva (period of holy festivals) too exists there. There need not be any doubt in this respect. If a man remembers the Tīrtha and goes there or dies there, he shall become an attendant of Rudra.

CHAPTER FIFTYTWO

The Story of Dīrghatapas

Īśvara said:

1-10. O king, I shall narrate another story that happened long ago. A sage of great austerities went to heaven along with his family.

Uttānapāda said:

How did the Brāhmaṇa, the great sage, go to heaven along with his family? O Lord, I am very much eager to know. Kindly tell me, O Lord.

Īśvara said:

Formerly there was a king of Kāśī well known as Citrasena. He was a brave warrior, a liberal donor and highly righteous. He had realised all his desires and he possessed great wealth.

The city was well-populated. It was full of different kinds of gems. It was situated on the banks of Gaṅgā and was well-known as Vārāṇasī.

It resembled the autumnal moon in splendour. It was well-adorned by learned men. Indrayaṣṭis (Flag-staff of Indra) were seen all over it. It was full of cows and cowherd colonies. There were many banners (fluttering over it). It reverberated with sounds of Vedic recitation. Various kinds of merchants engaged themselves in buying and selling. It was rendered resplendent by mechanical devices, well laid streets and many other lofty towers. Temples of divine features and majestic hermitages abounded there. It was beautified with trees, jack-fruit trees, Bakulas, Tālas, Aśokas, Āmrakas, Rājavṛkṣas, Kapitthas and Dāḍimas. Auspicious chants of Vedic recitations sanctified everything. It was beautiful with many varieties of fruits and flowers. It was embellished with clusters of Kadalī (plantain) trees.

On the northern side of that city there was a splendid hermitage. It is well-known in all the three worlds by the name Mandāravana.

11-17. It contained many Mandāra trees. Hence it came to be known by the name Mandāraka.

A Brāhmaṇa named Dīrghatapas lived there. In view of his prolonged severe austerities, he is remembered as Dīrghatapas. He resided there along with his wife, sons and daughters-in-law. His five sons always served him diligently. His youngest son Ṛkṣaśṛṅga was also a man of great austerities, richly endowed with Vedic study, celibate and endowed with good qualities. He always practised Yoga and took in bulbous roots, roots and fruits. He used to assume the form of a deer and move among the herds of deer. Everyday in the evening he used to come back to his parents. With great devotion, the son of the sage made obeisance to them and went again to forests and mountain caves. Thus the son of the sage sported about with young fawns everyday. Once by chance that Ṛkṣaśṛṅga passed away.

CHAPTER FIFTYTHREE

Ṛkṣaśṛṅga Goes to Svarga

Uttānapāda said:

1-7. O Lord, how did the younger son of Sage Dīrghatapas who was residing in the hermitage, meet death?

Īśvara said:

Listen with concentration to the divine story, O king. Merely by listening to it, one is rid of all sins.

The king of Kāśī was well-known on the earth, O king, as Citrasena. He was mighty, had great energy and was great in exploits. Righteousness always prevailed in his kingdom. There was no impiety anywhere. Engaged always in the Vedic rites, he protected the subjects righteously. He strictly adhered to his duty. He was fond of war as well as of hospitality to guests. Abiding by the conventional duties and rights of Kṣatriyas, he enjoyed worldly pleasures as he pleased. There is (was) no limit to the wealth in his treasury. He possessed elephants, horses, chariots and foot-soldiers. He used to discuss and discourse with the scholars well-versed in Itihāsas and Purāṇas. The king shone like Lord Śaṅkara in Kailāsa. While he was ruling the kingdom like this (once) the king spoke to the minister:

8-17. "I shall go ahunting. Stay here you all attending to the protection of the kingdom." When the ministers said, "You may go", the ruler of the land went off.

His vassal kings following him hurriedly riding on their respective horses even as their royal umbrellas got brushed with one another. Thus they followed him to the forest. Dust from the ground was kicked up by the hoofs of the horses and the elephants. Thereby the solar disc and the quarters were completely covered. Neither the sun nor the moon, neither the quarters nor the trees nor even the peaks of the mountains all round could be seen. They could not even see one another as if it were a mid-night in the rainy season.

There he espied a great herd of deer. Accompanied by all those princes, the king rushed at them. The herd was dispersed and the deer ran helter-skelter in various directions.

King Citrasena alone took a path and reached the place where those deer were present. He entered the impenetrable forest and the dark caves of the mountains completely overgrown with creepers and hedges. He stopped in a place where he could scarcely be seen. Thinking that the deer had disappeared, the king looked around and thought: 'In which direction shall I go? Where can I be in touch with the soldiers of the army?' Thus King Citrasena was in a great predicament. He resorted to the shade of the trees and took rest.

18-29. Distressed with hunger and thirst, he wandered all round in the forest and caves of the mountains. Then he saw a divine lake adorned with clusters of lotuses. It was full of swans and Kāraṇḍava variety of cranes. The Cakravāka birds rendered it splendid. On seeing it, the great king felt his hairs standing on ends. He gathered the lotuses and took his bath. After offering libations to the Pitṛs, Devas and human beings duly, he covered Śaṅkara with the lotuses and adored him. He drank the pure water adequately with mental concentration and purity. He came out of the water and saw a tree nearby. He spread his upper cloth on the ground and sat down. Then, as he sat there he began to think, 'What shall I do now?' Even as he was sitting there, he saw many deer in the forest region. Some were facing the east; others the south; some faced the west and a few the northern direction. Some deer were asleep. Others stood with their ears lifted up. In the centre of those deer, was standing Ṛkṣaśṛṅga, the Yogin of great austerities. On seeing the deer, the king thought about his food intake, 'I shall kill one from these deer and eat as I please. By eating the venison, I shall become normal in my physical state. I shall return to Kāśī assiduously enquiring about the pathway.' After thinking thus the king who was at the foot of the tree raised his bow and fixed an arrow therein. He discharged the arrow into those deer that had been herded together. That Ṛkṣaśṛṅga of great austerities who was in their midst was hit.

30-38. All those forest-dwellers (deer) became frightened and went from there crying. The sage who fell down cried "Kṛṣṇa! Kṛṣṇa!" and continued: "Alas! something horrible has been committed by him who has killed me now. Who is that evil-minded wretch, in whom this sinful thought has occurred? I was stationed amidst the deer. I do not harass or obstruct anyone." On hearing that human voice, the king was struck with dismay. Hurrying there he saw the Brāhmaṇa shining with Brāhmaṇical splendour.

Citrasena said:

Alas! Something horrible has been committed by me because the Brāhmaṇa was slain.

He then said to the Brāhmaṇa: "You have been unwittingly killed by me, O sinless one, because I mistook you for a deer. I shall now gather together much wood and immolate myself. Among things seen and unseen, there is nothing like the slaughter of a Brāhmaṇa. Unless I immolate myself, I will not be rid of the sin of Brāhmaṇa-slaughter."

Ṛkṣaśṛṅga said:

At my death you will not attain Siddhi (object desired). Now when I die, there will be many killings. On my death my mother, the aged father, the saintly brothers and their wives will die. When these deaths occur how can there be purity in you? If you are inclined to do so, I shall tell you a means.

Citrasena said:

39-45. May the means which is in your mind be mentioned. O great sage, I shall do everything even if I have to exert myself.

Ṛkṣaśṛṅga said:

I shall ask you something regarding yourself. Who are you? From where have you come? How did you come here? Who are you? One among Brāhmaṇas, Kṣatriyas or Vaiśyas? Or are you Śūdra-born?

Citrasena said:

O dear one, I am not a Śūdra. I am neither a Vaiśya nor a Brāhmaṇa. O Brāhmaṇa, I am not low-born. O great sage, I am a Kṣatriya. I know my duties. I am aware of what has been done by me. I am engaged in the welfare of all living beings. Unwittingly a sin has been perpetrated. What is the means of becoming purified?

Ṛkṣaśṛṅga said:

Take me to the hermitage where my parents are present. Introduce yourself as the slayer of their son and say that you regret it. On seeing me, perhaps they may have compassion for you. They will tell you the means whereby there can be (mental) peace.

After hearing his words, O excellent king, Citrasena took the Brāhmaṇa on his shoulder and went to the hermitage.

46-49. When he became unable to carry he began to take rest frequently. Presently he saw that the Brāhmaṇa had lost consciousness and that all his sense-organs had become impaired. Citrasena kept him in the shade of a banyan tree. He folded his cloth four times and began to fan him therewith frequently. Even as he watched, O great king, Ṛkṣaśṛṅga of great austerities quickly passed away by means of Dhyānayoga (meditation) because he was fully conversant with Yoga. He cremated the Brāhmaṇa according to the rites that have been enjoined. After taking his bath, he lamented with great sorrow.

CHAPTER FIFTYFOUR

Dīrghatapas Goes to Heaven

Īśvara said:

1-5. Thereupon the king became greatly anguished. (He thought:) 'How can I go back to my abode in Vārāṇasī? Afflicted by the sin of Brāhmaṇa-slaughter, I shall consign my body to fire. Or at the instance (of the son of the sage) I shall go to the hermitage and recount to the great sage everything in the way it had happened.'

After thinking thus, the king went to the hermitage taking the bones of Ṛkṣaśṛṅga. The excellent king stood within the range of the vision of that great sage of purified soul.

Dīrghatapas said:

Do come. Welcome unto you. May you be pleased to sit here on the seat so that I can offer you Argha and Madhuparka along with the seat.

Citrasena said:

6-17. O great sage, I am not worthy of being received with the offerings of Argha (materials of worship) or even being spoken to. Your son, the Brāhmaṇa stationed in the middle of the deer, was killed by me. Ṛkṣaśṛṅga, a Brāhmaṇa of great austerities, was killed as a result of the wrong impression that he was a deer. Know that I am the slayer of your son. Punish me with the severest form of punishment. Having consideration for my delusion and confusion, O excellent sage, do what is befitting in this regard.

The mother of the dead son became highly perturbed on hearing those words. She came out of the house and lamented, "Alas! I am killed." She fell on the ground and lamented with the profundity of her grief and affliction. "I am doomed," she lamented and cried in affliction very piteously like a female osprey. "O my son! My son! Reveal your face unto me. Honour me, your mother. O my son, when will I see you again at the threshold arriving there with the fullness of your Vedic study and eagerness for the performance of Japa and Homa. There is a popular saying that sandalpaste is cool but the embrace of the limbs of the son is cooler than sandalpaste, if the body becomes the subject of the close embrace of one's own son. Of what avail is sandalpaste or a drop of nectar? Of what avail is even the moon? O my beloved son! I wish to embrace you. Separated from you and grief-stricken I will surely die." Lamenting thus in her affliction and wretchedness due to having been bereaved of the son, she fell into a swoon on the ground. On seeing his wife fallen due to the affliction and grief for her dead son, the sage became extremely furious at King Citrasena.

Dīrghatapas said:

18-28. Go away, get away, O great sinner. Do not show me your face. Why was my son, a Brāhmaṇa, killed without any purpose? O king, many sins of many Brāhmaṇa-slaughters will befall you. You alone are the cause of the death of me along with the entire family.

After saying this, the sage thought over the matter again. Then he eschewed his fury as a true sage and said:

Dīrghatapas said:

O dear one, shed off your anguish. I have been rather very harsh. You have been reprimanded, O bestower of honour, by me who have been scorched by misery and assailed by the bereavement of my son. What does a wise man do when impelled by his own Karmas. Even at the outset, the intellect of men follows the Karmas. It is in accordance with this that death has been enjoined for me. Undoubtedly the (sin of) slaughters will befall you as uttered by me before. Among Brāhmaṇas, Kṣatriyas and Vaiśyas, among the castes of Śūdras and Cāṇḍālas who are you? Tell me the truth. Why was a Brāhmaṇa killed?

Citrasena said:

I shall submit, O Brāhmaṇa- sage, you must forgive me. I am not a Brāhmaṇa. O dear one, I am neither a Vaiśya nor a

Śūdra, neither a hunter nor a base-born one. O great sage, I am a Kṣatriya. I am the king of Kāśī. I have come to this excellent forest to hunt deer. By mistake, this sage in the guise of a deer was shot down. I have incurred sin. Now I am resorting to your feet. What should be done by me, O Brāhmaṇa? Tell me the true means.

Dīrghatapas said:

29-34. O Lord, even a single sin of Brāhmaṇa-slaughter cannot be redeemed. How can eleven such sins be redeemed? Listen, O king. On account (of the death) of Ṛkṣaśṛṅga, my four sons, their wives, the mother and I — all these will die. O dear one, I shall tell you a splendid way-out. Listen to it. See whether you can carry out that easy task, O king. Cremate the entire family including me in funeral pyre; O king, cast off the bones at Śūlabheda in the waters of Narmadā. On the southern bank of Narmadā is the well-known Tīrtha named Śūlabheda. It is an excellent Tīrtha that destroys all sins and all miseries. Be clean (physically and mentally) and cast off our bones into the Tīrtha. You will be rid of all sins undoubtedly. That is my word.

The King said:

35-45. O dear one, let the command be given. I shall undoubtedly carry it out. Whatever I have, the entire kingdom, the treasury, the friends and sons, O great Brāhmaṇa, all of them are yours, at your disposal. I shall give them to you. Be pleased (to accept it).

O king (Uttānapāda), even as the Brāhmaṇa and the king were conversing thus, the wife of the sage, whose heart broke into two died there. The woman assailed by the grief for the son fell on the ground, devoid of life. All the sons met with death on account of the bereavement of their mother. Along with the husbands all the daughters-in-law also died. O excellent king, all those saintly souls attained death. The king called together all those Brāhmaṇas, the residents of the hermitage. The excellent king informed them of everything in the way it had happened. On being permitted by them, he gathered firewood assiduously. King Citrasena performed the cremation and collected the bones of all the sages beginning with Ṛkṣaśṛṅga. O king, that king (Citrasena) proceeded towards the southern quarter on foot. When he could not walk, on being pressed down by the weight, he took rest and then proceeded after a short while. At every stage he set down the bones and took bath along with his garment. Without taking food but taking in water only, he thus proceeded facing the southern quarter. Before long he reached the banks of Narmadā. On seeing the Brāhmaṇas staying in the hermitage the king asked:

Citrasena said:

46-55. O excellent Brāhmaṇas, O highly blessed ones, may the path leading to Śūlabheda be shown to me, so that I can go there for the fulfilment of my task.

The sages said:

Within a Krośa (3 Kms) distance from here there is the highly splendid Tīrtha. You will see it on the southern bank of Narmadā.

At the instance of the sages the king went on hastily and ere long saw the Tīrtha full of many Dvijas (birds, Brāhmaṇas), overgrown with a number of creepers and trees and rendered splendid by numerous flowers. There were many bears and lions too and splendid devotees observing many kinds of vows. Some of them were standing on a single foot. Others had their eyes turned towards the sun. Some were standing on a single big toe. Others were standing with the arms lifted up. Some took a single meal a day. Some took in as food bulbous roots and fruits. Some took in food only once in three nights. Others observed the vow of Parāka. Some were engaged in Cāndrāyaṇa expiation. Some observed fast for a fortnight. Some observed fast for a whole month. Some broke fast at the end of a Ṛtu. Some were engaged in the practice of Yogic exercises. Some meditated upon '*That*' (*Tat-pada* i.e. Supreme Brahman). Some took in as food only withered and decaying leaves. Some ate bitter and estringent things. Some took in mosses for food. Some took in air as food. Some were householders and some were Agnihotrins. On seeing the Brāhmaṇas like these, the king knelt down on the ground, bowed down his head and spoke these words, O king:

Citrasena said:

56-64. O Brāhmaṇas, in which part of the land is that Tīrtha? Tell me the truth so that the thing desired may be made possible.

The sages said:

Go a distance of a hundred Dhanvantaras (Dhanus=four Hastas). On the peak of Bhṛgutuṅga you will see that large Tīrtha full of water. It is holy.

On hearing their words, he went near the Kuṇḍa. On seeing that Tīrtha, the king became confused again. He was struck with wonder and began to think over and over again. Then the king saw a flesh-eating Kurara (osprey) in the sky. It was hovering round holding a snake but was being attacked by those (birds) without a piece of flesh. Desirous of the piece of flesh they fought with one another. Struck by the beaks the osprey fell into the water where formerly the Trident-bearing Lord had split the ground. By the power of that Tīrtha, he immediately became a man. He (the king) saw that person in divine form seated in an aerial chariot. As he went ahead, Yakṣas, Gandharvas and Apsarās eulogized him. Even as he was being sung about by the Apsarās, he vanished on the top of the Sun. Citrasena was extremely surprised. He decided that the same was the Tīrtha as mentioned by the holy sage. On seeing the power of the Tīrtha, he experienced horripilation.

65-73. He thought, 'This is my blessed day since I have come here.' He then placed the bones down and took his holy bath in accordance with the injunctions. With water mixed with gingelly seeds he propitiated the Pitṛs and deities. Then the king took the bones and cast them into the water. For a moment, the king stood looking up with the face lifted up. He saw all of them (members of the family of Dīrghatapas) in divine forms and splendid features. They had divine garments and were adorned with divine ornaments. They were seated in various kinds of aerial chariots attended upon by celestial damsels. On seeing them separately seated in the aerial chariots, the king was delighted.

Then the sage seated on the aerial chariot spoke to Citrasena: "O gentle soul, O King Citrasena, O excellent king, thanks to your favour. I had this divine goal. Your task has been carried out excellently. Even a son cannot do like this unto his Pitṛs. O dear one, by the power of my utterance you will be free from sins. O great king, you will realize your cherished desires, whatever be in your mind." After blessing the intelligent Citrasena, sage Dīrghatapas went to heaven along with his sons.

CHAPTER FIFTYFIVE

Kāśīrāja Attains Mokṣa

Uttānapāda said:

1-5. On seeing the great efficacy of the Tīrtha, what did King Citrasena do? Where did he stay? What was his food?

Īśvara said:

After climbing on to the Bhṛgutuṅga peak and resorting to the north-eastern quarter the excellent king performed an elaborate penance in the Kuṇḍa there. Then he meditated upon all the Devas, Brahmā, Viṣṇu and Maheśvara and hurled himself down. Presently, Rudra and Keśava appeared before him and held him by the hand. Rudra spoke these words to the king;

Īśvara said:

O great king, do not unnecessarily abandon your life prematurely. You are still very young. It is not proper for you to die now. Hasten back to your abode. Enjoy all desired and desirable pleasures. Like another Śakra of heaven, rule your kingdom free from thorns (enemies).

Citrasena said:

6-12. O Lord, I desire neither the kingdom nor the sons nor kinsmen, neither the wife nor the treasury, neither elephants nor horses. Leave me, leave me, O great Lord, let there be no obstacles put in my way. With your favour, O Maheśvara, heaven has been attained by me today.

Īśvara said:

Of what avail is Svarga unto him, before whom there are Brahmā, Viṣṇu and Śaṁbhu? What will he do by going there? We three gods are pleased. Choose an excellent boon as you please. O great king, that shall undoubtedly be true.

Citrasena said:

If you, the three Lords: Brahmā, Viṣṇu and Maheśvara, are pleased, it behoves all the three of you to stay here permanently. In the same way as Gayāśiras has been rendered meritorious by all of you, this Śūlabheda also should be made sacred. I shall stay wherever all the three of you stay. Further, grant me the over-lordship of all the Gaṇas.

Īśvara said:

13-21. O king, we the three Devas, shall stay in Śūlabheda from today onwards in all the three divisions of time by means of a fraction. You shall certainly be the Lord of the Gaṇas. By the name 'Nandin' staying near me you shall be worshipped before I am. After your casting off the hones, as Dīrghatapas went to heaven seated in an aerial chariot along with the members of his family, so you too shall do.

Thus, O king, the Devas granted boons to Citrasena and stationed themselves on the top of the Kuṇḍa in the southern quarter. They said to one another, "This is a great meritorious Tīrtha. Just as Gayāśiras has already been cited as meritorious, so also on the banks of Revā this Śūlabheda is undoubtedly meritorious."

Īśvara said:

This Tīrtha is as meritorious as Gayāśiras. By offering balls of rice and libation even once a man shall attain purity. Excepting only Gayāśiras, O king, no Tīrtha is equal to even a sixteenth fraction of the Śūlabheda Tīrtha. From north to south the Kuṇḍa extends to ten Hastas and from north-east to west twenty-one Hastas. In regard to the rites of offering balls of rice and the like, that Tīrtha has these dimensions. Those who are engaged in impiety do not get a chance of offering *Dāna* here.

22-31. Viṣṇu stationed himself in the form of Pitṛ (i.e. father), Brahmā in the form of Pitāmaha (grandfather) and Rudra as Prapitāmaha (great-grandfather). Thus the three deities got themselves stationed, O king. The Pitṛs are always waiting like this: "When will my son visit the Tīrtha? When will he redeem us?" If a devotee takes the holy bath in Śūlabheda and visits but once Śūladhara (Trident-bearing Lord Śiva) he shall not be without sons or wealth for seven births. He will never become sick. He shall redeem twenty-one generations of his father's family, twenty-one generations of the mother's family and ten generations of his wife's family. O king, if a single Brāhmaṇa is fed in the Śūlabheda Vana with even greens, roots and fruits, it amounts to the feeding of ten million persons elsewhere. A devout man who performs Śrāddha at the five spots shall redeem all the members of the family, who have become *Pretas* (ghosts), with the favour of Brāhmaṇas and deities as well as of the Pitṛs. A person who offers Śrāddha should stay there where Lord Maheśvara is present. If a devotee performs Śrāddha with devotion in that Tīrtha, the following persons shall attain liberation undoubtedly for a Yuga: They are: those who commit suicide, those who have killed cows and Brāhmaṇas, those who have been killed by animals with curved fangs, or drowned in water, or struck down by lightning, those who were not cremated or on whose death Āśauca[1] was not observed or libation not offered. O king, merely by taking bath all the sins committed through ignorance or childish nature will be dispelled.

32-40. Just as a cloth washed by a washerman becomes pure and clean, so also a sinner who takes his bath in that Tīrtha becomes free from impurities. One who adopts Sannyāsa (life of a recluse) in this Tīrtha in accordance with the injunctions and meditates upon Mahādeva always shall attain the highest position. He shall sport about as he pleases and wishes

1. Non-performance of auspicious rites due to impurity caused by certain inauspicious happenings such as death etc.

for in the palace of Śiva and is later born in an auspicious family as one conversant with the principles of the Vedas and Vedāṅgas. He shall be endowed with handsome features and comeliness. He shall be devoid of all ailments. He may be born as a king or prince. He shall be endowed with piety and good conduct. Thus, O king, the excellent benefit of the Tīrtha has been recounted to you. On hearing this a man shall always be rid of all sins.

If one reads this narrative always to leading Brāhmaṇas, at the time of Śrāddha or in a temple during festival days, Devas become pleased with him. So also human beings along with the Pitṛs. All the sins of those who read or listen perish. He who writes the *'Greatness of the Tīrtha'*, and gives it to Brāhmaṇas attains the ability to recollect previous birth and also gets the desired benefit. He shall stay in Rudraloka as long as the written syllables stay on.

CHAPTER FIFTYSIX

Fruit of Dāna Described

Uttānapāda said:

1-8. I wish to know some more. By whom was Gaṅgā brought down? How did the holy River which was stationed on the head of Rudra, happen to come here? What is the efficacy of the holy Devaśilā? O Śaṅkara, if you are pleased, describe these things to me.

Īśvara said:

Listen with mental concentration as to how the highly esteemed Gaṅgā was brought down by all the Devas for the sake of the welfare of all the worlds.

O king, in the southern quarter, there is a mountain named Vindhya. All the Devas went to the top thereof , O king.

After adoring Īśa, the Lord of the universe, Lord of Devas, the preceptor of the universe, they requested him: "Release to the ground Gaṅgā stationed in the middle of your matted hairs." Thus Gaṅgā was invoked by all the Suras led by Brahmā. Thereupon the brilliant river was released to the earth by Rudra from his head.

This has been created as a highly meritorious river there in that spot by the Devas themselves. Therefore she has become Devanadī (divine river) for the welfare of men on the earth.

Those who always live on her banks, those who take their holy bath with devotion and those who always drink her water, do not go to the abode of Yama.

9-18. Prācī Sarasvatī is to the west of the celestial river, O king, in the Kuṇḍa of Śūlabheda where she had fallen.

There is an excellent Tīrtha to the south of Śūlabheda. It is there that the meritorious Devaśilā was created by the Lord himself.

If one takes his holy bath there with devotion and propitiates the Pitṛs and deities, they will become contented until the time of the annihilation of all living beings.

A person should feed Brāhmaṇas there with great devotion after taking a holy dip there. Even if a small quantity of cooked food is offered, there is no end thereof (in regard to efficacy).

Uttānapāda said:

What are those Dānas which when offered are highly esteemed in the world? By offering which devoutly is a man rid of all sins? Tell me the greatness of Devaśilā, the benefit that accrues from the holy bath, Dāna and the like and the good that would be attained through Vrata, Upavāsa (fast) and Niyama (restraints and observances).

Īśvara said:

O king, formerly there was a very powerful king of Cedi well-known as Vīrasena. He was the Lord of a vast region and he was superbly vigorous. There was no enemy throughout the land nor was there any pestilence. No thieves ravaged the land nor was there any impiety. Only righteousness prevailed everywhere and at all times.

The king had many sons and he was always joyous in the company of his wives. He had a single daughter as beautiful as the Daughter of the Mountain (Pārvatī). The girl was a darling of the parents and all the kinsmen. At the proper time her marriage was duly celebrated.

19-26. Thereafter the king of Cedi began a Yajña (a sacrifice) lasting for twelve years. In the meantime the husband of his daughter met with his death.

Seeing his daughter widowed the king became grief-stricken. He told his wife who too was afflicted with misery: "My dear, a great misery has befallen us. It shall be unbearable throughout our life. This girl is proud due to her beauty and youth. It is very difficult to keep her under restraint. Perhaps she may even spoil the family. How can this girl be guarded? There is no means whereby Bhānumatī (name of the girl) can be kept safe." On hearing the mutual discussion of the parents, the girl said:

Bhānumatī said:

O dear father, I am never ashamed to say what follows before you. Verily no defect or default shall assail you, O king, on my account. From now onwards I shall cease to have my tresses of hairs. At your place I shall wear half (of the usual length) of a coarse cloth. I shall observe the Vratas laid down in the Purāṇas. I shall cause myself to wither up and thus propitiate Janārdana. This is what I think, dear father, if you allow me to do so.

On hearing the words of Bhānumatī, the king became highly delighted.

27-35. In view of her intended pilgrimage, the king placed a vast amount of wealth at her disposal. To guard her he engaged many old men to accompany her. He sent Brāhmaṇas and priests, slaves and servants as well as foot-soldiers capable of protecting her.

Thus with the full consent of her father the chaste lady went to the banks of Gaṅgā, O king. She took holy dips in both the shores[1] of Gaṅgā. Honouring excellent Brāhmaṇas everyday with sweet scents, garlands, ornaments etc., she spent twelve years on the banks of Gaṅgā.

---

1. This probably implies that she performed a circumambulation of the river.

Thereafter, the princess left Gaṅgā and proceeded towards the South and arrived at the great river Revā along with her attendants and ministerial followers. At Oṁkāra at Amarakaṇṭaka she stayed for five years. She went from one Tīrtha to another Tīrtha both on the north as well as on the south bank (of Revā). Taking many holy ablutions and adoring Brāhmaṇas devoutly and without lethargy, she went to the West reaching the confluence of the celestial river.

There she saw a holy hermitage full of the congregation of sages. On seeing the saintly concourse she bowed down and said: "What is the greatness of this Tīrtha? What is the name? I may be favoured by ye, O venerable ones. Let this be spoken."

The sages said:

36-47. This is well-known as Cakra Tīrtha. It was here that the discus was granted to Hari by the Trident-bearing Lord of Devas, the delighted Maheśvara.

If a person takes his holy bath in the Tīrtha here and propitiates the Pitṛs and deities, he will undoubtedly reach that destination from where there is no return at all.

O Tapasvinī (ascetic woman), the next day the person should go to Śūlabheda and duly perform the holy ablution in accordance with the injunctions mentioned before.

He will undoubtedly be rid of sins committed in the course of three births. Three cavity-fuls of water and gingelly seeds (*Añjali* = cavity of palms joined together) alone should be offered as libation (to Pitṛs). There is no doubt that the Pitṛs thus become satiated for twelve years.

He who performs Śrāddha devoutly through Brāhmaṇas well-versed in the Vedas, O king, should avoid usuriousness. Whatever is offered to the Pitṛs becomes everlasting in its benefit.

The next day, he should go to the splendid and meritorious Devaśilā. There the meritorious Jāhnavī formerly created by Devas, is visible.

O king, one should take holy bath there and offer water mixed with gingelly seeds (to Pitṛs). Merely offering balls of rice once, one is rid of the sin of Brāhmaṇa-slaughter.

The person should observe fast on the eleventh day in either half (of the month) and keep awake at night. He should also read the story from a Purāṇa. He should perform the adoration of Viṣṇu with flowers, incense and Naivedya offerings. He should feed Brāhmaṇas in the morning and make gifts in accordance with his capacity.

On the fourth day he should go to the place where Prācīsarasvatī (flows) issuing forth from the body of Brahmā, for the purpose of sanctifying embodied beings. After taking bath the man should devoutly propitiate the Pitṛs and deities.

After duly performing the Śrāddha he should feed uncensurable (praise-worthy) Brāhmaṇas. Undoubtedly the Pitṛs become satiated for twelve years.

48-57. This spot consists of all Devas and all Tīrthas. The place is full of crores of deities and is the most excellent of all excellent Tīrthas with ten million Liṅgas.

If a person who is pure and has controlled his sense-organs, takes his bath for three nights, a fortnight, a month, six months and (sometimes) a year, he is sure to dwell in heaven. He will never be born again in the mortal world.

Strictly observing the restraints he will be rid of sins accumulated in the course of three births.

A woman of pure vows who remains there for a period of twelve years without a male associate, is honoured in Rudraloka for all times.

On hearing the words of the sages, she went ahead with great joy. She took holy bath in the Tīrtha and remained active and alert day and night.

On seeing the power of the Tīrtha she said again, "O Brāhmaṇas including the priests, may my words be listened to. I will not forsake such a holy spot as this either in the day or at night as long as I live. Kindly tell my mother and father these words: 'Your daughter is staying at Śūlabheda, regularly observing the vows.'"

After saying this, O king, Princess Bhānumatī continued her stay there. She began the observance of fast on alternative days. Gradually she increased the duration of the fast to a month. She always stationed herself at Devaśilā and meditated upon the Discus-bearing Lord. She burned incense day and night; offered sandalpaste and lights. She herself washed the feet and fed Brāhmaṇas. That queen (Princess) thus observed her vows and stayed there for twelve years.[1]

Īśvara said:

58-68. Now, O king, listen to another story showing the greatness of Devaśilā. I shall narrate, O mighty-armed one, an old legend along with the historical background.

There was a hunter, a forest-dweller of the Śabara tribe. Afflicted by famine he went to the forest accompanied by his wife for procuring some meat. He did not see birds or animals or fruits. Ultimately he espied a lake beautified with clusters of lotuses.

On seeing the excellent lake, the Śabarī (Śabara's wife) spoke these words: "Take these splendid lilies (lotuses) for the sake of getting the money for our food. Righteous and pious persons will be coming to Śūlabheda for the adoration of the Lord. The flowers can be sold."

On hearing the words of his wife, he gathered the lotus flowers. After coming out of the water he saw a Śrīvṛkṣa (Bilva tree) in front of him. He plucked ripe fruits of Śrīphala and reached Śūlabheda where he saw a great number of people.

On the eleventh day in the bright half of the month of Caitra, even children, old men and women should not eat anything.

He saw a pavilion erected there over the Devaśilā rock. It was divinely exquisite, embellished with flower garlands and covered with cloths.

The sages who lived in the hermitages came there. They undertook their fasts and holy observances. All of them had the holy fires with them and their wives too were there.

The entire bank of the Devanadī appeared very charming with the crowds of sages. O excellent king, the whole path was blocked by visitors.

69-79. On seeing the entire country present there, the Śabara said to his wife: "Go and ask someone as to why they

1. Upto verse 57 the story of Bhānumatī is narrated. The remaining part of her story will be told later. In the meanwhile the story of Sabarī, which is a part of Bhānumatī's, is told by Īśvara. The story is told to emphasize the Māhātmya of Devaśilā and is not a break in Bhānumatī's story.

are having the holy bath. Is it any of the Parvas (holy festival days) about which we hear? Is it the lunar or solar eclipse? Is it the transit of the Sun or the Akṣayatṛtīyā?"

Thereupon, at the instance of her husband the Śabarī set off. She saw a woman there to whom she gave two splendid lotus flowers and asked: "What is the Tithi (lunar day) today? What is the Parva today? Do tell me. Why do the people take the holy ablution? What is the reason for the holy bath?"

The woman said:

It is the holy Ekādaśī (eleventh day) today. It causes destruction of all sins. If even once anyone observes fast today, he will attain heaven.

On hearing her words, the Śabarī recounted to the Śabara without excitement, O excellent king, the entire statement of the woman. "It is a meritorious Ekādaśī today. It is named Madanaikādaśī. Even children and old men observe fast today. All sins will be destroyed thereby. It is heard that there is a splendid princess, regularly observing holy vows and restrictions in diet. The chaste lady is Bhānumatī by name. No woman on a par with this lady has been heard of in all the three worlds. She appears to be some divine lady incarnated on the earth."

On hearing the words of his wife, the Śabara said to her: "Sell the lotuses for whatever you get immediately and get your food. But this is my firm determination that I should not eat. O fair lady, evil-minded that I am, nothing auspicious has been done by me."

Śabarī said:

80-89. As far as I remember, I did not eat before you (have eaten). Whatever was left after your meal only that was eaten by me.

On coming to know of the resolute decision of his wife, the hunter went away to have his holy bath. Wearing half of his upper garment he devoutly took his holy bath. He paid respects to all the Devas and then went to Devaśilā. Though diffident (about results) he stood there bowing down to Janārdana.

The queen (Princess) was informed by that woman to whom the Śabarī had given the two lotus flowers. On seeing the pair of lotus flowers, she (Princess) said to the servant: "Wherefrom were the lotus flowers obtained by you. Do tell me presently. Go quickly and bring more such lotus flowers. Bring the lotus flowers in exchange of food grain or cash."

On hearing the words of Bhānumatī, she (the servant woman) went to the Śabara. "Give me more of the Śrīphalas and flowers."

Śabarī said:

Go and tell the queen that I shall give you the Śrīphalas along with the flowers. I do not covet anything nor do I wish for anything in return.

She hastened back and told the princess everything just as it happened and the words of the Śabarī in full detail.

On hearing her words, the queen herself went there and spoke lovingly to the Śabarī: "Give me the lotuses for the price."

Śabarī said:

90-97. O queen, I do not desire to get (any) price of the flowers and the fruits. Śrīphalas and flowers may be taken from me as you please. Do perform duly the adoration of Vāsudeva, the Lord of the universe.

The queen said:

I will not accept the lotuses from you without giving the price thereof. I shall give you a Khārikā (sixteen Droṇas) of food-grain. May it be accepted.

Accept ten, twenty, thirty, forty or even a hundred Khārikās and go across the ocean of famine.

For the sake of the lotuses, I shall surely give you money, jewels, gold or anything else desired by you.

Śabarī said:

O lady of fair countenance, I do not think of foodstuff now. Excepting the Lord, I do not think of anything else. My mind is not inclined to anything other than the thought of the Lord, O fair lady.

The queen said:

Food should not be discarded by you. Everything is established in food. Hence, by all means accept the foodstuff given by me. Sages of great esteem, those who dwell in forests—all diligently come and beg at the portals of householders.

Śabarī said:

98-110. It has been rejected earlier. Everything is established in Satya (Truth). It is due to Satya that the sun blazes. It is because of Satya that the fire burns. Through Satya the ocean stands (firm). The wind blows through Satya. Through Satya crops ripen and cows yield milk. The entire universe consisting of mobile and immobile beings has Satya for its support. Hence by all means, one should protect Satya through abiding by Satya. Excepting the task pertaining to the Lord, my mind is not inclined in regard to anything. Take the flowers, O queen, and perform the adoration of the mace-bearing Lord Viṣṇu.

It is learnt through the statements of Brāhmaṇas that there is no harm at all in accepting Kuśa grass, greens, water, fish, scents, flowers, raw rice-grain (for rituals), meat, bed, seat, corn etc., and water. These should not be rejected.

The queen said:

Flowers are of four types: those plucked from gardens; flowers (collected) from forest; flowers which are bought and flowers obtained as gift. The best one is a flower from the forest plucked by oneself. The middling is a fruit (flower) gathered from a garden. That which is bought is the base one. Learned men know that what is obtained as a gift is futile.

Purohita (Priest) said:

O queen, take the flowers and perform the adoration of the mace-bearing Lord Viṣṇu. Under some pretext you should render help in return at some other time.

Īśvara said:

Accepting the Śrīphalas given by the Śabara along with the

lotus flowers, the queen performed the auspicious adoration. She listened to the Purāṇic story and kept awake at night. Thereupon the Śabara spoke these words to his wife: "O beautiful lady, let the oil be taken as much as can be obtained for the lamps." Thereafter they lighted a lamp and performed the auspicious adoration of Hari.

They meditated upon the Upholder of the Earth and kept awake at night. At dawn they saw the people eager to take the holy bath. Some were bathing in Śūlabheda and others in the Devanadī. Some men took bath in Sarasvatī and others in the whirlpool of Mārkaṇḍa.

111-120. Some went to Cakrạtīrtha and took the holy bath in accordance with the injunctions. All those pure persons performed Śrāddha assiduously and faithfully on the Devaśilā rock after their holy bath. Their mind remained pure.

On seeing them, the Śabara too offered Piṇḍas with the Bilva fruits.

Similarly Bhānumatī offered the Piṇḍas to her husband. Uncensurable (praiseworthy) Brāhmaṇas who were devoid of hypocrisy and practice of usury were fed.

The queen fed them with Haviṣya (cooked rice), curd, sugar, honey and ghee, milk pudding made out of cow's milk and especially with Kṛtānna (rice mixed with condiments etc.). After feeding them, the queen made monetary and other gifts in accordance with the injunctions. The gifts were sandals and shoes, umbrella, bed, cow, bull, various kinds of jewels, gold and cash too.

O great king, if a person makes a gift of a tawny-coloured cow at Cakratīrtha, it is on a par with a gift of the whole earth along with the mountains, forests and parks.

Uttānapāda said:

O Lord of Devas, be favourably disposed towards me and recount to me all those esteemed gifts to be made over (in the name) of the Lord of the universe.

Īśvara said:

He who makes the gift of gingelly seeds obtains desired progeny; he who gives lamps gets excellent visual power; he who gives plot of land attains heaven and he who gives gold gets longevity.

The giver of a house becomes free from ailments; he who gives silver becomes handsome; he who gives clothes attains the world of the Moon; and he who gives horses becomes identical with the Sun-god.

One who gives a bull attains well-attained glory and fortune; a giver of cows goes to heaven; one who gives vehicles and bed obtains a (good) wife and one who gives succour from fear obtains prosperity.

121-129. A person who gives foodgrain attains permanent happiness; one who gives Vedic text attains the eternal Brahman. Of all Dānas, viz. water, food, earth, clothes, gingelly seeds, gold and ghee, Brahmadāna (gift of learning) is the best.

The donor gets correspondingly adequate return in accordance with the intention or the degree of emotional fervour with which he makes the gift, whatever it may be.

O king, listen to what the Śabara said to his wife on seeing the various gifts made by the queen: "O fair lady, I have heard entirely the Purāṇa as read by the Brāhmaṇas who have mastered the Vedas. The benefit of the Dānadharma is auspicious. The sin accumulated in the previous births has been wiped off through the holy bath, Dāna, Vrata etc. After casting off the body, that cannot be ordinarily cast off, one attains excellent goal. I am afraid of the ocean of worldly existence, O fair lady. I speak the truth unto you. I have committed many sins, O fair lady. Many animals have been killed by me. I have always burnt down many hills. I am scorched by those sins. Poverty never leaves me. The sinner that I am, I have never taken the holy bath in a Tīrtha. Therefore, O fair lady, I am miserable. I have incurred poverty that cannot be removed. You go to your mother's house. Cease to have love and affection for me. I wish to climb on to the peak of the mountain and hurl myself to death."

Śabarī said:

130-134. I have nothing to do with my mother or father. I have nothing to do with kinsmen and relatives. O my Lord, I shall attain the same goal as you. Women's Dharma does not allow that they should continue to live without their husbands.

In such a life many defects are possible as proclaimed by Dharmaśāstra texts, O Lord of Bhojas (i.e. Śabara clan). Do make the ritualistic breaking of the fast, lest the Vrata should be defective. Whatever is desired by you, you should dedicate to Viṣṇu.

On hearing the words of his wife the Śabara was pleased. He took the Śrīphala and duly performed the Homa. After bowing down to all the deities he took food with her. Coming to know that there was Viṣuva (Equinox) on the full-moon day of Caitra he stayed there for three days.

CHAPTER FIFTYSEVEN

The Śabara Goes to Svarga

Īśvara said:

1-8. After feeding Brāhmaṇas, Bhānumatī ate what was left after feeding them. After eating she took rest with pleasure, while the food got digested. On the Madanākhyā Trayodaśī day (thirteenth of the bright half named Madana), she took bath in the Hrada (whirlpool) of Mārkaṇḍa and adored Lord Guhāśaya (Śiva) (stationed in a cave as abode). She observed fast as enjoined. She bathed Maheśvara with Pañcāmṛta and sweet scents. Incense, lamps, *Naivedyas* were offered. She adored (the Lord) with different kinds of flowers and excellent *Naivedyas.* She kept awake in the night hearing Purāṇic stories and witnessing dances and hearing songs and prayers. She meditated upon Lord Maheśvara. The entire quantity of cooked food was duly spread in front of the Lord. All the people belonging to all the four castes were fed along with their attendants.

On the fourteenth day the whole day was spent in worshipping the Bull-emblemed Lord. She kept awake in the night keeping conchs blowing and drums and other instruments continuously being played. The sound of Paṭahas echoed everywhere. Many devotees thronged there. Then the whole night was spent in dancing and singing songs and prayers. At dawn the Brāhmaṇas were fed with milk-puddings, honey and ghee.

9-16. Gifts were made to Brāhmaṇas in accordance with own capacity as well as the qualifications of the ones. The Lord was adored with sweet-smelling flowers such as Madana and the like, and clothed all round with delicate clothes of various colours. Many garlands were kept hanging down and many lamps were kept blazing. There were various kinds of sweet cooked foods such as Modakas etc., round in shape.

Then all those Brāhmaṇas engrossed in the study of the Vedas glorified that Parva by the name *Padmaka*. Today is the day of the Sun (Sunday). The Tithi (lunar day) is fifteenth. The constellation is that pertaining to Tvaṣṭṛ. Today is the day of the transit of the Sun, the equinoctial time. Vyatīpāta is the Yoga and Viṣṭi is the Karaṇa. This Parva named *Padmaka* has four times more benefit than that of *Ayana* etc. Whatever is offered, consigned to the sacred fire, or repeated as Japa becomes everlasting.

Those Brāhmaṇas went to Śūlabheda along with Bhānumatī. They saw the Śabara standing at the Kuṇḍa along with his wife. O king, the Śabara went in the north-eastern direction. He climbed on to the Bhṛgu mountain along with his wife in order to leap down therefrom.

Bhānumatī said:

17-23. O noble-minded one, stop, stop. Listen to my words. Why do you give up your life? You are still a youth. What is your distress? What is the cause of your dejection? What is your misery? What is your ailment? You seem to be a child now. Pray, let the reason be mentioned.

Śabara said:

I have no reason to offer. I have no sorrow. I am afraid of the worldly existence and my intellect does not intend to do anything else. It is with very great difficulty that one fortunately obtains human birth. If, even after getting the human birth, one does not practise piety, O beautiful lady, one definitely falls into a terrible hell solely due to one's own defect. Hence I wish to hurl myself down into this Tīrtha that is destructive of sins.

The queen said:

You have yet ample time to acquire piety. Whether one has done one's duty well or ill, one becomes pure through Vrata and Dāna. I shall give you food-grain or clothes or adequate cash. Perform righteous actions always. Always meditate upon Maheśvara.

Śabara said:

24-31. I desire no money, no food-grains, no garments. If anyone accepts food from another, he accepts his sins as well.

The queen said:

One who has bulbous roots, roots and fruits for food or wanders begging for excellent alms or takes the holy bath in the excellent Tīrthas, is rid of all sins. Whatever the pure man does, he shall be free from sins. You will become pure through your holy rites and will certainly attain beatitude.

Śabara said:

Intake of food has been abandoned by me today, but I will not eschew Satya (Truth) which is greater even than my vital airs. O fair lady, do this favour to me. Excuse me.

After saying this the Śabara bound himself with half of his upper cloth, meditated upon Hari and fell down along with his wife.

When he fall down from the top of the mountain, O king, he died. They were seen smashed to smithereens over the Kuṇḍa. Within a period of three Muhūrtas the Śabara climbed on to an aerial chariot along with his wife and attained the excellent state (i.e. beatitude).

CHAPTER FIFTYEIGHT

The Greatness of Śūlabheda Tīrtha

Uttānapāda said:

1-8. Thereafter, O Lord of the chiefs of Devas, what did Bhānumatī do? This is my doubt. O Lord, do me the favour of mentioning this.

Īśvara said:

After reflecting for a short while, she went near the Kuṇḍa. Observing the greatness of the Kuṇḍa, the queen became filled with delight.

She invited many Brāhmaṇas and adored them duly at the same moment. The princess duly made gifts to the Brāhmaṇas. After making firm resolve, she stayed with calmness of mind.

Then, O king, she adored the Pitṛs and Devas. She spent a fortnight of the month of Madhu remaining there. Then on the new-moon day, the queen went near the mountain.

She climbed on to the peak of the mountain, joined the palms of the hands together and spoke these words of request to all those Brāhmaṇas: "May my mother, father, brother and all other friends and relatives be requested to forgive me. Let them be told these words of mine: 'Your daughter performed penance at Śūlabheda in accordance with her capacity. She cast herself into that Tīrtha and has gone to heaven.'"

The Brāhmaṇas said:

9-13. O lady of splendid vows, we shall convey the message given by you to your mother and father. O lady of excellent hips, let there be no doubt in your mind.

After dismissing those people, she, stood on the peak of the mountain and girdled herself with half of the upper cloth firmly. Then, O king, with concentration she hurled herself down from the top of the mountain.

When she fell down (half the distance from the mountain) the celestial damsels were delighted. They said: "O dear Bhānumatī, O highly esteemed fortunate lady of great penance, be pleased to get into the divine aerial chariot and proceed towards Kailāsa." Even as they were all watching, she went to heaven.

Mārkaṇḍeya said:

14-24. Thus the full details regarding Śūlabheda have been recounted to you as heard earlier from Śaṅkara in the assembly of sages and Devas.

He who devoutly reads this at a Tīrtha or in a divine shrine, is released from great sins incurred in the course of a hundred births.

All these (following) sinners are released from the sins by the power of Śūlabheda: Sinners such as a Brāhmaṇa-slayer, a drinker of spirituous liquor, a thief, a defiler of his preceptor's bed, a killer of cows, a murderer of women, a misappropriator of the property of gods (temples) and Brāhmaṇas, a traitor to his master, a killer of friends, a committer of breach of trust, one who takes away the deposits of others, destroyer of other people's treasures (or pawned things), a diluter of wine, a user of false weights, a usurer (with high rates) , a creater of impediments (with regard to marriages etc.) of girls, a seller of girls, one who indulges in sexual intercourse with wives of others or a brother, cows, daughter-in-law, daughters, a hater of others and defiler of piety. If anyone reads this at the time of Śrāddha, O king, while the Brāhmaṇas take their food, the Pitṛs become over-joyed with him.

One who devoutly listens to this when it is being read and has self-control shall be rid of all sins. He shall enjoy all pleasures and niceties of life.

This is conducive to great fame and longevity; this is sacred and excellent. It increases the life span and glory of those men who read and listen.

Thus the meritorious greatness of Śūlabheda has been recounted to you. It is not listened to by sinners. This Śūlabheda is situated on the southern bank of the river of the enemy of Madana (i.e. Gaṅgā). It is like a spade that digs up and uproots the bulbous roots of powerful sins.

CHAPTER FIFTYNINE

The Greatness of Āditya Tīrtha

Mārkaṇḍeya said:

1-8. Thereafter, a person should go to Puṣkariṇī that is destructive of all sins. When its power is listened to, one is rid of all sins.

There is a highly splendid Tīrtha on the northern bank of Revā, where Lord Divākara (Sun-god) is always present as Vedamūrti (the Veda incarnate).

This Tīrtha is meritorious and bestower of all desires just as Kurukṣetra is meritorious, excellent and conducive to the fulfilment of all desires.

O Lord of the Earth, just as Dāna increases in benefit at Kurukṣetra, so also undoubtedly it increases in Puṣkariṇī as well.

If a person gifts a grain of Yava at Puṣkariṇī, the place (in heaven) that he attains is proclaimed as the same as when one offers gold over the head, O king.

One should take his holy ablution at the time of solar eclipse and make duly gifts of elephants, horses, chariots, jewels, a house, cows, bullocks bearing the burden of the yokes etc.

If a person gives gold or silver to Brāhmaṇas till the thirteenth day, it shall give thirteen times the benefit.

He should propitiate the Pitṛs and deities by means of libations of water mixed with gingelly seeds. The person shall cherish love for that Tīrtha in the twelfth year, O king.

9-14. If a person performs Śrāddha there with milk-pudding, honey and ghee, the performer of Śrāddha attains heaven. Everything given to the Pitṛs shall be everlasting.

One attains never-failing benefit by offering raw rice grains, Badaras, Bilvas or oil extracted from Iṅguda along with sesamum in that Tīrtha.

There is no doubt about it. The devotee shall take his holy ablution in the Tīrtha, worship Lord Divākara, perform the Japa of *Ādityahṛdaya* and again worship the Sun-god. He shall attain the greatest world honoured even by Devas.

If a person makes the Japa of even a single Mantra from the Ṛgveda, Yajur Veda or a Sāman hymn, O king, he attains the benefit of (reciting) the entire Veda.

One who meditates upon Divākara and repeats the three-syllabled Mantra (i.e. Āditya) after the Japa of *Ādityahṛdaya*, is released from all sins.

O excellent king, one who duly gives up his life there, shall go to the greatest region where Lord Divākara is present.

CHAPTER SIXTY

The Greatness of Ādityeśvara Tīrtha

Śrī Mārkaṇḍeya said:

1-8. I shall further describe (the greatness of) the excellent Ādityeśvara which is destructive of all miseries and all obstacles, O son of Pṛthā. The Tīrtha is always conducive to longevity, increase in glory and prosperity. It grants sons, welfare and heavenly pleasures.

O scion of the family of Kurus, other (Ravi) Tīrthas have not attained the glory of this Tīrtha, whether in heaven, or mortal world or in Pātāla. O excellent king, all these Tīrthas, viz. Kurukṣetra, Gayā, Gaṅgā, Naimiṣa, Puṣkara, Vārāṇasī, Kedāra, Prayāga, Rudra-nandana, Mahākāla, Sahasrākṣa and Śukla Tīrtha do not merit even a sixteenth fraction of Ravi Tīrtha.

O excellent king, listen to what happened in Ravitīrtha. Though I am extremely distressed due to old age, I shall narrate it to you out of affection. May all the sages of great vigour engaged in austerities listen.

This has been heard by me in the presence of Rudra along with Nandin, Skanda and the Gaṇas. Śaṁbhu was asked by Pārvatī as to the benefit of Ravitīrtha. What was narrated by Śaṁbhu enthusiastically, everything sung about by Rudra, was heard by me with concentrated attention.

9-16. I shall recount it to you. Listen to it with caution. Brāhmaṇas oppressed by famine resorted to Narmadā. They were: Uddālaka, Vasiṣṭha, Māṇḍavya, Gautama, Yājñavalkya, Garga, Śāṇḍilya, Gālava, Naciketā, Vibhāṇḍa, Vālakhilyas and others, Śātātapa, Śaṅkha, Jaimini, Gobhila, Jaigīṣavya, Śatānīka. All those came there.

Pilgrimage was performed by them around Narmadā. Incidentally the leading sages came to the Ādityeśvara shrine too. It was splendid and was covered with various trees such as Dhava, Tinduka, Pāṭala, Jaṁbīra, Arjuna, Kubjaka, Śamī, Kesara, Kiṁśuka etc. That Tīrtha of highly meritorious nature was full of fragrant flowers. There were the trees of Punnāga, coconut, Khadira and Kalpa trees as well. The holy spot was infested by many beasts of prey, deer and cats. It was rendered splendid by bears, elephants and Citrakas (hunting leopards). All the sages entered the forest full of flowers.

17-23. At the end of the forest, they saw women of red complexion wearing red garments. They had smeared themselves with red sandalpaste and worn red-coloured ornaments. They were holding nooses in their hands and were terrifying (to look at). Near them were men resembling black clouds. Their faces (mouths) were large and they had huge bodies. They had nooses in their hands and they could be compared to Anāvṛṣṭi (Drought). They had tawny-coloured eyes.

O most excellent one among the descendants of Kuru, another old woman was seen by the leading sages. She had a long tongue. Her face was hideous and her curved fangs were sharp. She was unassailable. O descendant of Bharata, the old woman was very near that group. The Brāhmaṇas engaged in their self-study of the Vedas were seen by those people of evil actions.

They collectively spoke to the Brāhmaṇas engaged in austerities: "All our masters are standing in the midst of the Tīrtha. Those highly esteemed ones should be urged to start hurriedly by all means."

On hearing those words of theirs, all of them hurriedly went to the marshy land in Narmadā and the excellent Brāhmaṇas surveyed Revā.

24-37. Then some of the others began to eulogize: "Be victorious, O divine one, (we make) obeisance to you. Obeisance to you, O (river) resorted to by groups of Siddhas. Obeisance to you, the most auspicious and sacred one among all. Obeisance to you, the most excellent one issuing forth from the person of Rudra.

Obeisance to you, the holiest and the most sanctifying one of all. Obeisance to you, O divine one, O auspicious bestower of boons. I bow to you, O excellent one among the rivers, O bestower of happiness, O destroyer of sins, O river of diverse features and cool waters. Obeisance to you whose limbs (waters) are respectfully attended to by many groups of living beings. (Bow to you) whose waters have purified Gandharvas, Yakṣas and Serpents, one whose waters are drunk by herds of great elephants, buffaloes and boars; (to you) who wear water-waves as garlands. I bow down to you, the most excellent one among all, the bestower of happiness. Do release us fettered by the nooses of sins.

Men do wander through the hells only as long as they do not resort to your waters, touched by the rays of the moon and the sun. O divine one, if it is touched (by the devotees) it shall bestow the highest region.

O divine one with a face resembling a lotus, you are the ultimate goal unto the people harassed by many a fear of the worldly existence, enveloped by many sins and many *Dvandvas* (mutually opposing pairs like pain-pleasure etc.). There is no doubt about this, O divine one, that rivers become sanctified and free from impurities after having resorted to you. You bestow freedom from fear on those who are afflicted by miseries. You are adored by many Śiṣṭas (men of good conduct).

Men with their physical forms submerged in faeces and urine, wander in hells as long as they do not touch this water, the waves whereof are scattered with great power.

Even Mlecchas (barbarians), Pulindas (hunting tribe), Yātudhānas (demons) who drink thy meritorious water, O divine one, become released from terrible fear. More so in the case of the Brāhmaṇas afraid of the noose of worldly existence.

In this terrible Yuga brought in by Kali, lakes and rivers get decreased, but you, O divine one, shine with the waters full to the brim like Gaṅgā in the heavenly path of the galaxy.

O bestower of boons, O excellent one, after waiting this much of time we will, with your favour, attain liberation. Do this favour so that we will attain salvation.

Those who have resorted to you, those who have sought refuge in you, have you as the ultimate goal. You protect them like a mother or like a father who protects the sons. Protected by you, we pass off the terrible period of oppression due to drought."

Eulogized thus, O Yudhiṣṭhira, the divine river Narmadā, the most excellent one among the rivers, became visible to those Brāhmaṇas in the most excellent form.

Mārkaṇḍeya said:

38-46. O king, those who read and listen to this prayer with great devotion and mental calmness, attain Rudra by means of a vehicle yoked with a bull. Their limbs will be embellished with divine garments.

If persons take bath in the waters of Narmadā and repeat this prayer always, this excellent river shall ere long bestow on them, at the close of their life, the purest state (in the other world).

One should get up in the morning and repeat this excellent hymn everyday. When one goes to bed then also one should repeat this. Thereupon the holy River grants him the dissolution of his body in her own waters. O king of great esteem, she accords him support as well. They will be rid of sins and will rejoice in heaven enjoying all pleasures. Not otherwise.

The divine river Narmadā, on being propitiated by this hymn, O descendant of Bharata, nourished those Brāhmaṇas by means of her waters. She flowed through the southern tract of land. The River said: "I shall grant you Amṛtatva (immortality) which is not obtained even by Yogins. It is very difficult even for all the Suras to attain. You will get it with my favour."

After receiving this very excellent boon the Brāhmaṇas were delighted in their minds. As they were going, they saw a great miracle:

Śrī Mārkaṇḍeya said:

O son of Kuntī, persons stationed on the banks of Narmadā were seen by them. They were very powerful and engaged in holy ablution and adoration of the deity. They were five in number.

They were seen by all the Brāhmaṇas who had mastered the Vedas and Vedāṅgas. Understand, O great king, how they were enquired after by them:

The Brāhmaṇas said:

47-59. At the end of the forest was a pair of women extremely terrible and awe-inspiring. These old men too with nooses in their hands were terror-striking. They were unassailable, difficult to look at and moving about here and there. They spoke auspicious words: "There is no salvation there."

All of them began to look about here and there again and again, but not at each other. May the words uttered by them be narrated in full. "O excellent men, our five men (husbands) stay there. O blessed ones, they should be made to proceed promptly and hurriedly by all means."

Then those five men after hearing these auspicious words, looked at one another and began to say again and again: "Where are they? Whose? Where did they go? What was said by those terrible ones?"

The men said:

By all (of us) *Tīrthāvagāhana* (bathing in the holy waters) was performed with great devotion in all Tīrthas in eastern, southern, western and northern directions. But the sin has not been dispelled by them. But they (we) became free from sins by the power of this Tīrtha. May all the sages, the Brāhmaṇas, comparable to fire and god of Death (in brilliance) listen: Their sins were terrible, unthinkable unto the embodied ones. The wife of the preceptor was resorted to by one of the sinners. The wealth of a friend, gold and other assets, was taken away by another. The sin of Brāhmaṇa-slaughter, the highly terrible sin, was committed by another. Another unwittingly committed the sin of imbibing spirituous liquor. The slaughter of cows was committed by another sinner unwittingly. O king, the sins of all these were committed unintentionally. On hearing those words of the Brāhmaṇas they became surprised. Instantly all the sinners became rid of sins by the power of this Tīrtha, the power of Narmadā.

60-70. Nowhere can sins gain access here. All those sinners thought after consulting one another. Citrabhānu (Sun) was remembered by them after thinking about Hari in the heart. After taking the holy plunge in the auspicious waters of Revā, the Pitṛs and deities were propitiated by them. After meditating on Lord Janārdana in the heart and bowing to Lord Bhāskara (Sun-god) they circumambulated the blazing fire with devotion. O king, O excellent one among the sons of Pāṇḍu, they who were distressed due to the sins and were fallen, now regained the *sāttvikī bhāvanā* (mental predilection of Sāttvika type) and abandoned Rajas and Tamas.

On the northern bank of Narmadā everything was destroyed by them in the fire. Then, O Yudhiṣṭhira, they were seen seated in an aerial chariot.

An incomparable miracle was seen by the sages on the banks of Narmadā. Ever since then all of them were bereft of *Rāga* (attachment) and *Dveṣa* (hatred). The Brāhmaṇas who were delighted resorted to Ravi Tīrtha with a desire for salvation.

O king, listen to the auspicious merit of this Tīrtha. I am afflicted by old age, O king, but happy due to the devotion. I am stationed within two Krośas (1 Krośa = 3 Kms.). Hence I shall describe in a general way Ravitīrtha that is as auspicious as Kurukṣetra. It is what was recounted by Īśvara formerly to Ṣaṇmukha and heard by me. It was heard by them all from Rudra and I was present nearby.

Īśvara said:

When a solar eclipse takes place, O Ṣaḍānana, the (meritorious) benefit in Kurukṣetra and Ravitīrtha is on a par with each other. In regard to the holy bath, Dāna, Jāpya and Homa in particular the benefit in Kurukṣetra is the same (as here at Ravi Tīrtha). No doubt should be entertained in this connection.

71-78. Whether it is a village or a forest, Narmadā is auspicious and meritorious everywhere. Especially at Ravi Tīrtha Revā is the bestower of meritorious benefits.

Persons with the sense-organs under control should visit the Tīrtha on a sixth lunar day, Sunday, Vyatīpāta, Vaidhṛti, Saṅkrānti, eclipse day and new-moon day. They should be free from lust and anger as well as *Rāga* (attachment) and *Dveṣa* (hated). They should observe fast before the deity with great devotion. They should keep awake at night and offer light unto the deity. They must listen to the story of Viṣṇu or, O son of Kuntī, they should repeat Vedic Mantras, whether they be from Ṛgveda, Yajurveda, Sāmaveda or Atharveda. One who recites even one Ṛk shall obtain the benefit of (the recitation of) the whole Veda and by the recitation of the Gāyatrī the benefit of the recitation of all the four Vedas is obtained.

At dawn the persons should adore Brāhmaṇas with the gifts of cooked food and gold, or by giving plots of land, garments and cooked food in accordance with their capacity.

O son of Pāṇḍu, they may make gifts of umbrella, shoes, beds and houses. There shall be freedom from fear through the gifts of an elephant, a virgin, a horse, learning, a bull capable of bearing a yoke, vehicle etc.

79-86. Enemy becomes friend; poison becomes Amṛta. The Planets become highly pleased and the Sun becomes pleased.

Thus the entire merit-giving benefit of Ravitīrtha has been recounted to you, O king. Men who devoutly hear the auspicious benefit of Ravitīrtha shall be rid of sins. They reside in the world of Ravi. He who gifts a pot of gingelly seeds gets the benefit that accrues from the gift of a cow, by viewing Bhṛgu, by drinking the water in Kedāra and also the worship of an Aśvattha tree for a year. By glorifying Ādityeśvara one gets all these (above-mentioned) benefits. On listening to the efficacy, O prince, one ceases to be born again i.e. gets liberated. I shall mention all these to you, O king, out of devotion. All sins disappear like water when the pot (containing it) is broken. One should undoubtedly be face to face with the Tīrtha. There is no doubt about it. The greatest secret of the Tīrtha has been mentioned to you, O son of Pāṇḍu.

The auspicious narration of the Tīrtha should be kept concealed from all sinners, persons who kill masters, friends etc. This should be guarded always by sensible persons.

CHAPTER SIXTYONE

The Greatness of Śakreśvara Tīrtha

Śrī Mārkaṇḍeya said:

1-10. Thereafter one should go to the well-known meritorious Śakratīrtha on the southern bank of Narmadā. It is destructive of all sins.

Formerly a very severe penance was started by Śakra at that Tīrtha itself. With great devotion he performed penance with Lord Maheśvara in view.

Propitiated thereby, O king, the Lord, the Consort of Umā, granted him the over-lordship of Devas, the excellent kingdom and the destruction of Dānavas.

It (the boon) was acquired by Śakra, O king, by the power of Narmadā Tīrtha. Thereafter the Tīrtha became the most meritorious one on the earth.

By observing fast on the thirteenth lunar day in the dark half of the month of Kārttika with devotion, one is rid of all sins.

O dear son of Pāṇḍu, the devotee is released from the sins (evil effects) caused by inauspicious dreams, ill omens, malefic Planets and Śākinī (a kind of evil spirit).

O great king, there is no doubt that congenital sins of those who devoutly visit Śakreśvara, perish. Undoubtedly sins accrued due to a sexual approach to a woman who should not be so approached, marrying one who should not be married and killing one's master or a friend, perish. The auspicious gift of a cow should be made to a leading Brāhmaṇa. Or a yokable bullock beautiful in every limb should be given, O king. This should be given with great devotion by one who desires residence in heaven. Thus the entire benefit of Śakreśvara has been recounted to you, O king.

CHAPTER SIXTYTWO

The Greatness of Karoḍīśvara Tīrtha

Śrī Mārkaṇḍeya said:

1-7. Then, one should go to the excellent Tīrtha named Karoḍīśvara, O great king. O dear one, it was there that Dānavas along with their followers were killed by the delighted Devas led by Indra who always thought of victory. The Dānavas were killed in battle by the infuriated groups of Devas. Remembering again and again the previous enmity, sons and grandsons (of Dānavas) too were killed.

Remembering the kinship (with them) all the Devas including Indra gathered together their heads and cast them into the waters of Narmadā. All the Suras took their holy bath there and installed Umāpati (Śiva). All the Suras delighted in their minds went to their region in the firmament.

O blessed one, an excellent crore of the Dānavas was slain. Ever since then that Tīrtha is well known over the earth as Karoḍī. O son of Pāṇḍu, it is destructive of sins.

A devotee should observe fast devoutly on the eighth and fourteenth days of either half of a month and keep awake before the Trident-bearing Lord at night, engaged in reading (listening to) the stories of the good (meritorious stories) and in reciting and studying the Vedas.

8-16. In the morning he should then worship Tridaśeśvara. The idol (Liṅga) should be bathed in Pañcāmṛta and smeared with sandalpaste. He should with concentration offer worship with excellent sprouts (of Bilva tree) and flowers.

Facing the southern direction, he should recite the Mantras of various types. In accordance with the injunctions a handful of gingelly seeds should be offered by way of libation to the dead in the water coming upto the navel. Turning towards the southern direction, he should control his sense-organs and offer Śrāddha to the (departed) Brāhmaṇa. Śrāddha should be performed through Brāhmaṇas of uneven number eagerly engaged in the study and recitation of the Vedas. The Brāhmaṇas should be propitiated with gold, cows, foodstuffs, betel leaves, ornaments and a pair of sandals, O son of Pāṇḍu. His rite shall be effective a crore-fold more. No doubt need be entertained.

O king, listen to the merit that accrues to one who duly casts off his body in the Tīrtha.

That man of righteous soul resides in the rarely accessible Śivaloka as long as the bones remain in the waters of Narmadā.

After a long time, he may fall down therefrom and be born as a human being here. He shall then be glorious and owner of a lot of wealth. He shall be honoured by kings.

17-23. He shall be endowed with all piety. He shall be intelligent and have sons to perpetuate his line. The man shall be well-known all over the earth and long-lived. He will remember the Tīrtha once again, O excellent king, will go to that Tīrtha, worship Karoḍeśvara and attain the greatest goal.

Tridaśeśvara was installed by Indra, Candra, Yama, Rudra, Ādityas, Vasus and Viśvedevas on the northern bank of Revā with a desire for the welfare of all the worlds.

If a man endowed with devotion erects a palace (shrine) in that Tīrtha, O excellent one among men, he shall attain the goal of the good.

He should erect the same by means of timber, stone and bricks, all with wealth legitimately acquired.

Whether he be a Brāhmaṇa, a Kṣatriya or a Vaiśya or a Śūdra or even a woman, he should do everything within his capacity. When Śaṅkara is duly worshipped all those men too go to their respective goals.

If a person always listens to the greatness of the Tīrtha with devotion, his sins perish within six months.

CHAPTER SIXTYTHREE

The Greatness of Kumāreśvara Tīrtha

Śrī Mārkaṇḍeya said:

1-9. Then, O great king, one should go to the excellent Kumāreśvara. It is the most famous of all the Tīrthas. It is in the vicinity of Agastyeśvara.

Formerly, O king, spiritual power was achieved by Ṣaṇmukha after propitiating the destroyer of all sins, with great devotion.

By resorting to the Tīrtha, he became the commander-in-chief of the army of Devas. He destroyed all the enemies. That noble-souled one became endowed with fiery brilliance by resorting to the Tīrtha. Ever since then, that spot on the banks of Narmadā became a Tīrtha.

A person should go to that Tīrtha with concentration of the mind and control over the sense-organs. Especially on the fourteenth day of Kārttika and also on the eighth day, one should bath the Lord of the Daughter of the Mountain, with curds, milk and ghee.

There should be performance of music and the due offering of balls of rice.

Whatever is given by Brāhmaṇas who have mastered the Vedas and are duly engaged in the six holy rites, becomes everlasting, O son of Pāṇḍu.

This Tīrtha consisting of all other Tīrthas was created by Śikhivāhana (Skanda), O king.

Thus the entire benefit of (a visit to) Kumāreśvara has been narrated to you.

By visiting Kumāreśvara merit is obtained, O son of Pāṇḍu. On death, he attains heaven. What has been spoken by Īśvara is the truth.

CHAPTER SIXTYFOUR

The Greatness of Agastyeśvara Tīrtha

Śrī Mārkaṇḍeya said:

1-4. Then, O great king, one should go to the highly splendid Tīrtha, the excellent Agastyeśvara (created) for the sake of the destruction of the sins of men.

By taking the holy ablution there, O king, one is rid of the sin of Brāhmaṇa-slaughter.

On the fourteenth day in the dark half of the month of Kārttika the devotee should control his sense-organs and be engaged in meditation. He should bathe the Lord with ghee. Accompanied by twenty-one generations of his family he shall (not[1]) slip down (?) from the region of Īśvara.

He shall then make gifts of wealth, shoes, umbrella, ghee, blanket and food to all. All (the gifts) shall have crore-times more benefit.

1. 'na' (not) is not printed in the text due to oversight.

CHAPTER SIXTYFIVE

The Greatness of Ānandeśvara Tīrtha

Śrī Mārkaṇḍeya said:

1-11. O great king Yudhiṣṭhira, then one should go to the excellent Ānandeśvara where Rudra had the greatest delight. I shall describe that Tīrtha which destroys all sins.

Yudhiṣṭhira said:

O excellent Brāhmaṇa, Rudra had the greatest delight? May the entire episode be recounted to me succinctly even as I am accompanied by my kinsmen.

Śrī Mārkaṇḍeya said:

I shall describe the excellent Ānandeśvara, O great king. After slaying the Dānavas, Maheśvara, the Lord of Devas, was adored by all the Devas, Kinnaras, Yakṣas and Pannagas. The highly delighted Bull-vehicled Lord danced.

He had assumed the Bhairava (terrible) form with Gaurī stationed in half of his body. This Bhairava was surrounded by terrible Bhūtas (goblins), Vetālas (vampires) and Kaṅkālas (skeletons). O son of Pāṇḍu, he danced on the southern bank of Narmadā. The Lotus-seated One was installed by all the delighted groups of Maruts. Ever since then that Tīrtha is mentioned as Ānandeśvara. One should duly adore the Lord on the eighth, fourteenth and fifteenth (i.e. full-moon) lunar days, O king. He should smear him with sweet scents. O Yudhiṣṭhira, according to one's capacity he should adore Brāhmaṇas. A gift of cows should be made. A gift of garments causes prosperity and happiness. On the thirteenth day in Vasanta, he should perform Śrāddha too by means of Iṅgudas, Badaras, Bilvas, raw rice-grains or water. At the excellent Ānandeśvara Tīrtha the devotees should perform the Śrāddha unto the departed ones.

They shall be delighted until the destruction of all living beings. There shall be no snapping of the family-line in the course of seven births. O descendant of Bharata, bliss shall certainly come to them in every birth.

CHAPTER SIXTYSIX

The Greatness of Mātṛtīrtha

Śrī Mārkaṇḍeya said:

1-9. Then, O great king, a person should go to the excellent Mātṛtīrtha. It is situated on the southern bank of Narmadā very near the confluence.

The Mothers gathered together on the bank of Narmadā, O great king. The Lord of Devas, wearing a Vyāla (python) as his Yajñopavīta and with Umā as half of his body, was present there. The group of Yoginīs said: "O Hara, it is a pity indeed, O Maheśvara. That we are invincible to all Devas is due to your grace, O Maheśvara. (But now) may this Tīrtha be well-known by this procedure all over the earth." Śiva said: "O Yoginīs, let it be so." After saying this, he vanished.

Śrī Mārkaṇḍeya said:

The devotee should be invariably pure and observe fast at that Tīrtha with great devotion on the ninth lunar day. He should adore Mātṛgocara (Lord Śiva). The Mothers will be pleased with him. The Bull-vehicled Lord too will be delighted.

An excellent scholar well-versed in the Mantraśāstra should preside over the ritualistic holy ablution of a barren woman and of a woman whose dear child is dead or one who has no son, O Yudhiṣṭhira.

They should offer a water-pot with gold and five kinds of jewels therein.

The preceptor should bathe the woman desirous of a son with a brass-pot. That woman shall bear a vigorous son endowed with good qualities.

Whatever one desires shall be achieved by him, O king. There has never been a Tīrtha greater than Mātṛtīrtha and never shall be.

CHAPTER SIXTYSEVEN

The Greatness of Luṅkeśvara Tīrtha

Śrī Mārkaṇḍeya said:

1-8. The Tīrtha well-known as Luṅkeśvara is situated in the middle of water beyond (the previous Tīrtha). It is bowed to by Suras and Asuras.

This Tīrtha is highly meritorious and renowned as very miraculous all over the earth, O descendant of Bharata. Listen to the origin and greatness of this Tīrtha.

Formerly there was a demon of great power, who was arrogant due to (his) great strength. He was well-known as Kālapṛṣṭha. He was a grandson of Brahmā.

He resorted to the bank of Gaṅgā and performed a very severe penance. Remaining in topsy-turvy position he began to imbibe smoke day and night. The Lord happened to stand nearby in the company of Umā. On seeing him engaged in fierce penance, Pārvatī said: "See, see, O Mahādeva, there is a man imbibing smoke. Be pleased. (Make him happy.) O Lord, grant him a boon quickly."

Īśvara said:

The words spoken by you do not appeal to me. One's own affair should always be thought of. One should disregard other people's affairs. He who follows the whims and pleasures of fools, women, children and enemies invariably falls into a terrible distress. This is the truth that has been uttered.

The Devī said:

9-14. It is stated in scriptures that when a husband requested (for something) by the wife speaks of various causes (pleads excuses) that woman becomes humiliated. "If you do not honour me (my request), I shall commit suicide."

Thus urged by Pārvatī, the Lord went towards the Dānava.

Īśvara said:

Why do you imbibe smoke? Why do you perform these

austerities? What is your sorrow? What is your distress? Tell me the desired object. You still seem to be only a youth about twenty years old. Hence tell me the great cause or purpose of this penance.

The Dānava said:

May unflinching devotion to you and steadfastness towards you be granted to me. Another period of one thousand years has gone unobstructed, O Lord. O Lord, already two thousand days have been completed by me doing this penance.

Īśvara said:

15-23. Do request for whatever has been desired by you, O devotee of good Vratas. I am pleased with you.

On hearing the words of the Lord, the Dānava thought, 'Shall I request for heaven? Or shall I request for the entire earth?' Thus he thought on being afflicted by the arrows of Kāma.

The Dānava said:[1]

If you are pleased with me, O Lord, you will kindly grant me this boon, O Lord. I am not pleased with wars since I have no strength. O Lord, if I touch anyone on the head, whether he be a Deva, Dānava or Gandharva, let him be reduced to ash instantly.

Īśvara said:

Whatever has been thought of by you shall be fruitful. Get up. Go quickly to your abode, O Dānava.

The Dānava said:

O Lord of the chiefs of Devas, be pleased to stay so that I shall test your boon by placing my hand on your head. I can have the satisfaction and conviction.

1. This story seems to be a special contribution of Revā Khaṇḍa. As PE 127A notes, it is not traced in any other Purāṇa.

Thereupon Maheśvara began to worry. 'Neither Skanda nor Hari nor Brahmā can be competent to deal with this situation now.' After coming to know that the calamity had overtaken him, the Lord requested his bull, "Now, fight with this sinful one."

The Daitya extended his hand and was about to touch the Lord's head. By that time he was lashed with his tail by the bull and so he fell down distressed.

24-36. Accompanied by Umā, the Lord went in the southern direction. Extremely frightened, he turned his neck frequently to look back (to see how far he followed). When the Lord vanished from the scene, the Daitya fought with the bull. Both of them were very powerful, the most excellent ones among the mighty. They fought each other for three Ghaṭikās, striking each other with thunderbolt-like hits and the Daitya could not get the chance to touch the head of the bull with the hands.

Striking him with a lash of his tail, the bull came away. The Daitya too got up and closely followed the bull.

With the speed of wind, he came to the place where Lord Maheśvara was present. On seeing the Dānava coming, the bull spoke these words:

"O Lord, be pleased to ride on my back and go ahead quickly." Accordingly the Lord got on to his back along with Umā and sped ahead.

Then the Lord reached heaven and entered the palace of Śakra; but the Dānava in his arrogance due to his might did not leave off the pursuit of the Lord.

Leaving the world of Indra, he went to Brahmā's world. Wherever the Lord went in fright along with the heaven-dwellers, he saw the Dānava following closely his back.

After wandering in all the worlds the Lord was overwhelmed with surprise. There was no place where he could rest even for a moment.

On coming to know of a fierce fight between the Lord and the Dānava, sage Nārada became highly delighted in his soul. He began to dance saying, "I am blessed today. My birth and my life has been excellently lived." On seeing the great quarrel his satisfaction reached the maximum. Leaving them aside the Brāhmaṇa Nārada came to the place where Maheśvara, the Lord, was present.

On seeing the Brāhmaṇa the Lord adored him and spoke thus:

37-44. "O Nārada, O most excellent one among sages, do you know where Keśava is? Go there and inform Keśava about this."

Nārada said:

The Lord of Devas certainly dispels the disaster of Devas, Dānavas and Siddhas, Gandharvas, Uragas (Serpents) and Rākṣasas. The impossible should not be uttered, not even mentally thought of, O Lord; I am not aware of such calamity in your case.

Īśvara said:

O Nārada, do go quickly to the place where Lord Janārdana is present. Everything done by the Dānava has been already known to you. This Dānava cannot be slain by groups of Maruts even assisted by Indra. O great sage, go and intimate (this) to Lord Keśava.

Nārada said:

O Lord, I am not going now. Keśava is in sound sleep in the Ocean of Milk. For urging him, behest has to be given by you to these—mother, sister or daughter. One should not wake up a sleeping king, master or preceptor.

Īśvara said:

If a great fire catches the house and wise men do not wake up the people there, they will perish.

Nārada said:

45-52. Hurry up, Mahādeva; my good Lord, save yourself. No doubt, I shall go to the place where Lord Janārdana is present.

Thereupon the extremely terrible Nandin and Mahākāla took up weapons in their hands brawny like pillars and struck the Dānava with weapons like Mudgara etc.

All the three had huge bodies measuring seven palm trees in height. While they were fighting one another there was no question of subduing or resting at all.

Thereafter the Brāhmaṇa went towards Keśava who was asleep in the Ocean of Milk. He saw him lying on the couch of the serpent Śeṣa. The pair of his feet were held by Lakṣmī and kept on her thigh. Keśava was devoutly sung about by the Apsarās.

After bowing down devoutly (Nārada said:) "Today my birth has become fruitful. My life has become excellent one. O Lakṣmī, do wake up the Lord of Devas unhesitatingly."

On hearing the words of Nārada Lakṣmī pressed the big toe of the Lord and said, "Nārada is at the threshold. Do wake up, O Slayer of Madhu."

On seeing Nārada the Lord was highly pleased and said, "Welcome, O excellent one among sages. The night has well-dawned today."

Nārada said:

53-60. O Lord, this morning is fruitful unto me, thanks to thy vision. The Devas have ceased to be in good condition and safe. Get up and proceed to them.

Śrī Viṣṇu said:

It behoves you to recount the cause of the disaster to Brahmā, Indra, Rudra and the others, groups of Maruts.

Nārada said:

A great and severe penance was performed by a Dānava. A boon was granted by Rudra enabling (him) to reduce to ash (by the touch of his hand any one) as desired by him mentally. On the strength of the boon so granted, he attempts to kill the Lord. On coming to know such an attempt, the Lord has been brought here along with the Devas.

On hearing the words of Nārada, Hari went along with the sage and saw Īśāna going to the northern direction.

On seeing the Lord (Hari) Rudra embraced him again and again. Madhusūdana also bowed to the Lord (Rudra).

Viṣṇu said:

O Lord Maheśvara, may the cause of fear be mentioned. I shall send the Devas, Dānavas and Yakṣas to the abode of Yama. There is profuse perspiration on your forehead, O Maheśvara, undoubtedly breaking through the head, the limbs and the sense-organs (which are tired).

Īśvara said:

61-69. Fools have no happiness. Patients have no happiness. One who is not free has no happiness. Particularly a henpecked husband (dependent on another i.e. wife) has no happiness. O Viṣṇu, urged by a woman a boon has been granted to the Dānava by me: "If you place your hand on anyone's head he will be reduced to a heap of ashes." Told thus by me he has become invincible and immortal, O Keśava. The sinner wishes to kill me. Have you any means of remedy?

Viṣṇu said:

O Śaṅkara, I shall find out some means of killing the Dānava. May you and all the Devas go and stay on the banks of Revā. You must not delay. O Lord, hurry up.

A Tīrtha like that cannot be seen in the mortal world, a Tīrtha where there is Gaṅgā, the great river Revā and Prācī Sarasvatī flowing to the south.

If holy ablution is taken there and Dāna is performed devoutly, the sin committed in the course of seven births perishes undoubtedly. This Tīrtha is highly meritorious and destructive of all sins. O Lord of Devas, do go to the Luṅkeśa Tīrtha there along with the Devas.

At the instance of Viṣṇu he (Śiva) entered the excellent Hrada (whirlpool).

70-78. He diverted himself very much along with the groups of Maruts. Thereafter Lord (Kṛṣṇa) employed his Māyā in various ways. He created the month of Vasanta beautified with splendid gardens and forests abounding in the following trees: Aśoka, Bakula, splendid Brahmavṛkṣa (i.e. Palāśa), Śrīvṛkṣa, Kapittha, Śirīṣa, Rājacampaka, Śrīphala, Tāla, Kadamba, Udumbara, Aśvattha and various other trees. They had profuse collection of flowers of sweet scent with humming bees hovering round.

In the centre thereof there was a great splendid Nyagrodha tree. Many birds perched thereon. It was reverberated with the cooing of cuckoos. Kṛṣṇa instantly assumed the form of a girl of such physical charm as there was no other girl on a par with her (in beauty) in the three worlds consisting of mobile and immobile beings. A group of seven girls also (was created). They were very beautiful with splendid eyes. All of them had divine forms embellished with divine ornaments. They were desirous of a man.

A swing was tied to bamboos and decorated with beautiful garlands of pearls, jewels, rubies and splendid lapis lazuli. Those great girls sat on it and began to sing sweetly.

79-88. A cool breeze blew gently over the splendid forest. Sweet fragrance was wafted by wind and it tickled the sense of smell of the Dānava.

He was very much astonished by the sweet scent of flowers. He thought, 'Smelling it, I feel that such a (fragrant) flower[1] has been never seen or heard by me.'

Even as he was reflecting thus, a splendid sound of music (was heard by him). On hearing the sound of music he became deluded by the Māyā of Hari.

Just as a deer falls into the great snare of a hunter, so also the Kālaspṛṣṭa (one who is touched by Kāla) Daitya fell into the trap of Kṛṣṇa.

On seeing the girl the Daitya swooned and fell on the ground. Even as he fell down he saw a girl standing at the foot of a banyan tree.

Seeing the faces of the girls, he was again afflicted by the god of Love. He lifted up a golden staff and wished to topple her down.

The girl said:

No. No. Do not touch me. I am a virgin of an excellent family. Oh, leave me off so that I can go home quickly!

1. *puṣpam* is probably the original reading and not *puṇyam*.

The Dānava said:

O splendid girl, I wish to marry you. Thus, undoubtedly you shall become the queen of the entire earth.

The girl said:

In childhood father protects her (a woman). In youth husband protects her. In old age son protects her. Hence a woman does not deserve being independent. I am not free. I am born of a noble family. Either my father, brother or mother should be approached with the request.

The Dānava said:

89-96. O lady of splendid eyes, if you are not going to act independently, if you do not wish me (to be your husband), it will end in my death today. It is true.

The girl said:

Trust cannot be placed (indiscriminately) on every man. Men behave with women curiously. They are lascivious and infatuated with love. You may very well marry me and enjoy all pleasures with me. Later my whole life may be ruined. Neither you nor anyone else will be mine.

Whether one is a Brāhmaṇa girl, a Kṣatriya girl, a Vaiśya girl or a Śūdra girl, she cannot have a second husband. She will have to remain single throughout her life.

The Dānava said:

The statement made by you has been kept in mind by me. Whatever you may think of, I shall offer for convincing you.

The girl said:

Understand that I am a cowherd lass. I am playing with my companions. Only take the solemn oath taken in our family. It is not the ordeal known as 'poison' 'Kośa' or 'Tulā' (Balance). In all cowherd families the hand is placed on the head.

The hand was then placed on his own head by the Daitya,

blind with passionate love, O great king. Immediately he was reduced to ash. He was burnt down like a bundle of hay.

97-109. An auspicious shower of flowers was heaped upon Keśava by the Devas. Delighted and free from feverish mental anguish, all the Devas went to their respective abodes.

Keśava went to the Ocean of Milk after Kālaspṛṣṭa had been struck down.

He who devoutly listens to the story of the Dānava shall always be victorious as Śaṅkara had uttered already. For this reason it is well-known as Liṅgeśvara (Luṅkeśvara). (The sin) that is lying latent within perishes merely by the holy ablution. All the sins pertaining to the skin, bone, blood, flesh, suet, nerves, marrow and semen virile perish even if they had been perpetrated in the course of a crore births.

If a devotee devoutly drinks three cavity-fuls of the water at Luṅkeśvara, O great king, all his sins become split into a thousand smithereens. Particularly on the eighth and fourteenth days of either half of a month a man should observe fast, O son of Pāṇḍu, and perform the Śrāddha for the Pitṛs. All the Pitāmahas (grandfathers i.e. ancestors) condemned to hell become redeemed.

If a person offers even a Kākiṇī (worthless small coin) to a Brāhmaṇa who has mastered the Vedas, he attains thereby all the benefits of the Dāna rites performed in Kurukṣetra etc.

It is not otherwise. O king, it is Śaṅkara who says this.

O king, this Liṅga is Sparśa Liṅga (a Liṅga to be touched in adoration) made by Śaṅkara himself. Merely by touching it men attain residence in Rudra Loka. The same is the case with regard to the benefit of Dāna etc. performed here, as in the case of Kurukṣetra etc.

It is for this reason that the Lokapālas (Guardians of the Quarters) are made protectors. Durgā in an auspicious form having four hands is also created for the sake of protection.

Dhanada, the chief of the Lokapālas, is the bodyguard of Īśvara. He always protects through the activities of the Planets.

Luṅkeśvara is not left off even today, O great king, by the Devas who have assumed the forms of sons, brother, or someone related to the master.

CHAPTER SIXTYEIGHT

The Greatness of Dhanada

Śrī Mārkaṇḍeya said:

1-11. Then one should go to the Tīrtha of Dhanada, O Yudhiṣṭhira. It is on the southern bank of Narmadā and it causes the destruction of all sins. There is no doubt about this that the benefit of all the Tīrthas is obtained there.

A person with the sense-organs under control should observe fast with great devotion on the thirteenth day in the bright half of the month of Caitra and keep awake at night.

A wise man should bathe Dhanada with Pañcāmṛta, O great king. A *Dīpa* (lamp) supplied with ghee should be given. Arrangement for vocal and instrumental music should be made. Desirous of the welfare of himself, he should adore Brāhmaṇas in the morning. They should be persons deserving *Pratigraha* (religious gift) and expounders of the principles of various lores. They must be persons regularly performing rites enjoined in Śrauta and Smārta Texts. They should be indifferent towards the wives of others. They should be adored with gifts of cows, gold, garments, shoes, foodstuffs, umbrellas and beds. All sins shall thus be destroyed. The sins acquired in the course of three births shall be destroyed by the power of Dhanada. It is the giver of heavenly pleasures to the arrogant and salvation to the humble. It shall give food to the poor in every birth. Destruction of misery and birth in a good family shall be had naturally by the man.

By resorting to the waters of Narmadā, there shall be destruction of ailments. He who imparts Vidyā (learning) at the Tīrtha of Dhanada attains Bhāskara Loka (world of the Sun) which is free of all ailments.

Those who arrange a large procession of idols in accordance with their capacity, O son of Pāṇḍu, on the southern bank of Revā, go to the world of Śaṅkara bereft of all miseries.

CHAPTER SIXTYNINE

The Greatness of Maṅgaleśvara Tīrtha

Śrī Mārkaṇḍeya said:

1-8. Then one should go to the excellent Maṅgaleśvara installed by the Son of the Earth (i.e. Mars) with a desire for the welfare of all people.

The moon-crested Lord Śaṅkara was propitiated (by Maṅgala) with great devotion. On the fourteenth day, the Lord and preceptor, Maṅgaleśvara, manifested himself (and said): "Tell me, dear son, the splendid boon (you wish to have). I shall grant it to you, O Maṅgala."

Maṅgala said:

O Śaṅkara, O Śaṁbhu, do me this favour: May I be born of the sweat of your limbs and stay in every birth in the middle of the Planets.

O Īśāna, with your favour I am worthy of being worshipped by all the Devas. Today I have become blessed due to your appearance before and conversation with me. Stay at this holy spot, O Lord of the chiefs of Devas, after my name (Maṅgalamaheśvara).

The Lord said, "Let it be so, dear son" and vanished.

Maṅgala, the noble soul, installed Maheśvara by means of his own Yogic power and worshipped the Trident-bearing Lord.

The Liṅga named Maṅgaleśvara is the destroyer of all miseries. A wise devotee should propitiate Brāhmaṇas at that Tīrtha. He shall propitiate the Brāhmaṇas along with their wives.

9-16. O excellent king, (he should observe) the Caturthī-aṅgāraka-vrata, at the conclusion of which a cow along with bulls capable to carry the yoke is given to a Brāhmaṇa couple (man and wife). The Brāhmaṇa should be learned and a master of the Veda. The gift should be given with God Śiva in view saying, "May Mahādeva, the bull-emblemed Lord, accompanied by his wife be pleased." O son of Pāṇḍu, gift of a pair of red clothes should be made. The bearers of yoke (bulls) may be red in colour, or white or black. An umbrella, auspicious bed, red garlands and unguents should be given with a pure heart, O excellent son of Pāṇḍu.

Śrāddha too should be performed on the fourth and eighth days of both the fortnights, the dark and the bright. There should not be any hesitation in spending money. Thereby the departed souls become well-pleased, O king, for a period of one Yuga. In every birth the man becomes blessed with sons, O excellent king.

By the power of the Tīrtha, the devotee shall be handsome in every limb, O king. There shall be well-being in the family. There can never be any evil thing anywhere. The sin of the devotee who glorifies the Lord everyday is destroyed.

CHAPTER SEVENTY

The Greatness of Ravi Tīrtha

Śrī Mārkaṇḍeya said:

1-4. There is a highly splendid Tīrtha on the northern bank of Revā. It was inaugurated by Ravi. O son of Kuntī, it causes the destruction of all sins.

There, on the northern bank, Bhāskara (the Sun-god) stays with his sixteenth part. He is installed on Narmadā as an eradicator of all the ailments of men.

O excellent king, on every sixth, eighth and fourteenth lunar day, if a man bathes (the deity) and devoutly offers Śrāddha unto the departed, O son of Kuntī, his sins will be destroyed. He is honoured in the world of the Sun.

Falling down from heaven (later) he will be born in a family free from impurities. In every birth he shall live free of all ailments and will be wealthy.

CHAPTER SEVENTYONE

The Greatness of Kāmeśvara Tīrtha

Śrī Mārkaṇḍeya said:

1-4. Thereafter, O excellent one among the sons of Pāṇḍu, listen to another Tīrtha named Kāmeśvara. It was here that Gaṇādhyakṣa (Gaṇeśa), the highly powerful son of Gaurī, became a Siddha (i.e. one who had achieved spiritual perfection).

In that Tīrtha, a devotee should control his sense-organs, bathe the idol with Pañcāmṛta with great devotion and offer incense, Naivedya and other articles of adoration. By propitiating the Lord of the worlds thereby, he will be rid of all sins.

O Yudhiṣṭhira, a devotee should take his holy bath there on the eighth day in the month of Mārgaśīrṣa. Whatever be his desire in performing the adoration, he shall certainly attain it.

CHAPTER SEVENTYTWO

The Greatness of Maṇināgeśvara Tīrtha[1]

Śrī Mārkaṇḍeya said:

1-5. Thereafter, O great king, one should go to the auspicious Maṇināgeśvara on the northern bank of Narmadā. It causes the destruction of all sins. It has been installed by Maṇināga with a desire for the welfare of all the worlds.

Yudhiṣṭhira said:

How was Īśvara propitiated by a serpent with venom in the fangs? Even though they may be very small, venomous reptiles strike terror unto the world.

May everything conducive to the destruction of all sins be recounted to me. My misery due to the distress caused by

1. Herein the legend of Vinatā's enslavement and release (from Mbh, *Ādi* chs 19-20) is adapted for the glorification of this Tīrtha.

Duryodhana, that originating from Karṇa and Bhīṣma and the terrible distress caused to Pāñcālī is washed away by the current (of sane advice) from your lotus-like mouth and (thus) I have attained great peace (of mind). We have heard the sin-destroying story that issued forth from your mouth, O Brāhmaṇa. Still, it is unreasonable that our pain has not subsided.

6. Or, O dear one, the benefit (fruit) that is derived from Vidyādāna (imparting learning) is obtained by always listening to the stories or episodes concerning Hari.

Śrī Mārkaṇḍeya said:

7-15. As and when you go on speaking (by way of request), O king, fluency of speech comes to me naturally. Neither the laxity of limbs due to my old age nor your friendship becomes diminished, O dear one. Hence in the company of your kinsmen listen to this praiseworthy story that destroys sins.

I shall narrate to you the old legend in the manner it happened. It has been traditionally handed down by the ancestors, O descendant of Bharata.

Kaśyapa had two wives, the most excellent ones in all the worlds. Vinatā gave birth to Garuḍa and Kadrū to serpents.

O dear one, they stayed on contentedly in the abode of Kaśyapa. Both the ladies Kadrū and Vinatā were always delighted. Kaśyapa, the patriarch, sported along with them.

One day, the slender-limbed wife of Kaśyapa, who was staying in the hermitage and whose countenance was splendid, saw the horse Uccaiḥśravas that had the speed of mind and was white all over. He was running non-stop with his speed comparable to that of mind. On seeing the horse she (Kadrū) jealously spoke these words:

Kadrū said:

Tell me, fair lady, of what colour is the horse of Sahasrāṁśu (the Sun). (This is evidently a mistake, as the horse belonged to Indra?) I say it is black. What do you say? Tell me.

Vinatā said:

16-25. Is it not that you see only black (things) with your eyes and not white ones? O fair lady, by speaking the untruth you will go to the world of Yama. With regard to the truth or otherwise of (our) statement it is a wager between you and me. (If my statement turns out to be untrue) I shall be a slave in your palace for a thousand years. If my words prove to be untrue and Uccaiśśravas turns out to be black, then I shall be a slave in your palace. O mother of serpents.

Kadrū then said: "If Uccaiśśravas is white, I shall be your slave." Thus the dispute between the two increased.

The young lady in the hermitage was worried throughout the night. All her activities were reported to the kinsmen. She spoke to her sons, O son of Kuntī, "I have made a bet."

On hearing that a bet was made by their mother the Serpents shouted loudly: "There is no doubt that you have become a slave. The vehicle of Bhāskara (? of Indra) is white. The horse Uccaiśśravas is white, it is not black at all."

Kadrū said:

Now think of a means to prevent my becoming a slave. Do enter the hair-pores of the horse Uccaiśśravas, only for a short while, till he appears black. Within a moment she can be made my slave. After making the lady Vinatā who is proud of being true, my slave, you all will be back at your own places happily.

The serpents said:

26-34. O mother, you are our mother and hence worthy of being worshipped by us. In the same manner she is worthy of being worshipped (by her sons). Hence one should be particular in not deceiving mothers. Verbally, mentally and physically one should do whatever is conducive to the benefit of the mother, father's wife (step-mother), maternal and paternal grandmothers.

Kadrū became furious at their words. She blazed like the fire of death. "If there are serpents on the earth not willing to carry out my behest, all of them will unexpectedly get into the mouth of fire."

All the serpents heard those words of their mother. Some of them penetrated the pores of the hairs of the horse Uccaiśśravas.

Some vanished in the ten different quarters because they were afraid of the curse of Kadrū. Some of them disappeared under the waters of Gaṅgā; some in those of Sarasvatī. Some of them hid themselves in the great ocean. Some entered the caves of Vindhya. The excellent serpent Maṇināga resorted to the waters of Narmadā and performed extensive penance on the northern bank of Narmadā.

O son of Kuntī, to save himself from the fear of the curse of his mother, he meditated upon the destroyer of Kāma. He meditated on the Lord who is indivisible (impossible to be divided), incomprehensible and devoid of birth and death. For more than a hundred years he subsisted himself on air; for half of that period he fixed his eyes on the Sun. While he was thus engrossed in meditation, the Lord, the destroyer of Tripuras, appeared before him.

35-43. "Excellent! Excellent! O highly esteemed one. O serpent, you have intrinsic strength. I have been resorted to by you with devotion. I am pleased with you, O Lord of serpents. Request for any boon from me whatever may be in your mind."

Maṇināga said:

O Lord, it is out of fear from the curse of my mother that I subjected myself to austerities on the banks of Narmadā. May my mother's curse be ineffective in regard to me, with your favour, O my Lord.

Īśvara said:

O dear one, at my behest you will never get into the jaws of fire. O son, you will also reside in my world.

Maṇināga said:

O Mahādeva, may you be pleased to stay by a part of yours in this spot. May you be pleased to stay in the waters of Narmadā by a thousandth fraction of yours for the sake of obliging the worlds. O Śaṅkara, stay here after my name.

Īśvara said:

O serpent, install my great Liṅga here at my behest.

After saying this, the Lord vanished and went away with Umā.

Mārkaṇḍeya said:

Those who go to that Tīrtha with pure and clean minds on the fifth, eighth or fourteenth day, whether it be bright half or dark half of the month, and always adore the Lord, do not go to Yama, O son of Kuntī.

They must bathe with curds, honey, ghee or milk, Lord Virūpākṣa, half of whose body is that of Umā, the Lord who burned down the body of Kāma and who slew the demon Agha; or they must witness the great Lord being bathed with great devotion. They will therefore go to the great world devoid of all sins.

44-51. Śrāddha for the departed should be performed, O son of Kuntī, on the fifth and eighth lunar days through well-qualified Brāhmaṇas—those who study and ponder over Vedic passages, who are devoted to their own wives with scrupulous avoidance of other men's wives, who are gentle and polished, who invariably perform the six enjoined rites and who avoid sending Śūdras on errands (of spiritual nature).

Dear son, the following persons should never be employed in Śrāddha: lame ones, lepers, impotent ones, those who live on usury, husbandmen and those of an avocation different from the decent rites.

O king, in Vratas and Śrāddhas, that Brāhmaṇa should be avoided from afar, a Brahmaṇa who keeps a Śūdra woman in his abode or who keeps buffaloes.

In the auspicious Maṇināgeśvara Tīrtha the following Brāhmaṇas should never be honoured, if one wishes for upward progress of oneself along with the Pitṛs: one-eyed ones, mumblers (those who utter meaningless, indistinct words), mentally disordered and those devoid of self-study of the Vedas.

One who makes a gift of a cow beautiful in every limb, to a Brāhmaṇa, goes to the greatest world (and stays there) until the annihilation of all living beings. Thereafter, slipping down from the heavenly world, he will be born in a family devoid of impurities.

O king, if persons visit Maṇināgeśvara with great devotion, there shall be no fear from serpents in their family.

52-53a. By visiting Maṇināga shrine devotees appear to groups of serpents in the forms of Garuḍa and so the serpents are suspicious (afraid) of them.

Henceforth, O king, listen to the benefits of Dānas (gifts) made here.

53b-65. O great king, those excellent men, if desirous of their welfare (final beatitude), should give to a deserving (Brāhmaṇa) cooked rice with all condiments, water, bed, an umbrella, a virgin and a sweet-speaking maidservant (slave). Fragrant flowers, scents and garments, lamp, food-grains, a splendid well-furnished house should be given. Those who give with great devotion go to heaven.

Whatever gift is given at Maṇināga, residence in heaven becomes certain as a fruit of that Dāna. All sins disappear like water in a mud-pot not yet annealed and baked.

One who gives unto a Brāhmaṇa foodstuffs cooked and prepared in the waters of Narmadā becomes rid of all sins and sports about with Devas.

Hereafter I shall mention the characteristics of those who slip down from the heavenly worlds: They are long-lived. Their sons will be alive. They will be alive. They will be devoid of all types of ailments. They will be endowed with sons and servants. They will be persons ready to renounce. They will enjoy pleasures. They will always be engaged in the narration of pious stories. They will be devotees of Devas, Brāhmaṇas and preceptors. They will relish pilgrimages. They will be obedient to mothers and fathers. They will be devoid of hatred and anger.

O son of Pāṇḍu, all the people having these characteristics have truly come down from heavenly worlds and they will go to heaven again.

O excellent king, Maṇināga is a Tīrtha which is the most excellent one among Tīrthas. One who reads or listens to this narration about the Tīrtha shall be rid of all sins. He is honoured in the world of Śiva. No poison affects them. They move about as they please. By listening to this narrative one gets that benefit which one gets by viewing Bhāskara (the Sun-god) on the sixth lunar day in the month of Bhādrapada.

CHAPTER SEVENTYTHREE

The Greatness of Gopāreśvara Tīrtha

Śrī Mārkaṇḍeya said:

1-5. O son of Kuntī, there is an extremely splendid Tīrtha on the southern bank of Narmadā. The excellent Gopāreśvara is destructive of all sins. A meritorious Liṅga issued forth from the body of a cow on the surface of the earth there, O king.

Yudhiṣṭhira said:

How did it come to happen that a Liṅga that causes destruction of sins issued forth from the body of a cow on the southern bank of Narmadā very near Maṇināga? O Brāhmaṇa, may the origin of the Gopāreśvara Liṅga be narrated succinctly.

Śrī Mārkaṇḍeya said:

Formerly, O son of Kuntī, Kāmadhenu performed a penance there. She meditated on Maheśvara, the Lord of Devas, with great devotion.

Maheśvara, the Lord of the worlds, became pleased with the tawny-coloured cow. From within her body Parameśvara, the indivisible Lord, came out.

Maheśvara said:

O tawny-coloured one, O Parameśvarī, O mother of the universe, I am pleased with you. O one of fair countenance, say quickly why the propitiation was carried on.

Surabhi said:

6-15. I have been created by Parameṣṭhin for the sake of helping the worlds. It is with my favour that all the affairs of the world come to fulfilment. O Śaṅkara, if people will proceed towards heaven, it is due to my favour. O Śaṁbhu, do stay in my Tīrtha with a desire for the welfare of the worlds.

Saying "So it shall be", the Lord stayed there joyously. Ever since then, that Tīrtha became well known all over the earth.

By means of a single bath, O great king, one dispels a great mass of sins. The gift of a cow at Gopāreśvara should be made with great devotion. A suitable cow should be given to a deserving excellent Brāhmaṇa along with gold and calf.

The cow should be young, white in colour and yield profuse milk. It shall be given along with cloths also.

The gift should generally be made on the eighth or fourteenth lunar day in the dark half of a month.

Of all the months, the month of Kārttika is of special significance. The gift should be made over to a Brāhmaṇa eager to continue the self-study of the Vedas.

The gift is to be made with great devotion. One who makes the gift duly, he who accepts it gracefully and duly—both of them are meritorious. One who witnesses this also earns merit.

One should offer balls of rice to the departed ones with due reverence and devotion. Thus, O great king; the departed ones attain the great goal (heaven).

The sins of those who make devoutly obeisance everyday to Rudra become dissolved like water in a broken pot.

One who releases a bull ritualistically in that Tīrtha is honoured in Śivaloka. The Pitṛs are redeemed by him.

Yudhiṣṭhira said:

16-23. O excellent Brāhmaṇa, quickly explain assiduously the benefit that accrues to men when Vṛṣotsarga (ceremonial and ritualistic releasing of a bull) is done.

Śrī Mārkaṇḍeya said:

Listen, O son of Dharma. I shall explain fully the benefit that is attained when a bull fully endowed with all excellent characteristics, O king, is let loose on the full-moon day in the months of Kārttika and Vaiśākha. A person should take his holy bath and remain clean with all the sense-organs controlled. He should make the Vṛṣotsarga in the presence of Rudra uttering, "May Hara be pleased". Dear son, he should keep nearby four excellent female calves. After offering these possessing all essential features to a leading Brāhmaṇa, he shall say: "May Mahādeva be pleased. May Brahmā, Viṣṇu and Maheśvara be pleased."

He will be honoured in Śivaloka, O king, for as many years

as there are hairs on all the limbs. After staying in Śivaloka, when he is reborn in the mortal world, it shall be in a great family richly endowed with wealth and food-grains. He shall be endowed with handsome features and excellent learning. He shall be clean and truthful. He shall be devoid of ailments.

O Yudhiṣṭhira, the greatness of Gopāreśvara has been narrated by me. The Liṅga had issued forth from the body of the cow on the southern bank of Narmadā.

CHAPTER SEVENTYFOUR

The Greatness of Gautameśvara Tīrtha

Śrī Mārkaṇḍeya said:

1-6. There is an excellent Tīrtha on the northern bank of Revā. It is destructive of all sins in the mortal world. It is (known) by the name Gautameśvara. It has been established by Gautama himself, with a desire for the welfare of all the worlds. O Yudhiṣṭhira, this Tīrtha is in the form of a flight of stairs unto heaven for all men. Go there with great devotion to the place where the Lord, the preceptor of the universe, is present for the sake of the destruction of sins. He is also the bestower of a residence in Svarga.

The Tīrtha is conducive to the augmentation of blessedness. It bestows victory. It is destructive of miseries. By means of a single offering of balls of rice there a devotee shall redeem three generations of his family.

At the behest of Gautama, everything that is given with devotion, whether meagre or much, shall become a hundred thousand times (more beneficial) as stated by Rudra. This is the greatest Tīrtha of all Tīrthas.

CHAPTER SEVENTYFIVE

The Greatness of Śaṅkhacūḍa Tīrtha

Śrī Mārkaṇḍeya said:

1-5. There is a great and beautiful Tīrtha on the southern bank of Narmadā. It is well-known in the terrestrial sphere by the name of Śaṅkhacūḍa, O son of Pāṇḍu. Śaṅkhacūḍa is himself present there on the pleasant bank of Narmadā, due to the fear of Vainateya (Garuḍa).

A person should remain clean with mental concentration and purity and bathe Śaṅkhacūḍa with milk, honey and ghee.

He should keep awake at night before the Lord. After honouring Brāhmaṇas of esteemed holy vows, with cooked rice soaked in curds, a cow should be gifted to an eminent Brāhmaṇa. Thereby all sins will be destroyed.

Libation should be offered (to the Pitṛs) killed by serpent bite. He shall go to the greatest world, as said by Śaṅkara.

CHAPTER SEVENTYSIX

The Greatness of Pāreśvara Tīrtha

Śrī Mārkaṇḍeya said:

1-7. Thereafter, one should go to the excellent Pāreśvara (Tīrtha), O great king. The noble-souled Parāśara performed on the splendid banks of Narmadā a severe penance for the sake of a son, O son of Pāṇḍu.

Gaurī, the daughter of Himavān, was propitiated by him with great devotion on the northern bank of Narmadā.

The great goddess, the sharer of half of the body of Śaṅkara, became pleased with him. "Oh! O excellent sage! I am pleased by your devotion. O Brāhmaṇa, request for a boon from me, O highly intelligent Parāśara."

Parāśara said:

O goddess, if you are pleased with me, if a boon has to be

given to me, O goddess, grant me a son who is endowed with the qualities of truthfulness and cleanliness, who regularly studies the Vedas and is an expert in all scriptural texts.[1] O goddess, thanks to the boon; may there be your presence in this Tīrtha here. O Daughter of the Mountain, for the sake of helping the worlds, may you be pleased to stay on the southern bank of Narmadā by the name of Parāśara.

Śrī Devī said:

8-17. So be it, O Brāhmaṇa.

She vanished there itself. The noble-souled Parāśara installed Pārvatī. He established Śaṅkara, bowed down to by Suras and Asuras, the Lord who cannot be comprehended in an adequate manner, who cannot be divided and approached even by Devas. O king, Parāśara, the noble-souled one, became contented.

The Tīrtha there should be resorted to devoutly by a pure person with a controlled mind. Whether a woman or a man, she or he should be free from lust and anger.

The month may be Māgha, Caitra, Vaiśākha, Śrāvaṇa or Mārgaśīrṣa, but invariably it should be (visited) in the bright half of the month. There the devotee stays in a splendid place on the southern bank.

After observing fast with great devotion, he should perform the following Vrata. He shall keep awake during the night and offer lights in accordance with his capacity. There should be dance, vocal and instrumental music etc. The devotee should be devoid of lust and anger.

In the morning, Brāhmaṇas should be honoured in accordance with one's capacity, O son of Kuntī, by means of cash gifts, gold, garments, umbrellas, quilts, betel leaves and food. The devotee should propitiate Brāhmaṇas of esteemed Vratas. O excellent king, Śrāddha should be performed with libations of water or cooked or uncooked food.

18-24. In the case of women and Śūdras, Āma-śrāddha (Śrāddha with uncooked food) is recommended.

O Yudhiṣṭhira, four times the usual quantity should be given in case it is uncooked food to be given to the Brāhmaṇas.

1. Birth of Vyāsa as a son is suggested to be the fruit of this boon to Parāśara.

The Brāhmaṇas should be assiduously honoured in accordance with the injunctions of the Vedas, by means of Kuśa grass a Hasta (forearm, a cubit) in length as well as gingelly seeds and raw rice-grains.

The Brāhmaṇas should sit facing the north and the performer of Śrāddha himself faces the south. Uttering the following Mantra, the food should be placed on Darbha(?) before the Brāhmaṇa: "May the departed ones go to the great world by the power of this Tīrtha. May my sin be subdued. May auspiciousness always increase. O excellent Brāhmaṇa, may the family and the groups of kinsmen (always) flourish."

After uttering this, gifts should be made to the Brāhmaṇas in accordance with one's capacity. Cow, plot of land, gingelly seeds, gold etc., cooked food, garments etc. should be given, O excellent son of Pāṇḍu, in the splendid hermitage of Pāreśvara.

Those who devoutly listen are rid of all sins.

CHAPTER SEVENTYSEVEN

The Greatness of Bhīmeśvara Tīrtha

Śrī Mārkaṇḍeya said:

1-7. Thereafter, one should go to the Bhīmeśvara Tīrtha, which destroys all sins. It is resorted to by the groups of sages who are splendid and regular performers of severe Vratas.

A person controlling the sense-organs and observing fast, should take his holy bath in the Tīrtha. Raising his arms up towards the Sun, he should utter the single-syllabled Mantra. The sins accrued to him in the course of that birth perish instantly.

By (the recitation of) Gāyatrī, the sins acquired in the course of seven births perish certainly. A hundred repetitions destroy the sins committed before in the course of ten births. Gāyatrī destroys the sins arising in the course of three births by means of a thousand repetitions.

The Mantra whether Vedic or secular (non-Vedic) in origin that is repeated, O king, instantly burns down all sins like fire that burns blades of grass.

One should not wilfully commit sins on the strength of the power of a deity. If the sin is committed due to ignorance, it perishes quickly, but not the other one at any time.

A person should offer gifts at that Tīrtha according to his capacity. O son of Pāṇḍu, everything yields everlasting benefit.

CHAPTER SEVENTYEIGHT

The Greatness of Nāradeśvara Tīrtha

Śrī Mārkaṇḍeya said:

1-9. Thereafter, a person should go to the excellent Nāradeśvara Tīrtha, O great king. It is the greatest of all Tīrthas, established by Nārada.

Yudhiṣṭhira said:

O excellent one among sages, why was this Tīrtha established by Nārada? O excellent one, narrate all this to me if you are pleased.

Śrī Mārkaṇḍeya said:

Nārada, the son of Parameṣṭhin, the excellent sage, O son of Kuntī, performed penance on the northern bank of Revā formerly. The control of the nine Nāḍīs[1] (blood vessels?) reached its extreme limit and Paśubhartṛ (i.e. Śiva) was thus propitiated by Nārada.

Īśvara said:

O eminent Brāhmaṇa, O Lord of Yogins not born of a womb, I am pleased with you. O dear one, request for a boon, whatever desire you may have been cherishing in your mind.

---

1. In human bodies, there are ten Nāḍīs. Out of them Iḍā, Piṅgalā and Suṣumṇā are the main ones. Suṣumṇā is the most important as it leads to God-realization. There is no appropriate equivalent term in English as some of the Nāḍīs carry life breath and not blood.

Nārada said:

With your favour, O Śambhu, may my practice of Yoga be successful. Let my devotion to you be firm in me for all time. O Lord, I should be the master of the Vedas and Vedāṅgas and should have power of moving about as I wish. O Lord of the worlds, I should be one conversant with the events of the three divisions of time (past, present, future) and expert in music. Whenever a battle takes place among Devas, Dānavas and human beings, O Maheśvara, whether it be in Pātāla, mortal world or heaven, I should be competent to see the same everyday with your favour. I may also (be able to) see you and Pārvatī. Let this Tīrtha be well known as the destroyer of all sins.

Īśvara said:

10-14. O Nārada, undoubtedly everything shall occur thus. What has been thought of by you will be achieved. There is no doubt about it.

You shall be one roaming about wherever you wish, whether it be in Svarga, Pātāla or in human habitation. You wander everywhere and you will not be stopped by anyone.

With my favour, you shall certainly have (mastery over) the seven Svaras (notes), the three Grāmas (gamuts in music), the twenty-one Mūrcchanās (melodious keys) and forty-nine Tānas (protracted notes) (i.e. all the details of the Science of Music)

Your dance and divine music will be pleasing to me. Everyday you shall watch the quarrel among Devas, Dānavas and Kinnaras.

With my favour, your Tīrtha on the earth shall become meritorious. With my favour, you will be a singular master of the principles of the Vedas and Vedāṅgas, an adept in all branches of knowledge and yet, O Nārada, you shall be free from undue attachment.

15-23. After saying thus, the Lord vanished. Nārada installed the Trident-bearing Lord there, O great king. The Tīrtha renders help to all living beings. Installed by Nārada, it has become the most excellent Tīrtha in the world. O excellent king, one who visits that Tīrtha, should have control over all sense-organs. O son of Kuntī, with great devotion he should observe fast on the fourteenth day in the dark half of the month of Bhādrapada and keep awake at night.

An umbrella should be given to a Brāhmaṇa of auspicious characteristics. Śrāddha should be offered to those who were killed with weapons. By the power of the balls of rice offered, they will go to the greatest world.

With the Pitṛs in view, O descendant of Bharata, a tawny-coloured cow should be offered to a Brāhmaṇa after saying this Mantra: "Due to the purity of this Śrāddha and with the favour of the Brāhmaṇa, let them attain the greatest goal."

Monetary gift should be given to the Brāhmaṇa in accordance with one's capacity, uttering this Mantra: "Due to the purity of the waters of Narmadā, the power of the wealth legitimately acquired and their own intrinsic worth, let the departed ones go to the highest goal."

O wide-eyed one, Haviṣya rice should be given to Brāhmaṇas. the light should be given devoutly and there shall be dance and music. He who carries out these activities in the holy temple shall acquire everything. He attains the vicinity of Rudra--so said Rudra himself.

By the gift of learning alone, one shall attain everlasting goal.

24-32. Yoked bulls and arable land should be gifted, O king. There the devotee should propitiate Fire-god devoutly with auspicious Mantras, using plenty of ghee and other articles of Homa.

They should worship devoutly and perform dance in all the three parts (of the day).

In the Tīrtha named after Nārada on the northern bank of Revā, Fire-god is worthy of being propitiated. Devas have Fire for their mouth. The sage is identical with all the Devas. All are delighted by the sage. When Havyavāha (Fire-god) is worshipped poverty is averted.

With wealth there is happiness in every birth. Men of noble birth and excellent clothes will always be endowed with wealth.

The following revive and resuscitate youth that goes on receding: raft that of rivers, husband that of women, king engaged in good conduct that of the subjects, wealth that of men and seasons that of trees.

It was at that Tīrtha that Dhanadatva (status of being a giver of wealth) was obtained by Dhaneśa (Kubera), the power of restraining (Yamatva) was obtained by Yama, Indratva by the Thunderbolt-wielding Lord, and the status of being a king was obtained by other kings. By the efficacy of Nāradeśvara Dhruva attained stability (fixed position).

A Tīrtha that is the most excellent one among all the Tīrthas was created by Nārada on the northern bank of Revā on the ocean-girt earth. That is the most excellent one of all Tīrthas.

CHAPTER SEVENTYNINE

The Greatness of Dadhiskanda and Madhuskanda Tīrthas

Śrī Mārkaṇḍeya said:

1-7. Then, O great king, one should go to two excellent Tīrthas that destroy all sins, viz. Dadhiskanda and Madhuskanda. If the devotee takes his holy bath in Dadhiskanda and offers curd to Brāhmaṇas, O descendant of Bharata, neither sickness nor old age, neither grief nor jealousy assail him in the course of seven births. He is born in a pure family and stays there as long as a thousand Moons last.

One should offer gingelly seeds mixed with honey in the Madhuskanda Tīrtha. He will never see Lord Vaivasvata (Yama) for a period of seventy births. If the person offers balls of rice mixed with honey there shall be no poverty in the family till (the birth of) grandsons of his grandsons.

In the Tīrtha the man shall take his holy bath duly facing the south and offer balls of rice mixed with curd. His father, grandfather and great-grandfather will be contented for twelve years. No hesitation need be felt in this regard.

CHAPTER EIGHTY

The Greatness of Nandikeśvara Tīrtha

Śrī Mārkaṇḍeya said:

1-11. Then a person should go to the excellent Tīrtha called Nandikeśvara, O great king. It was here that Mahānandin became a Siddha (enlightened one). I shall narrate everything to you.

Formerly Nandin, the Lord of Gaṇas, faced Revā and proceeded from Tīrtha to Tīrtha performing austerities and achieving victory[1]. When he left Dadhiskanda and Madhuskanda, Mahādeva became pleased and spoke to Nandinātha.

Īśvara said:

O Nandīśa, I am delighted. Choose any boon that you desire. I am pleased with your penance performed in the course of your pilgrimage.

Nandīśvara said:

I do not covet wealth nor do I desire a family and progeny. Excepting your lotus-like feet, I do not desire anything else. Whether I am born amidst worms, insects and locusts or as a brute of lower order, let my devotion be steady towards you in all my births.

Saying "So it shall be" with great tenderness, O king, Mahādeva held that enlightened one by the hand and went to his abode.

A man who takes his holy bath in that Tīrtha with great devotion and worships the Three-eyed Lord, attains the benefit of Agniṣṭoma Yajña.

If a person bathes in the Tīrtha and casts off his life, then he becomes Śiva's attendant and rejoices for everlasting Kalpas. After a great deal of time, he will be born in a pure family well-

---

1. Here '*Jaya*' seems to be a misprint for '*Japa*'. There is no propriety of 'achieving victory' as there is no enemy to be defeated. In Devanāgarī script *pa* (प) and *ya* (य) appear alike and the printed text if emended as '*japam kurvan*, 'performing Japa' is more suitable in the context.

conversant with the principles of the Vedas and Vedāṅgas. He will live for a hundred years.

Thus, O dear one, the excellent greatness of the Tīrtha has been narrated to you. It is difficult of access for human beings but it destroys all sins.

CHAPTER EIGHTYONE

The Greatness of Varuṇeśvara Tīrtha

Śrī Mārkaṇḍeya said:

1-8. Then, O great king, one should go to the excellent Varuṇeśvara where the great Lord Varuṇa became a Siddha. O excellent king, subsisting on oil-cakes, vegetables and leaves, he observed Kṛcchra, Cāndrāyaṇa and other austerities and propitiated the Lord of the Daughter of the Mountain. Thereby he attained great Siddhi.

One who takes his holy bath there in that Tīrtha, offers libations to the Pitṛs and deities and devoutly worships Śaṅkara, attains the greatest goal.

Listen to the meritorious benefit of that person who offers along with cooked rice a Kuṇḍikā (pitcher), Vardhanī (pot) or a big water-pot. He attains that benefit which a man is likely to get by means of a Sattra (sacrifice) lasting for twelve years. No hesitation need be felt about it.

Of all Dānas, the gift of cooked rice is remembered as the greatest. O excellent king, water and cooked rice cause instant delight.

Men who die there in the Tīrtha attain residence in the city of Varuṇa until all the living beings are annihilated.

Afterwards, when the period is completed, he is reborn in the mortal world. A man who gifts cooked rice always lives for a hundred years.

CHAPTER EIGHTYTWO

The Greatness of Pañca Tīrtha(s)

Śrī Mārkaṇḍeya said:

1-7. Thereafter, O king, one should go to the excellent Vahni Tīrtha where the highly refulgent Hutāśana performed penance and became a Siddha. Formerly he had been made one that eats everything by a (certain) sage in Daṇḍaka. But Hutāśana resorted to the banks of Narmadā and became purified.

One who bathes there in the Tīrtha, worships Maheśvara and enters a blazing pyre attains identity with Agni. One who devoutly takes his holy bath there and offers libations to the Pitṛs and deities, undoubtedly obtains the benefit of Agniṣṭoma Yajña.

The excellent Kaubera Tīrtha is next to it, O king. It was there that Kubera, the Lord of Yakṣas, formerly became a great Siddha.

A man who takes his holy bath there in the Tīrtha and devoutly worships the Lord of the universe accompanied by Umā, becomes rid of all sins.

There one who, after taking bath and standing in water upto the navel, gives gold (as Dāna) to a Brāhmaṇa, will obtain a hundred million times the usual benefit.

8-15. The benefit that is obtained in Dadhiskanda, Madhuskanda, Nandīśa, Varuṇālaya and Āgneya is obtained merely by taking holy bath in that Tīrtha. Those by whom the five excessively meritorious Narmadā Tīrthas have been visited, are worthy of being saluted. They are blessed in the world of human beings and their wishes have been fulfilled.

They go to the world of Bhāskara, that is extremely great and destructive of sorrow. From Bhāskara's world they go to the Loka of Īśvara and from Aiśvara Loka they go to *Anivartaka* world (that from which there is no return to Saṁsāra). He is taken to the greatest world and stays there till fourteen Indras complete their reign. Thence slipping down from Svarga, the man becomes a righteous king. Free from all sins he will enjoy the entire world consisting of the mobile and immobile beings.

Those residents who always resort to the Narmadā Tīrtha and have Viṣṇu as their deity will undoubtedly be born as heroes with unbroken glory.

Gaṅgā is meritorious at Kanakhala; Sarasvatī in Kurukṣetra; but Narmadā is meritorious everywhere whether in village or in forest.

One should always reside on the banks of Revā. He shall be on a par with one who has bathed in all the Tīrthas and imbibed Soma juice everyday.

All the rivers beginning with Gaṅgā, seas and lakes perish at the end of the Kalpa. But Narmadā does not perish thereby.

CHAPTER EIGHTYTHREE

The Greatness of Hanūmanteśvara Tīrtha

Śrī Mārkaṇḍeya said:

1-8. Then, O great king, one should go the extremely splendid Tīrtha reputed as destructive of the sin of Brāhmaṇa-slaughter. It is installed on the banks of Revā. Here is an excellent Liṅga named Hanūmanta[1].

Yudhiṣṭhira said:

Do tell me, how the Tīrtha named Hanūmanteśvara originated (was established) on the southern bank of Revā and it is capable of destroying the sin of Brāhmaṇa's slaughter.

Śrī Mārkaṇḍeya said:

Well! Well! O mighty-armed king adorning the lunar race!

1. Here the Rāmāyaṇa hero, Hanumān, is charged with the sin of Brāhmaṇa-slaughter for killing Rāvaṇa's army of Brahma-rākṣasas in battle. Killing in battles is no sin and Hanumān did it as per Rāma's order. But according to this Purāṇa, he accrued the sin of Brāhmaṇa-slaughter from which he was redeemed by performing penance on the bank of Revā. He installed a Liṅga in honour of Śiva. It became known as 'Hanūmanteśvara' in his memory. Neither Rāmayaṇa nor Mbh nor other Purāṇas know this story.

This Tīrtha which is to be kept more secret than other secret Tīrthas, has never been disclosed to anyone else by me. It is due to my love unto you that I tell you. Further I have now been afflicted by old age.

Formerly, there was a great battle between Rāma and Rāvaṇa. Pulastya was the son of Brahmā and Viśravas was his son. Rāvaṇa was born of him. He was a Brahmarākṣasa with ten heads. With the favour of the Trident-bearing Lord, he became the conqueror of all the three worlds. All the Devas were conquered. Rāma's wife was abducted, though prevented by Kuṁbhakarṇa urging "Release, release Sītā." The sinner was implored again and again by Vibhīṣaṇa and Mandodarī: "You have been conquered by Kārtavīrya who was defeated by the Son of Reṇukā (i.e. Paraśurāma). That Paraśurāma has been defeated by Rāmabhadra. How can you have victory over him in battle?"

Rāvaṇa said:

9-16. I can never be conquered by monkeys, men, bears, boars etc. devoid of arms, nor by groups of Devas and Asuras.

Śrī Mārkaṇḍeya said:

But he was defeated by Rāmacandra with the assistance of Sugrīva, Hañumān, Kumuda, Aṅgada and others. The powerful Paulastya was killed in battle by Rāmacandra. The garden was demolished and heroes killed by the son of Prabhañjana (Vāyu). Rāvaṇa's son Akṣakumāra was killed in the battle. The huge and terrible army of the Rākṣasas was threshed by the Monkey.

Thus the main activity of Rāma was over and Sītā was set free. When Rāma went to Ayodhyā, Hanūmān, the great monkey, went to the mountain named Kailāsa for paying obeisance to Maheśvara.

That excellent monkey was then addressed by Nandin: "Stop! Stop! Due to the slaughter of the Rākṣasas you have incurred the sin of Brāhmaṇa-slaughter. Hence, O monkey, Bhairava's assembly certainly should not be witnessed by you."

Hanūmān said:

O Lord Nandin, ask Hara the expiation for the suppression

of the sin. Why I, a monkey, have become a sinner? What is the cause thereof?

Nandin said:

17-27. Was not (the river) born of Rudra's body and stationed in the earth heard of by you? By listening to her name, the sin incurred in the course of a birth perishes. By glorifying her twice the sin is destroyed. By taking bath in Revā, the sin acquired in the course of thirty births becomes annihilated. Hence go to the banks of Narmadā and perform a severe penance.

On hearing what was said by Nandin, the son of Wind-god went to the banks of Narmadā, to the southern confluence on the earth. He meditated upon the very auspicious Lord, the odd-eyed (three-eyed), trident-bearing one endowed with matted hairs as crown and python as the sacred thread, the Lord who smeared all his limbs with the holy ash, the Lord producing the reverberating sound of Ḍamaru, the quiescent sharer of half of Umā's body, who is seated on the bull-vehicle.

He adored the Lord for many many years. Ultimately the great Lord was pleased and he arrived along with Umā and spoke sweet words with the majestic rumbling sound of clouds. The Lord said: "Well! Well! O dear one, severe penance has been performed by you. Formerly by killing Rāvaṇa (and his followers) sin has not been committed by you. Indeed you were engaged in the task of your master. You have become a Siddha by seeing me."

On seeing Hara, the eternal Lord, the partner of half of Umā's body, Hanumān prostrated before him with eight limbs touching the ground and said: "Be victorious, O Śambhu, obeisance to you. Be victorious. Obeisance to the destroyer of Andhaka. Be victorious, O bearer of Gaṅgā on the head."

On being eulogized thus, Mahādeva, the bestower of boons, spoke these words: "O dear one, O son of the Wind-god, choose a boon from me."

Śrī Hanūmān said:

O Maheśvara, due to my conversation with you just for a moment, let not the sin arising from the slaughter of the Brahmarākṣasa be effective (in my case).

Īśvara said:

28-33. Dear Son, undoubtedly you are free from sins, due to the greatness of the Narmadā Tīrtha, the power of Dharma and Yoga and of seeing me. O great monkey, I shall grant you another boon. The following names of yours shall be conducive to the welfare of the worlds: *Māruti* (Son of Wind-god), *Hanumān, Añjanīsuta* (Son of Añjanī), *Vāyuputra, Mahābala* (Extremely powerful), *Rāmeṣṭa* (Darling of Rāma), *Phālguna, Gotra, Piṅgākṣa* (Tawny-eyed), *Amitavikrama* (Of unmeasured valour), *Udadhikramaṇa-Śreṣṭha* (Excellent due to feat of crossing of the ocean), *Daśagrīvasya Darpahā* (Destroyer of the arrogance of the Ten-headed One), *Lakṣmaṇaprāṇadātā* (Bestower of life on Lakṣmaṇa) and *Sītāśokanivartana* (One who has dispelled Sītā's sorrow).

After saying this, Lord Śaṅkara vanished along with Umā. Hanūmān installed Īśvara there devoutly.

That Liṅga is a bestower of cherished desires by the favour of Īśvara, by the power of his Brahmacarya (celibacy) and the strength of his Yogic soul. The Liṅga cannot be chopped off nor can it be comprehended adequately and is devoid of origin and destruction.

Śrī Mārkaṇḍeya said:

34-45. Dear son, listen to the directly perceived proof of the efficacy of Hanumanteśvara. O son of Pāṇḍu, it occurred at the end of Tretā and the beginning of Dvāpara.

There was a king named Suparvan on the earth. The king enjoyed perpetual happiness. The men (subjects) had a long span of life. He was endowed with sons and wealth and his reign was free from the harassment caused by thieves. Śatabāhu[1] of terrible valour was his son.

O Lord of men, this prince always indulged in sinful activities. He wandered all over the earth, mountains and forests. For hunting herds of deer he came to the Vindhya mountain. He was sporting about in the forest where different kinds of trees grew sprawling and herds of elephants wandered about.

1. The stories of Subāhu and Śikhaṇḍin are contributed to illustrate the greatness of Hanumanteśvara.

It was full of beautiful lions and leopards. It was infested by wild boars and deer. After sporting there, the king (prince) arrived at a certain place on Narmadā.

He arrived at the forest of Hanūmanta that extended to a hundred Krośas. It was splendid with groves of tamarinds. It was full of Kadamba trees. It was rendered splendid always on account of Pālāśa, Jambīra, Kārañja, Khadira, Pāṭala, Badara, Śamī and Tinduka trees. It was crowded with herds of deer. It reverberated with the sounds of peacocks. Droves of pigeons cooed all round with exquisite notes.

The king sported about there in autumn and during the dark half of the month of Āśvina. Arriving at the centre of the forest he saw a tawny-coloured Brāhmaṇa moving about. The restless Brāhmaṇa with a book in his hand was asked:

Śatabāhu said:

O excellent Brāhmaṇa, with a book in your hand you wander alone in the forest looking this way and that. Why do you wander thus?

The Brāhmaṇa said:

46-51. O king, I have come from Kānyakubja. I have been sent here by the Princess to deposit the bones (ashes) in the water of the Hanumanteśvara Tīrtha.

The king said:

O Brāhmaṇa, why is the throwing of the bones carried out in Hanumanteśvara? What is the purpose? It is something wonderful. Let it be explained to me.

The son of Suparvan left his vehicle and (got down on the ground). After bowing down, he joined his palms in reverence to the Brāhmaṇa, O king. Then he (the Brāhmaṇa) narrated his earlier story in full.

The Brāhmaṇa said:

There is a powerful king named Śikhaṇḍin in Kānyakubja. This king has no son. As a result of his long-cherished desire, a daughter was born to him.

By the power of Narmadā the girl of beautiful limbs could remember the previous births. Once the question of her marriage was raised by the father:

"Dear daughter, this worldly existence is not permanent. I wish to perform the rite of Kanyādāna (gifting away a virgin). One should perform tomorrow's task today itself, and the work of the afternoon in the foremoon itself. Death does not wait to see if one has completed his tasks or not."

The Virgin said:

52-61. Dear father, I must be given in marriage at the time when I wish for it.

The king was surprised at the statement of his daughter.

Śikhaṇḍin said:

O highly esteemed girl, what you have stated is surprising. Let it be fully explained.

On hearing what her father said, the excellent girl came near him, O king, and recounted what had happened in Hanumanteśvara.

"Father, at that time, I was a female peacock (peahen). My name was Kalāpinī and I lived with my husband on the southern bank of Revā very near the confluence of Revā and Aurvyā.

Once it chanced that I was sporting about in the meritorious Hanumantavana. At night I was asleep in the company of my husband on a Sarala tree. Hungry hunters came to that excellent forest.

I was seen by those sinners who thought of killing me even as I was in the company of my husband. I was tied up with a cord along with my master (husband). They wrung my neck and cracked the tail. Along with my husband they baked our flesh in fire and ate it as they pleased. Contented they went to sleep and the night came to a close.

In the morning the remnant of my flesh and the bones from (my) body covered with nerves and flesh were seized by one of those birds of prey. One piece fell down from the sky from the birds. On seeing the piece of flesh other birds too flocked there.

62-73. On seeing the flock of birds the bird dropped down the piece of bones even as the entire flock of birds moved about and watched.

O king, it fell into the waters of Narmadā in Hanumanteśvara. It was a piece of my bone that fell into the waters of Narmadā. By the power of the meritorious nature of the Tīrtha I was born as your daughter. I became a princess with moon-like countenance.

Born into your royal family, I became endowed with the power of remembering previous births. Hence I do not desire marriage. O excellent king, even now my husband is in a difficult situation among the birds and animals there. O great king, the remnant of his bones is sure to be in that Tīrtha. Dear father, despatch an excellent Brāhmaṇa to cast off those bones. Thus, O excellent king, the explanation has been given to you in full.

My husband is in a tight spot among birds and animals. If you do send someone, dear father, to the banks of Narmadā, I shall make him know (the bones) as indicated by the places and signs."

[*The Brāhmana said:*]

I was summoned there by Śikhaṇḍin, O king. (He had said:) "I shall give you twenty villages. Go to the banks of Narmadā." Thus my despatch was announced by him. I was afflicted by absence of glory and wealth.

The Virgin said:

You go to the meritorious Narmadā that destroys all sins. To the south-east of Somanātha is the great deity Hanumanteśvara. Within half a Krośa from Revā, there is a well-grown banyan tree. In the vicinity of the banyan tree, there is a Kārañja and a Kaṭaha tree. You will see the minute pieces of the bones very near the root of the banyan tree. O excellent Brāhmaṇa, carefully look out for them under the tree and collect them and go to Revā.

74-83. In the dark half of Āśvina on the lunar day pertaining to Tripurāri (i.e. 14th day) bathe the Trident-bearing Lord devoutly and keep awake at night. In the morning stand in the water upto your navel, O excellent Brāhmaṇa, and say "Let his liberation take place" and cast them off.

After casting off the bones, you must take the holy bath that is destructive of sins.

[*The Brāhmaṇa said:*]

As mentioned by the girl, O great king, by doing thus he will have his liberation. Everything that was narrated by the girl was recorded in the book (notebook). Then I came here, O great king, to this Tīrtha that annihilates sin.

After seeing the signs (remnants of bones), O king, I took the bones and scattered in the waters of Narmadā in accordance with the injunctions mentioned before.

There was an immediate shower of flowers, O son of Pāṇḍu, followed by the shout "Excellent! Excellent!" There came a divine aerial chariot and the peacock assumed a divine form and went to heaven.

After seeing this convincing proof, O king, in Hanumanteśvara, the Brāhmaṇa and the king, Śatabāhu, undertook a fast. Engaged in propitiating Īśvara, they reduced their own bodies by drying them up. The excellent Brāhmaṇa and Śatabāhu stayed meditating on the Lord.

Within half a month, Śatabāhu, the noble-minded king, died. An aerial chariot with splendid tinkling bells came there. (A voice spoke out:) "Excellent! Excellent! O excellent king, get into the aerial chariot."

Śatabāhu said:

84-90. I will not come along the path to heaven as long as the Brāhmaṇa is also not present. The excellent Brāhmaṇa is my very preceptor because he imparted instructions to me.

The celestial damsels said:

This Brāhmaṇa is overwhelmed with greed. Sins are gathered through covetousness.

O king, only men characterised by Sattva quality, who die in Hanumanteśvara go to the world of Śaṅkara that destroys all sins.

There is no destruction of the sin of this Brāhmaṇa, O king. The house and the housewife dominate the mind of this Brāhmaṇa.

Thereupon Śatabāhu said to the Brāhmaṇa politely: "Leave off covetousness, the cause of all disaster, O excellent Brāhmaṇa." After saying this the king went to heaven surrounded by the celestial girls.

After a few days the Brāhmaṇa went to heaven accompanied by panegyrists.

By the power of the Tīrtha, the peacock was reborn as son of the king of Kāśī. He recollected the previous birth given to him by the girl. Seeing him become major (in age) the chaste princess, with the leave of her father attained the prince as her husband in Svayaṁvara.

Śrī Mārkaṇḍeya said:

91-101. This is the event that took place in that Tīrtha, O excellent king. For this reason this Tīrtha is always very sacred.

The time of visit to this Tīrtha may be any month but the (lunar) eighth and the fourteenth days are good, especially so the fourteenth day in the dark half of the month of Āśvina.

A devotee shall bathe the deity with great devotion with honey, milk or ghee. Again the Lord is bathed with curds mixed with sugar-candy and ultimately with the water sprinkled with Kuśa grass.

The devotee should smear Maheśvara with sandalpaste and sweet scents. Then he should adore with sweet-smelling flowers and Bilva leaves.

The devotee should further adore with great devotion Śiva named Hanumanteśvara by means of various kinds of flowers available at the time and season such as Unmattamuni, Jāti, Kāśa, Kuśa etc., or by means of bulbous roots or fruits of Mucukunda tree.

The lamp should be lighted with ghee or, if it is not available, with gingelly oil.

Śrāddha should be performed through Brāhmaṇas who are householders and masters of the Vedas. They should have all the essential characteristics and possess nobility of birth.

Uttering the words: "May those who are detained in Naraka (Hell) proceed to heaven," he should bow down to the Brāhmaṇas. He should propitiate the Brāhmaṇas devoutly with garments, cooked food and gold.

All the fallen Brāhmaṇas should be avoided, especially one who has a Vṛṣalī as his housewife. Devas call a woman Vṛṣalī if she is libidinous and carnally approaches other lustful men in addition to her own husband. A Śūdra woman is not Vṛṣalī.

Śaṅkara said that through Śrāddha all sins of Brāhmaṇa-slaughter, imbibing liquor, resorting to preceptor's wife, stealing gold, acting treacherously towards friends and mis-using deposits entrusted, are destroyed.

Śrī Mārkaṇḍeya said:

102-111. Of what avail is my prattling, O dear one? Why should I recount much? Anyone having comnitted all kinds of sins should make gifts to a Brāhmaṇa.

Particularly at this Tīrtha, the gift of a cow should be made, because, O son of Kuntī, such a gift is far superior to all other kinds of gifts.

Cows are full of all the Devas and all the Devas are identical with a cow. O king, Śakra dwells always on the tips of the horns; Skanda occupies the chest; Brahmā the head; the Bull-emblemed Lord is in the forehead; the deities Moon and Sun are the two eyes. Sarasvatī dwells in the tongue. All the Sādhyas and groups of Maruts are her teeth, O king. One should know that all the four Vedas with the Aṅgas and duly arranged words are in the Huṁkāra (bellowing of cow). Sages, the innumerable ascetics, dwell in the pores of the hairs. Yama stands at the back always scrutinizing the auspicious and the inauspicious. He has a huge body. He is armed with a big staff. He is dark-complexioned and has a buffalo for his vehicle. The four meritorious oceans are the flowing currents of milk from her udders. Cow should be honoured by a sensible person always, because Gaṅgā who originated from the feet of Viṣṇu and destroys sins merely by her sight is stationed in the flowing milk. O son of Pāṇḍu, the sacred and all-auspicious Lakṣmī is always present in cowdung. Hence smearing with cowdung should be done. Gandharvas, Apsarās and Nāgas are well-established at the tips of the hoofs. Know that cow is identical with all the Tīrthas that are present on the ocean-girt earth. Hence *Gavya* (milk product) is sacred.

Yudhiṣṭhira said:

Dhenu (cow) full of all Devas is embellished with the Devas and others. Why have they resorted to cow?

Śrī Mārkaṇḍeya said:

112-118. Viṣṇu is identical with all the Devas. Cows are born of Viṣṇu's body. On account of these two things, the different Devas are attributed by the people (to the different limbs of cow).

Before the deity Hanumanteśvara a cow should be gifted with great devotion to a Brāhmaṇa, O son of Pāṇḍu. She should be a milch cow. She may be white or tawny-coloured. She should be accompanied by her calf and should be well-behaved. She should be covered with a white cloth. She should be well adorned with gold fitted to the horns. A milk pot made of brass should also be gifted along with the cow.

She should be given in front of Hanumanteśvara by one observing rules and regulations and desirous of heavenly pleasures and everlasting status.

Those who give cows to the indigent and the feeble go to the world of Viṣṇu. After slipping down to the world, O king, he is born in the abode of a Brāhmaṇa. He becomes an able son of the family with all good qualities, learning, wealth and prosperity.

The Hanumanteśvara Tīrtha destroys all sins, O king. One who hears about it becomes rid of sins resulting from admixture of castes.

There is no doubt about this that even one who sees it from far or thinks about it becomes free from sins and is liberated.

CHAPTER EIGHTYFOUR

Kapi and Other Tīrthas

Śrī Mārkaṇḍeya said:

1-8. In this context they cite an ancient legend. On the Kailāsa Mountain this was recounted by Śiva to Ṣaṇmukha who had devoutly asked him.

Īśvara said:

Formerly, O Skanda, in Tretāyuga, Rāvaṇa was killed by Rāma. At that time fourteen crores of Brahmarākṣasas were killed.

When they were killed for the sake of according protection to heaven-dwellers, dear son, there was a great deal of joy and merriment in all the three worlds.

After redeeming Sītā, Rāma came to Ayodhyā along with the leading monkeys. Bharata, the elder brother of Lakṣmaṇa, arranged for a great festival and handed over the kingdom to him. Thereafter Rāma began to rule the kingdom from which all thorns (enemies) had been eradicated. Hanumān who had completed his task, went to Kailāsa. Nandin, the door-keeper, did not allow the monkey, though he was a part of Rudra, to meet Rudra, the destroyer of a heap of sins.

Nandī was thereupon asked by him: "What sin has been committed by me? Wherefore am I denied the pleasure of seeing the meritorious body of Rudra accompanied by Aṁbikā?"

Nandin said:

O leader of monkeys, you had taken up (this) incarnation for the sake of the Devas. Yet the sin committed can be destroyed only through suffering the consequences thereof.

Hanumān said:

9-17. O Nandin, was it any sin that I committed, when I was carrying out the task of Devas? Of course the wicked Rākṣasas who desecrated the Yajñas of the Brāhmaṇas were killed.

Curious to hear their conversation, Hara peeped through another door and saw the monkey of terrible strength, who happened to be a part of himself. Afterwards, he saw the Lord of monkeys standing before him.

The Lord said:

Īśvara said:

O monkey, Gaṅgā, Gayā, Revā, Yamunā and Sarasvatī are the rivers that destroy all sins. Take the holy baths in them.

On the southern bank of Narmadā there is an extremely splendid Tīrtha situated very near Somanātha. O monkey, do go there. At my behest your great sin will perish by taking a holy plunge there.

* * *

Leaping up from there, Hanumān roared loudly and went to the southern bank of Revā. He performed a very severe penance there. After a short period, with the favour of Īśa, O son of Kuntī, the sin resulting from the slaying of the Rākṣasas became dissolved even as he performed the penance.

Thereafter, Lord Hara went to that Tīrtha along with the Devas. He embraced the monkey and granted him a boon: "Henceforth this shall undoubtedly be your Tīrtha."

Thenceforth it became Kapitīrtha and Hara himself remains stationed there by the name Hanumanteśvara. He dispels all sins resulting from all sorts of killings.

18-27. All the sins of that person who takes his holy bath there devoutly and worships the Liṅga, perish as averred by Hara himself.

If the bones are dissolved there and if Piṇḍas are offered there, there is everlasting benefit. Whatever is gifted there has a crore times benefit.

Hanumān went to Ayodhyā to see Rāma. He recounted to him what transpired in regard to himself in the course of their pleasant dialogue.

Śrī Rāma said:

As you carried out the task of the Devas as well as that of mine (you incurred sin). So I too have become a sinner. Undoubtedly I have to and I shall perform penance.

Thereafter Rāghava performed penance for twenty-four years there on the southern bank of Revā that destroys sins.[1]

He stayed in the city of Jyotiṣmatī and took a holy plunge in Revā. At his bidding Lakṣmaṇa rendered him regular service.

Both of them, Rāma and Lakṣmaṇa installed Liṅgas there. By the power of the genuine penance on the banks of Revā the two heroes of great intellect, Rāma and Lakṣmaṇa, attained relief from sins.

Then Hara, the leader of Devas, came to the Tīrtha along with the meritorious sages. After releasing his own Kalā (Part) into the Tīrtha he granted a boon.

---

1. There is no confirmation of this in the text of Rāmāyaṇa. This is for the glorification of that Tīrtha.

Potfuls of water of all the Tīrthas were poured on the ground by the sages. Gathering together it became a Liṅga by the name Kalākuṁbha.

The Lord became well-known as Kuṁbheśvara; he was adored by the groups of Devas. Rāma too worshipped that Liṅga that was resorted to by the Devas.

28-36. In order to enhance the glory of Rāma, the Lord granted another boon. On the twenty-fourth year of his penance, Rāma attained relief from sins, when Saturn was in Kanyā (Virgo) Zodiac along with Jupiter (Guru). Hence the Devas proclaimed gladly that the Devayātrā (divine procession) shall be conducted at that time.

Just as one obtains the benefit of all the Tīrthas in the Godāvarī Tīrtha, so also men get the benefit through the holy ablution in Revā and also by visiting the Liṅgas.

[*Śiva said:*]

O Ṣaṇmukha, listen to the benefit of those who remain in the vicinity of Kuṁbheśvara on the banks of Narmadā and perform the Śrāddha of Pitṛs. The Pitṛs will have the never-failing goal for as many years as there are pores of hairs in the body of all human beings.

By seeing the three Liṅgas men obtain that benefit which is usually obtained by visiting all the deities on the earth and taking ablution in all the Tīrthas.

A man without a son obtains a son. An impoverished man obtains wealth; a sick person is freed from ailments. No hesitation or doubt need be entertained in this respect.

O Skanda, in the vicinity of Kuṁbheśvara the benefit obtained is twelve times that of the bath taken in Godāvarī when Jupiter is in Siṁha (Leo) Zodiac.

Those who know but do not visit Kuṁbhaśaṁbhu, the consort of Umā, on the southern bank of Narmadā, have their very birth fruitless.

37-44. This is spoken by the Lord, that the Devayātrā should be conducted in the twenty-fourth year as in the case of Godāvarī Yātrā as per bidding of the sages.

The *Dāna* made in the vicinity of Revā in Kuṁbheśvara is everlasting in its benefit as long as the Moon, the Sun and the stars are present in the firmament.

There all great *Dānas* should be made by wise and learned people. They praise the *Dāna* of cows, gold and silver here. When a mass of sins perishes by a mere remembrance of the Tīrtha, what doubt is there, O Skanda, that it destroys the sin of Brāhmaṇa-slaughter through holy bath?

He who takes the holy bath there in the Tīrtha and performs the Śrāddha, O Yudhiṣṭhira, shall redeem one hundred one generations of his family at the bidding of Śiva.

Whatever Tīrthas, lakes and oceans there are, they do not deserve even a sixteenth fraction of the adoration of the Śivaliṅga.

Thus the Devas with Hari and Īśvara as their leaders granted the boon, left their excellent names and went to their respective abodes.

After granting the boon to this Tīrtha, Rāma, the elder brother of Lakṣmaṇa, entered Ayodhyā freed from sins by the waters of Narmadā.

45-50. Accompanied by sages, people, deities and the members of his family, and after making a gold idol of Sītā, he performed a sacrifice there at that Tīrtha. That Tīrtha was created formerly in Tretāyuga, and named after Skanda. Hence the Liṅga should be regularly visited by people.

Sins accrued due to great evil deeds affect the bodies only until a creature visits the Tīrtha resorted to by Devas.

Those who visit the great Lord Hara installed in the city of Jyotiṣmatī are noble-souled and blessed. Their birth and life are excellent.

Hence getting rid of ignorance, the Tīrtha named Kuṁbheśvara should be respectfully approached by people for the sake of obtaining all benefits.

Śrī Mārkaṇḍeya said:

After hearing these words of Śaṁbhu, Ṣaṇmukha respectfully bowed to the pair of lotus-like feet of his father, reached the southern bank of Śiva's river and visited (Liṅgas of) the leading monkey, Rāma and Kuṁbhaśaṁbhu.

CHAPTER EIGHTYFIVE

The Greatness of Somanātha Tīrtha[1]

Śrī Mārkaṇḍeya said:

1-10. Then, O great king, one should go to the age-old Tīrtha of Narmadā that destroys even the sin of Brāhmaṇa-slaughter. It is on a par with Vārāṇasī.

Yudhiṣṭhira said:

O Brāhmaṇa, let the wonderful thing that happened on the banks of Narmadā be recounted. O venerable Lord, how is it on a par with Vārānaṣī? Do tell me. My kingdom is taken away from me. I have sunk in the ocean of misery, O excellent Brāhmaṇa. Along with my kinsmen I have become rid of sorrows after having bathed in the water of your speech.

Śrī Mārkaṇḍeya said:

Excellent! Excellent! O mighty-armed one who are an ornament unto the lunar race, I have been asked about a very rare and inaccessible Tīrtha that has to be kept as the utmost secret.

At first there was the Pitāmaha (Grandfather Brahmā), the Lord of the entire universe. Ten leading sages were mentally born unto him, viz. Marīci, Atri, Aṅgiras, Pulastya, Pulaha, Kratu, Pracetas, Vasiṣṭha, Bhṛgu and Nārada.

The highly refulgent Prajāpati named Pracetas begot Dakṣa. It is well-known that fifty daughters were born to Dakṣa.

He gave ten of them to Dharma and thirteen to Kaśyapa. The illustrious one gave twenty-seven to Moon-god (Indu).

Among those girls there was one named Rohiṇī. She was the greatest beloved of Moon-god. Due to his compassion for the remaining ones, Dakṣa cursed Moon.

---

1. The story of Dakṣa's curse to Soma (Moon-god) for his special attention to Rohiṇī and neglect of other wives and his redemption from it by a bath in the confluence of Sarasvatī and Western Sea is given in Mbh, *Śalya* 35.45-86. Here the credit of the redemption is given to a bath in Narmadā to commemorate which Somanātha was installed.

By the power of the curse of Dakṣa, the Prajāpati (Patriarch), Candra (Moon-god), the Lord of the night, became afflicted by consumptive disease and lost all splendour.

11-20. Soma (Moon-god), the nectar-rayed one, went trembling to Pitāmaha and prayed: "O Lotus-born One, obeisance to you. O Vedagarbha (having the Vedas in the womb), obeisance to you. I have sought refuge in you. Protect me, O Lotus-seated One."

Brahmā said:

O Lord of the night, you appear to be bereft of your Kalās (digits) and hence lacking lustre. O dear one, what is the reason for which you have become dejected in mind?

Soma said:

"O Brahmā, O Lord of the universe, lack of lustre in me is due to the curse of Dakṣa. O Pitāmaha, may the expiation for this curse be suggested to me.

Brahmā said:

Revā is easily accessible everywhere but at three holy spots viz. Oṁkāra, Bhṛgukṣetra and the confluence with Aurvā it is difficult of access, O Lord of the night, go there where Revā has its bank (i.e. go to the banks of Revā).

He hurriedly went to the place where there is the confluence of Revā and Aurvī.

Soma who was at the terminal stage of sickness meditated upon the Enemy of Tripuras. When a hundred years were complete Maheśvara became pleased (with him). The Bull-seated Lord, the Consort of Umā, appeared before Somarāja who prostrated before the Lord and prayed loudly: "Be victorious, O Śaṁbhu, I make obeisance to you. Be victorious, O Śaṅkara; obeisance to the destroyer of sins. Be victorious, O Īśvara, O Lord of the universe, obeisance to you. Be victorious, O Lord having Vāsuki as an ornament. Obeisance. Be victorious. Obeisance to the Lord holding trident and skull. Be victorious, O destroyer of the body of Andhaka. Obeisance to the slayer of the groups of Dānavas. Be victorious, O Niṣkala (without Kalās, parts). Obeisance to the Sakala (with Kalās). Be victorious, O Kāla. Obeisance to the burner of Kāma. Be victorious. Obeisance to the one having blue neck. Be victorious. O subtle one, O unsullied one, O Lord of sound! Obeisance to you. Be victorious, O primordial one, O beginningless one, O endless one. O Śaṅkara, obeisance. Be victorious, O Īśa, save me, the servant."

21-25. On being eulogized thus by Somarāja, O son of Pāṇḍu, O excellent king, Mahādeva was pleased with him along with Śivā. Śaṅkara said:

Īśvara said:

O fair one, request for a boon from me, whatever may be in your mind. Very good! Very good! O mighty one, I am pleased with your penance.

Soma said:

O Maheśvara, I am burnt by the curse of Dakṣa and have become feeble without intrinsic strength. O Lord, stop the effect of the curse. O Lord, grant me welfare.

Īśvara said:

I have been captivated by your devotion. I, along with Umā, have been propitiated. You are Somanātha devoid of sins. By resorting to the Tīrtha you have become so (sinless).

Thus the Lord of the chiefs of Devas spoke (to Moon-god). After meditating for a while, the great Liṅga was installed by Indu. It is the bestower of cherished desires on all living beings in the world. It is destructive of all miseries. It is destructive of the sin of Brāhmaṇa-slaughter.

Yudhiṣṭhira said:

26-35. O venerable Lord, tell me succinctly the power of Somanātha. You have come to us, O excellent Brāhmaṇa, as the saviour of those who are submerged in the ocean of misery.

Śrī Mārkaṇḍeya said:

Listen to the efficacy of the Tīrtha.[1] I shall briefly recount to you what happened on the northern bank at the confluence of Revā and Uri.

There was a king named Śambara. Trilocana was his son and Kaṇva was the son of Trilocana. He was given to sinfulness.

He used to wander in forest everyday and looked for herds of deer. A herd of deer was killed by the son of Trilocana.

A Brāhmaṇa was wandering in the midst of the deer in the guise of a deer in the desolate forest. Due to his association with the herd of deer, the excellent sage was incidentally killed by Kaṇva.

Kaṇva who had thus incurred the sin of Brāhmaṇa-slaughter roamed over the earth lustreless and feeble. In the course of his wanderings he reached Narmadā at the confluence of Uri.

It abounded in trees like Kiṁśuka, Aśoka, Jambīra, Panasa, Kadamba, Pāṭala etc. The beauty was enhanced by Bilva and Nāraṅga trees. There were tamarind and Campaka trees too. An Agasti tree spread its shadow there.

The forest teeming with many living beings was splendid everywhere with beasts of prey like leopards, deers, cats, Śambara and Śūkara (wild boars). It was full of rabbits, Gavayas (blue oxen), peacocks and wild asses.

Hardly did he enter the forest when Kaṇva was overwhelmed with thirst and extreme fatigue. He then took his holy bath in the meritorious waters of Revā at the confluence that destroys sins.

36-40. With great devotion, Somanātha was adored by him, O Yudhiṣṭhira. He drank the excessively pure waters that destroy all sins.

Along with his servants, he tasted various kinds of fruits. Utterly tired due to the hunting of deer, he slept soundly in the shade of the trees.

In the meantime a certain Brāhmaṇa came to that confluence in the excellent Tīrtha for bathing. The Brāhmaṇa wayfarer was urged by delight with (his) mind resting therein.

---

1. The story of Prince Kaṇva to illustrate the efficacy of this Tīrtha, is a special contribution of this author.

A woman said to him: "O excellent Brāhmaṇa, stop, stop!" Even as the frightened Brāhmaṇa looked all round in every direction, O king, he saw a woman clad in red garments, wearing red garlands, smeared profusely with red sandalpaste. She held a noose in her hands.

The woman said:

41-46. O Brāhmaṇa, may this message be heard. If you are going towards the confluence, my husband is staying there. Send him to me quickly saying, "Your wife is waiting alone in the middle of the forest."

On hearing thus, the Brāhmaṇa repaired to the holy confluence, rare even to Suras. Kaṇva who was resting in the cool shade of the trees was seen by the Brāhmaṇa. Thereupon the excellent Brāhmaṇa spoke these words to him:

The Brāhmaṇa said:

A certain lotus-eyed maiden was seen by me in the middle of the forest. The maiden is clad in red garments. She has smeared her body with red sandalpaste. Wearing red garlands she appears highly splendid. The fawn-eyed damsel has a noose in her hands. Seated on the top of a tree, she spoke to me these words: " May my husband be sent."

Kaṇva said:

O eminent Brāhmaṇa, in which holy spot is that fawn-eyed damsel? To whom does she belong? For what reason is she staying there? Tell me all this.

The Brāhmaṇa said:

47-54. She is in the park itself half a Krośa away from the confluence.

The king could not understand (who she was) merely through these words of the Brāhmaṇa.

Thereupon, King Kaṇva commanded his own messenger.

Kaṇva said:

Do go there and ask her from which place she has come and where will she go.

The messenger thus sent hurriedly went near the woman. He saw the maiden seated on the tree and told her, O excellent king: "My master asks you who you are and where will you go?"

The girl said:

A preceptor instructs and trains those who possess Ātman (i.e. those who are good). A king chastises those with an evil-Ātman (i.e. the evil-minded ones). Here, Yama, the son of Vivasvān (Sun-god) is the chastiser of those who commit sins secretly. The sin of Brāhmaṇa-slaughter has befallen through the killing of the Brāhmaṇa in the guise of a deer. Though possessed by me, your king is liberated by the power of the Tīrtha.

Within a distance of half a Krośa the sin of Brāhmaṇa-slaughter cannot gain entry. Such is the power of Somanātha. It is remembered as one on a par with Vārāṇasī.

Do go; let the king be sent here quickly and without any hesitation.

The servant hurriedly came back trembling and greatly agitated. He recounted everything that happened earlier. At the statement of the servant the king fell on the ground.

The servant said:

55-63. O Lord, why do you grieve? Whether it is auspicious or inauspicious, it has already been acquired.

On hearing his words the king spoke these words: "I will cast off my life in the vicinity of Somanātha. May fire and plenty of fuel be brought."

Presently everything was brought by the servants who were under his control. The king took his holy ablution in the splendid water at the confluence that is destructive of sins. He adored Somanātha with great devotion. He circumambulated three times the blazing fire. After meditating in his heart upon Janārdana, the Lord clad in yellow garments and wearing matted hairs(?) and a crown, Kaṇva, the king, jumped into the fire.

He meditated upon the Lord who was accompanied by Śrī and was seated on Garuḍa, the Lord who held conch, discus and club and who invariably slew Asuras. (He prayed:) "May beatitude be attained by me."

A voice said: "Excellent! Excellent! O prince!" and a shower of flowers fell.

The servants witnessed the unprecedented miracle and looked at one another. They too meditated on Gadādhara (Lord Viṣṇu holding a mace) in their hearts and died by jumping into the fire. Thereafter, O son of Pāṇḍu, all of them were seen seated in aerial chariots.

By the power of Somanātha they were freed from sins and went to heaven as the Brāhmaṇa was meditating on the Bull-emblemed One.

Śrī Mārkaṇḍeya said:

64-70a. This is the power Somanātha.

Listen with attention to the ritual (of worship). The days for observance of fast are the eighth and the fourteenth lunar days. At all times the fast can be undertaken on Sundays especially in the bright half if Sunday coincides with the seventh lunar day. The man should observe fast and at night he should devoutly keep awake.

He should bathe Parameśvara with milk products and Pañcāmṛta. Thereafter he should apply sandalpaste and offer flowers, incense etc. The lamp shall be lighted with ghee therein and there should be dance and music.

In the morning of Monday and the eighth lunar day, Brāhmaṇas should be honoured. They should have great control on anger and be self-possessed. They should have avoided censuring others. They should be handsome in every limb. They should be worthy of being praised. They should be those who looked after their wives very well. They should be regularly reciting Gāyatrī. They should never indulge in prohibited rites. If a remarried widow, Vṛṣalī and Śūdrī frequent anyone's abode, he (such a Brāhmaṇa) should be abandoned even from a distance by one who wishes for one's welfare. In the course of Vrata,

Śrāddha and Dāna, the following should be avoided even from a great distance: those deficient in any limb, those who have additional limbs and those who have no proper antecedents.

70b-78. Brāhmaṇas bereft of Vedic study are like maidens of steel. Undoubtedly they cause the downfall of themselves along with those on whose behalf they perform holy rites.

Brāhmaṇas regularly performing the six Karmas are on a par with the rafts made of Śālmali tree (silk-cotton tree). They themselves cross and enable the donor too to cross (the ocean of existence).

One who performs a Śrāddha at Someśvara (of the departed ones) without feeling of jealousy, his ancestors, the departed ones, become deeply satisfied until the annihilation of all living beings.

This is my truthful statement that he who gifts cooked food, garments and gold to a Brāhmaṇa goes to the world of Śaṅkara.

One should gift a full-fledged horse, young and white in colour. It may be red or yellow but shall have all characteristic features. The Brāhmaṇa as well as the horse should be smeared with Kuṁkuma, adorned with garlands and covered with a white cloth.

He should tell the Brāhmaṇa, "Keep your feet on my shoulders and get on to the horse."

When the Brāhmaṇa is comfortably seated after mounting, the devotee should say, "May Bhāskara (Sun-god) be pleased." He shall be rid of all sins and go to the world of Śaṅkara.

79-89. If a person with his sense-organs under control goes to Somatīrtha on a day of eclipse, he shall become a righteous king even after falling down from Satyaloka. His residence shall always be there. It never perishes. His son becomes long-lived. His wife is always favourably disposed towards him. He shall be free from all miseries and shall live more than a hundred years.

A person should observe fast and eschew anger and (then) offer a cow to a Brāhmaṇa along with her calf. The cow should be a milch one and should be covered with a white cloth. The cow may be of any of these colours: variegated, yellow, smoke-gray, blue and spotted, tawny etc. She should be embellished with bells and ornaments. The hoofs should be covered with silver. A pot made of brass should be given for milking. O king, the horns should be capped with gold.

By offering a white cow a donor gets the family increased; a red cow increases good fortune. Variegated and yellow ones are reputed as destroyers of misery.

A tawny-coloured one destroys sin acquired in the course of seven births. The donor of a cow attains Satyaloka, O king.

At the end of a fortnight, during Vyatīpāta and Vaidhṛti, at the time of the transit of the Sun, when the day comes to a close, when there is the Gajacchāyāparva (?), solar eclipse etc., the noble-souled devotees should go to the confluence rare even unto the Suras. After smearing oneself with clay he enters the water. With water upto the level of the heart, he shall perform the Japa of Gāyatrī, of Viṣṇu, Sun-god or Śiva as he pleases and perform Prāṇāyāma. They too are relieved of their sins. Thus spake Śaṅkara. If one circumambulates the area around Somanātha, it is as though the entire earth consisting of the seven continents has been circumambulated by him.

90-99. There is no doubt that a slayer of a Brāhmaṇa, an imbiber of liquor, one who resorts to the wife of the preceptor, a killer of foetus, one who steals gold—all these are rid of their sins. A person with the sense-organs subdued, who listens to this narrative of the Tīrtha, becomes rid of the ailment if he is sick and if he is not sick attains happiness.

If your mind is burning with trouble you will do well, O Yudhiṣṭhira, to listen to me. In this world, O king, even a single foeticide is very difficult to get rid of. It is much more difficult, O son of Kuntī, in the case of Moon who was guilty of twenty-six sins of foeticide (due to his negligence of twenty-six wives). He too came to this Tīrtha, performed a very severe penance and became rid of all sins.

The Cool-rayed One thus became happy. O king, this ancient Gāthā (verse) is heard as sung by the great sages: "A single Liṅga installed duly shall dispel ten foeticidal sins." Hence, O descendant of Bharata, Soma (Moon-god) installed three Liṅgas: The first Liṅga was installed at the confluence of Revā and Uri; the second one at Bhṛgukacchaka; after attaining great Siddhi he installed the third one at Prabhāsa.

Thus I have told you entirely the greatness of the Tīrtha. It is conducive to piety, good fame, long life and heavenly pleasures. It sanctifies men.

He who seeks sons, gets sons and one without desire attains heaven. After performing the pilgrimage to the Tīrtha, O king, one becomes relieved of all sins. Thus the entire benefit of Somanātha has been narrated. Undoubtedly one who listens to this gets a son and one who bathes, eight sons.

CHAPTER EIGHTYSIX

The Greatness of Piṅgaleśvara Tīrtha

Śrī Mārkaṇḍeya said:

1-8. Thereafter, O great king, one should go to the excellent Piṅgalāvarta. It is on the northern bank in the vicinity of the confluence. O leading king, Piṅgaleśvara was installed by Havyavāhana (Fire-god).

Yudhiṣṭhira said:

O venerable one, how was Īśvara installed by Havyavāha? Narrate everything to me. It behoves you to recount it as a favour.

Mārkaṇḍeya said:

O king, *Retas* (semen virile) was sprinkled over Havyavāhana by Śaṁbhu who had attained the height of orgastic excitement while gleefully sporting with Gaurī.

The *Retas* was cast into the mouth of Havyavāha by Rudra of unmeasured lustre. Scorched by the *Retas* of Rudra, he became eager to undertake a pilgrimage.

Crossing the oceans and rivers he gradually came to Revā. Fire-god then performed a severe penance with great devotion and meditated.

Hutāśana (Fire-god) solely lived on air and continued the penance for more than a hundred years. Ultimately Mahādeva became pleased and was ready to grant boons to Jātavedas (Fire-god). Approaching him (Fire-god), he spoke these words:

Īśvara said:

O Havyāśa (Fire-god), choose a boon, whatever may be in your mind.

Vahni (Fire-god) said:

Obeisance to you, O Lord of all the worlds. O Lord of fiery form, I make obeisance to you. Scorched by your *Retas,* I have become leprous, O Maheśvara. Be compassionate, O Mahādeva; destroy (heal completely my) ailments.

Īśvara said:

9-15. O Havyavāha, be free from illness quickly with my favour. Taking your holy bath in the Tīrtha here, you will regain your original form.

After saying thus, Mahādeva vanished there itself. Thereafter Havyavāha hurriedly took his bath in the waters of Revā. Instantly he became completely free from ailments and attained a divine form. Vahnī (Fire-god) thereafter installed the Lord of Devas, named Piṅgaleśvara.

He worshipped him joyously and eulogized through prayers. Thereafter Havyavāhana went back to his own land, the land of Devas.

O king, it was thus that Piṅgaleśvara was installed by Havyavāha. Only he who has subdued anger should observe fast there. He will attain the benefit of the Yajña called Atirātra. In the end, he shall attain the status of Rudra.

O descendant of Bharata, one should offer a tawny-coloured cow with her calf to a Brāhmaṇa. She should be adorned in accordance with one's capacity. O great king, he who gives this shall attain the greatest goal.

CHAPTER EIGHTYSEVEN

The Greatness of Ṛṇa-tray-mocana Tīrtha[1]

Śrī Mārkaṇḍeya said:

1-5. Thereafter, O king, one should go to the highly excellent Tīrtha which was established by the groups of sages born of the family of Brahmā.

It is called Ṛṇamocana. It is situated on the banks of Revā. A person should devoutly offer libations to the Pitṛs and deities for six months.

Instantly the debt to Devas, Pitṛs, and human beings owed by himself becomes redeemed as soon as the man takes his bath in the waters of Narmadā.

There the sin is actually and directly seen as the result. If a person who has subdued his sense-organs takes his bath with concentration of mind in that Tīrtha and performs charity and worships the Consort of Girijā (Umā), he becomes free from the three kinds of debts and remains resplendent in the heavenly world.

CHAPTER EIGHTYEIGHT

The Greatness of Kapileśvara Tīrtha

Śrī Mārkaṇḍeya said:

1-7. Thereafter, O son of Kuntī, a person should resort to the Kāpila Tīrtha installed by Kapila. It is destructive of all sins.

O king, on the eighth and fourteenth days of a bright fortnight, the person should bathe the Lord, with great devotion, with the milk of a tawny-coloured cow or ghee. Then he should smear Maheśvara with sandalpaste and sweet scents. Then, O excellent king, he should adore with white, sweet-smelling flowers. Those who have conquered their anger and adore (Śiva) thus, never go to the abode of Yama.

1. The belief that everyone owes the obligations of and has to repay the 'debt' to parents or ancestors, to gods and to society is certainly noble. Dharmaśāstra works specified Śrāddha, performance of sacrifices etc. for this. But this text advises to take a bath in this Tīrtha and wash off the debts.

By adoring Kapileśvara, wise persons never see the terrible hell of Asipatravana and the fierce Yamacullī (Oven of Yama).

After taking the holy bath in the meritorious Revā waters, the devotee should feed auspicious Brāhmaṇas, O descendant of Bharata, and gratify them with the gifts of cows, garments, gingelly seeds, umbrella and quilts. He is reborn as a pious king.

His splendour will be dazzling but he will not be terrible (i.e. he will be quiescent). His sons will live long. He will speak pleasing words. O son of Pāṇḍu, he will never face hosts of enemies.

CHAPTER EIGHTYNINE

The Greatness of Pūtikeśvara Tīrtha

Śrī Mārkaṇḍeya said:

1-5. Thereafter, O great king, a person should go to the excellent Pūtikeśvara which is destructive of all sins. It is situated on the southern bank of Narmadā. It was installed by Jāṁbavanta who sought the welfare of all the worlds.

There was a king named Prasenajit. The jewel from his[1] chest was taken out, where a wound had been caused, which had become foul and putrid. He performed a penance there at the Tīrtha and the wound healed.

The excellent Pūtikeśvara Liṅga was installed[2] by him. O most excellent one among the descendants of Bharata, the man who devoutly takes his holy bath there attains all cherished desires after worshipping Parameśvara. O king, on the eighth and the fourteenth days in the dark half of a month and at all times, devotees should adore the Lord. They never go to the abode of Yama.

1. Here the reading should have been '*tasya*' and not '*tasyām*' as it cannot be construed in this context which refers to King Presenajit.
2. There appears some confusion of the author. According to BhP X.56.13-14 a lion killed Prasenajit and took away the dazzling Syamantaka gem from him; Jāmbavān killed the lion and took away the gem. Here Jāmbavān is said to have taken the gem from the chest of Prasenajit; so it was Prasenajit who was wounded and the wound was healed at this Tīrtha. So here '*tena*' stands for Prasenajit and not Jāṁbavān unless we imagine that seeing the healing effect of the water of the Tīrtha in the case of Prasenajit, Jāmbavān installed the Liṅga.

CHAPTER NINETY

The Greatness of Jalaśāyī Tīrtha

Śrī Mārkaṇḍeya said:

1-11. On the northern bank of Revā, there is an excellent Tīrtha dedicated to Viṣṇu. It's name *Jalaśāyī* is well-known all over the earth.

After slaying Dānavas Janārdana went to sleep there. The discus was also washed by the Discus-bearing Lord of Devas. By resorting to the waters of Revā, Sudarśana became free from sins.

Yudhiṣṭhira said:

Do recount the details of the Cakratīrtha bowed to by groups of sages, so also the inimitable prowess of Viṣṇu as well as the benefit accruing from Revā.

Śrī Mārkaṇḍeya said:

Well! Well! O highly intelligent Yudhiṣṭhira, you are indeed one without any attachment (for worldly pleasures). The Tīrtha that has to be kept as a great secret has been created by the Discus-bearing Lord himself. Hence I shall recount to you the story that is destructive of sins.

Formerly there was a great Daitya well-known as Tālamegha.[1] All the Devas were conquered by him, O king. Their kingdom was taken away. He claimed: "I am Viṣṇu. There is no doubt about it." He himself partook of the shares in the Yajñas. The wealth of Dhanada was taken away. The elephant of Śakra was snatched. The sinner coveted even Indrāṇī and the excellent horse of Sun-god.

O son of Kuntī, afraid of Tālamegha, Ravi, Rudras, Indra, Yama, Skanda, Varuṇa, Fire-god, Wind-god, Lord Dhaneśvara, Vākpati (Bṛhaspati) and Maheśa became morose. They went to Brahmaloka and met Pitāmaha. The Suras beginning with Vāgīśa (Bṛhaspati) eulogized with various hymns of prayer: "Obeisance to the Lord carrying out the differentiation of the three Guṇas and thereafter acquiring differentiation."

* * *

1. No such demon is known to Mbh, VR, and PE. This appears to be a new legend to glorify the Tīrtha.

On seeing the Devas devoid of enthusiasm and pallid in face, O king, the delighted Lord replied to the heaven-dwellers:

Brahmā said:

12-24. Welcome unto the group of Suras. Why? Your earlier brilliance has vanished? Your faces resemble the luminaries under the painful influence of overhanging mist and fog? The weapons of the Suras remain unmanifest due to the disappearance of their lustre. The Kuliśa (thunderbolt) of the Slayer of Vṛtra appears as though its glory has been checked and mitigated. Further, the noose in the hand of Pracetas (Varuṇa) which used to be impossible to ward off to the enemies has reduced to the helplessness of a serpent whose vigour and vitality has been checked by a *Mantra* (magic spell).

The mental gloom of Kubera seems to proclaim his discomfiture. Vāyu (Wind) with controlled gait appears like a tree with broken branches.

Though never-failing, Yama too, now goes on scratching the ground with his staff devoid of its intrinsic brilliance, bringing out the dimness of an extinguished firebrand.

How have these Ādityas (Sun-gods) unfortunately have become cool through the loss of their brilliance! They can be seen at pleasure like those painted in a picture. So, tell me, dear ones, why you have come here and what you seek from me. What is the purpose of your visit, O Suras? Tell me unhesitatingly. Only the creation of the worlds is vested in me. The onus of guarding it lies in you.

Thereupon Vṛtra's Slayer nudged his Guru as though by means of his thousand eyes that exhibited the lustre of a lotus-pond gently wafted by mild wind.

Indeed he was the eye (the seer) on behalf of Indra. Though he possessed only two eyes, they were more powerful than his (Indra's) thousand eyes. Vācaspati (Bṛhaspati) spoke thus to the Lotus-seated Lord with hands joined in deference.

"O dear father, the mighty Tālamegha born of your family, harasses the Devas like a comet that has come up.

All the groups of the Devas are miserable on account of that Dānava. Tālamegha, the powerful Lord of the Daityas, torments all of us. Hence we have sought refuge in you. O Vidhi (Brahmā), be our shelter and resort."

Thereupon the delighted Lord Brahmā spoke these words to them:

Brahmā said:

25-35. O Suras, except Lord Mādhava, there is no one among you who is on a par with that Tālamegha. That Dānava cannot be controlled by me too.

Thereupon, O king, all the groups of the Suras with Viriñci (Brahmā) as their leader started towards the Ocean of Milk. Utterly miserable on account of that enemy, the Devas hurriedly set off with a desire to see Keśava. After reaching the Ocean of Milk, they eulogized Lord Jalaśāyin (i.e. Viṣṇu).

The Devas said:

You are beginningless and the universe takes its origin from you. You annihilate the universe but you yourself are endless. The universe constitutes your form; otherwise you are formless. Be victorious, O Lord adored by the Devas.

Be victorious, O Lord lying in the Ocean of Milk. Be victorious, O Lord who are always wooed by Lakṣmī. Be victorious, O son of Devakī, for the purpose of the destruction of the Dānavas. Be victorious, O Lord having the conch and the club in the hands. Be victorious, O Lord holding the discus.

On hearing this eulogy sung by the Devas, Jalaśāyin woke up. He uttered sweet words with the majestic rumbling sound of clouds: "O Brahmā, why have I been awakened by your Suras and Asuras (?), though they are themselves powerful."

Brahmā said:

O Kṛṣṇa, they have come to your abode due to their fright of Tālamegha. O Janārdana, the sinner Tālamegha cannot be killed by anyone. Do kill that wicked fellow. Otherwise he will not die.

Śrī Kṛṣṇa said:

O Devas, return to your own abodes and take up the work of your own subjects. I shall kill the evil-minded, mighty Tālamegha. But let the Devas tell me the place where that Dānava stays.

The Devas said:

36-45. That Lord of Dānavas dwells in the caves of Himālaya surrounded by twenty-four thousand maidens and by innumerable horses and chariots, O Kṛṣṇa.

Actors[1] (? warriors) are of various kinds there, O Hari, and their qualities cannot be counted. The elephants are as huge as mountains and the horses are comparable to elephants. The mighty giant inspiring fear into the Devas stays there.

On hearing the words of those Devas who were extremely agitated within, the Lord thought about Garuḍa, the destroyer of multitudes of enemies.

The Lord wielding club and discus, took up the discus in the hand. With his other hands Janārdana held the bow, the pestle and the plough[2] and mounted the Lord of birds for the purpose of slaying the Dānava.

At that time evil portents, terrible in form, began to occur in the city of the Dānava.

Jackals entered the middle of vultures along with pigeons. Even when there was no wind blowing, his flagstaff fell down. There was a fight between serpents and mice as well as lions and elephants. Rivers deviated from their path and flowed with a mixture of blood. Untimely and off-season flowers were seen on the trees all round. Then the Lord of the universe reached Himālaya, the Lord of mountains. In the vicinity of the city, the conch, Pāñcajanya, was blown suddenly.

Due to that loud report, the Lord of Dānavas became highly infuriated. Then the mighty Tālamegha spoke these words:

---

1. The reading should be emended as *Bhaṭāḥ* (भटाः), soldiers, as *Naṭāḥ,* actors, is irrelevant here.
2. A pestle and a plough as weapons of war are associated with Balarāma, Kṛṣṇa's elder brother. They are shown to be Viṣṇu's weapons here!

Tālamegha said:

46-55. O Dhundhumāra, who is it that has unwittingly fallen into the clutches of Death without being aware of my power? O Dhundhumāra, at my behest, go quickly, surrounded by your own army; bind that professedly mighty one and bring him to me forcibly.

Dhundhumāra said:

Undoubtedly, I shall bring him whether he be a Sura, Yakṣa or Kinnara, even if he be fully equipped with multitude of chariots, elephants, horses and foot-soldiers.

Thereupon the source of origin of the universe, the powerful Lord, was seen seated on Garuḍa.

"Let him be caught. Let him be caught." The servants were ordered thus by him. As they ran about in the four directions all round, they were burned like locusts by Suparṇa (Garuḍa) of fiery form.

Dhundhumāra was hit hard with an arrow by Kṛṣṇa. Struck on his chest the sinful fellow fell on the chariot in a state similar to that of the dead. Thereupon all the Dānavas became excited and raised a great cry.

Thereafter the infuriated Tālamegha got into a chariot and set out. O son of Kuntī, he saw Keśava holding the conch, discus and club.

Tālamegha said:

O Kṛṣṇa, these other Dānavas who were killed by you in battle are on a par with Hiraṇyakaśipu. O Acyuta, they were not manly enough.

After saying thus, O son of Kuntī, the Dānava discharged a volley of arrows like a heavy downpour. Keśava cut and split the arrows discharged by the Dānava.

Garuḍa slew that part of the army that was indestructible by the Suras and Asuras. Twice the number of his (Tālamegha's) arrows was discharged by Kṛṣṇa.

56-65. The Dānava discharged twice the number further

(increasing) two-fold. Kṛṣṇa cut them off with arrows eight times that number.

Thereupon an excellent Āgneya (pertaining to Fire) arrow was discharged by the angry Daitya. Kṛṣṇa discharged Vāruṇa (pertaining to Varuṇa) and the Āgneya missile was suppressed by the Vāruṇa. Tālamegha then countered it by discharging Vāyavya (pertaining to the Wind). Hṛṣīkeśa discharged Sārpa (pertaining to the serpent) for suppressing the Vāyavya. Nṛsiṁha (Kṛṣṇa) discharged the Nārasiṁha arrow, O son of Pāṇḍu.

On seeing the Nārasiṁha, the highly powerful Tālamegha got down from the chariot quickly. He then seized a sword and shield and said, "O Kṛṣṇa, I shall send you along the terrible path of Yama." Saying this, O son of Kuntī, the Dānava approached Keśava.

The Daitya struck with his sword the club-wielding Janārdana. Delighted in his mind, Keśava caught hold of the tip of the Maṇḍala (Disc?) and struck Tālamegha on his chest in the course of that great battle. Thereupon the Daitya struck Hari and Janārdana struck the Daitya in that battle. On that Janārdana became all the more infuriated. O descendant of Bharata, he then took up the never-failing discus and hurled it on the head of Tālamegha. His head rolled down. Mountains quaked. The oceans became agitated, O son of Kuntī, and rivers deviated from their regular courses.

66-78. Then the Devas let down a shower of flowers on Keśava (saying): "O Keśava, one who could not be killed by the groups of Suras, has been killed by you!" Then the Devas became normal and happy when Tālamegha was felled down. O son of Kuntī, Janārdana resorted to the banks of Narmadā.

He considered Narmadā, the Ocean of Milk itself. Accompanied by Lakṣmī, Kṛṣṇa lay down on the serpent, Ananta, on the northern bank of Narmadā.

The terrific Cakra (discus) with the garlands of flames and sparks fell into the waters of Narmadā in the mortal world very near Jalaśāyin.

Due to the contact with the waters of Narmadā, it became rid of sins that had been acquired due to the killing of Tālamegha, O son of royal personage. The entire sin was immediately washed off in Narmadā waters, O descendant of Bharata.

Thereafter, O king, this Tīrtha became well-known as *Jalaśāyī*

Tīrtha; some call it *Kālāghanāśana* and others *Cakra Tīrtha*. The Tīrtha on Narmadā is very famous in Bhāratavarṣa.

May the power of that Tīrtha be listened to, O king. Just as Ananta is the most famous of all the serpents, Janārdana of all the Devas and Mārgaśīrṣa of all the months, so also is Narmadā the most famous of all the rivers.

In the month of Mārgaśīrṣa, on the eleventh day in the bright half, a man devoid of lust and anger should, meditating on Viṣṇu, go to Jaleśa.

One who takes a single meal at night and that too unsolicited, who observes fast, feeds Brāhmaṇas and offers gifts to them does not go to the abode of Yama.

Those people who are afraid of the world of Yama, O son of Pāṇḍu, should visit the Lover of Śrī lying on the couch of the Serpent. He is encircled by cowherdesses, has resorted to Yoganidrā (Yogic slumber) and is Cosmic-formed. He is the Lord of the universe and destroyer of the fear of worldly existence.

79-89. With great devotion, one should bathe the Lord with honey, milk, ghee or with water mixed with sugar candy. Those people bereft of jealousy who visit Janārdana, the source of origin of the universe, the deity as being bathed, go to the greatest world bowed to by Suras and Asuras.

A lamp should be lighted with ghee or with gingelly oil. The devotees should keep awake at night before the Lord, keeping themselves free from envious tendencies. O excellent king, with devotion they should listen to the story of Viṣṇu. There is no doubt that sins like that of Brāhmaṇa-slaughter perish.

If the men circumambulate the preceptor of the universe, Jalaśāyin, it is as good as if the earth consisting of the seven continents is circumambulated.

When the night dawns, with purity a person should propitiate the Pitṛs with the libations of water. O son of Pāṇḍu, the men should perform Śrāddha there through well-qualified Brāhmaṇas always devoted to their own wives, quiescent and avoiding other men's wives. They should regularly recite Vedic passages. They should be auspicious and be strictly engaged in their own duties and rites. They must regularly perform Yajñas everyday. They must perform Sandhyā rites twice a day. If one wishes for one's welfare, one should perform Śrāddha with great faith.

Those men are blessed in the mortal world, who, worthy of being saluted on the earth, always abide resorting to the lotus-like feet of Hari. Those who visit Jalaśāyin, the leader of Suras, directly, those who perform holy rites, such as fortnightly fast, Pārāka Vrata, the splendid Cāndrāyaṇa rites, the terrible monthly fast, eating only once in six days and the Pañcama Vrata, at that Tīrtha, shall get the everlasting goal.

Śrī Mārkaṇḍeya said:

90-101. Henceforth I shall explain the benefit of Tiladhenu[1] (a cow made of gingelly seeds), the procedure thereof, the time and the auspicious benefit of the gift.

This meritorious anecdote was formerly heard from Sage Dvaipāyana by Nārada and others on various occasions at the site of the holy Naimiṣa.

This is highly conducive to longevity and auspiciousness. It augments glory. A wise man who narrates this to Brāhmaṇas attains infinite benefit.

A cow, a house, a quilt, women etc. should not be gifted to many (i.e. more than one): On a gift being divided (among many) (*vibhaktadakṣināḥ*?) these do not attain (go back to) the donor.

One of these should be given, O Yudhiṣṭhira. If it is distributed among many, it will be subjected to sale and shall burn down the family (of the donor) upto the seventh generation.

Gingelly seeds are of various colours—some are white, some black and some resembling cow's urine. A person should make a cow and its calf with all these diverse kinds of gingelly seeds.

The cow should be made of four Droṇas (a measure of quantity of approximately 60 or 30 Kgs) of the gingelly seeds as much of each colour as are available. The calf should be made of one Droṇa of gingelly seeds or more if desired.

The cow of gingelly seeds can be made by the measure or weight current in the particular region and doing so a devotee attains everlasting benefit.

It should be placed comfortably on a clean ground strewn with flowers, incense and raw rice-grains. Two Ratnas (jewels)

1. This topic is not directly related to this Tīrtha. It is probably an interpolation out of context.

should be placed in the ears and two lamps in the eyes. A piece of sandal should be placed in the chest and gold at the navel. Honey and ghee should be given above and mustard seeds will constitute the hairs. A blanket should be thrown on the back and honey and ghee on the hips. Yavasa (fodder), milk-pudding and ghee along with honey also are to be given.

The horns are bedecked with gold and the hoofs with silver. The tail is also bedecked in gold. Ratnas are placed on the back. A brass vessel as one intended for milking should be given.

102-111. Tiladhenu purifies from all the following sins: those committed in the childhood; those unwittingly committed; verbal ones; physical ones; mental ones; the sins of spitting into water, crossing over a threshing rod, carnally approaching a Vṛṣalī, the wife of the preceptor, a virgin etc.; stealing gold; and imbibing liquor. Other sins too are quelled.

After observing fast for a day and a night, the devotee should gift it in accordance with the injunctions.

The various obstacles in the path towards the abode of Yama are easily countered by this gift: for example, the river Vaitaraṇī in the terrible city of Yama; the sandy expanse, the iron pieces, the rocky region etc. where a sinner is roasted and fried; the hell Avīci, the Yāmala mountains, where there are steel-beaked crows and terrible hounds; the hell Asipatravana where there is the Kūṭaśālmalī etc. The devotee shall easily cross over these and proceed towards the abode of Dharmarāja. O descendant of Bharata, on seeing him, Dharmarāja speaks pleasing and wholesome words: "There is an excellent, befitting Vimāna (aerial chariot) embellished with gems and jewels. O excellent man, get into it and attain the greatest goal." Do not give this to a clever soldier; do not give it to a mere priest; do not give it to a squint-eyed one or an ugly one, one deficient in limbs and one who lives on shrines. Do not give it to a Brāhmaṇa not familiar with the Vedas, nor to one who sells everything, one who is treacherous towards friends, one who is ungrateful, and one devoid of Mantras.

112-117. It should be given to one who has mastered the Vedānta, to a Śrotriya having a large family. It should be given to a son of a master of Vedānta, to a householder, to a Brāhmaṇa of handsome features in all limbs, one of good conduct and pleasing words.

The full-moon days of Māgha, Kārttika, Vaiśākha, Mārgaśīrṣa, Āṣāḍha and Caitra are good for the gift. The Ayana (transit of the Sun), Viṣuva (equinox), Vyatīpāta, at all times on the holy occasion of Ṣaḍaśīti etc. and the holy period/moment of Hasticchāyā (also are good).

Thus the Kalpa of Tiladhenu has been recounted to you by me.

They go to the world of Viṣṇu after placing the foot on Yama. After the extinction of life, they go undoubtedly to the world of Viṣṇu. They break through the solar zone and go. No hesitation need be entertained.

Thus the benefit of Cakratīrtha has been entirely recounted to you, O king. On hearing this devoutly, a man is rid of all sins.

CHAPTER NINETYONE

The Greatness of Caṇḍāditya Tīrtha

Śrī Mārkaṇḍeya said:

1-9. Thereafter, O king, one should go to the highly splendid Tīrtha called Caṇḍāditya. O excellent king, it was established by Caṇḍa and Muṇḍa.

Formerly there were two great and terrible Daityas named Caṇḍa and Muṇḍa. Resorting to the banks of Narmadā, they performed very severe penance.

They meditated on Lord Bhāskara (Sun-god), the destroyer of darkness in all the three worlds. Pleased with their penance, the Thousand-rayed Lord said: "Excellent! Excellent! Request for a boon, O heroes, as you wish, whatever has been desired by your mind."

Caṇḍa and Muṇḍa said:

O Divākara, we should be invincible to all the Devas. We should be mentally very alert. At all times, we should be beyond the reach of all the ailments.

"Let it be so", said Bhāskara, the stealer of waters. After saying so, Bhānu (Sun-god) vanished. With great devotion Bhāskara was installed there by them. One should go there for the fulfilment of oneself. There one should propitiate by means of libations etc., Gīrvāṇas (Devas), human beings and the Pitṛs. He shall stay in the world of Bhāskara for a period of a day of Viriñci (Brahmā), O king.

He should light a lamp on the sixth lunar day, O king. He is liberated from all sins. He goes to the city of Ravi (Sun-god).

He who listens to the origin of Caṇḍabhānu (i.e. Bhānu installed by Caṇḍa), O leading scion of the family of Bharata, shall be always victorious. He shall be free from mental suffering and physical ailment.

CHAPTER NINETYTWO

The Greatness of Yamahāsya Tīrtha

Śrī Mārkaṇḍeya said:

1-5. Thereafter, one should go to the excellent Yamahāsya Tīrtha which dispels all sins. It is situated on the banks of Narmadā.

Yudhiṣṭhira said:

O eminent Brāhmaṇa, how did this Yamahāsya come into existence on the earth? Narrate this entirely to me. I have got great curiosity about it.

Śrī Mārkaṇḍeya said:

Well! Well! O highly intelligent one! I have been pertinently asked, O prince. Formerly your father (Yama/Dharma) came to the sacred Narmadā for taking his holy bath. Just as a cloth washed by a washerman becomes free from impurities, so also, O Yudhiṣṭhira, Dharmarāja (Yama) became free from impurities. On seeing his body devoid of impurities, he was surprised and he laughingly said:

Yama said:

6-18. How do men loaded with sins come to my city? Merely through a single holy bath in Revā, the position in the world of Viṣṇu is obtained.

Those who are physically fit but do not visit the auspicious Revā of meritorious waters, should be known as persons congenitally blind or on a par with dead and lame men.

O king, it is for this reason that the chastiser of the worlds laughed: Those who are physically fit, yet do not visit the river Revā of meritorious waters!

Yama installed the Lord there and went to heaven. O king, a devotee who has conquered anger and sense-organs should devoutly observe fast, particularly on the fourteenth lunar day in the dark half of the month of Āśvina. He shall be liberated from all the sins.

He should keep awake at night and light the lamp of the Lord with ghee, O great king. Listen to the benefit thereof.

He is redeemed of all sins such as those resulting from carnally approaching a prohibited woman, from eating prohibited foodstuffs and from drinking prohibited beverages.

The sin that results from riding what should not be ridden and by milking what should not be milked, is dispelled merely by the holy ablution. Thus all types of sins do perish.

That man never sees the world of Yama. O king, this is the greatest secret of the Pitṛs on the Earth.

Undoubtedly, to those who make gift at Yamahāsya everything becomes everlasting. A devotee should subdue anger and adore Brāhmaṇas on a new-moon day by means of various gifts such as gold, plot of land, gingelly seeds, skin of a black antelope, cow of gingelly seeds etc.

Those who gift in accordance with what is laid down in the scriptures, a horse, an elephant along with ploughshare, a girl, a cow, a buffalo that yields good quantity of milk etc. do not go to the world of Yama.

19-24. Yama becomes delighted at every birth, O Yudhiṣṭhira. Buffalo is the vehicle of Yama and buffaloes are the mothers of his vehicle, buffalo. Certainly Yama becomes pleased as a result of their gift.

Even if one is surrounded by sins, one does not go to Yama.

For this reason the gift of a buffalo here is excellent. Water should be sprinkled on its horns. The buffalo should be covered with a smoke-coloured cloth. Hoofs should be made of iron and copper (red cloth?) should be placed on the back. On the east there shall be a hillock of salt; on the south-east there shall be a mountain of jaggery. Cotton constitutes the portion of the south; butter on the south-west; seven food-grains on the west. Rice grains should be placed on the north-west. Gold is placed on the northern side and ghee on the north-east. These things should be offered uttering "May Yamarāja be pleased with me."

25-30. Before the Brāhmaṇa, one shall utter these words: "Yama's world is highly frightening. Asipatravana is terrible. Yamacullī is extremely terrifying. Vaitaraṇī is horrible. Kumbhīpāka causes terror. Kālasūtra is extremely terrifying. So also the Yamala mountains, Krakaca (scissors), Tailayantra (oil-extracting machine), the hounds, the vultures are hideous. Nirucchvāsa is highly noisy, Raurava is excessively terrible. O excellent Brāhmaṇa, we hear that all these are present in the world of Yama. With your favour and by the power of this Tīrtha, let them be gentle. By the power of this Dāna and with the favour of Yamarāja, may I not go to Naraka in any birth whatsoever."

Men who listen to this account of Yamahāsya shall be rid of sins. They will not see the abode of Yama.

CHAPTER NINETYTHREE

The Greatness of Kalhoḍī Tīrtha

Śrī Mārkaṇḍeya said:

1-10. Thereafter, one should go to the excellent Kalhoḍī Tīrtha which is well-known all over Bhārata as destroyer of the sins of (even) Gaṅgā.

It is difficult of access to men, O son of Kuntī, and is situated on the banks of Revā for the sake of destruction of the sins of living beings like the Ūṣara[1] (arid) Puṣkara. "That is the Tīrtha. This is meritorious." These are the words of the Trident-bearing Lord.

Gaṅgā came there in the form of a cow for the purpose of holy ablution. Hence it became well-known as the excellent Kalhoḍī Tīrtha.

Three nights should be spent there around a full-moon day, O Yudhiṣṭhira. If a person eschews Rajas and Tamas Guṇas as well as anger, hypocrisy and jealousy, O son of Kuntī, the benefit of salvation is obtained by him.

The devotee shall bathe the Lord three times a day on all the three days. The milk should be that of a cow and the cow should have its calf alive. The milk is to be kept in a copper vessel. Honey should be mixed therewith.

Uttering "*om namaḥ śrīśivāya*" (Om, obeisance to Lord Śiva), the deity is to be bathed. He goes to heaven surrounded by celestial damsels.

The person should duly take his holy ablution and offer *Dāna* on behalf of the departed ones. He should make gift of a white cow to a Brāhmaṇa of great cleanliness who is always devoted to his wife. He should say, "May my grandfathers be pleased."

The devotee should adopt Sāttvika qualities. The cow shall be accompanied by her calf and should be covered with a cloth and placed on gold. Such a donor shall attain the world of Śaṁbhu.

---

1. *Ūṣara* seems to be a special name of the sacred places, such as Reṇukā Tīrtha (Panjab), Śūkara, Kāśī, Kāliñjara, Mahākāla (Ujjain). According to *Padma Purāṇa* they are nine in all. (De 102)

CHAPTER NINETYFOUR

The Greatness of Nandikeśvara Tīrtha

Śrī Mārkaṇḍeya said:

1-4. Beyond that itself, O king, one should go to the auspicious Nanditīrtha that is destructive of all sins of men. It was formerly created by Nandin.

It accords salvation to creatures overwhelmed by masses of sins. It is on the banks of Narmadā. A devotee should observe fast for a day and a night, O Yudhiṣṭhira, there at Nandinātha. He should adore Nandikeśvara with the full complement of the five Upacāras. O son of Dharma, he should gift gems to Brāhmaṇas.

He should then go to the greatest place where the Pinākabearing Lord resides. He will be endowed with all types of comforts and ease and will rejoice along with celestial damsels.

CHAPTER NINETYFIVE

The Greatness of Nārāyaṇa Tīrtha

Śrī Mārkaṇḍeya said:

1-10. Thereafter, one should go to the excellent Badaryāśrama, O great king. It has been formerly mentioned by Śambhu as the most meritorious and excellent Tīrtha of all Tīrthas.

Kirīṭin (i.e. Arjuna), your brother, also called Phālguna, became a Siddha there for the sake of the descendants of Bharata. Know that he is Nara with divine features.

Both of them, Nara and Nārāyaṇa came to the banks of Narmadā. Knowledge is attained only by him who is devoted to Janārdana.

One who is impartial towards all beings, mobile as well as immobile, Brāhmaṇa as well as Cāṇḍāla, gets the favour of Janārdana. He is pleased with him.

O son of Kuntī, see the identity between me and other Ātmans. There never is any difference. The Badarikāśrama penance-grove has been made by Nara and Nārāyaṇa.

For the purpose of blessing the worlds, Śaṅkara was installed there. The Liṅga installed by the triad of deities opens the path to heaven and then to salvation.

After going there, a devotee should remain clean and observe fast for a night. Eschewing Rajas and Tamas, he should adopt Sāttvika attitude. At night he should keep awake. The festival days are the eighth day in the month of Madhu and the fourteenth day of either half. Particularly that of Āśvina month has been spoken to you, O son of Pāṇḍu. With great devotion he should bathe the Bull-emblemed Lord with milk along with honey. This mixed with curds and sugar-candy to which ghee is added, is the holy Pañcāmṛta with which the Lord is to be bathed.

11-21. If a devotee perceives Śiva being bathed duly, and he has devotion and absence of envy, his residence is near Śiva in the world of Śakra. There is no doubt at all.

If obeisance is made to the Trident-bearing Lord even insincerely, it shall act as the unraveller of the bondage of the worldly existence.

If the practice of reciting the Mantra "*oṁ namaḥ śivāya*" is stabilised by the devotee, it is as good as everything is studied and heard and performed by him.

The devotee with sense-organs subdued should take one meal a day and devoutly bathe the Lord. O son of Kuntī, I shall mention a bit of the benefit he is sure to attain.

Though afflicted by old age I shall speak out of my affection for you. They pierce the solar zone and enter the greatest place (supreme position).

He and people like him become full of all happiness in the world. The fact that they are the abodes of pious rites shall be a surprise to the kinsmen. O Lord of the earth, they are endowed with the fulfilment of all desires on the earth.

The devotee shall perform Śrāddha there itself with the mixture of the waters of Narmadā through well qualified Brāhmaṇas of noble birth and mastery over the Vedas, who are of handsome features and good conduct, who are virtuous and devoted to their own wives, who have been born in the Āryadeśa, who are adepts and possess excellent physical forms.

The offering of the balls of rice should be done when the Sun is in the last Muhūrta of the day, if the person wishes for the greatest world of the Pitṛs, O son of Dharma.

A person should cautiously avoid those Brāhmaṇas who are squint-eyed, wicked and hypocritical, who are ruthless men, eunuchs and those who slander Brāhmaṇas. One shall avoid these Brāhmaṇas if one wishes for one's welfare.

22-28. Hence with all efforts one should resort to a deserving, well-qualified Brāhmaṇa. He shall then redeem the departed ones from hells, the chief whereof is Kuṁbhīpāka.

Thus there shall be salvation of all the Pitṛs, O Prince. Uttering "May my Pitāmaha be pleased" the devotee should give gold to Brāhmaṇas.

To them he should give cooked rice, and garments with devotion. He should give a cow, bullock, land and an umbrella, all of good qualities. That man attains Svarga. So said Lord Śaṅkara.

One who gives up his life through fire, water or starvation shall go to Śiva's palace.

On the banks of Naranārāyaṇī or in Devadroṇī, O king, one should perform holy rites. He dwells in the presence of Īśvara as long as fourteen Indras complete their reign. Slipping down again from heaven he becomes a powerful king endowed with all prosperity and good qualities and alert in protecting the subjects. Then he remembers that Tīrtha and comes back to the same Tīrtha.

CHAPTER NINETYSIX

The Greatness of Koṭīśvara Tīrtha

Śrī Mārkaṇḍeya said:

1-6. Thereafter, O great king, one should go to the great Koṭīśvara Tīrtha where, O descendant of Kuru, a crore of sages came there for the sake of the welfare of Kṛṣṇadvaipāyana.

The eminent sages took counsel with all the Brāhmaṇas who recited auspicious Vedic passages. Śaṅkara, the cause of the destruction of bondage, was installed there. The Lord causes severance from the worldly existence (Saṁsāra) and destroys the distress of all living beings.

It is called Koṭīśvara on the earth, O prince. One who bathes the Lord devoutly, on a full-moon day, especially of the month of Śrāvaṇa, O Yudhiṣṭhira, after offering libations of water and balls of rice to the manes in accordance with the injunctions will give everlasting satisfaction to the Pitṛs until the annihilation of all living beings.

This is the greatest secret of the Pitṛs that have resorted to the banks of Revā. It accords salvation to all creatures. It has been created by the excellent sages.

CHAPTER NINETYSEVEN

The Greatness of Vyāsa Tīrtha

Śrī Mārkaṇḍeya said:

1-8. Thereafter, a person should go to the excellent Vyāsatīrtha, O king. It is rarely accessible to men. It is meritorious and is stationed in the air-space between heaven and earth.

Yudhiṣṭhira said:

Why is that Vyāsatīrtha well-established in the atmosphere? Recount this succinctly. Do avoid verbose details.

Śrī Mārkaṇḍeya said:

Well! Well, O mighty-armed one! You are a favourite with good men and pious too. You are engaged in your own duties, O son of Kuntī, and you have respect and interest in pilgrimage.

Vyāsatīrtha is well-nigh inaccessible to all the creatures, O king. Afflicted by old age, O prince, I have become incapable.

Having lost alertness, my mind is out of tune and devoid of the power of recollection. This great secret Tīrtha has not been divulged to anyone by me.

Kali cannot enter that region, O great king, because it is the place of rest of Vyāsa. It came to be established in the atmosphere due to the activity of Revā.

Even Viriñci is incapable of glorifying adequately the good points of Revā. How can I then know the excellent greatness of Revā?

Hence I recount a bit of (the greatness) of Vyāsatīrtha. Here there is direct, convincing evidence seen in the Kali age.

9-17. No bird crosses beyond the terrible trident. O prince, I shall succinctly mention its region.

Formerly there was, O king, an honoured sage named Parāśara. A fierce penance of great benefit was performed by him in the waters of Gaṅgā.[1]

He entered the waters of Gaṅgā and stayed therein restraining his breath. When the twelfth year was complete, he came out from within the water.

Seeking alms he roamed about in the village. In a certain place he saw a boat in which he saw an extremely charming woman too.

On seeing her he became overwhelmed with love and so spoke to her sweetly: "O lady seated in the boat, you agitate my mind. O fawn-eyed one, on the banks of the river who may you be? Take me to the other bank."

On being asked thus by him, she bowed down to the eminent sage. On seeing him infatuated with love, she told about herself:

"I am a slave in a household of fishermen. I am a virgin, O excellent Brāhmaṇa. O venerable one, I have been directed by my master to look after the boat. It behoves you to know that the entire fact concerning me has been revealed to you."

On being told thus by her, he meditated for a short while and spoke thus:

Parāśara said:

18-28. O fair lady, by my knowledge (insight) I know your nativity. You are not the daughter of a fisherman. O beautiful woman, you are the daughter of a king.[2]

1. VV 10 ff describe the story of Vyāsa's birth from Parāśara and Satyavatī. The story is the same as in Mbh, *Ādi* 63.50-85.
2. VV 18-49 describe how Satyavatī, though a daughter of King Vasu (called Uparicara Vasu in Mbh), was born of a fish as the tube of Vasu's semen fell in the river while it was being carried to his queen. This story is the same as in Mbh, *Ādi.* 63.70-83.

The girl said:

O Brāhmaṇa, who is my father? Let it be mentioned. In whose womb was I born? In which family was I born? How did it happen that I became known as the daughter of a fisherman?

Parāśara said:

I shall narrate everything that has been asked by you. There was a king named Vasu who was an ornament unto the lunar race.

He was the overlord of Jambūdvīpa, O fair lady, and he heightened terror in the minds of the enemies. He had seven hundred wives and a thousand sons. He righteously protected the people and he was honoured always like a god. Mlecchas (Barbarians), the residents of Kṣīradvīpa, did not recognize his suzerainty.

Accompanied by his sons and attendants noted for their valour, he went beyond the ocean in order to exterminate them. The battle with Vasu was started by the Mlecchas. O fawn-eyed one, the entire host of Mlecchas was overpowered by Vasu and made to pay tribute. The whole host inclusive of the sons, vehicles and army was subdued. The chief of his queens was your mother, O fawn-eyed one.

While the king was away, she had her monthly course. Usually the emotion of love in women is inordinate at all times. Especially during the days of menses, they are pierced by the arrows of the god of Love.

On being tormented by the god of Love that splendid-eyed lady thought, 'I shall send a messenger to King Vasu now.' The messenger was called and instructed "O messenger, go immediately to the king."

The Messenger said:

29-35. King Vasu, the chastiser of enemies, has gone to the other shore. O splendid lady, without boats it is impossible to go there. All the boats are taken to the other shore.

The love-lorn queen became all the more upset at the words of the messenger. Her companion told her: "Why are you worried?

May your own letter expressing your state of mind correctly, be sent through a courier parrot. O beautiful lady, birds do go across the sea."

At the words of her companion the queen regained peace (of mind), O king. A scribe was instructed: "At my behest write the letter: 'O King Vasu, it is impossible for Satyabhāmā to continue to live without you. The days of menses have started already.' O scribe, do write the letter." When the letter was duly written on a Bhūrja leaf by the scribe, the parrot kept in a cage was immediately brought near.

Satyabhāmā said:

36-47. Take this letter and go quickly to the presence of King Vasu.

Parāśara continued:

The bird bowed down, took up the excellent letter, flew up into the sky, O king, and went through the firmament. Soon the bird reached the vicinity of King Vasu.

When the letter was dropped down by the parrot, the king took it with his hand and understood that it was sent by Satyabhāmā. Thinking over the purport of the letter, the king squeezed out his never-failing semen virile and put it in a tube. He entrusted it along with a letter in reply stating, "Go to the queen." The bird took the tube of semen, bowed down to the king, and flew away. The parrot was flying over the sea when it was spotted by a hawk.

Thinking that the parrot had some meat with it the falcon attacked it. It was pecked with the beak and killed by the vulture, O descendant of Bharata. When the parrot swooned the semen virile fell into the waters of the sea. The semen virile of King Vasu was swallowed by a fish. A girl appeared within the womb of the fish, O beautiful lady.

That fish was caught by fishermen who brought it home. When the fish was cut open, O excellent girl, you were seen there resembling the Moon in lustre and having the dazzling brilliance of the Sun. On seeing you all the fishermen on the banks of Gaṅgā became delighted.

All the delighted people went to the abode of the chief of

the fishermen and said: "There is a jewel of a girl whom you do take. She is highly brilliant." As he had no issue he adopted the fawn-eyed maiden. He said to his wife, "O fair lady of fawn-eyes, bring up this girl."

Śrī Mārkaṇḍeya said:

48-56. Then she (the girl with the boat) reflected upon the words of Parāśara and said: "Well, O dear Brāhmaṇa, there is the odour of fish emanating from me." After saying this, O king, she was willing to surrender herself.

Thereupon, the girl was rendered divinely fragrant by the sage by means of his Yogic power. By the same power, he enkindled fire and circumambulated it and duly married her out of love.

Then the sage began to touch the erotic centres of the girl in the boat itself. On coming to know that the Brāhmaṇa was eager to make love, she became afraid, O son of Dharma. She laughingly told him: "O Lord, O wise one, in the presence of the public you are on the verge of doing what the rustic people are accustomed to do. How is it that you are not ashamed!"

The sage then meditated for a short while and remembered the Tāmasī Māyā in his heart. The dark Māyā arrived and the entire world of mobile and immobile beings was enveloped by her.

The girl was dismayed thereby but was highly humoured. The happiness of being with a woman was attained by the sage who had been tormented by the compulsion of celibacy for long and he sported about diverting himself.

The girl was afflicted by the burden of conception instantly and she quickly delivered a boy holding a staff and having matted hairs. He was quiescent and held a waterpot too. A girdle embellished his waist. There was an upper cloth over his shoulder. (Apparently,) he was unafflicted by Viṣṇu's Māyā.

57-64. On seeing that boy of her own family, O son of Kuntī, the maiden became suspicious and nervous. Tremblingly she sought refuge in the sage saying: "O excellent sage, save, save my son, the wonderful son with a loin cloth and excellent girdle, holding a staff, having matted hairs and embellished with an upper cloth."

Parāśara said:

Do not be afraid. Even when your son is born you will still be a virgin and you will be known by the name Yojanagandhā (one whose fragrance reaches a Yojana) and Satyavatī.

A king named Śantanu will be your husband. You will be his chief queen and a crest-jewel of the lunar race.

Go back, O blameless lady, to your resort and remain there as before. Do not be sad. Here you have seen the power of my knowledge.

[Śrī Mārkaṇḍeya continued:]

After saying this, the Brāhmaṇa went away. The maiden approached her son. He humbly bowed down and prostrated with great devotion to his mother and said:

"O mother, I may be forgiven for what I am going to say. Be pleased with me. O my mother, I will make efforts at the propitiation of the Lord."

Upset at the words of her son she spoke these words:

Yojanagandhā said:

65-76. O dear son, do not go away now abandoning me, your sinless mother. Due to separation from you, there is no doubt, I will die soon.

No one is more affectionate than a son, no greater kinsman than a brother, no greater pious activity than truthfulness, and no greater sin than falsehood.

In spite of your childhood, dear son, you will be my support. I have no husband; (and if you go) I will have no son. See the mockery of Karmas.

Vyāsa said:

Do not be vexed within. What is uttered by me is the truth. O divine lady, at the time of any danger I may be remembered for the accomplishment of a task. I shall redeem you from danger. My haughty reply may be pardoned.[1]

1. Cf. Mbh, *Ādi* 63. 84-85

Śrī Mārkaṇḍeya said:

After saying thus, Vyāsa went away. That maiden too went home. At the close of Tretāyuga and the beginning of Dvāpara, O king, the son of Parāśara was in a predicament in the middle of a forest. The Devas with Śakra as the leader thought about Vyāsa (i.e. about his consecration etc.). It was told by Nārada himself: "He (Vyāsa) is the son of Parāśara. He was born of a daughter of a fisherman on the bank of Gaṅgā. He is endowed with (spiritual) knowledge." Then at the instance of Nārada, the excellent Suras too came there. Rāma, Pitāmaha and Śakra were surrounded by groups of sages. Seats were offered to all separately. They said, "Excellent! Excellent!"

Garbhādhāna (the rite of conception) and other consecratory rites of the boy were performed by Pitāmaha (god Brahmā). He was named Dvaipāyana because he was born in an island. He was called Pārāśarya because he was born of Parāśara. Since he was a part of Kṛṣṇa, he was named Kṛṣṇa. He would be arranging the Vedic texts. Hence (he is named) Vyāsa.

He was given the sacred ablution by Viriñci and blessed again and again by the groups of sages. "You are Vyāsa in all the worlds." After saying thus the Devas went away.

Pilgrimage was begun by Kṛṣṇa Dvaipāyana.

77-85. He took bath in Gaṅgā. Kedāra and Puṣkara were visited by him. So also Gayā, Naimiṣa, Kurukṣetra and Sarasvatī. He visited Mahākāla at Ujjayinī and Somanātha at Prabhāsaka. The great sage took his holy ablution everywhere on the earth girt by the ocean.

Ultimately he reached the immortal, splendid Narmadā that originated from Rudra's person. On seeing Narmadā, he became glad and obtained peace of mind.

He performed an elaborate penance after resorting to the banks of Narmadā. In summer he stood in the midst of five fires; in rainy season he lay on bare ground; in Hemanta (early winter) he stood wearing wet cloth and meditated upon Maheśvara. He meditated on Parameśvara abiding in the lotus of his heart. He meditated upon the splendid bestower of boons, the Lord who is the cause of creation and is indivisible. Engrossed in meditation he worshipped the Siddheśvara Liṅga everyday.

Due to the adoration of Siddheśvara Liṅga, and the power of Dhyānayoga, Śaṅkara became directly visible to Kṛṣṇadvaipāyana.

Īśvara said:

O dear one, I am pleased with you. Choose a splendid boon.

Vyāsa said:

O Lord, if you are pleased, if a boon has to be given to me, then (I ask) you will become directly visible on the banks of Narmadā. Let me be the knower of the past and the future, O Consort of Umā, with your favour.

Īśvara said:

86-96. Let it be so in your case, dear son, undoubtedly with my favour. I have been captivated by your devotion. I shall be visible on the banks of Narmadā by a half of one-thousandth part in your hermitage.

[Śrī Mārkaṇḍeya continued:]

After saying so the Lord went to the excellent Kailāsa mountain.

Kṛṣṇadvaipāyana duly took a wife[1] and he protected his wife in accordance with the injunctions in the scriptures. The son of Parāśara who had no son before begot a son. He was nourished and brought up by all the Devas, the leaders of whom were Viriñci and Indra.

At the time of the birth of the son Vasiṣṭha and other eminent sages came there: So also those led by Parāśara, in the course of their pilgrimage. Manu, Atri, Viṣṇu, Hārīta, Yājñavalkya, Uśanas, Aṅgiras, Yama, Āpastaṁba, Saṁvarta, Kātyāyana, Bṛhaspati and thousands, hundred thousands and hundred crores of sages of estimable conduct came with their disciples and camped on the banks of Narmadā.

1. But Mbh does not mention Vyāsa's marriage. It was at the sight of the celestial lady Ghṛtācī that Vyāys had emission of semen and Śuka was born. (Mbh, *Śānti* 324. 4-10)

All came to the splendid hermitage of Vyāsa with great pleasure, O king. On seeing the eminent Brāhmaṇas, he stood up by way of welcoming them. At the outset he bowed down to the feet of his father and then to all the others duly. He gave them seats with devotion and then offered *Pādya* and *Arghya*. After keeping the palms joined together in deference he spoke these words:

"There is no doubt. I have been elevated (to a higher position) by the conversation and adoration of all of you. With great pleasure, I shall offer you all the vegetables and fruits available in the forest."

97-102. He bowed to them severally and invited all of them. On seeing the sage Kṛṣṇadvaipāyana humbly bowing down, they blessed him with benedictions for success and looked at one another. All of them then looked at Parāśara.

The eminent sages said to him, "O dear one, reply suitably to Kṛṣṇadvaipāyana." On being told thus by all of them, the venerable Parāśara spoke to his son Vyāsa about what was decided by the sages to be done.

Śrī Parāśara said:

The sages do not wish to partake of your hospitality on the southern bank lest it should cause a break in their Vrata. Particularly they wish to partake of food in a Śrāddha.

Vyāsa said:

I shall do what you say. Kindly stay here for a short while. I shall propitiate the River and perform the excellent rite.[1]

[Śrī Mārkaṇḍeya continued:]

After saying this and remaining pure, he resorted to the bank of Narmadā. He recited the following prayer promptly. Know it, O king.

103-112. "Be victorious, O venerable goddess. Obeisance to you, O bestower of boons. Be victorious, O destroyer of sins

1. The miracle of change in the course of Narmadā is found only in this Purāṇa.

and bestower of many benefits. Be victorious, O you who hold the skulls of Śuṁbha and Niśuṁbha. I bow down to you, O destroyer of the distress of Devas and human beings.

Be victorious, O divine form having the moon and the sun as eyes. Be victorious, O excellent one of divine form with the face embellished by Fire-god. Be victorious, O great one submerged in Bhairava's body. Be victorious, O divine form drying up the blood of Andhaka.

Be victorious, O suppressor of Mahiṣa (demon in the form of a buffalo) with trident in the hand. Be victorious, O destroyer of the sins of the entire world. Be victorious, O goddess bowed down to by Rāma and Pitāmaha. Be victorious, O divine form bowed down to by the heads of Bhāskara and Śakra.

Be victorious, O divine lady eulogized by Ṣaṇmukha and Īśa, the armed one. Be victorious, O divine river flowing towards the ocean, O divine one eulogized by Śaṁbhu. Be victorious, O destroyer of misery and poverty. Be victorious, O divine form causing increase of sons and wives.

Be victorious, O goddess adopting all bodies. Be victorious, O guide unto Nāka (heaven), O destroyer of misery. Be victorious, O destroyer of ailments, O cause of salvation. Be victorious, O bestower of all desired things, O most excellent one among those who have achieved spiritual perfection."

[Śrī Mārkaṇḍeya continued:]

Vyāsa will be pleased and so also the Bull-vehicled Lord with one who reads in the presence of Śiva this prayer composed by Vyāsa, or in the house with pure feelings devoid of lust and anger. The divine river Narmadā will also be pleased. She is the destroyer of all sins.

Those on the earth by whom Narmadā is eulogized will never come within the sight of Yama.

"O goddess, in the matter of glorifying your good qualities, even Pitāmaha will be at a loss. O Narmadā, even Vākpati (Bṛhaspati) does not know how to eulogize your form adequately. How then can I endeavour to comprehend your good qualities, O divine river."

In view of these, the divine river Narmadā understood the state of purity (of Vyāsa) verbally, mentally and physically and became pleased with him. Then she spoke these words:

113-121. "O Vyāsa, O great sage, I am delighted with your truthful utterance. If at all you desire to be granted any boon, I shall fully grant it to you."

Vyāsa said:

O divine one, if you are pleased with me, if a boon has to be granted to me, it behoves you to provide hospitality unto the sages on your northern bank.

Narmadā said:

An improper boon has been requested for, O Vyāsa, that of deviating from the path. Even by Indra, Candra and Yama, it is not possible to make me flow through a wrong path. Dear son, request for another boon even if it be difficult of access on the earth.

[Śrī Mārkaṇḍeya continued:]

On hearing these words of the divine river Vyāsa fell into a swoon. Thinking 'My arduous endeavour has become futile', he fell down.

The entire earth consisting of mountains, forests and parks trembled. On seeing Vyāsa fallen into a swoon, the Devas including Vāsava raised a loud cry of lamentation and came there in thousands.

They lifted up Vyāsa who was engaged in arranging the Vedic text. They said: "O excellent River, he is straining himself for the sake of Brāhmaṇas and not for his own sake. He would presently cast off his life for the sake of cows and Brāhmaṇas." Thus Narmadā was told by the excellent Suras beginning with Brahmā.

Revā who became afraid, sprinkled him with her own waters and fanned him with many cool gusts of wind. The son of Satyavatī, who regained consciousness, bowed down to the Devas and said to the river:

Vyāsa said:

122-130. Benefit has been indicated by all the Tīrthas for resorting to them; yet due to my deficiency of fortune, O divine river, my meritorious hope has become futile like forest-flowers in the case of people.

Narmadā said:

O sage of great esteem, wherever on the surface of the earth you may desire to lead me I shall follow your path closely behind you even as you may hold the staff and proceed along with Vindhya.

[Śrī Mārkaṇḍeya:]

On being told thus, Vyāsa, the highly refulgent son of Satyavatī, made the excellent river flow on the southern side of his hermitage.

The highly brilliant sage wielding the staff made a Huṁkāra (gruff sound). On being afraid of the Huṁkāra of Vyāsa the daughter of Rudra quietly moved on.

With his staff he pointed out the path. The divine river became active there. The divine river was seen going along the path of Vyāsa by Devas with Śakra as their leader. Then the Devas along with Kinnaras made a shower of flowers.

The Brāhmaṇas, the chief of whom was Parāśara, became glad with blossoming eyes. (They said:) "Dear son, tell us what we have to do. We have been delighted by your act."

Vyāsa said:

Performing an elaborate penance and making gifts attended with great benefits, men should do what is conducive to the happiness of good people.

If the highly fortunate ones (like you) are pleased, if I am to be blessed, may all of you unhesitatingly stay in my hermitage.

My hospitality through greens and leaves with an admixture of Revāmṛta (nectarine water of Revā) should be accepted by you all with Parāśara as the chief guest. All of you do stay in my hermitage on the northern bank of Revā.

Mārkaṇḍeya said:

131-142. Holy ablution, libations and the Nitya rites (described as daily rites) were performed by the excellent Brāhmaṇas. Thereafter they went to Vyāsakuṇḍa and performed Homa by means of Śrīphalas and Bilva leaves in the holy fire.

More than a thousand sages performed the Homa in the

holy fire. They were: Gautama, Bhṛgu, Māṇḍavya, Nārada, Lomaśa, Parāśara, Śaṅkha, Kauśika, Sage Cyavana, Pippalāda, Vasiṣṭha, Naciketā of great austerities, Viśvāmitra, Agastya, Uddālaka, Yama, Śāṇḍilya, Jaimini, Kaṇva, Yājñavalkya, Uśanas, Aṅgiras, Śātātapa, Dadhīci, Kapila, Gālava, Jaigīṣavya, Dakṣa, Bharata, Mudgala, Vātsyāyana of great brilliance, Saṁvarta, Śakti, Jātukarṇya, Bharadvāja, Vālakhilya, Āruṇi etc. etc.

They had Akṣamālā (rosary) in their hands and they were engaged in meditative absorption.

All the Brāhmaṇas performed the Homa rite with full concentration. Thereupon a Liṅga destructive of ailments and bestowing salvation rose up there.

On seeing the greatest deity that is indivisible, Vyāsa became delighted. The Devas showered flowers and the excellent Brāhmaṇas pronounced benediction.

On seeing the Three-eyed Lord, Vyāsa prostrated with eight limbs touching the ground and adored the Brāhmaṇas with greens, roots and fruits.

After feeding the Pitṛs at the outset, all the Brāhmaṇas were duly served meals, O son of Pāṇḍu. After pronouncing holy blessing, the Brāhmaṇas went away. Ever since then that Tīrtha is called Vyāsatīrtha by learned men.

Yudhiṣṭhira said:

143-152. Do tell me in its entirety, whatever is meritorious as associated with Vyāsatīrtha. At what time do Snāna, Dāna and the other rites yield great benefit?

Śrī Mārkaṇḍeya said:

I shall speak everything to you in the company of your brothers, O son of Pāṇḍu.

A person should observe fast on the fourteenth day in the bright half of Kārttika. Remaining pure and controlling the sense-organs, he should keep awake at night with great devotion.

He should devoutly bathe the Lord with honey, milk and ghee, curds mixed with sugar candy and finally with water poured through Kuśa grass. He should then smear Parameśvara with sweet-smelling sandalpaste. Thereafter he should perform worship with fragrant flowers and Bilva leaves, and also with various flowers such as Mucukunda, Kunda, Kuśa, Jāti, Unmattamuni flowers and other seasonal flowers.

He should adore Dvīpeśvara, the excellent deity, with great devotion. Parameśvara is pleased by the gift of jaggery made of sugarcane. By gifting eight Gaḍukas (pieces of jaggery?) sin acquired during the day is dispelled. By gifting eight hundred Gaḍukas sin acquired in the course of a month is dispelled; by twice that sin of a year is destroyed; by ten thousand Gaḍukas sin of the whole life ever since the birth is destroyed. By twice that ailment is destroyed and by thrice there shall be acquisition of wealth. By six times that number one becomes eloquent in speech and by twice that one becomes a Siddha. There is no doubt that the status of Rudratva is achieved by one million (Gaḍukas gifted).

153-164. O great king, one should devoutly take the holy ablution on a full-moon day in accordance with the injunctions while uttering the prescribed Mantras. It destroys all sins.

The Vāruṇa, Āgneya or Brāhmya type of holy ablution causes everlasting benefit. A sensible man should duly offer libation to Devas, Pitṛs and human beings.

If a Ṛk verse is recited, he shall obtain the benefit of (reciting the whole of) Ṛgveda. If a Sāman verse is recited he shall get the benefit of Sāma Veda recitation. By reciting a Yajur Mantra he gets the benefit of (reciting) Yajurveda and by reciting Gāyatrī he obtains everything (benefits of reciting all the Vedas). He should recite the single-syllabled Mantra (*Om*) or the Saura (pertaining to the Sun-god) Mantra or the Mantra with Śiva as the deity or the Vaiṣṇava Mantra known as twelve-syllabled Mantra, namely "*om namo bhagavate vāsudevāya.*"

With great devotion he should adore Brāhmaṇas marked with all characteristic features of Brāhmaṇahood, devoted to their own wives and devoid of hypocrisy or covetousness.

The following Brāhmaṇas shall be excluded: those following different occupations, sinners, fallen ones, those who serve Śūdras, those who have accepted a Śūdra woman (as wife), those in whose house a Vṛṣalī is always present, backbiters, wicked ones, those who censure preceptors and elders, those who habitually hate the Vedas, those who argue endlessly and those with cunning behaviour characteristic of cranes. Such persons should be excluded in Śrāddha, Dāna and all *Vratas.*

A Brāhmaṇa of great self-control is better even if he knows only the essence of Gāyatrī. He is better than a master of all the four Vedas, should he be bereft of self-control, eating indiscriminately and selling everything.

One should honour deserving Brāhmaṇas by gifts of cooked food and gold. One who makes the gift of shoes, garments, quilt, umbrella, seat etc. to a Brāhmaṇa with devotion is honoured in heaven.

A real cow, or a Jaladhenu, or Ghṛtadhenu, Tiladhenu or buffaloes also should be given (as religious gift).

A man who gifts antelope skin, gingelly seeds and ghee, a virgin and a book shall obtain the everlasting world.

165-171. I have made a true statement that he who desires heavenly pleasures should make the gift of bullocks with well-adorned hoofs (with silver plate) along with food-grains and sundry articles of daily use.

The devotee should (symbolically) tie a thread round a Dvīpa (continent) or the auspicious earth, a temple or even the great Lord (Liṅga) with devotion.

If the man performs circumambulation in accordance with the injunctions, it is as good as circumambulating the seven continents viz. Jambū, Plakṣa, Śālmali, Kuśa, Krauñca, Kāśa and Puṣkara which are encircled by seven oceans.

O great king, the devotee shall perform the rite of Vṛṣotsarga (ceremonial release of a bull) at the shrine of Dvīpeśvara. By means of reddish-coloured bull the devotee attains the world of Maheśa.

A bull that has grey face, forehead and legs and is white in the tail is a guide (leads) to heaven. A blue one also is said to be like this. One who makes thus dedication in the Dvīpeśvara shrine, lives in heaven for as many years as there are hairs on its body, O descendant of Bharata.

172-178. By the power of Vyāsatīrtha he successively goes to the worlds of Sun-god, Śaṅkara, Viriñci and Viṣṇu and enjoys the pleasures there as he pleases.

Then the devotee should honour devoutly a Brāhmaṇa and his wife together. White and red garments are presented to the Brāhmaṇa. The couple should be circumambulated uttering this Mantra: "May the preceptor of the universe be pleased with me."

There is no other kinsman in this world or in the other world on a par with a Brāhmaṇa. It is he who saves from falling into the highly horrible world of Yama.

The devotee should, with great devotion, adore a Brāhmaṇa who is conversant with Itihāsas and Purāṇas, is a devotee of Viṣṇu, who has subdued his sense-organs and who has mastered the Sāmaveda in particular.

If people remember Dvīpeśvara with devotion even while staying at home, neither grief nor loss nor sin harasses them.

At the outset the devotee should adore the Siddheśvara Liṅga and thereafter the shrine where the illustrious Vyāsa, the son of Satyavatī, became a Siddha.

It is by adoring this (Liṅga) that the highly intelligent Dhārāsarpa became a Siddha.

179-185. O king, one who casts his life in that Tīrtha goes to the presence of Śiva after piercing the world of Sun.

The goal attained after casting life at the Tīrtha varies thus: If a devotee gets drowned in the water there, he lives in the world of Śiva for seven thousand years. If he immolates himself into the fire, he lives in the other world for eleven thousand years. If he falls from a precipice, he lives in the other world for sixteen thousand years. If he dies in a great battle, he lives for sixty thousand years in the world of Śiva. If he dies as a result of the attack of a cow, he lives in Śivaloka for eighty thousand years. O descendant of Bharata, if he dies fasting, his goal is everlasting.

The father, the grandfather, and the great-grandfather look at the scion of their family arriving in the form of air. They fondly yearn: 'Who is such a son in our family as offers us gingelly seed water as libation in that Tīrtha on the full-moon day of Kārttika or Vaiśākha months?'

By resorting to that Tīrtha we will attain heavenly pleasures. Thus the excellent Dvīpeśvara has been recounted to you entirely.

One who reads this with great devotion or listens with due attention thereto shall be rid of all sins. He rejoices in the palace of Śiva.

The Arid land (*Ūṣara*) of all Tīrthas has been created by the leading sages. O excellent king, there is no doubt that Vyāsatīrtha bestows all desires.

CHAPTER NINETYEIGHT

The Greatness of Prabhāsa Tīrtha[1]

Śrī Mārkaṇḍeya said:

1-7. Thereafter, O great king, one should go to the excellent Prabhāseśvara which is well-known in all the three worlds as an excellent flight of stairs unto heaven.

Yudhiṣṭhira said:

O dear one, do recount to me, how did Prabhāsa originate as the bestower of a flight of stairs unto heaven and as a visible one having great benefits. Do describe it to me succinctly without delay.

Śrī Mārkaṇḍeya said:

The wife of Ravi well-known as Prabhā was unfortunate. Śaṁbhu was formerly propitiated by her through a very severe penance.

For a year she stood taking in only air and for another year she was engaged in meditative absorption. Thereupon, O son of Pāṇḍu, Mahādeva was pleased with Prabhā.

Īśvara said:

Why do you undergo suffering, O maiden? What is desired to be said may be spoken. Indeed I am one with Bhāskara. There is no duality between us.

Prabhā said:

O Lord Śaṁbhu, excepting her husband no woman has any other Lord anywhere. He may or may not have good qualities; he may be wealthy; he may be amenable to love or prone to hatred; husband is a deity unto women.

But, O Lord of Sureśvara, it is my misfortune that I am

1. This is different from the Prabhāsa which is on the western coast of Kathiawar and is famous for its Somanātha temple. This one is a sacred place associated with Revā.

scorched and distressed in the midst of my companions as I do not get the happiness due from a husband. Hence I undergo very great distress.

Īśvara said:

8-15. With my favour you will be a darling unto Bhāskara.

Pārvatī said:

If Bhāskara does not take your word as an authority, the sufferings (i.e. penance) of this Prabhā would become futile, O Parameśvara.

The dispeller of darkness was thought about (mentally summoned) by Maheśa at the instance of Umā. Bhānu (Sun) came down from the sky on to the bank of Narmadā.

Bhānu said:

O slayer of the demon Aghāsura, O Lord, why have I been summoned?

Īśvara said:

O Bhānu, protect Prabhā according her the greatest contentment.

Umā said:

O destroyer of fog and mist, may you be pleased always to stay in the palace of Prabhā. O Ravi, let her be made the chief wife among all the wives.

Bhānu said:

O lady of excellent countenance, O goddess, I shall carry out your words of advice.

On hearing this, Prabhā was summoned. She requested Maheśvara:

Prabhā said:

O Lord, O Consort of Umā, O slayer of Manmatha, may you

be pleased to be present here permanently by a part of yours. Let one part be placed here for opening the Tīrtha.

Śrī Mārkaṇḍeya said:

16-25. A Liṅga constituted by all the Devas was installed there, O son of Pāṇḍu. It is a rare Liṅga well-known in all the worlds as Prabhāseśa.

All the other Tīrthas yield benefit in due course, but, O great king, Prabhāseśa bestows the desired benefit immediately.

Especially on the seventh day in the bright half of the month of Māgha, a devotee should offer a horse to a Brāhmaṇa of the qualities mentioned before. Indratva (status of Indra) or the region of Bhāskara is obtained by him, O king.

One should make the gift over to a Brāhmaṇa after taking holy bath with great devotion. A donor of cow attains heaven or Satyaloka, O king.

The cow should be auspicious, beautiful in every limb. She should be young, splendid and yielding plenty of milk. She should be adorned with a bell. She should have her calf with her (in that Dāna). A brass pot for milking should be given along with her. Those who make this gift, O excellent king, do not go to the abode of Yama.

One who bathes the deity with great devotion attains the highest world and stays there until the annihilation of all living beings. Merely by the bath all wretchedness is dispelled, O Pāṇḍava.

A person who devoutly offers at this Tīrtha a virgin in marriage to a Brāhmaṇa of the proper age and on a par with him in respect of nobility of the family, character and financial status, O great king, even if he is a great sinner, gets his sins dissolved like salt in water.

26-35. All these sins (mentioned below) are dissolved, O son of Pāṇḍu, through the gift of a virgin (in marriage): sin resulting from an act of treachery against the master; that of one who misappropriates money deposited; that of a slayer of a friend; that of an ungrateful person; sin arising from perjury; sin arising from demolishing a park in a village; carnally approaching other men's wives; sin due to usury; sin due to committing a theft; sin of destroying a well; sin of one guilty of Biḍālavrata (vow of a cat i.e. hypocrisy); arrogance; sin of felling trees; sin of prohibiting marital alliance; sin of cutting down a tree in a park; sin of cohabiting with a woman of the prohibited type; sin of coveting other man's wife after forsaking one's own wife; sin due to misappropriating a Brāhmaṇa's wealth; sin of a person administering poison; that of a cow-killer; sin arising from selling learning; sin in associating (with sinners); the terrible sin of killing dogs and cats, serpents and Śūdras; sin of a person unlawfully possessing landed property after taking it by force; sin of prevention of gifts to Brāhmaṇas; and misdeeds against cows and fire etc.

After going to the world of Bhāskara, he proceeds to the auspicious Rudraloka. He sports about in Rudraloka for a period of the reign of fourteen Indras. When all the sins are dissolved, the faith in Śiva is generated in him. One who visits this Prabhāsa Tīrtha, O son of Pāṇḍu, attains the benefit of all the Tīrthas and that of a horse-sacrifice.

Gift of a cow is highly meritorious and destructive of all sins. It is praiseworthy on every occasion but particularly on the fourteenth lunar day.

CHAPTER NINETYNINE

The Greatness of Nāgeśvara Tīrtha

Śrī Mārkaṇḍeya said:

1-5. Thereafter, O great king, a person should go to the Vāsukīśa Tīrtha that destroys all the clusters of sins and that was established on the southern bank of Narmadā.

Yudhiṣṭhira said:

O dear one, for what reason was the deity Vāsukīśa installed on the southern bank of Narmadā? O my preceptor, do narrate it in detail.

Śrī Mārkaṇḍeya said:

After creating and stabilising all these (visible) worldly objects,

Śambhu began to dance. Due to excess of activity sweat issued forth mixed with the waters of Gaṅgā coming out of the head (matted hairs). As it fell down, a serpent began to lick it.

Thereupon, O descendant of Bharata, Mandākinī became angry with the serpent and cursed: "O serpent, O insignificant creature, you will become a python."

Vāsuki said:

6-11. O divine river duly honoured by Hara, I am a sinner guilty of misdemeanour but worthy of being blessed by you. You are the meritorious, splendid river sanctifying the three worlds. You are the deliverer from mundane existence and the destroyer of the distress of the distressed ones. You are stationed at the threshold of heaven (Svarga), O goddess, take pity on me.

Gaṅgā said:

Perform an elaborate penance on Vindhya with Śaṅkara in view. Thereafter you will regain your original position and the state of a serpent at my behest.

Śrī Mārkaṇḍeya said:

Then the serpent hastened to the splendid mountain Vindhya and engaged in the propitiation of Śaṅkara. He began to perform the penance.

Everyday he meditated upon the three-eyed Mahādeva engaged in playing the Ḍamaruka (hand-drum). When a hundred years were completed, the preceptor of the universe was moved (with pity) and approaching him spoke these soft, loving words, "O dear serpent, with due deference, choose your boon from me."

Vāsuki said:

12-21. O Lord, if you are pleased with me, O Śaṅkara if you grant me a boon, O Lord of Devas, let there be redemption from sin unto me. Do mention any Tīrtha that is destructive of all sins.

Īśvara said:

O serpent of great might, do go to Revā, the bestower of welfare. Take your holy ablution in accordance with the relevant injunctions on its meritorious southern bank.

After saying so, the Lord vanished. Vāsuki in great haste entered the waters of Narmadā in his python form.

The excellent current of Jāhnavī flowed along with his path; he became a serpent again redeemed of all his sins in the waters of Narmadā.

Śaṅkara was installed there in Narmadā, O Yudhiṣṭhira. Thereafter, the Nāgeśvara Liṅga became famous as the destroyer of sins.

A devotee should bathe Śiva with honey on the eighth or fourteenth day. Undoubtedly he will become rid of sins immediately.

O son of Kuntī, those men without sons who take their holy bath at the confluence will get an excellent and splendid son comparable to Kārtavīrya.

One who observes fast and performs Śrāddha there itself, O Prince, shall release the departed ones from hell.

Neither in the family nor among his kinsmen shall there be fear from serpents. With the favour of Nāgas his family shall be free from defects and hence rejoice.

Thus, O excellent king, everything has been recounted to you due to my affection for you.

CHAPTER ONE HUNDRED

The Greatness of Mārkaṇḍeśvara Tīrtha

Śrī Mārkaṇḍeya said:

1-9. Thereafter, O king, one should go to the extremely splendid Tīrtha on the southern bank of Narmadā, well-known as Mārkaṇḍeśa.

Dear son, it is the most excellent of all the Tīrthas, saluted by Devas. It is to be kept as the utmost secret of all secrets. It has not been told to anyone by me.

It was installed by me formerly and it is like a flight of stairs unto heaven. Knowledge dawned upon me there itself, with the favour of Śaṅkara.

Anyone else who goes there and recites the Drupadā prayer under the waters becomes liberated from all sins, verbal, mental or physical, O son of Pāṇḍu. Clasping the Piṇḍī (of Śiva Liṅga) the devotee should face the southern quarter and devoutly worship the Trident-bearing Lord with a form having thirty-two hands. I am sure, O king, that after the fall of the body he will go to Śiva.

At night on the eighth lunar day, O descendant of Bharata, he should light lamps (filled) with ghee and he will attain the heavenly world. So said Śaṅkara.

O prince, thereby the Pitṛs become contented until the time of the annihilation of all living beings and they become pleased with him too.

A person should offer libations there with Iṅguda, Badara, Bilva, raw rice-grains or mere water to the ancestors of his family. He shall obtain the benefit (fruit) of his birth.